Publications of the Richard Rawlinson Center

THE RECOVERY OF OLD ENGLISH

THE RECOVERY OF OLD ENGLISH

ANGLO-SAXON STUDIES IN THE SIXTEENTH AND SEVENTEENTH CENTURIES

edited by

Timothy Graham

Medieval Institute Publications

WESTERN MICHIGAN UNIVERSITY

Kalamazoo, Michigan, USA — 2000

Library of Congress Cataloging-in-Publication Data

The recovery of Old English : Anglo-Saxon studies in the sixteenth and seventeenth centuries / edited by Timothy Graham.
    p. cm. -- (Publications of the Richard Rawlinson Center)
    Includes bibliographical references and indexes.
    ISBN 1-58044-013-4 (alk. paper) -- ISBN 1-58044-014-2 (pbk. : alk. paper)
    1. English philology--Old English, ca. 450-1100--History. 2. English philology--Old English, ca. 450-1100--Study and teaching--England--History--16th century. 3. English philology--Old English, ca. 450-1100--Study and teaching--England--History--17th century. 4. English literature--Old English, ca. 450-1100--History and criticism--Theory, etc. 5. Great Britain--History--Anglo-Saxon period, 449-1066--Historiography. 6. English language--Old English, ca. 450-1100--Historiography. I. Graham, Timothy. II. Series.

PE115 .R43 2000
429'.09--dc21

99-085971

ISBN 1-58044-013-4 (casebound)
ISBN 1-58044-014-2 (paperbound)

Printed in the United States of America

Cover Design by Linda K. Judy

CONTENTS

FIGURES

PREFACE

The papers in this volume chart selected major aspects of the progress of Old English studies from their beginnings in the third quarter of the sixteenth century to their coming of age by the early eighteenth. The book is both a reflection of and a response to the recent expansion of interest in the early history of Anglo-Saxon studies. It is the first collection wholly devoted to the subject since the publication in 1982 of *Anglo-Saxon Scholarship: The First Three Centuries*, edited by Carl T. Berkhout and Milton McC. Gatch. The preface to *Anglo-Saxon Scholarship* stated the editors' wish that that book—which was the outcome of two sessions at the Thirteenth Conference on Medieval Studies at Western Michigan University in 1978—should "stimulate new research in the history of Anglo-Saxon scholarship." The years since its appearance have indeed witnessed fruitful work within the field, and certain key figures not there covered in depth—among them John Joscelyn, William L'Isle, Abraham Wheelock, and Francis Junius—have since come under increasing scrutiny, with a developing appreciation of the full scope and importance of their contributions and their influence upon their contemporaries and successors. At the same time, the upswing in Anglo-Saxon manuscript studies during the 1980s and 1990s helped to bring into focus a large body of hitherto under-studied evidence relevant to the early modern history of Old English studies. Much more of the work of the first generations of Anglo-Saxonists survives in unpublished than in published form, in their annotations in the margins of Anglo-Saxon manuscripts, in their personal workbooks, and in materials carefully prepared for publication projects that ultimately foundered. It is the special intention of the present book to bring such unpublished materials, so richly remunerative of study, onto center stage while also taking a fresh look at several of the published works.

Five of the papers here presented were first delivered at the Twenty-Ninth International Congress on Medieval Studies at Western Michigan University in May 1994. They have subsequently been revised and expanded for publication, and now incorporate the results of new research conducted in the intervening period. The other three papers (those by Angelika Lutz, Kathryn Lowe, and Kees Dekker) have been prepared especially for this volume.

Lutz's extended essay presents a comprehensive overview that provides a broad introduction to the period as a whole. Taking as her subject the study of the manuscripts of a critically important historical text, the Anglo-Saxon Chronicle, Lutz tracks the changing fortunes of Anglo-Saxon studies, as the geographical center of gravity for Anglo-Saxonists moved from London in the late sixteenth and early seventeenth centuries, to Cambridge in the second quarter of the seventeenth century, and finally, from the 1650s, to Oxford, where the subject became firmly anchored in a university context. She includes an outline and assessment of the contributions of all the major figures in the period.

The other papers in the volume isolate specific themes and individuals, investigating, for example, the influence over a period of some two hundred years of Richard Verstegen's descriptions and engraved depictions of the pagan gods of the Saxons (Bremmer), or tracing the development of responsiveness to Old English poetry and the early history of its formatting in printed editions (Plumer). The two papers on William L'Isle reflect the recent flowering of interest in this still somewhat shadowy figure who bridges the gap between the sixteenth-century endeavors of the Parker circle and Henry Spelman's foundation of the Cambridge Anglo-Saxon lectureship in the late 1630s; while L'Isle has hitherto been best known for his 1623 publication *A Saxon*

Treatise Concerning the Old and New Testament, Phillip Pulsiano and Stuart Lee focus on the evidence of his handwritten workbooks, which enable precise identification of the Anglo-Saxon manuscripts that he studied and which reveal ambitious, but finally unrealized, plans for further publications. Of the three studies focusing on lexicography, one (Lowe) tracks the reputation and the utilization of the work of William Somner, who was responsible for the first published dictionary of Old English, while the other two (Graham, Dekker) consider the evidence that the unpublished dictionaries of John Joscelyn and Francis Junius bring to light about the full scope and the methodology of the work of these two scholars who were the leading experts on Old English in their respective times. The book ends with a list of Works Cited that provides the key for the references within the footnotes given in author-date format. It is intended that this list, although not exhaustive, can also serve as a working bibliography for the field.

This volume inaugurates a new series, Publications of the Richard Rawlinson Center. The series will include collections of essays and monographs dedicated to the study of the history and culture of Anglo-Saxon England broadly defined, with particular emphasis on manuscript studies. The series will thus embody and express the underlying aims of Western Michigan University's Richard Rawlinson Center for Anglo-Saxon Studies and Manuscript Research, which in 1999 celebrated the fifth anniversary of its foundation.

Timothy Graham
November 1999

Postscript, August 2000. As this book was about to go to press, the community of Anglo-Saxonists was saddened by the news of the death of Phillip Pulsiano, for many years one of its most energetic, committed, and popular members. May his contribution to the book serve as a memorial to a deeply valued colleague and friend. "Her mon mæg giet gesion his swæð."

ABBREVIATIONS

BL   London, British Library

Bodleian   Oxford, Bodleian Library

CCCC   Corpus Christi College, Cambridge

CUL   Cambridge University Library

DNB   Leslie Stephen and Sidney Lee, eds., *The Dictionary of National Biography*, 2nd edn., 22 vols. (London: Smith, Elder, 1908–09)

DNB: Missing Persons   C. S. Nicholls, ed., *The Dictionary of National Biography: Missing Persons* (Oxford: Oxford University Press, 1993)

DOE   *Dictionary of Old English*, issued in microfiche format (Toronto: Pontifical Institute of Mediaeval Studies, in progress)

EEMF   Early English Manuscripts in Facsimile

EETS   Early English Text Society
  OS   Original Series
  SS   Supplementary Series

Pat. Lat.   J.-P. Migne, ed., *Patrologia Latina*, 221 vols. (Paris, 1844–64)

TCC   Trinity College, Cambridge

THE STUDY OF THE ANGLO-SAXON CHRONICLE IN THE SEVENTEENTH CENTURY AND THE ESTABLISHMENT OF OLD ENGLISH STUDIES IN THE UNIVERSITIES[1]

Angelika Lutz

I. THE FIRST CONCERTED EFFORTS: ARCHBISHOP PARKER AND HIS CIRCLE

The beginnings of Old English studies in the sixteenth century are known to have been closely linked with the efforts of the early Elizabethan regime to represent the break with the Catholic Church under Henry VIII as a return to the greater independence from Rome that the English Church had known in the Anglo-Saxon period. What had essentially been a revolutionary change in the structure of power was thus retrospectively justified in the late Tudor period as a return to an earlier position from which the official Roman Church, not the English Church, had deviated.

[1]I am very grateful to Martha Berryman, Rolf H. Bremmer, Jr., Kees Dekker, Helmut Gneuss, Peter J. Lucas, J. C. T. Oates, Eric G. Stanley, Roland Torkar, and Andrew G. Watson for allowing me to use unpublished material and/or making valuable suggestions at various stages of the long history and prehistory of this paper. My greatest thanks go to Timothy Graham, without whose help, encouragement, and patience it might never have been completed.

1

These were the circumstances that engendered the organized study of Old English. Under the leadership of Archbishop Matthew Parker (1504–75) and with the support of Secretary (later Lord Treasurer) Sir William Cecil (1520–98), extensive studies of Anglo-Saxon historical sources and of the Old English language were undertaken. The aim was to demonstrate through these studies that the Anglo-Saxon Church had enjoyed a greater degree of independence than the English Church of the later Middle Ages. Textual and linguistic studies were thus intended to promote the consolidation of the Tudor regime.[2] This ideological and political intent, which lay at the heart of the studies of Parker's circle in the 1560s and early 1570s, was pursued above all, where Old English was concerned, by Parker's Latin secretary John Joscelyn (1529–1603), and also by Laurence Nowell (d. ?1569), who until his

---

[2] The best concise survey of these early studies, of those who participated in them, and of the most important publications (with citation of their full original titles) is still Adams (1917), where the sixteenth century is discussed in ch. I; see also esp. Flower (1935); Wright (1951); McKisack (1971), ch. II; Page (1993), 87–106; and Lucas (1999), 41–52. The view that the repudiation of Rome represented a return to an earlier and purer state of affairs is expressed with particular clarity in the preface to John Foxe's edition (with translation) of the Old English Gospels, *The Gospels of the Fower Euangelistes* of 1571, a publication in which Parker played an active part: "the religion presently taught & professed . . . is no new reformation of thinges lately begonne, which were not before, but rather a reduction of the Church to the Pristine State of olde conformitie" (cited in Adams [1917], 32–33). In the context of vernacular translations, great importance was attached to King Alfred's preface to his Old English translation of the *Regula pastoralis* of Pope Gregory the Great, as Alfred there called upon his bishops to promote the vernacular: see Page (1992), 36–41; and Page (1993), 101–04. The propagandistic aims of the work of Parker's circle have been most clearly described in Sanders (1983), but are also discussed in the chapter of Adams cited above; see also Fussner (1970), 238 and 248–52; Leinbaugh (1982), 51–59; and Graham (1997a), 33–35. These concentrated efforts of Parker's circle are to be distinguished from the multifarious antiquarian interests of various individuals in this period.

departure for the Continent in 1567 served in Cecil's household. It found its clearest expression in the first edition of Old English texts, *A Testimonie of Antiqvitie* of 1566, a publication sponsored by Parker in which John Joscelyn played a leading part.[3]

It would, however, be a mistake to see the achievements of Joscelyn and others in the study of Old English texts and of the Old English language, and Parker's and Cecil's provision of the personal and material preconditions of that study, as nothing more than the planning and execution of a propaganda exercise in the modern sense. Parker and Cecil themselves had a longstanding interest in antiquarian studies, and they could hope that their plan would be successful only because there already existed among their contemporaries a circle of educated people with antiquarian interests, including in particular highly trained clergy, but also teachers, lawyers, and noblemen in official positions. Antiquarian interests mingled inextricably with ideology and politics in the leaders and their co-workers, as also in the prospective readers.

Moreover, most of the historical and legal sources published by Parker's circle were not suitable as propaganda in the modern sense, on account of their length and their linguistic difficulty. These publications included the first edition of Anglo-Saxon laws, issued in 1568 by Nowell's friend William Lambarde (1536–1601), a distinguished antiquary in his own right,[4] and Asser's

---

[3]See Adams (1917), 23–25; Flower (1935); Bromwich (1962); Page (1993), 94–97; Graham (1997a), 33–38; and Lucas (1997a). For biographical information on Nowell see esp. Torkar (1981), 44–47; Hahn (1983); Berkhout (1985); and Berkhout (1998). The extensive Old English studies of Nowell and Joscelyn, which influenced the work of the later antiquaries, are considered in greater detail below.

[4]*Archaionomia, sive de priscis Anglorum legibus libri*, partly based on Nowell's transcripts, with a Latin translation; see Wormald (1997). The font used for the Old English text, which was modeled on Insular minuscule, had first been used for *A Testimonie of Antiqvitie*. Lambarde's publication also served the propagandistic aims of Church and State, although in a rather broader sense than

Latin life of King Alfred, issued by Parker and Joscelyn in 1574.[5]
It must, however, be emphasized that these works appeared within
the period when Archbishop Parker, in his role as leader of the
Anglican Church, actively engaged in promoting the dissemination
of Anglo-Saxon historical sources and the study of the Old English
language. By contrast, important projects that were started but not
finished during his lifetime, such as the first dictionaries of Old
English by Nowell and Joscelyn, were unable to achieve publication in the period following his death.[6] The first publications

---

A Testimonie: see Adams (1917), 27–31 and 157–59; Warnicke (1973), ch. 4;
Grant (1996), 18–22; and Lucas (1999).

[5] *Ælfredi regis res gestæ*. The special font was used for this publication also,
which led many to the erroneous view that the manuscript containing Asser's
biography, BL MS Cotton Otho A. xii—largely destroyed in the Cottonian fire
of 1731—was written in Insular rather than Carolingian minuscule. On this, and
more broadly on the respective roles of Parker and Joscelyn, see Adams (1917),
33–36; McKisack (1971), 42–48; Gneuss (1976), 296–97; Sanders Gale (1978),
10–19; Page (1993); and Graham (1994). Page (at pp. 88–99) convincingly
argues that Parker's part in utilizing Anglo-Saxon manuscripts for such purposes
was not restricted to texts written in Latin.

[6] This is clear from the survey of the most significant sixteenth-century
publications in Adams (1917), 191. For the period following Parker's death
Adams cites only Lambarde's local history, *A Perambulation of Kent* (1576), as
having Old English content worthy of mention. The legally trained Lambarde,
who belonged to the landed gentry, continued to enjoy a reputation at court as an
antiquary in the period after Parker's death, but he also possessed his own
financial means through which he could secure publication both of *A Perambulation* and of his historico-legal study *Eirenarcha*, published in 1581, which
contains only a small amount of Old English (see Adams [1917], 29–31 and 160;
Fussner [1970], 278–79; McKisack [1971], 78–82 and 133–38; and Warnicke
[1973], chs. 4–12). Nowell's Old English dictionary (Bodleian MS Selden supra
63), which includes additions by Lambarde, has been published by Marckwardt
(1952) (see also the critique by Torkar [1981], 47 and 61); Joscelyn's much more
extensive dictionary (BL MSS Cotton Titus A. xv–xvi; see Sanders Gale [1978],
34–35) has unfortunately not been published hitherto, but on its scope and

in Old English owed their appearance to the fact that the study of Old English had achieved a quasi-official status, guided and supported in the highest ecclesiastical and political circles.

My purpose in providing this introductory outline of the known causes of the principal achievements in Old English studies during the sixteenth century is to demonstrate:

1. that it required particular conditions for what began as just one of many fields of contemporary antiquarian interest to develop into an intensively pursued branch of study;
2. that the motives underlying the ensuing studies were ecclesio-political and ideological;
3. that the principal aim of these studies was to make accessible the earliest and most authentic sources for the history of Anglo-Saxon England, both those in Old English and those in Latin.

The study of Old English in Parker's circle was determined by these conditions. At that time it still had no institutional links with the universities.[7] It was over seventy years after the first publication of an Old English text that the study of Old English

method see Graham (1997a), 37–40, and the paper by Timothy Graham in the present volume. For the esteem in which later antiquaries held Joscelyn's dictionary and also his and Nowell's transcripts of Old English manuscripts, see below.

[7]Most of those involved, however, were graduates of Cambridge or Oxford. Even the fact that both Cecil and Parker held high office in the University of Cambridge in the course of their careers—the former as Chancellor (1559–98), the latter as Master of Corpus Christi College (1544–53) and as Vice-Chancellor (1545 and 1548) (see *DNB* s.nn.)—did not lead to the establishment of Old English studies in the university. Joscelyn, who aside from Nowell was the outstanding Old English expert of his time, bequeathed £100 to his old Cambridge college, Queens', but with the aim of promoting the study of Hebrew, not of Old English (see *DNB* s.n.; and Adams [1917], 38–39).

became established as a university discipline, when in 1639 a lectureship in "Antiquitates Britannicæ et Saxonicæ" was created at Cambridge. And only in the second half of the seventeenth century was the study of Old English introduced into the University of Oxford.

The stages in this process and the contributions of the leading individuals involved are already fairly well known. However, from existing accounts it is not sufficiently clear why, following the sixteenth-century beginnings described above, the further development of the study of Old English took the course that it did. Nor is it clear what external and internal conditions caused the study of Old English to become established as a university discipline, before any other branch of English studies.

I seek in what follows to throw light on these issues. In attempting to do so, I shall focus on the seventeenth-century study of a small, self-contained group of manuscripts, namely the seven surviving manuscripts of the Anglo-Saxon Chronicle.[8] Given the markedly historical orientation of Old English studies in the early modern period, the attention that the antiquaries paid to this text—the most important narrative source for the history of the later Anglo-Saxon period—is especially instructive for the history of the subject, and in particular for the investigation of the causes that led to the introduction of the study of Old English into the

---

[8] The seven manuscripts, referred to throughout this essay by their modern sigla A–G, are as follows. **A**: CCCC MS 173, fols. 1–32 (Ker [1957], no. 39); **B**: BL MS Cotton Tiberius A. vi, fols. 1–34 + MS Cotton Tiberius A. iii, fol. 178 (Ker [1957], no. 188); **C**: BL MS Cotton Tiberius B. i, fols. 115v–164r (Ker [1957], no. 191, art. 4); **D**: BL MS Cotton Tiberius B. iv, fols. 3–90 (Ker [1957], no. 192); **E**: Bodleian MS Laud Misc. 636 (Ker [1957], no. 346); **F**: BL MS Cotton Domitian A. viii, fols. 30–70 (Ker [1957], no. 148); **G**: BL MS Cotton Otho B. xi, fols. 39–47 (this copy was reduced to a few fragments in the Cotton fire of 1731; Ker [1957], no. 180, art. 3). There is in addition the fragment MS **H**, a single leaf containing annals for the years 1113–14: BL MS Cotton Domitian A. ix, fol. 9 (Ker [1957], no. 150). For all these manuscripts, see Table 1 below.

universities. For one thing, this is because of the antiquaries' pronounced and persistent interest in this text as a historical source. Then, this interest was intensified by the fact that the Chronicle is a complex textual entity: much of it is a homogeneous text deriving from a shared common stock, but in some sections, especially the later ones, the manuscripts comprise a group of texts that are independent of one another and that describe the same events from differing standpoints, or even narrate entirely different events for the same period.[9]

The antiquaries soon became aware of the complexity of the relationships among the seven manuscripts. They conducted their study of the Chronicle by comparing the different texts and frequently exchanged among themselves both the original manuscripts and the various early modern transcripts that were made from them. As will be described in greater detail below, these aspects of their work are attested by antiquarian records concerning the ownership, use, and loan of the Chronicle manuscripts; by extensive textual evidence witnessing to the work of the antiquaries;[10] and, not least, by the publication during the seventeenth century of two complete editions of the Chronicle, of which the first appeared in Cambridge and the second in Oxford. My aim is to show that the gradual institutionalization of the study of Old English can be seen to be closely related to the availability of manuscripts, transcripts, and eventually editions of the Chronicle. Moreover, the history of the study of the Chronicle also exemplifies the way in which the geographical center of gravity of Old English studies shifted during the period: from Canterbury and London (Lambeth) during Parker's lifetime, to London (City/

---

[9]See Plummer (1892–99), II, §§11–30; Whitelock (1979), 109–25; and Bately (1991).

[10]For example, complete or partial transcripts; passages of text which were copied from one manuscript into another; and extracts from the Chronicle which appeared in a broad range of historical works of the period.

Westminster area) in the late Elizabethan and early Stuart period, then, in the 1630s, to Cambridge, and finally, in the 1670s, to Oxford. It will emerge that along with this shift in location there was an accompanying shift in the focus of the content of Old English studies.

II. INSTITUTIONALIZING THE STUDY OF HISTORY OUTSIDE THE UNIVERSITIES: THE SOCIETY OF ANTIQUARIES AND THE FORMATION OF THE COTTON LIBRARY

In order to understand what caused Old English to become a subject of study in the universities, it is important to consider the endeavors of the late sixteenth and early seventeenth centuries that preceded the establishment of the Cambridge lectureship. Those endeavors, belonging to the period following Parker's death, should again have resulted in Old English studies gaining an institutional base outside the universities. The period is of significance because the principal individuals who participated in these early but abortive efforts gradually pointed the way, by means of their own work, toward the alternative path of establishing Old English in the universities, a path which they themselves partly prepared. Three people are of particular importance:

1. the antiquary and politician Robert Cotton (1571–1631), whose library in London for decades provided the focal point of efforts to establish the study of history outside the universities;[11]

---

[11]See esp. Sharpe (1979), an outstanding study that considers Cotton's achievement both as a promoter of historical and legal studies and as a political advisor and intermediary; see also *DNB* s.n.; Wright (1958); Fussner (1962), ch. 5; Tite (1994); Parry (1995), ch. 3; and Wright (1997).

2. the chorographer and historian William Camden (1551–1623), who worked in London throughout his life and used the Cotton library, but who shortly before his death endowed England's first chair of history at Oxford;[12]
3. the historian Henry Spelman (ca. 1564–1641), who also made extensive use of the Cotton library for his publications, but who in his old age established the Cambridge lectureship for "Antiquitates Britannicæ et Saxonicæ."[13]

All three belonged to the inner circle of the Elizabethan Society of Antiquaries, which had been founded in London ca. 1586[14] to study the history and antiquities of England; all three belonged to the small group of founder members. By this time William Camden had already gained a reputation as an antiquary through his ten years of work that led to the first publication of his *Britannia* in 1586; Cotton and Spelman were at the outset of their careers.

The development of the Society as an institution can best be sketched in conjunction with the scholarly and political biography

---

[12]The life and work of Camden—in contrast to those of his younger friend and spiritual foster-son Cotton—have not hitherto been the subject of a comprehensive assessment. See, apart from the *DNB* s.n., Powicke (1948); Piggott (1951); Fussner (1962), esp. ch. 9; Levy (1964); Fussner (1970), 277–83; McKisack (1971), esp. 150–54; Trevor-Roper (1971); and Parry (1995), ch. 1.

[13]The scholarly work of Henry Spelman has likewise not hitherto been comprehensively studied. See *DNB* s.n.; Adams (1917); 47–55, 73, and 117–18; Powicke (1930), with a valuable partial survey of Spelman's writings; Cronne (1956); Fussner (1962), esp. chs. 4–6 and 12; Fussner (1970), 240–41; Sharpe (1979), esp. chs. I–V; Kenyon (1983), 14–16; Oates (1986), chs. 7 and 8; Pocock (1951), 191–92; and Pocock (1987), ch. V.

[14]Not during Archbishop Parker's lifetime, as was for long wrongly believed. See Van Norden (1949–50), 136–40; Wright (1958), 179–82; McKisack (1971), 155; and Sharpe (1979), 17 n. 1.

of Robert Cotton.[15] With the foundation of the Society in London there came into being a club of private individuals with shared antiquarian interests. Most of them were young; but the membership included older antiquaries like Lambarde who provided some continuity with the work of Parker's circle.[16] The members gathered at Derby House near St. Paul's once a week to discuss two subjects which had been agreed upon at the previous week's meeting; they prepared themselves by the study of relevant sources. Materials for their studies included official records, manuscripts from the Royal Library, and manuscripts and records of the most varied kinds from the antiquaries' own private collections.[17]

Robert Cotton's library became increasingly important for the members' studies. Like the libraries of other well-to-do antiquaries of the period, it originated in an enthusiastic passion for collecting all kinds of memorabilia of the past; but Cotton developed a particular interest in manuscripts concerning the early history of England, manuscripts which he himself put to scholarly use and which he liberally made available to contemporaries who shared his interest.[18] In the spirit of the national enthusiasm of the late Elizabethan period, Cotton regarded this granting of access as an important public duty, as is clear from the petition which he, James Ley (1550–1629), and John Doddridge (1555–1628)

---

[15]See Wright (1958); McKisack (1971), ch. VII; Sharpe (1979), ch. I and pp. 198–203; and Tite (1994), 4–14.

[16]See Wright (1958), 183–85; and Sharpe (1979), 197–99. In the case of Lambarde, this continuity resulted from his early publications—his *Archaionomia* influencing Spelman's historical studies of the law and his *Perambulation*, Camden's *Britannia*—as well as from his activities among the public records in the last years of his life; see Fussner (1962), 75–76; Fussner (1970), 25, 240–41, and 278–79; and Warnicke (1973), chs. 4, 8, and 9.

[17]See Wright (1958), 185–89.

[18]See Wright (1958), 192–96; Sharpe (1979), ch. II, esp. 50–57 and 75; and Tite (1994), 6–24. See also below.

presented to the queen, probably in 1602.[19] The petition proposed the foundation of a royal academy and library for antiquarian studies, to be called "the Library of Queene Elizabethe" and "the Accademye for the studye of Antiquity and Historye founded by Queene Elizabeth." Two points of this petition are of interest for the history of the establishment of the study of Old English in the universities in the seventeenth century:

1. the readiness expressed in the petition to make available to the library of such an academy the private collections of members of the Society of Antiquaries.[20] This offer applied principally to Cotton's own library, which at the time was already of outstanding importance as a collection of historical manuscripts and of texts written in Old English;

2. the assurance that the academy "will not be hurtfull to eyther of the vniversiteis for yt shall not medle with the artes, philosophy, or other fynall Studyes their professed. For this Society tendeth to the preservation of historye & Antiquity of which the vniversityes being busyed in the Artes tak little care or regard."[21]

I shall return to the attitude toward the universities evinced by this statement—an attitude typical of its time—when I come to discuss the reasons for the change in attitude that later took place.

---

[19]This is the most likely date according to Wright (1958), 189–90, and Sharpe (1979), 27. The petition, on fols. 89–90 of BL MS Cotton Faustina E. v, is printed in Flügel (1909), 265–68.

[20]See Flügel (1909), 265.

[21]Flügel (1909), 268. For similar attempts to establish such institutions outside the universities, see Curtis (1959), 64–70 and 227–34.

The fate of Cotton's petition during the queen's lifetime is unclear. When in 1605 it was presented to King James I, it was dismissed, most probably on political grounds, as will be discussed below in relation to the later fate of the Society of Antiquaries. First I wish to show, using the Anglo-Saxon Chronicle as an example, what Cotton's offer to incorporate his library in the library of such an academy would have meant for the study of Old English in particular, and the actual significance that his library attained despite the rejection of the petition.[22] I shall attempt to show this in two ways: with reference to sources concerning the possession of manuscripts of the Chronicle during this period; and with reference to sources concerning those who used these manuscripts and the different types of use to which the manuscripts were put. The sources in question—references in the manuscripts themselves, in transcripts, in letters, in prefaces to printed books, and also in Cotton's memoranda in BL MS Harley 6018—mostly offer information about somewhat later phases in the history of the Cotton library. Nonetheless, in demonstrating the significance that the library attained despite the rejection of the petition and despite later additional difficulties, they give an impression of the value that both Cotton and his contemporaries attached to the library. Table 1 below presents a summary of the available information on manuscript ownership in the sixteenth and seventeenth centuries. Within the table, the second column shows the situation in the later sixteenth century; it is partly based on information given in a list of Chronicle manuscripts compiled by Joscelyn in 1565/6 (now BL MS Cotton Nero C. iii, fol. 208r),[23] partly on owners' dates

---

[22]On this, see esp. Wright (1958); Sharpe (1979), ch. II; and Tite (1994), 4–24.

[23]Printed in Wright (1951), 218–19 and 234, and Lutz (1982), 307–08; see also the new edition with commentary in Graham and Watson (1998), 54–59. Within this column, 1565/6 is cited within square brackets for those five manuscripts for which Joscelyn's list names an owner at that time. The dates of death of owners of the manuscripts are also cited in square brackets, as providing further information about the possible length of the private ownership of manuscripts;

TABLE 1. OWNERSHIP OF THE MANUSCRIPTS
OF THE ANGLO-SAXON CHRONICLE
IN THE LATE SIXTEENTH AND THE SEVENTEENTH CENTURIES

MS siglum	16th-century owner(s)	17th-century owner(s)	Present owner and library pressmark
A	1. Wotton [1565/6; d.1567] 2. Parker (until 1575) 3. Corpus Christi College, Cambridge (since 1575)	Corpus Christi College, Cambridge	Cambridge, Corpus Christi College, MS 173
B	Twyne [1565/6; d. 1581]	Cotton [1606]	BL MS Cotton Tiberius A. vi
C	1. W. Bowyer [1565/6; d. 1576] 2. R. Bowyer [d. 1606]	Cotton [1606]	BL MS Cotton Tiberius B. i
D	1. Worcester Cathedral [1565/6] 2. Joscelyn [d. 1603]	Cotton [1606]	BL MS Cotton Tiberius B. iv

for this see also Tite (1994), 11–12. All certain dates for the extent of the periods of private ownership as listed in columns 2 and 3 of the table are noted within parentheses; fuller information is given in the text and notes.

(Table 1—*Continued*)

MS siglum	16th-century owner(s)	17th-century owner(s)	Present owner and library pressmark
E	Cecil [1565/6; d. 1598]	1. ?Cotton [1618] 2. L'Isle [1622; d. 1637] 3. Laud (1638–39) 4. Bodleian Library (since 1639)	Bodleian MS Laud Misc. 636
F	?Camden	1. Camden (until 1623) 2. Cotton (after 1623)	BL MS Cotton Domitian A. viii
G	?	Cotton [1621]	BL MS Cotton Otho B. xi
H	?	Cotton	BL MS Cotton Domitian A. ix

of death. Joscelyn's list includes six of the surviving manuscripts (Joscelyn did not mention MS F and the fragment, MS H), and of these six, at least four had come into the possession of private individuals in the wake of the Dissolution of the Monasteries of 1536–40; sometime after the list was compiled, Joscelyn himself acquired MS D.

These private individuals included, in addition to Parker (MS A) and Cecil (MS E),[24] Nicholas Wotton (ca. 1497–1567),

---

[24]Cecil perhaps also owned MS G. Joscelyn did not list an owner for this manuscript but only remarked that Nowell had a transcript of it, whereas in the

Dean of Canterbury and York (from whose possession MS A passed into Parker's collection);[25] John Twyne (ca. 1501–81), Master of the Free Grammar School of Canterbury (MS B);[26] and William Bowyer (d. 1576), Keeper of the Records in the Tower of London (MS C).[27] The identities of these individuals make clear not only the general antiquarian interest of the time but also the concern of both Church and State to utilize historical sources for ecclesiastical and political issues. In this connection it is noteworthy that the ownership of Chronicle manuscripts at this early stage was concentrated in Canterbury and London.[28] Only one of the seven manuscripts reached its present owner in the late sixteenth century, a few years after Joscelyn's list of 1565/6, namely MS A: Parker bequeathed it to Corpus Christi College in

---

case of MS E he mentioned Cecil as owner of the manuscript and Nowell as owner of a transcript. Nowell himself noted at the end of his transcript of MS G (now BL MS Add. 43703, for which see Lutz [1981], ch. 3, Lutz [1982], 301–12, and below, Table 2, no. 1) that he wrote it in 1562 "in ædibus Secilianis" (fol. 264v). On the significance of Cecil's library see *DNB* s.n., pp. 1320–21; Wright (1958), 156, 170, and 199; Fussner (1962), 63–64; Tite (1994), 11–12; and Keynes (1996), 114–23.

[25]Through his activities as a leading diplomat in the service of the queen, Wotton embodied the close link between Church and Crown; see *DNB* s.n.; Ker (1957), no. 39; and Bately (1986), xiv.

[26]See *DNB* s.n.; Ker (1957), no. 188; McKisack (1971), 65–66; Taylor (1983), xi–xvii; and, with particular reference to Twyne as a collector of manuscripts, Watson (1986), with references to MS B on pp. 137 and 149.

[27]See Ker (1957), liv; Lutz (1982), 343–44; and Taylor (1983), xiv–xv.

[28]Parker probably kept MS A at Lambeth Palace in London, his official archiepiscopal residence and apparently the base of his book-collecting activities. He may also have kept some manuscripts at his country house at Bekesbourne, near Canterbury. After his death, his son John (1548–1619) kept books in his houses at both Bekesbourne and Lambeth; see Strongman (1977), 1–2; and Graham (1997a), 30.

Cambridge, along with most of the large collection of manuscripts he had obtained as a result of his efforts to overcome the effects of the dispersal of the monastic libraries.[29]

During the first half of the seventeenth century—as the third and fourth columns of Table 1 show—the other six manuscripts obtained the library pressmarks that reflect their very last private owners. Five of them (B, C, D, F, G) and the fragment, MS H, arrived one by one in Robert Cotton's library. This library, although remaining in private hands under his son and grandson, had already effectively become a quasi-official collection during the lifetime of its founder.[30] Its status is attested by numerous early seventeenth-century comments, and by the fact that antiquaries to whom the library had always stood open during their lives bequeathed their manuscripts to Cotton. Thus MS F passed to the Cotton library from the ownership of William Camden at the latter's death in 1623;[31] and Cotton probably obtained MS D at

---

[29]See Plummer (1892–99), II, §15; Ker (1957), no. 39; and Bately (1986), xiv–xv and xix–xx. In addition to his bequest to Corpus Christi, Parker had also given twenty-five manuscripts to the University Library in Cambridge in the year before his death. See McKisack (1971), 32–34; Oates (1958), 213–15; and Oates (1986), 96–110. Although this had not been part of his intention, Parker's donation and bequest helped prepare the way for the later establishment of the study of Old English in Cambridge.

[30]See Fussner (1962), 136 and 146–48; Sharpe (1979), 74–80; and Tite (1994).

[31]It is not known when this bilingual Old English and Latin version of the Chronicle, written at Christ Church, Canterbury, in the late eleventh or early twelfth century, came into Camden's possession, nor whether it had other private owners before him. It was used—but not necessarily owned—by the antiquary Robert Talbot (ca. 1505–1558; see *DNB* s.n., Graham [1997b], 295–96, and Graham [2000], 271–82), and may formerly have been bound with CUL MS Hh. 1. 10, a copy of Ælfric's *Grammar and Glossary* which Parker gave to the University Library in 1574. It is not mentioned in Joscelyn's list of 1565/6. Camden's ownership is attested by the churchman and ecclesiastical historian James Ussher in a letter to the historian John Selden (for both see below) dated

Joscelyn's death in 1603.[32] Over the decades Cotton also exchanged manuscripts in order to build up his library into a specialist collection of historical source materials; it was thus that he acquired MS C from Robert Bowyer (d. 1606),[33] Clerk of the Parliaments and William Bowyer's son. As for MSS B and G, it is not known when and how they came into Cotton's possession, although notes by Cotton in MS Harley 6018 concerning his loan of them in 1606 (MS B) and 1621 (MS G) provide a *terminus ante quem* for his acquisition of each.[34] (Several of the dates in square brackets in the third column of Table 1 refer to entries in Cotton's loan lists, for which see also below.)

MS E passed from private hands into public ownership in 1639, when Archbishop William Laud (1573–1645) gave it to the Bodleian Library in Oxford. Before that, it seems to have passed

---

19 September 1625, where Ussher refers to the manuscript having been "sometime . . . Mr Camdens" (see Ker [1957], no. 148, p. 188). By his will Camden left to Cotton all his manuscripts except those concerning heraldry. See *DNB* s.n. "Camden," p. 735; Ker (1957), no. 148; Sharpe (1979), 57–59; and Dumville (1995), 15–18.

[32] A note by Cotton in MS Harley 6018, fol. 156r, concerning the loan of MS D in 1606, comments that "it was Mr Gocelins" (see Ker [1957], no. 192, p. 255). Other manuscripts owned by Joscelyn also ended up in Cotton's library, along with a large part of his antiquarian writings and his work on Old English, including his two-volume dictionary of Old English (see Ker [1957], lii and 565); it seems likely that Cotton obtained these materials either by bequest or by purchase following Joscelyn's death.

[33] As is attested by a note by Cotton in MS Harley 6018, fol. 154v. See Ker (1957), lvi and 253; and Sharpe (1979), 57–58, where further cases of Cotton's exchanges of manuscripts are mentioned. On Robert Bowyer see Fussner (1962), 75–76, 93, and 142; McKisack (1971), 160; and *DNB Missing Persons*, s.n.

[34] See Ker (1957), liv–lvi, 234, and 250; for these lists see also Wright (1958), 200–01; Tite (1994), 1–39; and below. No mention is made in these lists of MS H, which comprises only two fragmentary twelfth-century annals (BL MS Cotton Domitian A. ix, fol. 9; see Ker [1957], no. 150, and Whitelock [1979], 116–17).

through the hands of two, possibly three, more private owners. According to Joscelyn's list, the manuscript had come into the possession of Sir William Cecil in or before 1565/6. From there it has been assumed to have passed directly into the hands of the antiquary William L'Isle (ca. 1569–1637), who owned it until his death.[35] When and how L'Isle got possession of MS E is not known. He mentioned it in 1622 in a letter to Cotton as "a faire Saxon Chronicle," quoting the beginning of annal 1052,[36] and there is also a reference to it by Richard James (1592–1638), Cotton's librarian from about 1625, who copied parts of annal 1125, referring to it as "Cronica Saxon. M^{ri}. W. Lisle."[37] But there is an earlier reference to "the *Saxon* Chronicles of *Peterborough*, *Canterbury*, and *Abingdon*" by the jurist and historian John Selden (1584–1654) in his *Historie of Tithes* (1618), and in a marginal note to this reference, all three manuscripts are stated to be "in Bibl. Cottoniana"; also, in Selden's long list of manuscripts in the index of sources to this work, the same three Chronicle manuscripts are listed under the heading "In Sir *Robert Cottons* Library."[38] This leads to the assumption that MS E may have

---

[35]On L'Isle see *DNB* s.n.; Adams (1917), 45–47 and 140–45; and Tuve (1939), as well as the papers in the present volume by Phillip Pulsiano and Stuart Lee. Whitelock (1954), 26, suggests that L'Isle, who received his university education at Cambridge, could have obtained the manuscript directly from Cecil, but more probably acquired it after Cecil's death in 1598. On the fate of Cecil's library in the seventeenth century, see Whitelock (1954), 26; and Tite (1994), 11–12.

[36]Cited by Whitelock (1954), 26.

[37]Bodleian MS James 17, fol. 115r, cited by Whitelock (1954), 26. On Richard James, see Tite (1994), 57–63.

[38]Selden (1618), 206 and sig. f3^{v}. The manuscript versions mentioned by Selden can be identified as MSS E, B, and C. On Selden, see *DNB* s.n.; Adams (1917), 66–68; Fussner (1962), chs. 2–6 and 11–12; Sharpe (1979); Tite (1994), 63–64 (who describes him as "the most active user of the Cotton library"); and Parry

belonged to Cotton's collection for some time and from there have passed into the ownership of L'Isle, possibly in exchange for another manuscript,[39] before L'Isle began his extensive comparative study of MSS E, A, and G, for which see below. After L'Isle's death in 1637, MS E was acquired by Archbishop Laud, who then gave it to the Bodleian Library in 1639, together with many other manuscripts from his private collection.[40] Thus all the Chronicle manuscripts, having passed out of monastic ownership into private hands in the course of the sixteenth century, became publicly available to scholars in the first half of the seventeenth century, most of them in Cotton's library in London.

This shift from private to public or semi-public ownership, which also applied to numerous other Anglo-Saxon manuscripts,[41] is reflected in the Chronicle manuscripts in the number of entries by early modern users that they contain. Sixteenth-century owners and users of manuscripts such as Joscelyn and Parker made numerous entries in the manuscripts, treating them more or less as

---

(1995), ch. 4. Fussner (1962), 135, states that "John Selden was greatly in Cotton's debt and dedicated his best-known and most controversial book, *The Historie of Tithes*, to Cotton."

[39] For exchanges of manuscripts between Cotton and other antiquaries, among them L'Isle, see Wright (1958), 202–04; Fussner (1962), 103; Sharpe (1979), 62–63; Tite (1992), 110–11; and Graham (2000), 290–93. Since MS E does not exhibit any traces of Cotton's ownership, this cannot be proved.

[40] On Laud's benefactions to the University of Oxford, see *DNB* s.n., pp. 629–32; Bennett (1938), 16; Trevor-Roper (1962), ch. 8; Philip (1983), 39–42 and 83; and Rogers (1991), 82–98. Folio 1r of the manuscript carries Laud's ownership mark of 1638. In the following year the manuscript formed part of a sizable gift that Laud made to the Bodleian Library; see Whitelock (1954), 25; and Ker (1957), no. 346 (with no. 344), pp. 424 and 426.

[41] See Fussner (1962), 35–37 and 60–69.

their personal property.[42] By contrast, the antiquaries of the seventeenth century made very few entries. An exception was William L'Isle, who seems to have planned an edition of the Chronicle presumably based on MS E, which belonged to him. Most of his entries occur in E; MSS A and G, which he used but did not own, have only isolated entries in his hand.[43]

Apart from users' entries in the manuscripts themselves, some small impression of the circle of the users of the Cotton library can be gained from allusions to the Chronicle in letters, from Chronicle extracts in various historical works, and from Cotton's notes in MS Harley 6018 concerning the loan of manuscripts.[44] According to Cotton's notes, the Chronicle manuscripts were lent

---

[42]For annotations and additions by Joscelyn in MSS A, B, C, D, and E and on his interleaved pages in MS D, see Classen and Harmer (1926), 5–12; Whitelock (1954), 22–26; Ker (1957), nos. 39, 188, 191, 192, and 346; Sanders Gale (1978), 206–15; Lutz (1982), 339–56; Taylor (1983), xii–xvii; and Bately (1986), xiv–xv and xliv. For Parkerian underlinings in red crayon in MSS A and E and the corresponding extracts from E in Parker's *A Defence of Priestes Mariages* of 1566/7, see Adams (1917), 25–27; Whitelock (1954), 22–24; Bately (1986), xlv; and Page (1993), 90–92. Nowell, who had made a complete transcript of MS G in 1562 (mentioned by Joscelyn in his list of 1565/6; now BL MS Add. 43703, see below, Table 2, no. 1), used this transcript for his later additions from other manuscript versions and did not annotate the manuscripts themselves; see Lutz (1981), xlix and li–lxv; and Lutz (1982), 303–38. For Robert Talbot's notes in MSS C and F see Ker (1957), l (roman numeral), 187, and 253.

[43]L'Isle interleaved MS E with paper to provide extra room for his notes. For his annotations in MSS A and G, and particularly his copious additions in E and its interleaved pages, see Whitelock (1954), 13 and 24–26; Ker (1957), nos. 39, 180, and 346; Lutz (1981), xlix–l; and Bately (1986), xv and xlv–xlvi. See also below, p. 23 and n. 52.

[44]Most of the details about users derive from Cotton's loan notes in MS Harley 6018. These give no information about the purpose of the use; the latter can in some cases be ascertained from entries in the manuscripts (L'Isle) and from the use of extracts from the Chronicle in publications (Selden, Spelman, and Ussher), for which see below.

repeatedly to antiquaries, historians, and also various office holders. Thus in 1606, MS B was loaned to both Arthur Agarde (1540–1615), Deputy Chamberlain in the Exchequer, and George Buck (d. 1623), historian and Master of the Revels, and in 1612 to Agarde again.[45] MS D was on loan to the antiquary Francis Tate (1560–1616) in 1606,[46] and MS G to William L'Isle in 1621.[47] Cotton's notes reveal some of the importance attached to the study of medieval manuscripts at the time, even beyond the restricted circle of antiquaries and historians.

Yet these notes do not provide a complete record of the borrowing of manuscripts, and they leave the use of the manuscripts within the library itself entirely out of account.[48] This somewhat slanted impression of the use of the Chronicle manuscripts of the Cotton library can in one case be supplemented by the evidence of an exchange of letters between two of the most active users of the library, namely the historian John Selden and the ecclesiastical historian and archbishop of Armagh James Ussher (1581–1656).[49] In a letter dated 4 August 1625, Selden

---

[45]See *DNB* s.nn. "Agard," "Buc"; Van Norden (1949–50), 154–55; Ker (1957), lv and 250; Fussner (1962), 73–76, 79–83, and 141; and McKisack (1971), 85–92.

[46]See *DNB* s.n.; Wright (1958), 183–86; Ker (1957), lv and 255; and McKisack (1971), 68–69.

[47]See Ker (1957), no. 180, p. 234.

[48]Scholars who are known to have used the Cotton library regularly and frequently, such as John Selden and Sir Henry Spelman, do not appear as users of Chronicle manuscripts in Cotton's loan lists, but they repeatedly refer to the Chronicle in their works. For Selden's use of Chronicle manuscripts in his *Historie of Tithes* (1618), see above (p. 18 and n. 38); for Spelman's references to the Chronicle in his *Archæologus* (vol. I, published in 1626) and his *Concilia* (1639), see below (nn. 79 and 99).

[49]On Ussher's importance as an ecclesiastical historian and orientalist, on his extensive scholarly contacts, and on the significance of the Cotton library for his

informed Ussher that at a recent meeting with Cotton "he gave me leave to send to your Lordship to spare me the two Saxon Chronicles you have of his . . . and (if you command it) they shall be sent you again in reasonable time"; a few weeks later (14 September) he wrote, "I have returned the *Saxon* Annals again, as you desired, with this suit, that if you have more of them (for these are very slight ones) . . . you will be pleased to send me them all, or as many as you have of them by you, and what else you have of the History of *Scotland* and *Ireland*, and they shall be returned at your pleasure."[50] In his answer to Selden dated 19 September 1625, Ussher stated: "I now onely have remayning in my hands . . . one booke onely of Annals in Saxon and Latine, which sometime was Mr Camdens, and that I send unto you."[51] These letters, which mention three of Cotton's Chronicle manuscripts (besides several other historical works) but specify only one, namely the bilingual MS F, provide a rare glimpse of the scholarly exchange between two of the most regular users of the Cotton library.

---

studies of ecclesiastical history, which culminated in his *Britannicarum ecclesiarum antiquitates . . .* (1639), see Parr (1686); Ellis (1843), 131–42; *DNB* s.n.; Adams (1917), 73 and 115; O'Sullivan (1956); Oulton (1956); Styles (1956); Wright (1958), 196 and 202; Fussner (1962), esp. 136–37; Watson (1966), 9–10, 21, 30, and 42; Knox (1967), ch. VI; Sharpe (1979), esp. 33–34, 58, 75, 107, 139, and 210–11; Tite (1994), 63; and Parry (1995), ch. 5. Ussher first met Cotton (and also Camden) in 1606, on his second visit to England, and from then on he came to London, Oxford, and Cambridge every three years (see *DNB* s.n., p. 65). We may therefore assume that, as a rule, Ussher used the resources of the Cotton library on his regular visits and that for him the borrowing of a manuscript represented an exception. Richard Parr notes in his biography that Ussher's visits to London were spent "chiefly in the Cottonian library, the noble and learned master of which affording him a free access not only to that but to his conversation" (Parr [1686], 10). For Selden's use of the Cotton library and its Chronicle manuscripts see above, p. 18 and n. 38.

[50]Printed by Parr (1686), 332 and 338.

[51]Bodleian MS Smith 21, p. 63, cited by Ker (1957), 187–88.

The purpose of the loan of a manuscript does not emerge from Cotton's notes nor from this correspondence, but in a few cases it can be determined from the results of the work of the borrowers. This is certainly the case with William L'Isle, who borrowed MS G in 1621. He collated it with his own manuscript (MS E), and also with MS A, which similarly contains traces of his work. Moreover, a letter of Ussher has survived, written to L'Isle in 1624, in which Ussher proposes that L'Isle should edit the whole Chronicle.[52] L'Isle's borrowing of MS G must thus have been linked with his extensive comparative studies of the Chronicle text, studies that may have had the underlying purpose of producing a conflated version of the text, the same purpose as had motivated Nowell and Joscelyn some decades before.

In the case of James Ussher's borrowing of MS F and two other Chronicle manuscripts in 1625, we may assume that it was connected with his studies toward his *Britannicarum ecclesiarum antiquitates* (1639), judging from his letter to Cotton of 20 December 1624, in which he mentions this project and some manuscripts from the Cotton library that he considers to be particularly useful for the initial phase of his work.[53]

---

[52]L'Isle was engaged upon the study of the manuscripts of the Chronicle from the early 1620s, as is shown by his entries in MSS A, E, and G (see above) and by the note in MS Harley 6018 concerning his borrowing of MS G in 1621; but Ussher's suggestion in the letter of 1624 (mentioned in Bennett [1938], 13) that he should produce a full edition with translation was never realized. In a letter to Cotton of 16 March 1631, L'Isle stated that "the Saxon Bible and Chronicles lye dead by me" (BL MS Cotton Julius C. iii, fol. 242r, cited in Whitelock [1954], 25). On L'Isle's single publication on Old English, *A Saxon Treatise Concerning the Old and New Testament* (1623), and on his various unfulfilled plans see also *DNB* s.n.; Adams (1917), 45–47 and 140–45; and Graham (2000), 306–12.

[53]BL MS Cotton Julius C. iii, fol. 156, printed by Ellis (1843), 131. Ussher's *Britannicarum ecclesiarum antiquitates* makes several specific references to manuscripts of the Chronicle. For example, on p. 36, Ussher prints part of annal 167 from the bilingual version, MS F (cf. Thorpe [1861], 15; specified as "quos

Especially noteworthy is the way in which manuscripts of the Chronicle and other manuscript sources in Cotton's possession were consulted for their relevance to questions concerning the constitution and the history of institutions. This happened in the case of the Society of Antiquaries, at whose meetings such questions became increasingly the focus of antiquarian interest.[54] And in later years, both Cotton and his contemporaries called upon the library's resources for such purposes in connection with their political work;[55] by this time Cotton enjoyed a distinguished reputation for his antiquarian and jurisprudential knowledge and acted as advisor to leading politicians while also serving several times

---

à V. Cl. Guil. Camdeno acceptos in instructissimâ suâ Bibliothecâ reposuit D. Robertus Cottonus" ["which, after receiving it from the noble William Camden, Robert Cotton placed in his excellently furnished library"], and cf. also his description of this manuscript in his letter to Selden cited above, p. 22 and n. 51). On p. 62 he quotes a short passage taken from annal 894 of MS G (cf. Lutz [1981], 65; specified as "ex Annalibus Anglo-Saxonicis Bedæ subnexis" ["from the Anglo-Saxon annals appended to Bede"]), and on p. 899, annal 430 from MS E ("id Petroburgensium Annalium collector de *Patricio* hunc in modum extulerit" ["the compiler of the Peterborough Annals expressed this in this way, with reference to 'Patricius'"]), which he contrasts with the reading *Palladius* in other Chronicle manuscripts ("alij Annales Anglosaxonici"; cf. Thorpe [1861], 18–19). For Ussher's works on ecclesiastical history see *DNB* s.n. Cotton himself took a keen interest in the subject and supplied Ussher with books and manuscripts, and Ussher pointed out on several occasions how much he owed not only to Cotton's library but also to his expertise and encouragement over a long time (see Sharpe [1979], 33–34, 88, 108, 139, and 211).

[54]Sharpe (1979), 30–31 and 152–54.

[55]See Fussner (1962), xvi–xvii and 127–34; and Sharpe (1979), chs. IV and V. That antiquarian studies could go hand in hand with political purposes is shown by the cases quoted by Sharpe (pp. 137, 146–48, 152–54, and 189) of antiquarian researches into such terms as *constable* and *bretwalda*, and into questions concerning the powers and privileges of office holders that could be resolved by study of the sources.

as a member of the lower House. From 1622 the Cotton library was housed directly opposite Parliament,[56] and it served increasingly for the investigation of precedents for determining political and constitutional issues. The loans recorded by Cotton in MS Harley 6018 demonstrate this broadening and partial shift of antiquarian interest from the history of the Church to matters of legal and constitutional history, a shift that accompanied the movement of the center of gravity of antiquarian studies to the very heart of London's political life.[57]

It was probably just this potentially dangerous political usage of historical sources that led to the king's rejection of the petition in 1605 and the disbanding of the Society of Antiquaries two years later.[58] As its younger members—especially those with legal training—had grown in age and influence, the Society had developed into a significant political institution; at its weekly meetings questions concerning the origin of institutions figured increasingly among the subjects for discussion.[59] There is no direct evidence that political pressure from above was the cause of the dissolution of the Society. In Sharpe's opinion, however, this is indicated by a comment made by Spelman in connection with the attempt to refound the Society in 1614: according to Spelman, the king "took a little Mislike of our Society"—despite the fact that it

---

[56]Before that, it had been first at Blackfriars and then in the Strand. See Sharpe (1979), 74–75; and Tite (1994), 19–20 and 80–112.

[57]Compare Sharpe (1979), 78: "The list of those borrowing from the library reads like a *Who's Who* of the Jacobean administration"; see also Fussner (1962), 127. Despite the shift in emphasis of antiquarian interests, there was no real antithesis between the Parker circle and the Society of Antiquaries, as is shown by William Lambarde's first edition of Anglo-Saxon laws, which was published with Parker's assistance, but also established an important foundation for the work of the later antiquaries, esp. that of Henry Spelman.

[58]Sharpe (1979), 28–29.

[59]Sharpe (1979), 29–32.

was expressly intended that the revived Society should steer clear of "Matters of State." In view of the king's attitude, the plan to refound the Society was abandoned.[60] The Society seems to have become a casualty of the growing tensions between king and Privy Council on the one hand and Parliament on the other.

Cotton himself was to run into increasing political difficulties despite considerable care on his part and sincere efforts to remain impartial. In 1626 his library came under threat of closure. In 1629 it was closed by order of the king, and Cotton was briefly arrested under the pretext of sedition. His repeated requests for the return of the library remained unanswered, and the prolonged uncertainty over its fate was partly responsible for his premature death in 1631.[61]

Thus to a certain extent, despite the continuing growth of the Cotton library, its history was a string of disappointments and defeats for Cotton himself, when measured against his endeavor to establish the study of history (and thereby indirectly of Old English also) outside the universities and in close association with the political sphere. He had to accept the rejection of the proposed Academy, the dissolution of the Society of Antiquaries, the failure of the attempt to refound the Society, and finally even the closure of the library itself. It is symptomatic of the change in attitude Cotton's experiences produced in him that in his later years he no longer offered to unite his own library with the royal collection.[62]

III. REORIENTATION TOWARD THE UNIVERSITIES: CAMDEN AND SPELMAN

Cotton's experiences must also have made a significant impression on those most closely associated with him in London,

---

[60]Powicke (1930), 353 with n. 1; Van Norden (1949–50), 134–55; and Sharpe (1979), 36. Spelman was one of those who wished to refound the Society.

[61]Sharpe (1979), 80–82 and 143–46; and Sharpe (1997), 15–22.

[62]Sharpe (1979), 80.

especially on his two long-standing friends, the distinguished historians Camden and Spelman, who for decades relied upon the Cotton library for their scholarly projects. In their later years both men became proponents of the establishment of the study of history in the universities: in 1622 Camden endowed the chair of Civil History in Oxford, while in 1639 Spelman established the Cambridge lectureship in "Antiquitates Britannicæ et Saxonicæ" to which I have already referred. As will be shown in what follows, the reasons for these endowments are to be sought principally in the experiences that the two historians underwent in London, but partly also in the changes that had taken place in the universities since the time of Cotton's petition.

This is especially clear in the case of William Camden.[63] He had studied at Oxford in his youth under the patronage of Dr. Thomas Cooper (ca. 1517–1594) and Dr. Thomas Thornton (1541–1629), and it was during these years that he developed his antiquarian inclinations. However, his efforts to obtain a fellowship and the Master's degree failed for religious and political reasons, and it is unclear whether he received his Bachelor's degree.[64] How much these early, unhappy Oxford experiences still hurt him even decades later is clear from the fact that in 1613, when he was offered an honorary M.A. as the celebrated author of the *Britannia*, he turned it down.[65] Even as late as 1618, in a letter to James Ussher, he wrote with bitterness about the injustices he had suffered in his student days.[66]

---

[63]In addition to the *DNB* s.n., see esp. Trevor-Roper (1971).

[64]*DNB* s.n., pp. 729–30.

[65]*DNB* s.n., pp. 730–31.

[66]"And to make you my Confessor *sub sigillo Confessionis*, I took my Oath thereunto at my Matriculation in the University of *Oxon.* (when Popery was predominant) and for defending the Religion established, I lost a fellowship in *All-Souls*, as Sir *Daniel Dun* could testifie, and often would relate how I was there opposed by the Popish Faction. . . . I know not who may justly say that I was

That only four years later he established the first chair of history at the very same university therefore requires explanation. Camden has left no direct statement of the reasons for his action. However, the repeated negative experiences of his efforts to pursue the study of history in London within the environment of the court, as free as possible from political pressures, seems to have been of decisive importance.[67] In particular, he must have acquired such experiences while working on his biography of Queen Elizabeth I, which he began in 1608 more or less at the king's commission. His work on both parts of the biography provoked the king to repeated attempts at censorship.[68] Camden dedicated the first part, which appeared in 1615 and which extended to the year 1588, "to God, my country and posterity, at the altar of truth" —not to the king.[69] As for the second part, completed in 1617 and delivered to the king,[70] Camden stipulated in 1621 that it should be published posthumously in Leiden.[71]

---

ambitious, who . . . refused a Mastership of Requests offered. . . . *Sed hæc tibi uni & soli*" (10 July 1618; printed by Parr [1686], 65; and Ellis [1843], 125–26).

[67]See *DNB* s.n.; Trevor-Roper (1971); and Kenyon (1983), 9–10. From these accounts it is abundantly clear that during the reign of James I Camden came under increasing political pressure because of his historical studies.

[68]*Annales rerum Anglicarum et Hibernicarum regnante Elizabetha* . . . . See *DNB* s.n., p. 733; Fussner (1962), 235–50; and Trevor-Roper (1971), 13–14.

[69]In contrast, in 1586 Camden had dedicated his *Britannia* to Sir William Cecil, who ten years later was the first to encourage him to write a history of the reign of Queen Elizabeth, as Camden wrote in the preface to the first part of the *Annales*. See *DNB* s.n., pp. 730 and 733–34; and Trevor-Roper (1971), 6–10 and 18. See also Collinson (1998), 152–63, who mentions Cotton's supportive and mediating role in this project over several years.

[70]To "his Majesty's judicious censure, whether it please him that they [sc. the *Annales*] should be suppressed or published, for I am indifferent" (Trevor-Roper [1971], 19).

[71]*DNB* s.n., pp. 733–34; and Trevor-Roper (1971), 20–21. Compare also the remark in his letter to Ussher cited above (10 July 1618; printed by Parr

In the case of his Oxford initiative, which he pursued in his last years, Camden was presumably stimulated in part by the direct precedent of his long-standing friend Sir Henry Savile (1549–1622), who founded the chairs of geometry and astronomy at Oxford in 1619.[72] Camden secured the finances of his chair by endowing it with the rents of a property he had purchased from Spelman.[73] The chair was to be expressly for Civil History, that is, political history founded upon the study of sources, as opposed to ecclesiastical history, which was still strongly colored by the Christian view of the history of salvation. Camden thereby brought a new subject into the university curriculum, and not without opposition from conservative circles within the university. Outside the universities, this new orientation of historical studies had already been discussed and taught for some years, under the influence of continental ideas.[74] Camden's endowment should therefore not be seen as a late acknowledgment by him of the traditional structures of his university; rather, it was an attempt to establish new structures, after conditions for studying history outside the universities, particularly in London, had become too difficult.[75]

[1686], 65): "I never made suit to any man, no not to his Majesty . . . ," which seems to express his general attitude during those years.

[72]See *DNB* s.n. "Savile, Sir Henry," pp. 857–58; and Powicke (1948), 69–70, who states that Savile "applauded his intention."

[73]*DNB* s.n. "Camden," p. 735.

[74]In a letter to the university, Camden explicitly referred to "the practice of such professors in all universities beyond seas" (Curtis [1959], 117, and Trevor-Roper [1971], 34; see also Hill [1965], 309). On Camden's contacts with continental historians and on the development of historical studies, see Dean (1941); Trevor-Roper (1971); Sharpe (1979), ch. III; Parry (1995), 26–28; and above all Fussner (1962), the fundamental account of the development of historical studies in England in the early modern period.

[75]Sharpe (1982) comes to a very similar conclusion, and draws attention to the fact that only two decades earlier, when Cotton had referred in his petition to the

It was through the foundation of this new chair, rather than through his own use of Old English for his publications,[76] that Camden contributed to the establishment of the study of Old English in the universities. This was despite the fact that, with Camden's consent, the first holder of the chair, Degory Wheare (1573–1647), taught Roman rather than Anglo-Saxon history.[77] The significance of Camden's Oxford chair for the establishment of Old English studies becomes clearer when one considers the career and work of his old friend Sir Henry Spelman. During these years of increasing political tensions between king and Parliament, Spelman had to undergo experiences very similar to those of Camden.

Spelman's historical interests were colored by his background as a member of the landed gentry and by a lengthy legal dispute concerning land ownership. This led him to conduct an investigation into the origins of English law, and this in turn led him in 1612 to establish his residence in London, close to Cotton's library.[78] He soon realized that in order to fulfill his purpose he

---

value of historical studies for the education of diplomats and had thereby sought to distinguish the aims of his project from those pursued by the universities, the state of the libraries in Oxford would in no way have facilitated such studies (see above all Sharpe [1982], 27–28, and, on the history of the Oxford libraries, Butt [1938], 64–66; Myres [1958]; Fussner [1962], 36–37; Philip [1983], chs. 1 and 2; and Rogers [1991], chs. II and III). Noteworthy also in this connection is Sharpe's observation that from 1620 Cotton increasingly sought contact with the universities (Sharpe [1979], 215).

[76]*Anglica, Normannica . . . scripta* (1603) and *Remaines of a Greater Worke, Concerning Britaine . . .* (1605). See Adams (1917), 43 and 191; and Gneuss (1990), 42, 45, and 67.

[77]See *DNB* s.n. "Camden," pp. 734–36, and Curtis (1959), 117, for Camden's aims in setting up the chair. For Degory Wheare's lectures, see Powicke (1948), 70–74, and Fussner (1962), 169–70. For the later expansion of the study of history to include English history, see Curtis (1959), 131–32.

[78]See *DNB* s.n., p. 737; Adams (1917), 48; Powicke (1930), 351–52; and Sharpe (1979), 212.

would require knowledge of the fundamentals of legal terminology. In 1619 he completed the first volume of his *Archæologus*, a glossary of English legal terminology that drew upon both Latin and Old English sources;[79] the volume covered the letters A–L. He offered the volume to the royal printer, who turned it down. He therefore had it printed at his own expense in 1626.[80] The second volume, accompanied by a reissue of the first, did not appear until 1664, when it was published by Sir William Dugdale (1605–86).[81]

---

[79]See Adams (1917), 47 and 176; and Pocock (1987), 93–103. The work contains a number of references to sources written in Old English, among them one to the Chronicle, namely in his entry s.v. *Gersuma*: "Chron. Sax. An. 1035. . . . His gersumā namon, &c. *ærarium ejus fregerunt*. . . ." This may be based on the annal for 1035 in MS C (which has *gærsuma*) alone, or it may be a conflation of the readings of C and D (which has *gærsaman*); cf. Rositzke (1940), 68; and Cubbin (1996), 65.

[80]*Archæologus in modum glossarii ad rem antiquam posteriorem . . .* (1626); see Adams (1917), 47–48, who adds that the book sold poorly. *DNB* s.n., p. 738, also reports the difficulties surrounding the publication and the sale of the first volume but states that in 1619 Spelman merely sent "sample sheets" to foreign colleagues, then continued his work after receiving positive reactions; and that the response of the scholarly world after the appearance of the first volume was similarly very positive. Powicke (1930), 354, mentions "general applause" as the reaction to the publication of the first volume and says nothing of Spelman's difficulties over the publication; however, he perhaps leaves a letter of Spelman, to which he refers at another point (p. 357), to attest to the difficulties. In this letter, which Spelman sent to Ussher in May 1637, along with a copy of the first volume, Spelman notes that the book was ready by 1626, the date carried on the title page, but that it could not be published, in Powicke's words, "until an imperial privilegium, necessary to prevent piratical or unauthorized publication in Germany, had been obtained."

[81]See Adams (1917), 47 and 176; on the importance of the *Archæologus* for historical studies, see Fussner (1962), 101–04 and 116.

In the meantime, Spelman had set to work on his other major work, the *Concilia*: an edition of sources for the history of the medieval English Church, many of these sources being in Old English.[82] There has been much speculation about what caused Spelman to shift the focus of his scholarly work. Against the background of the fate of the first volume of the *Archæologus* and the experiences of Spelman's friend Camden mentioned above, it seems plausible that (as one version has it) Archbishop William Laud, with whom Spelman was linked through shared antiquarian interests, found the definitions of terms such as *Magna Charta* and *Magnum Concilium* in the second part of Spelman's glossary so politically objectionable that he refused to license its printing.[83]

---

[82] *Concilia, decreta, leges, constitutiones.* . . . The first volume, which covers the period up to the Norman Conquest, appeared in 1639; the second was published by Dugdale in 1664 along with a reissue of the first. See *DNB* s.n., pp. 738–39; Adams (1917), 49–51; Powicke (1930); and Parry (1995), 168–73.

[83] Adams (1917), 49, cites this version as "a story long current" but also mentions other possibilities such as the financial failure of the first volume and declining interest in this project. It seems quite credible that against the background of growing political tensions Laud might have dissuaded Spelman from early publication of the second volume (for Laud's attitude toward the universities in the 1630s see Curtis [1959], 32–34 and 172, and Kearney [1970], 91–97). In this connection see the appraisal by Pocock (1951), 191–92, and Parry (1995), 177–78, of the influence of Spelman's entry *Parlamentum* for late seventeenth-century political discourse; and see also Fussner (1962), 103–04. Less conclusive is the view of Powicke, who sees the second volume of the *Archæologus* as simply uncompleted and as "very inferior to the first," citing Du Cange and others. On the one hand Powicke gives the impression that in the course of working on the *Archæologus* Spelman lost interest in it, but on the other he believes that he can infer from Spelman's papers that Spelman began work on the *Concilia* "as soon as the *Archæologus* or glossary was off his hands"; see Powicke (1930), 355 and 357. According to *DNB* s.n., p. 738, and Pocock (1987), 105–19, Spelman worked on the *Archæologus* and on some short papers on legal history until 1638.

In any event, with the *Concilia* Spelman was working in territory that was politically far less risky. Nonetheless, political circumstances soon brought his scholarly work into yet greater jeopardy, this time through the closure of the Cotton library in 1629–31, as a result of which Spelman was temporarily deprived of the most important resources for his work. Those resources included not only the manuscripts that provided the source materials for his researches in legal and ecclesiastical history. The library also contained the most important aids for interpreting those sources written in Old English. These aids included Ælfric's *Grammar* of Latin written in Old English, which had long been used by antiquaries as a grammar of Old English;[84] and, more especially, John Joscelyn's two-volume manuscript dictionary of Old English.[85] Only under these altered external circumstances in London did the lack of printed aids for the study of Old English become acutely felt, and it must have been in this situation that Spelman developed the idea of establishing the study of Anglo-Saxon history and of the Old English language as a university subject.[86]

---

[84]The library contained two manuscripts of the work, Faustina A. x and Julius A. ii; see Ker (1957), nos. 154A and 158.

[85]MSS Titus A. xv and A. xvi, described by Dugdale in a letter of 13 April 1640 as "the Cottonian Dictionarie" (see Watson [1966], 10). On the importance of Joscelyn's dictionary for Spelman's project of publishing a dictionary of Old English, see below.

[86]A more detailed investigation of the origins of the Cambridge lectureship would require a thoroughgoing analysis of the correspondence between Spelman and those in his circle, and also of Spelman's writings; the work in this direction that has been accomplished hitherto—above all that of Ellis (1843); Adams (1917); Powicke (1930); Fussner (1962); and Oates (1986)—represents only a beginning. But the evidence adduced so far suggests that the assessment by Adams (1917), 42, that the seventeenth century "witnessed the gradual absorption of the study of Old English by the universities," assigns the universities a more active and positive role than they actually played in connection with

IV. ABRAHAM WHEELOCK AND THE CAMBRIDGE LECTURESHIP
IN "ANTIQUITATES BRITANNICAE ET SAXONICAE"

Spelman conceived the plan for a lectureship in "Antiquitates Britannicæ et Saxonicæ, cum ecclesiasticæ tum politicæ"—the latter aspect probably under the influence of Camden's establishment of the Oxford chair in Civil History—as a result of consulting Cambridge manuscripts for his *Concilia* and, through the agency of Ussher, becoming acquainted with Abraham Wheelock (1593–1653), the University Librarian and Professor of Arabic, whom he recognized as the appropriate person for the post.[87] Wheelock was suited to Spelman's purpose in several ways. He had unimpeded access to the manuscripts in the University Library, and access under certain restrictions to those in the college libraries; as an expert linguist, he was better prepared for tackling what was in effect a foreign language than were the antiquaries, most of whom had had a legal or theological training; and as a man of insubstantial means he was dependent on the income that Spelman offered him.[88]

Camden's and Spelman's endowments. The initiative seems to have come from outside the universities.

[87]Wheelock held the University Librarianship from 1629 and the Professorship of Arabic from 1632. His study of Arabic had brought him into contact with Ussher as early as 1625. Spelman made Wheelock's acquaintance as a result of using Cambridge manuscripts for the *Concilia*, and he made frequent use of Wheelock's services for transcribing both Latin and Old English manuscripts. See Parr (1686), 310; Kennett (1693), 107–08; Ellis (1843), 145–50 and 153; *DNB* s.n. "Wheelocke"; Adams (1917), 73; Bennett (1938), 11–13; Utley (1942), 244–46; Murphy (1967); Murphy and Barrett (1985); and Oates (1986), chs. 7–9.

[88]On Wheelock's financial situation and his exaggerated financial worries, see Murphy and Barrett (1985), 170–74; and Oates (1986), 179–90. Spelman knew from the example of his kinsman William L'Isle—who had worked on the manuscripts of the Anglo-Saxon Chronicle from the early 1620s without any resulting publication (see above)—that prolonged work on Old English without any consequent publication did not advance the subject.

The Cambridge lectureship was historically orientated, and the study of Old English was to serve the purpose of making available in printed form historical sources that were written in Old English and of providing linguistic aids for the study of the sources. Spelman also specified which tasks should be undertaken first. According to him, they were to be:

1. the publication of the most important historical sources in Old English;
2. the preparation of an Old English grammar;
3. the preparation of an Old English dictionary.[89]

Wheelock, whom Spelman had prepared for the task over a period of several years, was to furnish the textual editions, Spelman's son John (1594–1643) was to contribute the grammar after completing his edition of the Old English Psalter,[90] and the antiquary Sir Simonds D'Ewes (1602–50) wished to provide the dictionary.[91] In

---

[89]This program is formulated most clearly in a letter from Spelman to Wheelock of 28 September 1638, printed in Ellis (1843), 154–55, and Adams (1917), 52–53, and quoted in extracts in *DNB* s.n. "Spelman," p. 739, where it is incorrectly dated to 1635.

[90]John Spelman's role is mentioned in the same letter. On his 1640 edition of the Psalter, see Adams (1917), 50–51, and Kimmens (1979), xxiv–xxv; see also *DNB* s.n.; Fussner (1962), 157–58; and Oates (1986), 187, 197–98, and 200–01.

[91]D'Ewes's proposal to produce a dictionary was not particularly welcome to Spelman, as the latter observed in a letter to Wheelock of 24 April 1640; see Oates (1986), 196. D'Ewes had already commenced work on an Old English dictionary in 1631, but by the time of his death in 1650 he had done little more than make a transcript of Joscelyn's dictionary; similarly, he began several other projects with initial enthusiasm but failed to complete them. See *DNB* s.n.; Adams (1917), 56–57 and 116–17; Bennett (1938), 359–60; Watson (1966), 8–15; and (less critical) Hetherington (1975) and (1980), 102–24. On Spelman's efforts to discourage the Dutch scholar Johannes de Laet (1582–1649) from

1640 the lectureship was officially instituted with Ussher's support.[92] Wheelock edited the two most important narrative sources for Anglo-Saxon history, namely the Old English translation of Bede's *Historia ecclesiastica* accompanied by the original Latin (the principal source for early Anglo-Saxon history), and the Anglo-Saxon Chronicle (the principal source for the later Anglo-Saxon period) together with a Latin translation. The volume containing both these works appeared in 1643, two years after Sir Henry Spelman's death.[93]

The choice of manuscripts for both texts reflected Sir Henry Spelman's long-standing familiarity with the Cotton library on the one hand and the change of orientation to Cambridge on the other. For the Old English version of Bede's text Wheelock used the Cambridge University Library copy (MS Kk. 3. 18) as his base manuscript, and he supplemented it with variants from the copies at Corpus Christi College (MS 41) and in the Cotton library (MS Otho B. xi).[94] For the Chronicle he used only two of the seven

---

publishing his Old English dictionary and on its later fate, see Ellis (1843), 154–55; Adams (1917), 56; Bennett (1938), 313–14 and 357–58; Hetherington (1980), 97–101; Bremmer (1988), 176–77; and Dekker (1999), 216–17.

[92]See *DNB* s.n. "Spelman"; Adams (1917), 53 and 73; Bennett (1938), 13–14; Oates (1986), 185–87; and Bremmer (1988), 176–77.

[93]*Historiæ ecclesiasticæ gentis Anglorum libri V . . . quibus in calce operis Saxonicam chronologiam . . . editam* (1643). See Adams (1917), 54–55 and 163–65; Murphy (1967); Lutz (1981), ch. 4; and Oates (1986), 204–09. The Cambridge University press created a special font for the edition, modeled on Insular minuscule. The font was employed for the first time in 1641 in *Irenodia Cantabrigiensis*, a volume dedicated to King Charles I and published at Cambridge: *Irenodia Cantabrigiensis* contained a poem composed in "Old English" by "Abrahamus Whelocus, Bibliothec. pub. Arab. & Saxo-Brit. Pr."; see Utley (1942), 244–53, and see also below. The full poem is quoted in the essay by Danielle Cunniff Plumer in the present volume.

[94]Lutz (1981), lxx–lxxi, and Oates (1986), 205–06, based on Wheelock's preface "Ad Lectorem," where Wheelock describes MS Kk. 3. 18 as the manuscript

surviving manuscripts: as his base manuscript he used MS G (also contained within MS Otho B. xi), which had a full copy of the Winchester text to 1001;[95] to complete the text he used MS A, the exemplar of MS G, which included many late additions and alterations to the original text as preserved in MS G, most of these additions and alterations having been made at Canterbury in the late eleventh or early twelfth century by the scribe of MS F.[96] In both the Bede and the Chronicle, base text and variants were scrupulously distinguished—by no means a standard feature of editions of the period.

Because it restricted itself to two manuscripts only, Wheelock's edition of the Chronicle came in for much criticism, as will be seen in greater detail below. This criticism seems unjustified, for there is evidence that there was a conscious intention

---

"quem omnino praecipue sequimur"; for his use of CCCC MS 41 see Graham (1997c). On the three manuscripts, see Ker (1957), nos. 23, 32 art. 1, and 180 art. 1; for a survey of them and of their interrelationships, see Whitelock (1962), 81. For the parallel Latin text of his edition Wheelock's principal manuscript was Cambridge, Trinity College, MS R. 5. 22, as he indicates in his preface; he also used Cambridge, Sidney Sussex College, MS Δ. 5. 17, and the Cottonian MS Tiberius C. ii. From a letter of Wheelock to Sir Thomas Cotton of 31 March 1640 (printed in Ellis [1843], 160), it appears that Wheelock also borrowed another Cottonian copy of the Latin text, MS Tiberius A. xiv, although he did not make use of it.

[95] Lutz (1981), lxxi–lxxviii. For an assessment of Wheelock's work on the Chronicle, see also Douglas (1951), 61 and 69–70.

[96] Lutz (1981), chs. 5 and 6. For the contents and textual relationship of MSS G, A, and F, see also Whitelock (1979), 109–11 and 115–16; Bately (1986); and Bately (1991). The textual similarities between these additions to MS A by the scribe of F and the text of MS E had been pointed out by Joscelyn in MS A in several notes (see, for example, s.aa. 423 and 443 in Flower and Smith [1941], fol. 4v). Wheelock noted Joscelyn's observation in his edition (p. 503) in the margin opposite annal 11, pointing out that this and all subsequent alterations in MS A were printed in brackets in his edition.

not to produce a conflated edition based on all the surviving manuscripts but to restrict the edition to the Winchester text, which until the fire in the Cotton library in 1731 was best preserved in MS G;[97] also, this restriction was not the result of Wheelock's lack of acquaintance with the manuscript tradition of the Chronicle, but was based on a decision of Henry Spelman, or at least on his advice.[98] From his work on the *Archæologus* and the *Concilia* Spelman appears to have known the other four versions of the Chronicle in the Cotton library (MSS B, C, D, and F), and also MS E, which until 1637 was owned by his kinsman William L'Isle.[99] It is therefore hardly likely that Wheelock's reason for confining himself to MS G among the Cottonian manuscripts was that he was given only restricted access to the Cotton library's holdings; after all, for the Latin text of Bede he was able to borrow both Cottonian manuscripts dating from the Anglo-Saxon period,

---

[97]The Winchester component of the text of the other Chronicle versions contained gaps in certain places, or had clearly been altered by later regional additions. See Whitelock (1979), 109–25; Lutz (1981), esp. chs. 1, 2, 5, and 6; and Bately (1991).

[98]See Wheelock's letter of 27 December 1639 to Spelman (printed in Oates [1986], 205), in which he reports that "I am at leasure fitting Bede his historie (by the help of six auncient MS. three in Lat. & three in Sax.) for the presse" and asserts that "I have learned, & shall learne more after yor methode. . . ."

[99]Compare his reference to "Chron. Sax. An. 1035" in the first volume of his *Archæologus*, cited above (n. 79), which may be based on both C and D. In his *Concilia*, vol. I (1639), he prints two Chronicle extracts: on pp. 163–68 the annal for 675 from MS E, which contains a long Peterborough insertion with Pope Agatho's privilege (cf. Plummer [1892–99], I, 35–37; and Whitelock [1979], 166 n. 9), and on p. 496 the annal for 977 from MS B or C (or both) on the assembly at Kirtlington (cf. Thorpe [1861], 230; Taylor [1983], 56; and Rositzke [1940], 51). Spelman does not specify these as extracts from the Chronicle, but this is in keeping with his treatment of all the sources he used for the *Concilia*.

although in the event he used only one of them for his edition.[100] In any case, it seems to me that the prevailing judgment of Wheelock's edition of the Chronicle suffers from being confined to the Chronicle and to Wheelock, without taking into consideration Wheelock's edition of Bede, Henry Spelman's *Concilia*, John Spelman's edition of the Psalter,[101] and James Ussher's expertise exhibited in his *Britannicarum ecclesiarum antiquitates*;[102] such consideration would enable a more rounded assessment of the editorial principles that underlay the first edition of the Anglo-Saxon Chronicle. Wheelock's work was reissued in 1644, enlarged by an expanded reprint of Lambarde's *Archaionomia*.[103]

The later fate of the Cambridge lectureship is overshadowed by the civil disorders of the time, which sorely afflicted Cambridge. The hardest blow was probably the death of John Spelman,

---

[100]See above, n. 94.

[101]*Psalterium Davidis Latino-Saxonicum vetus* . . . (1640); see Adams (1917), 50–51, who describes it as "the first scholarly edition of an Old English text with collations."

[102]Ussher's work makes specific reference to three Chronicle manuscripts (E, F, and G; see n. 53 above). Taken together, the Chronicle references in the works of Henry Spelman and Ussher suggest that both scholars were familiar with the complex textual tradition of the Chronicle and that Wheelock's selection of manuscripts for his edition could rely on their advice.

[103]See Adams (1917), 54; Bennett (1938), 15; and Oates (1986), 208–09. In his preface "Ad Lectorem" to the reissue of *Archaionomia*, Wheelock stated that he had used a copy belonging to John Selden of the original edition of 1568 which contained annotations by Lambarde (see Oates [1986], 208–09). Wheelock's reissue included some material not in Lambarde's original edition, for example some texts from Cambridge, Corpus Christi College, MS 201, a manuscript that seems to have been unknown to Lambarde at the time of the first edition, although there is evidence that he came to know it later; see Berkhout (1993–94), 284–85.

who died of camp fever in 1643.[104] With both Spelmans dead (Henry had died in 1641), no further publications ensued in direct connection with the lectureship. Sir Simonds D'Ewes's project for a dictionary resulted in little more than the provision of a transcript of Joscelyn's dictionary.[105] From Wheelock's hand there survives only some scanty preparatory work toward a dictionary and a grammar, although he presumably continued to teach Old English until his death in 1653.[106]

V. FROM CAMBRIDGE TO OXFORD:
WILLIAM SOMNER'S
DICTIONARIUM SAXONICO-LATINO-ANGLICUM

Following Wheelock's death, the financial provision for the lectureship was divided: one half remained in Cambridge,[107] while

---

[104]For his political involvement see *DNB* s.n.; for the afflictions caused the University of Cambridge by the Civil War, see Kearney (1970), 40–41, and Twigg (1990).

[105]Similarly, many others of D'Ewes's projects bore little fruit; see n. 91 above.

[106]A rough draft of the dictionary survives in BL MS Harley 761, and a fair copy of the A–B sections in CUL MS Gg. 2. 2; an attempt at a grammar is preserved in BL MS Add. 34600, art. 6. See Wülker (1885), 17; *DNB* s.n. "Wheelocke"; Bennett (1938), 356–57; Lutz (1981), lxix; and Oates (1986), 180 and 196. In an undated but apparently late letter to Ussher (printed by Parr [1686], 545–46), Wheelock wrote: "by my constant attending on my Lectures, I am prevented of doing what I otherwise might. Sir *Henry Spelman's* Saxon Lecture, honoured by your Lordship's first motion to the Heads of Houses . . . hath made me your Grace's Scholar . . . but my Saxon Imploiment will bind me much to be acquainted with your *Primordia Eccles. Britannicarum.*" For Wheelock's teaching see also Bennett (1982), 200.

[107]For the subsequent fate of the Cambridge lectureship, see Adams (1917), 55; and Bennett (1938), 16.

the other half was given to William Somner (1606–69)[108] as a research stipend toward the completion of his Old English dictionary, which had been in progress for some time. Somner had not received a university education. He had been trained at the Free Grammar School at Canterbury and afterwards became clerk to his father, who was registrary of the court at Canterbury; from there Somner was advanced by Archbishop Laud to be registrar of the ecclesiastical courts of the diocese.[109] His early works, particularly *The Antiquities of Canterbury* (1640), the *Observations on the Laws of King Henry I* (1644), and *A Treatise of Gavelkind* (completed in 1647), betray a keen interest in both local and legal history and thus may be placed in a tradition going back to William Lambarde.[110]

In the course of his work on the *Observations* he became acquainted with the classical scholar Meric Casaubon (ca. 1599–1671), who advised him to study Old English,[111] and this acquaintance with Casaubon gave his work a new, more linguistic turn: Somner soon became competent not only in Old English but also in other Germanic languages, and he employed this linguistic competence in drawing up glossaries for Casaubon's *De quatuor linguis* (1650) and for the *Historiæ Anglicanæ scriptores X* (1652)

---

[108]For Somner's correct date of birth see Urry (1977), vi–vii.

[109]See Kennett (1693), 4–7; *DNB* s.n.; Adams (1917), 58–59; Urry (1977), vii–viii; and Hetherington (1980), 125–27.

[110]Somner dedicated *The Antiquities* to Archbishop Laud. *A Treatise of Gavelkind* (on which see the study by Kathryn Lowe in the present volume) was published only in 1660. See *DNB* s.n., p. 669; Adams (1917), 58–69 and 177; Douglas (1951), 55; and Urry (1977), viii–ix and xvii–xix.

[111]See Somner (1659), "Ad lectorem," paragraphs 1–2 and 5; Kennett (1693), 22–30; *DNB* s.nn. "Casaubon" and "Somner," p. 669; Adams (1917), 59–62; Bennett (1938), 18–19; Hetherington (1980), 126–41; and Dekker (1999), 231–35.

of Sir Roger Twysden (1597–1672).[112] In the course of this work he gained a growing reputation as an expert in Old Germanic languages and became acquainted with several leading scholars of his time, among them Archbishop Ussher, John Selden, Sir Simonds D'Ewes, Sir William Dugdale, and the Dutch scholar Francis Junius (1591–1677), the most important philologist and expert in the Germanic languages of his time.[113] They supported Somner in various ways when, encouraged by Casaubon, he began to compile a "Saxon Dictionary."[114] Archbishop Ussher was once again instrumental in promoting the study of Old English as a

---

[112]See *DNB* s.nn. "Casaubon" and "Somner," p. 669; Adams (1917), 59–60; Bennett (1938), 19; Hetherington (1980), 126–28 and 131–32; and Dekker (1996), 515–21.

[113]For Junius's correct date of birth see Kerling (1984), 93; Breuker (1990), 46; and Lucas (2000), ix and n. 2; older studies note it as 1589. For Junius's life and career see von Raumer (1870), 106–29; *DNB* s.n.; Bennett (1938), 14 and 22–40; Sisam (1953a), 260; Morison and Carter (1967), 23 and 63; Sharpe (1979), 100; Hetherington (1980), 129–30 and 222–36; Philip (1983), 57–58; Stanley (1987), 50 and 55–56; Gneuss (1990), 43; Voorwinden (1992), v–xxiv; Berryman (1996), ch. I; Dekker (1999), ch. VI; and Lucas (2000), ix–xvi. Junius had studied theology and classical languages at Leiden and in 1621 went to England where, at the recommendation of Ussher, he joined the household of Thomas Howard (1586–1646), earl of Arundel, as keeper of his library and tutor to his son. From 1642 until 1646 he spent much time in the Netherlands, accompanying the young earl of Oxford, then returned to England and stayed there until 1651. The following years were predominantly spent in the Netherlands, until in 1674 he returned to England where he spent his last years until his death in 1677 in Oxford. For his publications and his extended manuscript studies and their importance for the institutionalization of the study of Old English at Oxford, see below.

[114]See Somner (1659), "Ad lectorem," paragraph 2; Kennett (1693), 108–09; *DNB* s.n. "Somner," p. 669; Adams (1917), 59–65; Bennett (1938), 20; Urry (1977), xii; and Hetherington (1980), 126–56 and 170–73. Somner's acquaintance with Junius presumably dates to the late 1640s. See Hetherington (1980), 130; and Dekker (1996), 522–23.

university subject in Cambridge, when in 1657 or earlier he suggested to Roger Spelman (1625–78), Henry Spelman's grandson, that he use one-half of the provision for the Cambridge lectureship to supply Somner with a stipend toward the completion of his dictionary; Ussher thus helped carry out the second part of the plan drawn up by Spelman in 1638.[115] Somner's *Dictionarium Saxonico-Latino-Anglicum* appeared in 1659, supplemented by the first printing of Ælfric's *Grammar*,[116] which in the form of manuscripts and transcripts had served the antiquaries as a grammar of Old English for a century.[117]

At that stage of the development of Old English studies it had become possible for Somner to base his dictionary to some extent on printed sources. Yet he did not content himself with printed material but also made a number of transcripts from manuscript texts, as he pointed out in his preface.[118] Thus for the Chronicle Somner used Wheelock's edition based on MSS G and A and in

---

[115]See Kennett (1693), 72–74; *DNB* s.n., p. 669; Adams (1917), 55 and 62; Urry (1977), xii–xiii; and Hetherington (1980), 143. Somner dedicated the *Dictionarium* to Roger Spelman, "viro vere generoso." For Ussher's role in selecting Wheelock for the Cambridge lectureship and for Henry Spelman's research plan, see above, pp. 34–36 and n. 89.

[116]*Dictionarium Saxonico-Latino-Anglicum, voces, phrasesque præcipuas Anglo-Saxonicas . . . complectens* (Oxford). For Somner's *Dictionarium* and for previous work toward the publication of a dictionary of Old English, see Somner (1659), "Ad lectorem," paragraphs 2–6; Kennett (1693), 70–81; Adams (1917), 55–66; Urry (1977), xii–xiii; Hetherington (1980), esp. ch. 4 and Appendix 4; Lutz (1988); and Gneuss (1990), 42–43.

[117]For antiquarian transcripts of Ælfric's *Grammar*, see the list by Helmut Gneuss in Zupitza (1966), viii–ix. See also above, p. 33 and n. 84.

[118]See "Ad lectorem," paragraphs 2 and 3, for his list of the transcripts he made, the printed texts and unpublished antiquarian materials he used, and the libraries he consulted; see also Cook (1962), 236–59; and Hetherington (1980), 145–56 and Appendix 4 (pp. 209–21). For his use of his own transcripts for the *Dictionarium* see Lutz (1988).

addition made a complete transcript of MS C from the Cotton library. Both this transcript and his copy of Wheelock's edition (now respectively Canterbury, Cathedral Library, MSS Lit. C. 8 and W/E 6.20)[119] contain numerous underlinings, many of which are reflected in his dictionary entries.[120]

In the exploitation of the Chronicle and other historical sources, Somner's *Dictionarium* betrays the strong historical interests of the antiquaries,[121] which also found expression in the historical orientation of Spelman's lectureship. But his dictionary entries also reveal a partial shift of interest in Old English scholarship in the seventeenth century, namely toward the study of Old English as a Germanic language and toward the study of Old English poetry. The inclusion of comparative and etymological information in the *Dictionarium* reflected recent scholarly trends which had their roots in the humanist study of the Bible in Latin, Greek, and Hebrew and in a growing awareness of the value of the vernaculars.[122] Somner had developed an interest in the comparative study of Old English through his cooperation with Casaubon on *De quatuor linguis* (1650), which attempted to establish correspondences among Latin, Greek, Hebrew, and Old English, and for this work Somner adduced much comparative evidence from Old High German and

---

[119]On MS Lit. C. 8, see Woodruff (1911), no. 84; and Lutz (1988), 6–15. See also below, Table 2, no. 9.

[120]See Somner (1659), "Ad lectorem," paragraph 15; Adams (1917), 63; Urry (1977), xvi; and Lutz (1988), 1–15. For Somner's work on the Chronicle see below, Table 2, nos. 9 and 10 and nn. 11–12 to the table; for his papers in the Cathedral Library see Woodruff (1911), 42–51; and Urry (1977), v and n. 1.

[121]See Somner (1659), "Ad lectorem," paragraphs 2 and 15; Hetherington (1980), 145–56 and Appendices 3 and 4; Stanley (1987), 16–17; and Lutz (1988), 1–14.

[122]See Adams (1917), 57–62; Gneuss (1990), 35–36 and 45–46; and Dekker (1999), esp. chs. I and V.

Dutch.[123] For his *Dictionarium* he extended his comparative studies and also included Old Norse evidence.[124]

In this phase of his work he received much inspiration and support from Francis Junius. The beginnings of Junius's comparative studies can be dated to ca. 1645, but on account of his family background he must have been familiar with comparative and etymological research long before that.[125] In the course of his extended comparative studies he gradually developed a truly novel concept of language relations and of the Germanic languages as a closely related group. In the preface to his *Observationes in Willerami abbatis Francicam paraphrasin Cantici canticorum*, which he published at Amsterdam in 1655, Junius offered a first sketch of his views on the relations of the Germanic languages.[126] The year 1655 also saw the publication of Junius's *Cædmonis monachi paraphrasis poetica*, an edition of the biblical poetry contained in one of the four Old English poetic codices.[127] The manuscript had been given to him by Archbishop Ussher in 1651, before Junius left England for the Netherlands. While it was still

---

[123]Mostly on the basis of Cornelis Kiliaan's *Etymologicum Teutonicæ linguæ* (1642). See Adams (1917), 59–60; and Dekker (1996), 518–22.

[124]For Somner's references in his dictionary to West and North Germanic cognates, see "Ad lectorem," paragraph 8; Bennett (1938), 20; Cook (1962), 150–62; Hetherington (1980), 170–74; and Dekker (1996), 522 and 538–39. For the later use of the *Dictionarium* by the Dutch scholar Jan van Vliet (1622–66) for his study of Old Frisian, see Dekker (1999), 125–28 and 168.

[125]See von Raumer (1870), 114–15; Breuker (1990), 50; Voorwinden (1992), vi–vii; Lucas (2000), x–xv; and Dekker (2000), 284.

[126]See Stanley (1987), 50–51; Voorwinden (1992), viii–xiv; Dekker (1996), 524–27; Dekker (1999), 257–60; and Lucas (2000), xv.

[127]Now Bodleian MS Junius 11. See Adams (1917), 70–72; Gollancz (1927), xiii–xv; Krapp (1931), ix; Bennett (1938), 25–27 and 343; Ker (1957), 408; Stanley (1987), 49–51 and 78; Rogers (1991), 146; and Lucas (2000), xiii–xxvi. With the exception of Nowell (see Flower [1935], 70), the antiquaries had not taken any interest in Old English poetic texts.

in Ussher's possession, Somner made a complete transcript of it, and later possibly received help from a commentary on the poems and a glossary drawn up by Junius after the publication of the texts.[128] Junius's main incentive for printing these texts, which he attributed to Bede's Cædmon,[129] was to make them accessible to lexical and etymological analysis as evidence for early Old English; but he was the first to recognize them as poetry, and for this reason his publication also marked an important beginning for the study of Old English poetry, as will become apparent below with regard to the study of the Chronicle poems in Oxford. Somner used both of Junius's books for his dictionary, and his praise of Junius's erudition in his preface betrays how much he valued his work.[130] Thus both the comparative study of Old English and the

---

[128]Now Bodleian MSS Junius 73 and 113, respectively. See Hetherington (1980), 175–76 and n. 58; and Lucas (2000), xxiv–xxvi and Appendix 1. The glossary refers to page numbers of the printed text. Whether Somner received assistance from these fragmentary studies remains open. In "Ad lectorem," paragraph 2, Somner expressed his frustration at the fact that Junius's edition did not contain a Latin translation: "ac utinam etiam (in majorem omnium utilitatem) Latinè versam" ("and would that [for the greater benefit of all] it had been translated into Latin"). But his shift from singular to plural pronoun in paragraph 7, where he described the extreme difficulties encountered in the language of the texts in MS Junius 11, points to help from someone else, though whether this person was Junius is not clear. See Somner (1659), "Ad lectorem," paragraphs 2, 7, and 10; Bennett (1938), 20; Hetherington (1980), 144 with n. 22 and 175–77; and Lutz (1988), 17–19. For the Chronicle poems see below, pp. 62–64 and nn. 183–86.

[129]See Gollancz (1927), xlviii–xlix; Stanley (1987), 24–25; and Lucas (2000), xv–xvi.

[130]In "Ad lectorem," paragraph 2, he described Junius as "in his learning most distinguished, a model of paternal esteem and erudition," and in paragraph 10 as "endowed with the greatest judgement and wisdom" (translation by Cook [1962], 238 and 249). See von Raumer (1870), 115–16; Voorwinden (1992), xviii–xix; and Lucas (2000), xxviii.

inclusion of poetic texts in the *Dictionarium* received support from Junius,[131] who later was to exercise great influence on the study of Old English in Oxford.

William Somner's dictionary, although supported by the Cambridge stipend, was printed at Oxford. The Cambridge types employed for the printing of Wheelock's Bede and Chronicle were too large for the purpose and, on account of the severe and long-lasting disorders of the Civil War in the Cambridge region, the university could not afford more suitable new types.[132] The association with the University of Oxford seems to have developed in 1653. It received strong support from Gerard Langbaine (1609–58), Provost of Queen's College from 1646 until 1658 and a friend of Selden and Ussher who made great efforts to draw the *Dictionarium* to Oxford by providing suitable types, as becomes apparent from a letter to Dugdale dated 6 December 1653.[133] In 1654 Junius wrote to Selden from Amsterdam about the possibilities of obtaining suitable Old English types, and the Oxford types, which were founded in 1655 by Arthur Nichols and first

---

[131] The extent of this support deserves further investigation. According to Adams (1917), 62, Junius spent much time at Oxford in 1658–59 and "probably helped in the actual compilation." Yet, although the Codex Argenteus had become available to Junius as early as 1654, and although he mentioned in a letter to Dugdale dated 28 January 1656 (cited by Bennett [1938], 29 n. 1) that he was busy comparing his manuscript dictionary with the Codex Argenteus, Somner's *Dictionarium* did not take note of Junius's work on Gothic in connection with his parallel edition of the Gothic and Old English Gospels (for which see below). See Cook (1962), 51–53; Voorwinden (1992), viii; and Dekker (1996), 522–23.

[132] See Adams (1917), 58, 64–65, and 163–65.

[133] For the letter see Bennett (1938), 17 n. 3. Langbaine had planned an edition of the Chronicle earlier on, possibly on the basis of Laud's gift of MS E to the Bodleian in 1639 (see above, n. 40), but he was anticipated by Wheelock. See Plummer (1892–99), II, cxxviii n. 6; *DNB* s.n.; Adams (1917), 55 n. 1; Bennett (1938), 16–17 and 21; and Bennett (1982), 200–01. See also below.

used for the *Dictionarium*, closely resemble the Junian types.[134] Thus although Somner himself remained outside the structures of both universities, his dictionary may be viewed as a kind of link between the first attempt at institutionalizing the study of Old English at the University of Cambridge and the later efforts at Oxford.

VI. FRANCIS JUNIUS AND THE OXFORD SAXONISTS

Somner's *Dictionarium*, although printed at Oxford, was nevertheless clearly associated with the Cambridge lectureship in "Antiquitates Britannicae et Saxonicae," particularly by later Oxford scholars, who viewed this dictionary as providing them with an opportunity to prove their superiority over Cambridge by producing a yet more comprehensive dictionary of Old English.[135] This attitude toward Somner's work must be viewed against the background of a more general competition between the two universities, which is reflected in the dates of endowment of several chairs and lectureships in the seventeenth century. Thus in 1624, two years after the foundation of Camden's chair for Civil History at Oxford, Cambridge likewise founded a chair for Civil

---

[134]See Adams (1917), 64 and 165–67; Dickins ([1946]), no. 10; Morison and Carter (1967), 229 and 244; Carter (1975), 124–25; Bennett (1982), 201; Stanley (1987), 78–79; Rogers (1991), 160; Lucas (1997a), 158–59; Lucas (1998), 178; and Lucas (2000), xix–xx.

[135]Somner himself soon became aware that his dictionary could be improved upon and worked toward a revised edition, as he wrote in a letter to Casaubon as late as 1664. He did not live to realize his plan: see Adams (1917), 64 and n. 4; Bennett (1938), 20–21; Cook (1962), 14; and Hetherington (1980), 178–79. That Somner's dictionary had firmer links with Cambridge is also indicated by the fact that fourteen Cambridge colleges subscribed to it but none at Oxford did so; see Bennett (1982), 201.

History.[136] Similarly, the Cambridge chair for Arabic endowed by Sir Thomas Adams (1586–1668) in 1632 and first held by Wheelock soon received competition at Oxford through Archbishop Laud's endowment of a chair in 1636, which was first held by Edward Pococke (1604–91).[137]

In the case of Old English studies it was also Cambridge that took the lead—with Henry Spelman's endowment of the lectureship in "Antiquitates Britannicae et Saxonicae" in 1639, the publication of Wheelock's edition of Bede and the Chronicle in 1643 and the enlarged reprint including the laws in 1644, and also with the publication of the *Dictionarium* and Ælfric's *Grammar* in 1659, which Somner dedicated to Sir Henry Spelman's grandson Roger.[138] Langbaine's frustrated attempts of the 1640s to publish the Chronicle[139] and his successful efforts of the 1650s to get the *Dictionarium* printed at Oxford betray that Old English was soon viewed as a subject that was considered attractive enough to be brought into play in this competition; but it was only in the 1670s that Oxford entered into the contest seriously. The leading figure behind the Oxford efforts was John Fell (1625–86), Dean of Christ Church and bishop of Oxford, an energetic university politician

[136]It was endowed by Camden's friend Sir Fulke Greville (1554–1628). Thus in both cases the initiative came from outside the university: see *DNB* s.n.; Hill (1965), 309; and Trevor-Roper (1971), 34. For the enormous expansion of university education and the curriculum in this period, see Curtis (1959), chs. III and IV; Stone (1964), 47–57 and 68–80; Stone (1966), 44–46; and Kearney (1970), chs. I and II.

[137]See *DNB* s.nn. "Adams" and "Pococke"; Utley (1942), 245; Curtis (1959), 91–92, 102, and 116; Trevor-Roper (1962), 281–83, 410, and 429; and Oates (1986), ch. 7.

[138]See n. 115 above.

[139]See above, n. 133, and below, n. 173.

with strong antiquarian and linguistic interests,[140] who wanted to turn the study of Old English into some kind of advertisement for the University of Oxford.

His initiative appears to have been inspired by Thomas Marshall (1621–85), who was offered a fellowship by Lincoln College in 1668, and who from 1672 until his death served as that college's Rector. Marshall had matriculated at Oxford in 1640 and presumably became acquainted with Junius through Ussher in the late 1640s, before he left for Holland for political reasons.[141] During his long stay in Rotterdam and Dordrecht he collaborated with Junius on his Gothic–Old English Gospels, which was published at Amsterdam in 1665;[142] the copious notes Marshall contributed in his *Observationes in evangeliorum versiones perantiquas duas, Gothicam scil. et Anglo-Saxonicam* won him the fellowship at his former college.[143] From 1668 until his final return to Oxford in 1672, Marshall spent much time in Holland on Fell's behalf, assisting him in his plans to equip the university press for the printing of texts in various languages, in which Old English

---

[140]See *DNB* s.n.; Bennett (1938), 39–48 and 315–19; Sisam (1953a), 260; and Morison and Carter (1967).

[141]See *DNB* s.n.; Adams (1917), 72–73; Bennett (1938), 33–34; Morison and Carter (1967), 23, 30–31, and 59–64; Bennett (1982), 202; and Rogers (1991), 162–64.

[142]*Quatuor D. N. Jesu Christi euangeliorum versiones perantiquæ duæ, Gothica scil. et Anglo-Saxonica . . .*; the book contained a Gothic glossary with much comparative material from other Germanic languages. The Codex Argenteus, the manuscript source for the Gothic Gospels, had come into the possession of the classical scholar Isaac Vossius (1618–89), Junius's nephew, in 1654. See von Raumer (1870), 117–29; *DNB* s.n. "Vossius, Isaac"; Adams (1917), 72–73; Cook (1962), 51–53; Voorwinden (1992), viii–x; Dekker (1996), 522–23 and 529–30; Dekker (1999), 99–102; and Lucas (2000), xvi.

[143]See Bennett (1938), 27–28 and 33–35; Rogers (1991), 162; Harris (1992), 5–6; and Lucas (2000), xxvi.

was to have a part.[144] Marshall planned two publications on Old English, an edition of the translation of Orosius's *Historiae adversum paganos* and an Old English grammar, the latter at Fell's suggestion, but neither project ever went beyond an early preparatory stage.[145]

Marshall's most important contribution to the institutionalization of Old English studies at Oxford consisted in persuading Junius to spend his last years with him at Oxford and to bequeath his private library to the Bodleian.[146] On the basis of their long cooperation and friendship, Marshall thus provided "the main link between the monumental but isolated work of Junius and the concerted studies of the Oxford 'Saxonists' at the close of the century."[147] Besides some extremely valuable original manuscripts[148] and his collection of printed books, many of which contained copious additions from his own hand,[149] Junius's bequest of

---

[144]See Bennett (1938), 36–38 and 315–16; Morison and Carter (1967), 31, 39–40, 58–68, and 158–60; Bennett (1982), 202; and Rogers (1991), 162. Fell's strong interest in the improvement of the printing facilities at Oxford becomes most obvious from his program for the university press dating from 1672, which proposed to publish texts in several Oriental languages and "the Liturgicks and homilies of the Ancient English-Saxons" (Morison and Carter [1967], 39).

[145]See Adams (1917), 73; Bennett (1938), 35–36 and 344; Bennett (1982), 202; and Fairer (1986), 810. His sketch of an Old English grammar is preserved as Bodleian MS Marshall 78.

[146]See *DNB* s.n.; Bennett (1938), 33–38; Morison and Carter (1967), 63; Fairer (1986), 809–12; Rogers (1991), 161–64; Harris (1992), 6–7; Stanley (1998); and Lucas (2000), xii–xiii. Junius's bequest may not have included his books on classical authors which, according to Bremmer (1998b), 213–14, Junius may have given to Isaac Vossius.

[147]Bennett (1938), 33.

[148]See Bennett (1938), 32; Philip (1983), 57–58; and Rogers (1991), 161–62.

[149]See von Raumer (1870), 122–23; and Bennett (1938), 31–32. For his copy of Somner's *Dictionarium* (now Bodleian MS Junius 7), see Adams (1917), 65 n. 4;

1677 comprised over thirty transcripts of Old English texts,[150] several manuscript dictionaries and glossaries,[151] and his valuable collection of types, which was later put to good use for the publication of works on Old English and other Germanic languages.[152] The transcripts and dictionaries were to form the basis for a large share of the publications that ensued from Oxford in the late seventeenth and the eighteenth centuries.

On the basis of Junius's bequest, Bishop Fell, together with Sir Joseph Williamson (1633–1701), an influential patron of Queen's College and a friend of Fell's, planned a regular lectureship, which was also to provide regular teaching of Old English.[153] The person selected for the lectureship was William Nicolson (1655–1727), who had entered Queen's College in 1670, and in 1678 was sent to Leipzig for one year in order to study German and Scandinavian languages. Before that, Nicolson had frequently been with Junius and had presumably also received instruction in Old English from Marshall. Nicolson's studies in Germany were financed by Williamson, who subsequently

---

for his collation of Wheelock's edition of the Chronicle with MS F, see below, Table 2, no. 11.

[150]See Bennett (1938), 31–32; Watson (1966), 9–10 and 43–44; and section III of the paper by Kees Dekker in the present volume.

[151]Especially the "Dictionarium Saxonicum" and the "Etymologicum Anglicanum," for which see below, as well as the study by Kees Dekker in this volume. Some smaller glossaries are preserved in Bodleian MSS Junius 77, 84, 112, 114, and 115–16. See Wanley (1705), 324; von Raumer (1870), 126–28; Adams (1917), 71–72; Bennett (1938), 28–30 and 363–69; Morison and Carter (1967), 115; and Hetherington (1980), 231–34.

[152]See Adams (1917), 72–74 and 167–68; Bennett (1938), 36–40; Morison and Carter (1967), 31, 71–72, 114–16, and 244–45; Bennett (1982), 201–02; Philip (1983), 57–58; Rogers (1991), 162; and Lucas (1998).

[153]See *DNB* s.n. "Williamson"; Adams (1917), 75; Bennett (1938), 41; Morison and Carter (1967), 31; Bennett (1982), 202–03; and Fairer (1986), 809.

founded the "Saxon Lecture" at Queen's, which Nicolson held from 1679 until 1682; he offered regular classes until he left Oxford for a parsonage in Cumberland.[154]

The competitive character of Fell's initiative becomes apparent when one considers the research projects he assigned to Nicolson, namely an edition of the Chronicle, a grammar, and a dictionary.[155] These projects were almost identical with the plan that Sir Henry Spelman had formulated for his Cambridge lectureship in the 1630s, and it seems to have been Fell's express aim to surpass Cambridge in exactly these targets. The grammar, which Fell had originally entrusted to Marshall, was a true desideratum, as Anglo-Saxonists still had to make do with Ælfric's Old English *Grammar* of Latin. Fell's plan was to have an Old English grammar appended to an edition of Junius's monumental "Dictionarium Saxonicum,"[156] in much the same way as Somner had appended Ælfric's *Grammar* to his *Dictionarium*. Nicolson produced a carefully rearranged transcript of Junius's dictionary in eleven folio volumes but left the project unfinished when he went to Cumberland in 1682; despite some later attempts by Oxford scholars, the dictionary was never printed.[157]

---

[154]See *DNB* s.n. "Nicolson"; Adams (1917), 75; Bennett (1938), 41–42 and 48; Bennett (1948), 29; and Fairer (1986), 809–12. For his frequent contacts with Junius, see Fairer (1986), 809, and Lucas (2000), xvii–xviii, who both cite a letter from Nicolson to George Hickes dated 12 March 1698, in which Nicolson described Junius as "very kind and communicative, very good, and very old."

[155]Presumably on the advice of Junius and Marshall. See Bennett (1938), 41–42, 48, and 63; Bennett (1948), 29; and Fairer (1986), 809–12.

[156]Junius's dictionary is preserved as Bodleian MSS Junius 2–3. See Bennett (1938), 28–30, 41–42, 50, 316–19, and 363–69; Hetherington (1980), 231–32; Fairer (1986), 810; Harris (1992), 6–7; Dekker (1999), chs. VI and VII.1; and Dekker in the present volume.

[157]Nicolson's rearranged transcript, entitled "Dictionarium septentrionale sive promptuarium vocum Goth. Anglo-Sax. Franc. Run. et Island., Latinè et Anglicè

When Nicolson left Oxford, Fell and Marshall entrusted the task of compiling a grammar to George Hickes (1642–1715), who in 1689 fulfilled it with his *Institutiones grammaticæ Anglo-Saxonicæ et Moeso-Gothicæ.*[158] The *Institutiones*, for which the Junian types were employed for the first time at Oxford, reflect Junius's concept of the study of Old English as part of the study of all Germanic languages.[159] Hickes had received a fellowship from Lincoln College in 1664 and, under Marshall's and Fell's influence, became interested in Old English and other Germanic languages.[160] He completed his work on the grammar many years after he had left the university for an ecclesiastical position at Worcester. For this reason his contribution to the institutionalization of Old English studies at Oxford is of a somewhat indirect nature, but he nevertheless exercised a strong influence on

---

redditarum," is Bodleian MSS Fell 8–18. Fell had every intention of fulfilling Junius's wish to get the dictionary published, but the project seems to have been beyond his financial means. In 1772 a version based on a Harleian transcript of Junius's dictionary and prepared by Edward Lye (1694–1767) appeared posthumously as *Dictionarium Saxonico et Gothico-Latinum*, without acknowledgment of the source. Before that, Lye had edited Junius's *Etymologicum Anglicanum*, his second full-scale dictionary (preserved as Bodleian MSS Junius 4–5), which came out at Oxford in 1743; Junius's etymological dictionary was not included in Fell's plan but it was used extensively by George Hickes for his *Thesaurus*, for which see below. See *DNB* s.n. "Lye"; Adams (1917), 72 and 104–05; Bennett (1938), 374; Cook (1962), 14–15; Hetherington (1980), 179 and 231; Harris (1992), 6–8; Berryman (1996), ch. I; Dekker in this volume, esp. section IV; and Lucas (2000), xvi.

[158]See von Raumer (1870), 129–39; *DNB* s.n.; Adams (1917), 75–90 and 167; Bennett (1938), 43 and 50–56; Bennett (1948), 28–31; Douglas (1951), ch. IV; Morison and Carter (1967), 114 and 117; Bennett (1982), 203–04; Fairer (1986), 816–20; Harris (1992), 18–28; Dekker (1999), 339–42; and Lucas (2000), xxvii.

[159]See Hickes (1689), "Præfatio," sigs. b3^r–c1^v; von Raumer (1870), 134–38; Bennett (1938), 50–56; and Dekker (1999), 340–42.

[160]See Harris (1992), 4–6.

its further development through his continuing contacts with the developing school of Saxonists at Oxford and with other persons who were closely associated with Oxford. This becomes most obvious from his monumental *Linguarum veterum septentrionalium thesaurus grammatico-criticus et archæologicus* (1703–05),[161] on which he started work after the publication of his *Institutiones*. For this project, which also contained a detailed study of Old Germanic poetry,[162] Hickes was able to secure the cooperation of former Oxford Saxonists such as William Nicolson and of several Saxonists at Queen's, in particular Edmund Gibson (1669–1748), the leading figure among the Oxford Saxonists in the 1690s until he left Oxford in 1698,[163] and his successor Edward Thwaites (1667–1711).[164] Most importantly, he enlisted the help

---

[161]See Adams (1917), 86–91; Bennett (1938), 82–151; Bennett (1948); Douglas (1951), 84–91; Harris (1992), 39–107; Fairer (1986), 815–20; and Dekker (1999), 341–42.

[162]Chapter 23, "De poetica Anglo-Saxonum" (pp. 177–221), includes the Chronicle poem *The Battle of Brunanburh* on pp. 181–82 and the *Menologium* and *Maxims II*, which serve as a preface to Chronicle MS C, on pp. 203–08; see Dobbie (1942), lx–lxvii and clxiv, and see also below. For his close cooperation with Nicolson on this matter, see his letter to Nicolson dated 6 December 1698 (printed by Harris [1992], as no. 94): "In your translation of the Saxon verses of Durham I will let Socij stand, and only make those two alterations you will allow off. I intend to send you the Dano-Saxonick Menologium and my version of it, which I desire you to revise, and tell me your free opinion of every thing. I think I told you formerly it was in the Cedmonian verse, and it and the notes I have written upon it are to Conclude the Chr. De poetica Anglo-Saxonum." See also Bennett (1938), 106a–106b and 112–17; and Stanley (1987), 7 and 36. See also below for a comment by Edmund Gibson on the Chronicle poems.

[163]For Gibson see Plummer (1892–99), II, §124; *DNB* s.n.; Adams (1917), 76–77, 119–20, 131, and 138; Sykes (1926); Bennett (1938), 63–66; Fairer (1986), 811–12; and Harris (1992), 44–45. For his edition of the Chronicle see below.

[164]See *DNB* s.n.; Bennett (1938), 68–81; Bennett (1982), 205; Fairer (1986), 812–13 and 820; and Harris (1992), 68–69.

of the great paleographer Humfrey Wanley (1672–1726), assistant librarian at the Bodleian Library from 1696 to 1700, whose repeated attempts to enter the university structures were eventually frustrated;[165] Wanley's *Catalogus* of 1705, which offered a detailed description of both original manuscripts and antiquarian studies of the sixteenth and seventeenth centuries in Britain and thus transcended the domain of the Oxford Saxonists,[166] formed the second volume of Hickes's *Thesaurus*.

Thwaites's importance for the institutionalization of Old English studies as a university subject at Oxford is mainly based on his role as "Anglo-Saxon praeceptor" at Queen's College from 1698, after Gibson had left the university. In this capacity he gathered a considerable number of students[167] and did much to improve the conditions for the teaching of Old English, in particular by engaging one of his pupils, Thomas Benson (1679–1734), to compile a condensed student version of Somner's *Dictionarium* which came out at Oxford in 1701;[168] and by publishing his *Grammatica Anglo-Saxonica* of 1711, an abridged

---

[165]For Wanley and his collaboration with Hickes, see Ellis (1843), 283–94; *DNB* s.n.; Adams (1917), 90–91 and 123–31; Bennett (1948), 30–31; Douglas (1951), 99–101; Sisam (1953a); Ker (1957), xiii–xiv; Wright (1960); Wright and Wright (1966); Heyworth (1989); Gneuss (1990), 43 and n. 24; Harris (1992), 63–68; and Keynes (1996), 126–31.

[166]For his *Catalogus* see the references in n. 165 above and Stanley (1987), 4–5; Harris (1983), 169 and 181–82; Harris (1992), 85–96; and Gneuss (1993), 101–03. See also section VII below. For its predecessor, which had been compiled by Hickes and published as part of his *Institutiones grammaticæ* in 1689, see Bennett (1938), 56; and Gneuss (1993), 91–101.

[167]See Adams (1917), 78; Bennett (1938), 69; Douglas (1951), 56 and 66–68; Fairer (1986), 813; and Lucas (2000), xxvii.

[168]*Vocabularium Anglo-Saxonicum, lexico Gul. Somneri magna parte auctius.* See Adams (1917), 78–79 and 132–33; Bennett (1938), 362; and Douglas (1951), 56–57.

student version of Hickes's grammar in his *Thesaurus*.[169]

Thus both the grammar, in the form of Hickes's *Institutiones*, of its further development in the *Thesaurus* and of Thwaites's *Grammatica*, and the dictionary, in the form of Benson's *Vocabularium Anglo-Saxonicum* and of Junius's "Dictionarium Saxonicum," which was closely studied but never printed, give an impression of the forces that—to differing degrees—were of particular importance for the success of the Oxford Saxonists:

1. the work of Francis Junius, who with his scholarly expertise, his advice, and a great number of textual and lexicographical studies provided the intellectual and material foundations for the publications that ensued from Oxford in the late seventeenth and early eighteenth centuries;
2. the initiative of Bishop Fell, an energetic and enlightened university administrator, who provided the printing facilities and assigned the research tasks;
3. the personal continuity of Old English studies over a period of several decades, mostly at Queen's College; this continuity was ensured both by regular teaching and by a kind of corporate spirit among Oxford Saxonists under the intellectual leadership of George Hickes, a spirit that persisted beyond individuals' respective stays at the university.[170]

---

[169]*Grammatica Anglo-Saxonica, ex Hickesiano linguarum septentrionalium thesauro excerpta* (Oxford). For other publications and projects, see *DNB* s.n., p. 840; Adams (1917), 78–79; Bennett (1938), 68–75 and 320–23; and Fairer (1986), 812.

[170]See Fairer (1986), who (at p. 808) states that "the revival of Saxon studies in Oxford was due to a combination of enlightened leadership by powerful university figures and the vital impetus given by the arrival in Oxford of the great continental scholar, Francis Junius," and (at p. 824) concludes that "Oxford's achievements in Anglo-Saxon studies had rested on three foundations: . . . organized teaching of the language . . . the sense of communal effort . . . and Hickes's mantle as an inspiring leader."

The combination of all three factors may also be observed in the third task that Fell had assigned to Nicolson, that is, a second edition of the Anglo-Saxon Chronicle: the *Chronicon Saxonicum* came out at Oxford in 1692, having been edited (following Nicolson's departure from Oxford[171]) by Edmund Gibson, at that time a twenty-three-year-old student who had just completed his B.A.[172] Gibson saw his edition of the Chronicle as an expression of the competition between Oxford and Cambridge, as becomes abundantly clear from his preface, at the beginning of which he relates how Gerard Langbaine, former Provost of Queen's, had planned an edition but had been anticipated by Wheelock, who had thus wrenched away the "palm of victory."[173]

Gibson considered his own edition far superior to Wheelock's work and criticized the earlier scholar's edition mainly for two reasons, one being that Wheelock's Latin translation was full of mistakes (for which see in more detail below), and the second that

---

[171]Notwithstanding his departure for Cumberland, Nicolson maintained an active interest in antiquarian work and stayed in close contact with the Oxford Saxonists: see Adams (1917), 74–75 and 124–25; Harris (1983), 173–74 and 183; and Fairer (1986), 814. For his *Historical Library* (1696), see below.

[172]*Chronicon Saxonicum ex MSS codicibus nunc primum integrum edidit, ac Latinum fecit Edmundus Gibson A. B. è Collegio Reginæ.* See Gibson (1692), "Præfatio," sig. b1[r]; Adams (1917), 75–76; Bennett (1938), 41–42; Douglas (1951), 69–71; and Fairer (1986), 811–12.

[173]"Præfatio," sig. b1[r]: "De eo publicando cogitasse jam olim eximium illud Collegii nostri & Academiæ decus, *Gerardum Langbanium*, ut apparet ex Schedis ejus MSS. in Bibliotheca Bodleianâ; in quibus dicit, ad prelum destinanti sibi hos Annales, Wheelocum *palmam præripuisse*" ("Gerard Langbaine, that outstanding adornment of our college and university, had already formerly planned to publish it, as appears from his papers in the Bodleian Library in which he says that, as he was preparing those annals for the press, Wheelock snatched the palm of victory from him"). For Langbaine's subsequent efforts to draw the publication of Somner's *Dictionarium* to Oxford and for the continuation of his Chronicle studies, see above, p. 47 and n. 133.

he considered Wheelock's text to be incomplete because it was based on only two manuscripts. This view was expressed on the title page, where Gibson announced that he had edited the Chronicle "ex MSS codicibus nunc primum integrum," and, in more detail, in his preface, where he explained that Wheelock had in fact printed only one manuscript and extracts of a second which, moreover, offered little additional information, as one manuscript appeared to be a copy of the other; he also remarked that both manuscripts selected by Wheelock were incomplete.[174] He conceded that Wheelock was the first to save this famous national monument from earwigs and woodworm,[175] but emphasized that his own edition adduced the texts of another three copies. Yet, as becomes clear from his description of the sources,[176] Gibson's edition was in fact based on only one original manuscript, MS E (Bodleian MS Laud Misc. 636), which had been given to the Bodleian Library by Archbishop Laud in 1639. Gibson's knowledge of the other four Chronicle versions considered for his edition derived from transcripts and from Wheelock's edition. His text of MS B was taken from a Parkerian transcript which had

---

[174]"Præfatio," sig. b1ᵛ: "Verùm malo fato evenit, ut neuter integrum Chronicon complecteretur, sed ipsius fragmenta (quod integrum nacti jam discimus) hinc inde parum feliciter excerpta. Ad hæc, non longe ultra annum millesimum hujus gentis Historiam deducunt; in rebus vero ita paucis discrepant, ut alterum alterius Apographum esse omnino videatur" ("But it came about by ill fate that neither contained the complete chronicle, but rather [as we now learn after having obtained the full work] fragments of it infelicitously excerpted here and there. Further, they take the history of this nation not far beyond the year 1000, and they differ from one another in so few things that the one seems entirely to be a copy of the other").

[175]"Præfatio," sig. b1ᵛ: ". . . primusque omnium præclarum istud hujus nationis monumentum à blattis ac tineis vindicavit."

[176]See "Præfatio," sigs. b1ᵛ–b2ʳ.

come into the Bodleian Library from Laud's collection in 1639.[177] MSS A, G, and F were accessible to him in the Bodleian Library through the legacy of Junius, namely in the form of a copy of Wheelock's edition (now Bodleian MS Junius 10)[178] which Junius had carefully collated with MS F in the Cotton library. Thus, Gibson's edition was based entirely on material from the Bodleian Library and to a considerable extent on the work of Francis Junius.

Gibson produced a conflated edition of this complex textual entity. In his text he used superscript letters to point to the apparatus at the foot of the page, where under the same letter he either noted the manuscript or transcript from which he had taken his text for the passage following that letter or, alternatively, added the reading of another textual version. Gibson seems to have aimed at a complete text ("integrum") in the sense that it should contain as much Chronicle material as he could get hold of at Oxford, and he appears to have used the available sources without any principled preference.[179] By contrast, Wheelock's (and

----

[177]How it came into Laud's possession is unknown. For its relationship with Joscelyn's work see below, Table 2, no. 6 and n. 8.

[178]A copy of the reissue of 1644. See below, Table 2, no. 11. In his preface (sig. b2ʳ), Gibson stated that in his view Junius had collated Wheelock's Chronicle edition with MS F with the aim of producing a new edition: "Hunc cum Chronico Wheelociano contulerat, ac variantes illius Lectiones suo Libro inseruerat Cl. *Franciscus Junius*, novam, opinor, *Chronici Saxonici* editionem orbi daturus" ("The noble Francis Junius collated this manuscript with Wheelock's edition of the Chronicle, and entered its variants into his book, with the intention [as I believe] of providing the world with a new edition of the Saxon Chronicle").

[179]Whether and to what extent the plan for this conflated text goes back to Junius is not clear. Junius's collation of Wheelock's edition with MS F may be a mere reflection of his awareness of the close connection between MS A and the Canterbury additions to this manuscript inserted by the scribe of MS F, but since many of those additions derive from the archetype of MS E (see Whitelock [1979], 110–11 and 115–16), Junius may well have considered a conflated edition which incorporated the extensive additional material of MS E to be an

presumably Spelman's) aim seems to have been a consciously selective edition of the Winchester text based on MS G and supplemented by additions from MS A, these additions being clearly marked by insertion in brackets. The two seventeenth-century editions thus represented different editorial concepts. Gibson's criticism of Wheelock's selective Chronicle text as being mutilated and incomplete was certainly plausible from his own point of view, but it was in fact unfounded, and his own edition, though offering much more textual material, did not really do justice to the structure and historical development of this complex source.[180]

With respect to the Latin translation of the text, Gibson's edition clearly represented an improvement on Wheelock's, as it could profit from Hickes's *Institutiones*[181] and from Somner's dictionary, including the additions that Junius later entered into his own copy of the *Dictionarium*.[182] Moreover, owing to the work of

---

adequate solution. Bennett (1938), 31, rightly points out that "We misconceive Junius's purpose if we regard his transcripts as mere copies. It is clear from the numerous instances in which he collates his transcript with other manuscripts of the same text . . . that he intended not only to copy but to edit these texts" (see also Bennett [1938], 343–47; and Dekker (2000), 285 and 295–96. Yet in view of Junius's intimate knowledge of the manuscripts in the Cotton library it seems doubtful whether Junius would have excluded the detailed eleventh-century annals of MSS C and D from such a conflated edition, as Gibson did (for Junius's transcript of the *Menologium*, the metrical preface to MS C, see below, Table 2, no. 13). Concerning the nature and extent of the information that Gibson had about Junius's Chronicle studies, presumably through Nicolson, we can only speculate; cf. Bennett (1938), 48.

[180]See Plummer (1892–99), II, §120, who rightly criticized Gibson's method as a "misconception." See also Sykes (1926), 10–11; Bennett (1938), 64–65; and Douglas (1951), 70–71.

[181]In his "Præfatio," sig. b1ᵛ, Gibson emphasized the great help that Hickes's *Institutiones* had been to his work; see also Bennett (1938), 63.

[182]Now Bodleian MS Junius 7; see Wanley (1705), 102. According to Kees Dekker (personal communication), Junius made very few real additions but

Junius and Somner, Gibson was able correctly to identify as poetry the Chronicle poems *sub annis* 937 (*Battle of Brunanburh*), 942 (*Capture of the Five Boroughs*), 973 (*Coronation of King Edgar*), and 975 (*Death of Edgar*). From Wheelock's marginal note to the beginning of the *Battle of Brunanburh* ("Idioma, hic & ad annum 942. & 975. perantiquum & horridum, Lectoris candorem, & diligentiam desiderat" ["The language, here and at the years 942 and 975, is very ancient and rough, and requires the reader's goodwill and attentiveness"]), it appears that Wheelock did not recognize that these annals were written as poetry and that he attributed his difficulties with their language to its great age and inferior quality.[183] That Wheelock was ignorant of the linguistic structure of Old English alliterative poetry may also be inferred from his attempt, dating from 1641, at writing a poem in Old English in praise of King Charles I on the occasion of his return from Scotland: he composed it in rhyming couplets (and preceded

---

mostly added corrections to his copy of the *Dictionarium*. For the quality of Wheelock's Latin translation see Somner (1659), "Ad lectorem," paragraph 15, where he characterized it as "valde mendosam" ("very faulty"). See also Plummer (1892–99), II, cxxviii; and Cook (1962), 25–26.

[183]Wheelock (1643), 555. His marginal note is reflected by John Milton (1608–74) in his *History of Britain* (1670), 225, where he remarks on the language of the Chronicle s.a. 938 (i.e., 937): ". . . the bloodiest fight, say Authors, that ever this Island saw, to describe which, the *Saxon* Annalist wont to be sober and succinct, whether the same or another writer, now labouring under the weight of his Argument, and over-charg'd, runs on a sudden into such extravagant fansies and metaphors, as bare him quite beside the scope of being understood. *Huntingdon*, though himself peccant enough in this kind, transcribes him word for word as a pastime to his Readers. I shall only summe up what of him I can attain, in usuall language." Milton had to rely on the Latin translation. Books IV and V of his *History*, which make frequent use of Wheelock's edition referred to as "Sax. an." in the margins, seem to have been written in the late 1650s; see the introduction to the 1991 facsimile edition by Parry (pp. 38–48).

it by a version in Hebrew).[184] But however flawed Wheelock's attempts at writing Old English poetry may have been, they serve to make the point that for a member of the University of Cambridge, verses in Old English (besides Hebrew and Greek) had by this time become something to show off with on such a celebratory occasion.

Wheelock's knowledge of Old English was based on prose texts; his linguistic competence was therefore bound to fail when confronted with the Chronicle poems, which exhibit lexical and syntactic features alien to Old English prose, such as kennings and variation. Gibson, in his note to the same Chronicle poem, cited Wheelock's note and then remarked: "Perantiquum proculdubio, horridum interim haud dicendum: quippe quod stylum Cædmonianum, elegantissimum plane, & in quo Ducum res gestæ ob ejus sublimitatem decantari antiquitus solebant, aliquatenus saltem referat" ("'Very ancient,' to be sure, but it is hardly to be called 'rough,' inasmuch as it displays, at least to an extent, that most elegant Caedmonian style in which, on account of its loftiness, they were accustomed in former times to recite the deeds of their leaders").[185] But despite the scholarly progress reflected in

---

[184]See Utley (1942), 248–61, for Wheelock's text (signed "Abrahamus Whelocus, Bibliothec. pub. Arab. & Saxo-Brit. Pr.") and a second by a certain William Retchford (signed "Guil. Retchford, Art. Bac. Aul. Clar."), who appears to have been Wheelock's student. Utley also provides a Modern English translation of both texts and a study of their language. See also Bennett (1982), 200; Oates (1986), 203–04; and the discussion of Wheelock's poem by Danielle Cunniff Plumer in the present volume.

[185]Gibson (1692), 112. He nevertheless printed the poems margin-to-margin and not in verse lines, presumably after the example of Junius, who in his *Cædmonis monachi paraphrasis poetica* and also in his transcripts of other poetic texts such as the *Menologium* preceding Chronicle MS C (now Bodleian MS Junius 67, for which see below, Table 2, no. 13) followed the practice of the Anglo-Saxon scribes by not adopting verse lines but rather by using metrical pointing; cf. Krapp (1932), xliv, Lucas (1995), 47–48, Lucas (1997b), Lucas (2000), xxi,

Gibson's remark, seventeenth-century students of Old English, with their fragmentary knowledge of the poetic vocabulary and of the Old English grammatical system, continued to find the linguistic analysis of alliterative poetry extremely difficult in detail.[186]

VII. The Concentration of Antiquarian Studies in Libraries

Gibson's use of the works of earlier antiquaries for his Chronicle edition points to an important aspect of the gradual institutionalization of the study of Old English in the seventeenth century, that is, the concentration of antiquarian materials in public or semi-public institutions. This can be seen clearly in the case of the Chronicle transcripts and partial transcripts (made from both original manuscripts and other transcripts) that were produced in the sixteenth and seventeenth centuries. Several of them had been handed on from one generation of private owners

---

and Plumer in the present volume. For this reason, Bennett's remark about Junius in the context of a comment on the poetic passages in Christopher Rawlinson's 1698 edition of the Old English Boethius (for which cf. n. 191 below)— "Rawlinson . . . rightly prints as verse the renderings of the Metres in the Cottonian manuscript, which Junius had taken as prose" (Bennett [1938], 77; cf. also Fairer [1986], 813–14)—is unfounded.

[186]See Plummer (1892–99), II, cxxix and n. 2. The difficulties of the seventeenth-century editors of the Chronicle poems may be illustrated with one example from *Brunanburh*, line 3b *ealdorlangne tyr* 'eternal glory' (acc.), which exhibits an adjectival poetic compound and a specifically poetic noun. Wheelock translated it as "longâ tiarâ (*ornatus*,)," Gibson as "longa stirpis serie [splendentes,]." Somner's translation for *Tir* (s.v.), "Imperium, principatus, dominatus, dominatio," was not very helpful, and the hapax legomenon *ealdorlang* 'eternal' (literally "lifelong"; cf. Campbell [1938], 96) was not recognized as such by any of the three scholars. For Somner's difficulties with the poetic vocabulary see also Somner (1659), "Ad lectorem," paragraph 7; Cook (1962), 45–46 and 123–27; Hetherington (1980), 175–76; Lutz (1988), 17–20; and Frank (1998), 210.

to the next, but in the course of the seventeenth century most of them likewise passed into the possession of public or semi-public institutions. This is shown in Table 2, appended to this essay, which lists these transcripts in roughly the chronological order of their production; the references to the entries in Humfrey Wanley's *Catalogus* of 1705 in the rightmost column are in themselves a reflection of the strong interest that early modern scholars took in such transcripts.[187]

Only three of the transcripts (nos. 1, 3, and 8) remained in private hands beyond the seventeenth century. Those that passed into public or semi-public ownership were often acquired by the same persons and institutions that acquired original manuscripts. An early example for the collecting of antiquarian materials had been set by Sir Robert Cotton, who, probably following Joscelyn's death, obtained not only original manuscripts that had belonged to Joscelyn, among them Chronicle MS D, but also his antiquarian papers such as his "notebook" which, among various other transcripts, contained several extracts from versions of the Chronicle (no. 5), and presumably also the collection of Chronicle extracts (no. 7) copied by Nowell for Joscelyn. This practice was then continued in Oxford. Among the volumes given by Archbishop Laud to the Bodleian Library in 1639 were not only original manuscripts such as Chronicle MS E but also the Parkerian copy of MS B (no. 6).[188] And when in 1677 Junius bequeathed his library to the Bodleian, Oxford came into possession of some of its most valuable manuscripts containing medieval English but also

---

[187]This list does not include transcripts of Chronicle material that were entered in the original manuscripts, either on vellum or on inserted paper leaves, such as Joscelyn's extensive additions to MSS A and D or William L'Isle's copious additions to MS E, although it is clear that a detailed study of the purpose of, e.g., Joscelyn's work on the Chronicle has to take into account the entire corpus of his transcripts and notes, for which see the references in n. 42 above.

[188]On Laud's benefactions to the University of Oxford, see n. 40 above.

received a great number of studies of Old English texts that Junius had made from manuscripts in other libraries: these included his collation of his copy of Wheelock's edition with MS F (no. 11), his transcript of the Regnal List that originally formed part of MS B (no. 12), and his transcript of the *Menologium* that serves as a metrical preface to MS C (no. 13), all made from manuscripts in the Cotton library. Some time after Somner's death, the dean and chapter of Canterbury acquired for the Cathedral Library Somner's collection of books and antiquarian studies. The collection included, besides Somner's own transcripts (among them his copy of MS C; no. 9), Nowell's copy of the eleventh-century annals from MS D that had come into Somner's possession from Lambarde's family (no. 4).[189] And in 1661 Ussher's entire library (including Lambarde's copy of Nowell's transcript of MS G; no. 2) was presented to Trinity College, Dublin, as the gift of Charles II.[190] Thus by the late seventeenth century, ten out of thirteen Chronicle transcripts, some of which had already passed through the hands of several private owners, came into public or semi-public ownership and thus became more accessible to the scholarly community.

This concentration of antiquarian transcripts in libraries in the course of the seventeenth century reflects the increasing awareness of the need for the institutionalization of Old English studies and of the value attached to earlier antiquarian studies for the advancement of scholarship in the field. In this context, Gibson's exclusive use of material from the Bodleian for his edition of the Chronicle may be viewed as an extreme case: for one thing, it was an expression of his youthful pride in the resources of Oxford that

---

[189]See Kennett (1693), 137; *DNB* s.n. "Somner," p. 669; Woodruff (1911), 42–51; and Urry (1977), v and n. 1.

[190]See *DNB* s.n. "Ussher," p. 71; for the development of Trinity College, Dublin, during the later seventeenth century see Kearney (1970), 139–40, 152–53, and 172–73.

enabled him to produce a text that outmatched the Cambridge edition in textual volume. And in his undifferentiated use, alongside Chronicle MS E, of the Parkerian transcript of MS B and of Junius's collation of MS F against Wheelock's edition, Gibson betrayed his total though indirect reliance on the textual expertise of Junius with his firsthand knowledge of the original manuscripts.[191]

But there was another, more scholarly reason for the growing interest in the transcripts and collations produced by the antiquaries of the sixteenth and earlier seventeenth centuries, namely an increasing awareness of the lack of a catalogue that provided a reliable survey of the medieval manuscripts containing Old English texts. In the case of the Anglo-Saxon Chronicle, on account of the complexity of the text, the interest in transcripts was particularly keen right from the beginning of the concerted antiquarian efforts of the Parker circle, as Nowell's transcripts (Table 2, nos. 1, 3, 4, and 7) and Joscelyn's Chronicle studies and his 1565/6 list of Chronicle manuscripts and transcripts illustrate.[192] This interest persisted during Cotton's lifetime and after, as is shown in Table 2. It did not even abate after the publication of Gibson's edition, as becomes apparent from the first volume of William Nicolson's *English Historical Library* published in 1696,

---

[191]For a similarly important role of Junian transcripts cf. Christopher Rawlinson's edition of the Old English Boethius, published at Oxford in 1698. According to Bennett (1938), 76–77, "That text was not so much Rawlinson's as Junius's. Junius had made a transcript (now MS Junius 12) of the Bodleian manuscript of the Anglo-Saxon Boethius, adding variant readings from the Cottonian MS Otho A 6 which was later destroyed in the disastrous fire of 1731. Rawlinson prints variant readings of the prose parts from Junius's transcript at the foot of the page; it is therefore fitting that Van Dyck's portrait of Junius should serve as frontispiece for the book." For Junius's motives behind his transcripts see Dekker (2000), esp. 292–96.

[192]For Joscelyn's list (now BL MS Cotton Nero C. iii, fol. 208r), see pp. 12–14 above.

which was intended as a review of previous historical research and a survey of the materials available for further study.[193] In chapter IV, where Nicolson—the former Oxford Saxonist, who had originally been assigned the task of producing an edition which was then carried out by Gibson—dealt with the Chronicle, he followed Gibson in criticizing Wheelock for using only two manuscripts. He pointed out that "Mr. *Gibson* had the advantage of three Copies more,"[194] which he listed as "1. *Laud*: A fair one in Vellum, given by Archbishop *Laud* to the University of *Oxford*; which corrects those that *Wheloc* had seen, and continues the History down to the year 1154" (i.e., MS E);[195] "2. *Cant*. Another Gift of the same Archbishop to the publick Library at *Oxford*. 'Tis a Paper transcript of some Copy (now lost) differing from all the rest. . . . It ends with the year 977" (i.e., the Parkerian transcript of MS B; see Table 2, no. 6);[196] and "3. *Cot*. A better Copy than it had been Mr. *Wheloc*'s Fortune to meet with in the *Cotton*-Library: which was accurately compared with *Wheloc*'s Edition by *Fr. Junius*, and ends *A. D.* 1057" (i.e., Junius's collation of Wheelock's edition with MS F; see Table 2, no. 11).[197]

This description of the textual sources used by Gibson suggests that Nicolson considered Gibson's edition superior to Wheelock's mainly because it represented the complex textual tradition more fully, and that he did not find fault with using

---

[193]See Butt (1938), 74–77; and Fairer (1986), 814–15.

[194]Nicolson (1696–99), I, 114. He also criticized Wheelock for using MS A as his second manuscript, pointing out that the textual material from this manuscript (i.e., the Canterbury additions to MS A inserted by the scribe of MS F and taken from the archetype of MS E) was clearly inferior in quality and extent to the text of the extant Peterborough MS E that was used by Gibson.

[195]Nicolson (1696–99), I, 114.

[196]Nicolson (1696–99), I, 115.

[197]Nicolson (1696–99), I, 115; but in footnote (m) Nicolson incorrectly associated Junius's extracts with "Tiber. B. 4," i.e., with MS D.

transcripts instead of the original manuscripts as long as the transcripts offered additional textual material. In fact, he seems to have been of the opinion that Gibson's edition could still be improved upon by adducing even more texts; and he called attention to manuscripts and transcripts of the Chronicle that had come to his attention through the publications of William Somner, James Ussher, and Henry Wharton (1664–95).[198] Most of them can be identified:

> 1. The *Saxon* Chronicle from *Julius Cæsar* down to the Reign of King *Edward* the Martyr, in Sir *John Cotton*'s Library [i.e., MS B]. . . .[199]
> 2. Another, in the same Library, from *Julius Cæsar* down to the Conquest; which was transcrib'd by *Somner*, and is now (under the Title of the Chronicle of *Abingdon*) amongst his MSS. at *Canterbury* [i.e., MS C and Somner's transcript thereof, now Canterbury, Cathedral Library, MS Lit. C. 8; see Table 2, no. 9]. . . .[200] 3. A Third, in *Latin* and *Saxon*, at the same place, which is frequently referr'd to by Mr. *Wharton*, and seems to have recorded many particulars of Note not mention'd by any of the rest. This Book was given to Sir *Robert Cotton* by Mr. *Camden*, says Archbishop *Usher* [i.e., the bilingual

---

[198]Wharton's *Anglia sacra* had come out in 1691.

[199]Nicolson (1696–99), I, 116. In footnote (o) he correctly identified it as "Tiber. A. 6." Wharton's information in his *Anglia sacra*, I, 176, that this manuscript ended s.a. 975 (*recte* 977) led Nicolson to the correct conclusion that its text was different "from what was perus'd by *A. Wheloc*," but it also seems to have led him to the wrong conclusion that there was no connection between this manuscript and the Parkerian transcript of it that Gibson had used for his edition (as "Cant.").

[200]Nicolson (1696–99), I, 116. In footnote (q) he correctly identified the manuscript as "Tiber. B. 1." In this case, Nicolson did not mention the source of his information. Somner's descriptions of the text in his transcript and in the preface to his *Dictionarium* do not mention the library pressmark of his exemplar.

MS F];[201] who also mentions a Copy of his own, worth the enquiring after [i.e., Dublin, Trinity College, MS 631; see Table 2, no. 2]. . . .[202]
4. The Book of *Peterburgh* [i.e., MS E], which was never thoroughly compar'd with any Copy, hitherto publisht, and differs from them all.[203]

Nicolson concludes by asking, "May we not also bring into this List those hinted at by Mr. *Kennet*;[204] and that which Mr. *Somner* had from Mr. *Lambard*?" This last information is misleading. It appears to point to Canterbury, Cathedral Library, MS Lit. E. 1, the partial transcript of MS D by Nowell, which passed from the possession of the Lambarde family into Somner's hands (Table 2, no. 4). But Nicolson's reference in his footnote (y) to *"Roman Ports*, &c. p. 32" leads to a specific Chronicle reference to Dover ("to Dofran gewende") that is found only in MS E and that Somner

---

[201]Nicolson (1696–99), I, 116–17. Identified in footnote (r) as "Domitian. A. 8." In footnote (s) he mentioned "Angl. Sac. par. I. p. 332" as the source of his information (Wharton's *Anglia sacra* contains frequent references to MS F). Since Junius had restricted his collation of MS F with Wheelock's edition (see Table 2, no. 11) to the Old English entries, Nicolson was not able to associate the bilingual manuscript mentioned by Wharton with the exclusively Old English extracts from this manuscript by Junius that Gibson had used for his edition (as "Cot.").

[202]Nicolson (1696–99), I, 117. This somewhat vague remark suggests that Ussher may not have been aware that the text of this transcript derived from MS G. For Ussher's frequent consultations of the Cotton library and for specific references to Chronicle MSS E, F, and G in his *Britannicarum ecclesiarum antiquitates*, see n. 53 above.

[203]Nicolson (1696–99), I, 117. This implies that Nicolson did not know that "The Book of Peterburgh" referred to by various antiquaries and Gibson's "Laud" were in fact the same manuscript.

[204]Nicolson (1696–99), I, 117. His reference in footnote (x) to "Life of *Somn.* p. 30. 66" leads to Kennett (1693), 66: "4. *Fragmentum Annalium* Saxonum *ab An.* 726. *ad An.* 1055," which cannot be identified with any of the transcripts listed in Table 2.

notes on page 32 of his *A Treatise of the Roman Ports and Forts in Kent* (1693). Somner's statement there that he had found this reference "in a small Saxon MS sometime belonging to Mr. *Lambard*, and procured for me by my late deceased friend *Thomas Godfrey*"[205] should therefore be interpreted as a reference to Nowell's partial transcript of MS E (now BL MS Add. 43704; Table 2, no. 3), which was made accessible to Somner by Godfrey but remained in private ownership until the twentieth century.

Nicolson's list of Chronicle manuscripts and transcripts betrays that he had no precise knowledge of the Chronicle manuscripts and transcripts he mentioned, and this judgment applies both to the material that had been used by Gibson and to the manuscripts and transcripts that Nicolson listed as worth checking; otherwise he would have noticed that most of the additional material mentioned by him had already been taken into account by Gibson in one form or another. Only his item 2 (MS C and Somner's transcript of it) would in fact have offered additional material. Thus, Nicolson's attempt at a state-of-the-art report of historical studies at the close of the seventeenth century makes it particularly clear with regard to the Anglo-Saxon Chronicle that further progress could only be achieved on the basis of a comprehensive firsthand assessment of the entire textual tradition of the original manuscripts and the transcripts that had been produced since the later sixteenth century.

This assessment became available less than a decade later, when in 1705 Humfrey Wanley published his *Librorum veterum septentrionalium catalogus historico-criticus* as part of George Hickes's *Linguarum veterum septentrionalium thesaurus grammatico-criticus et archæologicus*. The detailed descriptions of the antiquarian materials in Wanley's *Catalogus*, very much like those of the Anglo-Saxon manuscripts, reflect the importance that was

---

[205]For Godfrey see n. 6 to Table 2.

attached to these materials by early modern scholars. As regards the Anglo-Saxon Chronicle, two of the transcripts made by Nowell listed in Table 2 below (nos. 1 and 3) remained in private hands until the twentieth century and thus escaped Wanley's attention, as did Lambarde's transcript of MS G, which had come into the possession of Archbishop Ussher and was taken to Ireland after Ussher's death (Table 2, no. 2). Wanley's catalogue was superseded in the twentieth century by Neil Ker's *Catalogue of Manuscripts Containing Anglo-Saxon* (1957), but only for the original manuscripts; a correspondingly detailed overview of the transcripts of Old English texts does not exist so far.[206]

VIII. CONCLUDING REMARKS

In this paper on the study of Old English in the seventeenth century I have concentrated on the factors that resulted in its institutionalization as a university discipline. I have tried to show that Sir Henry Spelman's endowment of a lectureship at Cambridge must be viewed against the background of several abortive attempts by the historians around Sir Robert Cotton to create a firm basis for the study of medieval English history outside the universities. The growing political tensions between king and Parliament in the early Stuart period led former leading members of the Society of Antiquaries such as Camden and Spelman to the conclusion that the future for the study of history (and with it the study of Old English) had to be pursued within the structures of the universities. With their endowments they contributed to a more general change of orientation of the universities toward a stronger emphasis on research and a diversification of the syllabus. When the Oxford Saxonists began to establish Old English studies at Queen's College, these changes to the English

---

[206]For much valuable information about early modern transcripts see Ker (1957), l–lvi, 506–10, 562–67, and the descriptions of their Anglo-Saxon exemplars.

university structures had become effective or were well under way, and the study of historical sources of the Anglo-Saxon period and of the Old English language had developed into a field of research that appeared suitable to university politicians at Oxford as an advertisement for their university in its competition with Cambridge.

Despite the clearly distinct historical causations for the introduction of the study of Old English at the two universities, the lines of its development at Cambridge and Oxford exhibit some remarkable parallels. This is partly due to the factual necessities of the study of any dead language, specifically, the need to make accessible the most important texts by producing editions, dictionaries, and grammars. Yet the reasons for these parallels must also be sought in the rivalry of the two universities, which in Oxford resulted in the concentration on practically the same research targets as had first been formulated by Spelman for Cambridge and in the attempts of the Oxford Saxonists to surpass Cambridge's achievements. This can best be illustrated by the two seventeenth-century editions of the Anglo-Saxon Chronicle: Gibson's Oxford production was expressly aimed at outmatching Wheelock's *editio princeps*.

Due to the complexity of the Chronicle text and to the strong historical orientation of Old English studies throughout the early modern period, the study of the Chronicle not only serves to illustrate the rivalry between Cambridge and Oxford but also has proved suitable for a more general investigation of the institutionalization of Old English studies: from the beginnings of its concerted study in the later sixteenth century, the Anglo-Saxon Chronicle attracted much scholarly exchange and cooperation, and called for precise listing and evaluation of the manuscript sources, for reliable transcripts and collations, and for an adequate method of editing. For these reasons, the study of the Chronicle in the early modern English period played a particularly important role in the institutionalization of Old English studies in general. In this development, the universities of Cambridge and Oxford gained increasing importance, but the initiative for the incorporation of Old English studies came from outside the universities—after the subject had been intensively pursued outside the universities for almost a century—and it was determined by political conditions to a greater extent than has hitherto been assumed.

TABLE 2. SIXTEENTH- AND SEVENTEENTH-CENTURY CHRONICLE TRANSCRIPTS
AND THEIR OWNERS UP TO THE EARLY EIGHTEENTH CENTURY

No.	Library pressmark	Transcriber	Copied from	16th–18th-century owners	Ref. in Wanley's *Catalogus*
1	BL MS Add. 43703[1]	Nowell	MS G, with additions from MSS E, C, B, D[2]	1. Lambarde 2. Lambarde family	—
2	Dublin, Trinity College, MS 631[3]	Lambarde	No. 1 (G-text only)	1. Lambarde 2. Ussher 3. Trinity College, Dublin	—
3	BL MS Add. 43704[4]	Nowell	MS E (part), with additions from MSS C and D	1. Lambarde 2. Lambarde family	—
4	Canterbury, Cathedral Library, MS Lit. E. 1[5]	Nowell	MS D (annals 1043–79)	1. Lambarde 2. Godfrey[6] 3. Somner 4. Cathedral Library, Canterbury	p. 271

(Table 2—*Continued*)

No.	Library pressmark	Tran-scriber	Copied from	16th–18th-century owners	Ref. in Wanley's *Catalogus*
5	BL MS Cotton Vitellius D. vii[7]	Joscelyn	MSS A, B, C, E (extracts)	1. Joscelyn 2. Cotton library	p. 240
6	Bodleian MS Laud Misc. 661[8]	Parker circle	MS B	1. Laud 2. Bodleian Library	p. 84
7	BL MS Cotton Domitian A. xviii[9]	Nowell	Nos. 3 and 4	1. Joscelyn 2. Cotton library	p. 248
8	BL MS Harley 312[10]	D'Ewes	MS F (intro-duction and annal 60 B.C.)	1. D'Ewes 2. D'Ewes family 3. Harley	p. 308
9	Canterbury, Cathedral Library, MS Lit. C. 8[11]	Somner	MS C	1. Somner 2. Cathedral Library, Canterbury	p. 271

No.	Library pressmark	Tran-scriber	Copied from	16th–18th-century owners	Ref. in Wanley's *Catalogus*
10	Canterbury, Cathedral Library, MS W/E 6.20[12]	Somner	No. 9 (variant readings entered in his copy of Wheelock's edition)	1. Somner 2. Cathedral Library, Canterbury	p. 272
11	Bodleian MS Junius 10[13]	Junius	MS F (extended extracts entered in his copy of Wheelock's edition)	1. Junius 2. Bodleian Library	p. 103
12	Bodleian MS Junius 66[14]	Junius	MS B (Regnal List)	1. Junius 2. Bodleian Library	p. 95
13	Bodleian MS Junius 67[15]	Junius	MS C (*Meno-logium* and intro-ductory lines of the Chronicle text)	1. Junius 2. Bodleian Library	p. 95

Notes to Table 2

[1]This Chronicle transcript, which forms part of a complete transcript of BL MS Cotton Otho B. xi made by Nowell in 1562, is first mentioned by Joscelyn in his list of Chronicle manuscripts in BL MS Cotton Nero C. iii, fol. 208r, as part of his description of MS G ("habet eius exemplar Laur. Nowel"); and after that by Nichols (1780–90), 510, as no. I.3, "Chronica conservata in Monasterio Sancti Martini," of the "Collectanea of Lawrence Nowell and William Lambarde, in the possession of Multon Lambard, Esq;." For the author and antiquary John Nichols (1745–1826), see *DNB* s.n. The transcript came into the possession of the British Museum only in 1934. See Flower (1934), 130–32; Ker (1957), 234; British Museum (1967), 196; Lutz (1981), ch. 3; Torkar (1981), 37–65; Lutz (1982), 304–11; and Grant (1996), 25–26.

[2]The additions from MSS E, C, B, and D (in that order) were entered by Nowell from 1565 onwards. These additions must be seen in conjunction with his extracts from MSS E, C, and D in BL MS Add. 43704 (see no. 3 in the table) and from D in Canterbury, Cathedral Library, MS Lit. E. 1 (no. 4 in the table). Taken together, they form a conflated Chronicle text based on five out of seven manuscripts, a text which may have been intended as the basis for an edition of the Chronicle. See Lutz (1981), lvii–lxv; and Lutz (1982), 304–33.

[3]See Abbott (1900), 105; and Lutz (1981), lxv–lxvii. Lambarde copied the Chronicle from Nowell's transcript of MS G in BL MS Add. 43703 (no. 1 above) in 1563/4, before Nowell supplemented it with material from MSS E, C, B, and D: see Campbell (1938), 133–44; and Lutz (1982), 305–06 and 313–14. The transcript may have come into Ussher's possession on one of his first visits to England; he presumably acquired it from Lord William Howard (1563–1640), together with other manuscripts from Lambarde's library (see O'Sullivan [1956], 39). Since Nowell's entire collection of Chronicle transcripts (see nos. 1, 2, 4) had passed into Lambarde's possession at Nowell's departure from England in 1567 (see Torkar [1981], 44–47), Lambarde no longer needed his early copy of Nowell's transcript of MS G and possibly for this reason passed it on to Howard, from whose collection it eventually came into Ussher's hands. Ussher's entire library was sent to Ireland after his death and reached Trinity College in 1661: see *DNB* s.n. "Ussher," p. 71; and O'Sullivan (1956), 58.

[4]These extended extracts from MSS E, C, and D form a supplement to Nowell's transcript of MS G and the shorter additions from MSS E, C, B, and D in BL MS Add. 43703 and to the eleventh-century annals in Canterbury, Cathedral Library, MS Lit. E. 1 (see nos. 1 and 4 in the table). This supplementary transcript is first mentioned by Joscelyn in the description of MS E in his list of 1565/6, "habet eius exemplum Laurentius Nowel," and again by Nichols (1790), 510, as no. IV, "Chronica Peterburgensis. A transcript by L. Noell, 1565." See Lutz (1981), lx–lxii; and Lutz (1982), 308–30.

[5]See Todd (1793), 294; and Canterbury (1802), 126. This transcript of the late entries of MS D supplements Nowell's extracts from the earlier entries of MS D in BL MSS Add. 43703 and 43704 (nos. 1 and 3 above); see Lutz (1982), 330–31 and 337–48. Wanley mentions Lambarde, Godfrey, and Somner as consecutive owners of this "Fragmentum Chronici Saxonicè."

[6]For Thomas Godfrey (1615–75), William Lambarde's grandson and Somner's contemporary, who seems to have taken great interest in his grandfather's antiquarian studies, see Warnicke (1973), 138–39.

[7]The Chronicle transcripts in Joscelyn's "notebook" do not make sense as an independent document but only as different stages of his extensive study of the original manuscripts of the Chronicle. That study included his transcribing into the manuscripts themselves substantial passages copied from the other manuscripts, and entering numerous remarks on the textual relations between the manuscripts: see Sanders Gale (1978), 70, 73–75, and 206–15; Lutz (1982), 339–53; and the references in n. 42 above. Just like his other antiquarian materials, the "notebook" seems to have reached Cotton's library shortly after Joscelyn's death; see above, p. 17 and n. 32.

[8]This Parkerian transcript of MS B, which includes the Regnal List at the point at which it originally appeared in B, i.e., following the Chronicle text, incorporates Joscelyn's additions from MS A and also his references to MS C entered in MS B; it can on these grounds be dated to 1565 or later. The transcript may have been commissioned by Joscelyn but was made by a professional scribe with little knowledge of Old English: see Ker (1957), no. 188; Lutz (1982), 305–06 and 342–45; and Taylor (1983), xiv–xv and xix–xx. For its use by

Edmund Gibson for his edition see above. For other Parkerian transcripts of that type see Graham (1994), 425–30; and Parkes (1997), 124–25.

[9]See Wanley (1705), 248, art. II: "Excerpta quædam Saxonica (ex historia Petroburgensi)," stated by him to have been identified as such by James Ussher, and art. III: "Excerpta alia nonnulla (ex Annalibus Saxonicis aliis)." Nowell copied these Chronicle extracts from versions E and D from his transcripts, BL MS Add. 43704 and Canterbury, Cathedral Library, MS Lit. E. 1 (nos. 3 and 4 above), not from the original manuscripts; see Lutz (1982), 333–38. He seems to have made these transcripts for Joscelyn, at a time when Joscelyn had studied MSS B, A, and C (in that order) but had not yet had access to MSS E and D; for the complex interrelations between these extracts and Joscelyn's Chronicle studies see Lutz (1982), 333–55. The extracts presumably reached Cotton's library as part of Joscelyn's antiquarian materials shortly after Joscelyn's death.

[10]This copy of the preface and annal 60 B.C. is entitled by D'Ewes, "Transcriptum vetustissimi in membrana Chronici Anglo-Saxonici-Latini in Bibliotheca Cottonianâ reperti in uno volumine inter alia compacti (quod nota sive charactere Domitianus A. 8. ab alijs ibidem codicibus MSS. distinguitur)" ("Transcript of a very old Anglo-Saxon–Latin Chronicle on parchment to be found in the Cotton Library, joined with other items in a single volume [which is distinguished from the other manuscripts there by the note or mark Domitian A. 8]"); see also Harley (1808), 193, no. 4. His rationale for this isolated partial Chronicle transcript is not clear. For D'Ewes's various antiquarian projects see also above, n. 91. D'Ewes's antiquarian collection was sold to Robert Harley by his grandson in 1705: see *DNB* s.n. "D'Ewes," pp. 902–03; and Wright and Wright (1966), II, 445.

[11]This is a transcript of the Chronicle text only (BL MS Cotton Tiberius B. i, art. 4); it does not include the *Menologium*, which is commonly assumed to function as a kind of metrical introduction to the Chronicle in MS C (for Junius's transcript of the *Menologium*, see no. 13 in the table). Somner did, however, mention the *Menologium* in his introductory description of the manuscript context, as also the Orosius which follows the Chronicle in this manuscript. See Woodruff (1911), 46, no. 84; and Ker (1957), no. 191. Somner used this transcript extensively for his *Dictionarium*; see pp. 43–44 above with nn. 118 and 119.

[12]These variant readings that Somner inserted in his copy of Wheelock's 1644 reissue of the Chronicle are taken from his own transcript of MS C (no. 9 in the table), not from the original manuscript. They are related to his work on the *Dictionarium*; see Lutz (1988), 9 and n. 20.

[13]The transcript ends: "1056. Her forðferde Victor papa . . . monte cassino - - - - -"; Junius seems to have found fol. 70v of his exemplar too difficult to read. In Thorpe's edition of 1861, p. 329, this annal is dated 1057 and continues for two more lines, and the text ends imperfectly with the annal for 1058: ". . . to Rof."; cf. the hardly legible verso of the final page in Dumville's 1995 facsimile. In Junius's transcript, the annals for 1002–56 are prefixed to Wheelock's Bede on five paper leaves, most variants and additions to the earlier entries are added to the respective annals or annal numbers of Wheelock's Chronicle text, and two passages from annals 694 and 796 are inserted on the originally blank paper leaf after the laws. Taken together, these extracts from MS F seem to form a complete copy of the material not found in Wheelock's edition; see Dumville (1995), 16–17. For Gibson's use of Junius's collation for his edition, see above, p. 60.

[14]This transcript contains in fact two items taken from different sections of BL MS Cotton Tiberius A. iii: (I) Ælfric's *Colloquy* (fols. 60v–64v; see Ker [1957], no. 186, art. 11, and for numerous other transcripts made by Junius from this miscellaneous manuscript see Ker [1957], pp. 240–41); and (II) the Regnal List of the West Saxon kings (fol. 178), which originally concluded Chronicle MS B (see Ker [1957], no. 188, arts. 1, 2; and Taylor [1983], xviii–xxii). Junius headed his transcript of the Regnal List "Ejusdem Cottoniani codicis folio 175 sequentia hæc antiquâ manu descripta invenias, vide Chronologiā Wheloci ad annum ccccxcv" ("On fol. 175 of the same Cottonian manuscript you can find the following, copied in an ancient hand; see Wheelock's *Chronologia* at the year 495"). Wanley described it as "Chronici veteris fragmentum," like Junius with a reference to "*Chron. Whel. ad annum ccccxcv.*," the entry describing Cerdic's and Cynric's coming to England; this means that Junius and Wanley failed to note the manuscript connection between MS B and this Regnal List.

[15]Ending on fol. 8r with "Ær Cristes geflæscnesse . . . rice gewinnan. &c." (cf. Rositzke [1940], 12); the transcript is headed "Hoc Abbingdoniensis chronici initium in Cottoniano codice Ms° cui titulus TIBERIUS B. 1. pag. 110" ("This

is the opening of the Abingdon Chronicle in the Cottonian manuscript marked Tiberius B. 1, p. 110"). Junius seems to have copied the first lines of the Chronicle text only in order to indicate the manuscript context for the *Menologium* and *Maxims II*, which he rightly viewed as a preface to the Chronicle in MS C; cf. Dobbie (1942), lx. Wanley did not mention the introductory lines of the Chronicle in his description but characterized the content of Junius's transcript as "*Initium* Abingdoniensis Chronici *Poetice scriptum, & è Codice Cottoniano cui Titulus* Tib. B. I *per* cl. Junium *descriptum*" ("The opening of the Abingdon Chronicle poetically written, and copied by the noble Junius from the Cottonian manuscript marked Tib. B. I").

JOHN JOSCELYN, PIONEER
OF OLD ENGLISH LEXICOGRAPHY

Timothy Graham

John Joscelyn (1529–1603) was the principal student of Old English within the group that, under the direction of Matthew Parker, archbishop of Canterbury (1559–75), actively engaged in manuscript studies in Parker's household at Lambeth Palace in London. Having taught Latin and Greek at Queens' College, Cambridge, in the 1550s, and having resigned his fellowship in 1557 perhaps on religious grounds, Joscelyn joined the household as Latin secretary soon after Parker became archbishop in 1559.[1] His entry into the household is presumably datable to before October 1560 when Parker made him a prebendary of Hereford Cathedral, perhaps as a means of remunerating him for his services. Joscelyn participated in Parker's program of publishing Anglo-Saxon religious and historical texts. He is believed to have written the introduction for *A Testimonie of Antiqvitie*, an edition of one of Ælfric's Easter homilies and other Old English texts that appeared, under Parker's auspices, probably in the autumn of 1566 and was the first-ever publication in Old English.[2] He

---

[1] For the details of Joscelyn's career, see *DNB* s.n.; and Venn and Venn (1922–27), II, 490.

[2] *A Testimonie of Antiqvitie, Shewing the Auncient Fayth in the Church of England Touching the Sacrament of the Body and Bloude of the Lord Here Publikely Preached, and Also Receaued in the Saxons Tyme, aboue 600. Yeares*

cooperated in the edition of the Old English Gospels published under John Foxe's editorship in 1571,[3] and in Parker's 1574 edition of Asser's *Ælfredi regis res gestæ*, which included the first edition of King Alfred's preface to the Old English translation of the *Regula pastoralis* of Gregory the Great.[4] He drafted the Latin lives of the archbishops of Canterbury published in Parker's *De antiquitate Britannicæ ecclesiæ* of 1572,[5] and in writing the lives of the Anglo-Saxon archbishops he made use of the magnificent collection of Anglo-Saxon manuscripts that Parker had assembled. The *De antiquitate* included, in its life of Dunstan, the first printed reference to Wulfstan's *Sermo Lupi ad Anglos*, which is there summarized in Latin.[6]

Apart from his role in Parker's publications, Joscelyn made significant contributions to Anglo-Saxon studies that remained unpublished. Principal among these were an Old English grammar and dictionary. Both of these passed into the manuscript collection of Sir Robert Cotton (1571–1631), probably on Joscelyn's death in 1603. The grammar has long been lost. Cotton noted in a loan list dated 17 November 1612 that he had lent both it and the

---

Agoe (London: John Day). See Pollard and Redgrave (1976–91), I, nos. 159 and 159.5. On the date of publication, see Adams (1917), 23 n. 4; Bromwich (1962), 270 n. 1 and 271 n. 2; and Lucas (1997a), 148 n. 9.

[3] *The Gospels of the Fower Euangelistes Translated in the Olde Saxons Tyme out of Latin into the Vulgare Toung of the Saxons, Newly Collected out of Auncient Monumentes of the Sayd Saxons, and Now Published for Testimonie of the Same* (London: John Day, 1571); Pollard and Redgrave (1976–91), I, no. 2961.

[4] *Ælfredi regis res gestæ* (London: John Day, 1574); Pollard and Redgrave (1976–91), I, no. 863. The edition of Alfred's preface (with interlinear English translation) occurs on sigs. F.i^r–F.ii^v.

[5] *De antiquitate Britannicæ ecclesiæ & priuilegiis ecclesiæ Cantuariensis, cum archiepiscopis ejusdem 70* (London: John Day, 1572); Pollard and Redgrave (1976–91), II, no. 19292.

[6] *De antiquitate*, pp. 63–64.

dictionary to his former teacher, the antiquary William Camden (1551–1623).[7] Some time thereafter, the grammar went missing. In the preface to his *Institutiones grammaticæ* of 1689, George Hickes mentioned his fruitless efforts to locate it.[8] All that survives is a lengthy index for it, now Bodleian MS Bodley 33. The dictionary has had a happier fate. Comprising two volumes, it survives in the British Library as MSS Cotton Titus A. xv and A. xvi. It is by far the most significant sixteenth-century contribution to Old English lexicography.

The dictionary is the work of Joscelyn and one other hand. It appears to have been Humfrey Wanley who first stated in print that Joscelyn's collaborator was Matthew Parker's son John (1548–1619). In his catalogue of Anglo-Saxon manuscripts, Wanley described MS Titus A. xv as "codex chartaceus in Quarto per Joannem Josselinum & Joannem Parkerum D. Matth. fil. (ut videtur) scriptus" ("paper volume, in-quarto, written by John Joscelyn and John Parker, the son of Matthew [as it seems]").[9] Wanley's description was repeated by Joseph Planta in his 1802

---

[7]BL MS Harley 6018, fol. 162v, within a section of loans headed "M Camden": "Saxon Grammar that was Mr Gocelin [*sic*] . . . Saxon Dixonary in two volumes Mr Gocelins." Cotton described both the grammar and the dictionary as being bound "in velum."

[8]George Hickes, *Institutiones grammaticæ Anglo-Saxonicæ, et Moeso-Gothicæ* (Oxford, 1689), 2: "a Viris eruditis, præsertim Bibliothecarum Præfectis, de Josselini Grammatica diligenter sciscitatus sum, hoc consilio, ut ipsam forte suis latebris ereptam, cum nostra Grammatica, jam tum Typographo tradita, conferrem" ("I diligently enquired about Joscelyn's Grammar among learned men, especially librarians, with the intention that, should it perhaps be rescued from its hiding-place, I might compare it with our Grammar, which by then was already in the printer's hands").

[9]Wanley (1705), 239.

catalogue of the Cotton manuscripts,[10] and the identification of Joscelyn's collaborator as John Parker has been accepted by modern scholars.[11] The script of Joscelyn's collaborator is formal and neat; it shows some differences from the script of John Parker in his memorandum book, London, Lambeth Palace Library, MS 737. John Parker was, however, capable of varying his hand, and the memorandum book generally shows him in his more informal mode. The script of the collaborator matches that of Bodley 33, the index to Joscelyn's grammar. Bodley 33 includes on fols. 1 and 2a a title and a preface written in the same hand as the rest of the manuscript. The title describes the index as the work of "Jo. P.," and the preface is signed with the same initials. The initials no doubt stand for "Johannes Parker"; the traditional identification of Joscelyn's collaborator is evidently correct.

The two volumes of the dictionary are made up of paper leaves that now measure ca. 224 × 149 mm but that were formerly somewhat larger. Both volumes are now in British Museum bindings of the 1950s.[12] Within these bindings, the quires of the first volume are sewn onto meeting guards; those of the second volume are not. The sewing onto guards renders the quire structure of MS Titus A. xv easily visible. Most of its twenty quires have sixteen or eighteen leaves, but quire 3 (fols. 32–46) has fifteen

---

[10]Planta (1802), 513. Planta altered Wanley's text by placing the four words "Matthæi filium ut videtur," not just the words "ut videtur," in parentheses. From the positioning of Wanley's parentheses it is unclear whether he meant that it seemed that the dictionary was the work of Joscelyn and John Parker, or that it seemed that John Parker was the son of Matthew; Planta's adjustment establishes that he interpreted Wanley's comment as applying to the identity of John Parker.

[11]See, for example, Rosier (1960), 28 n. 3; and Hetherington (1980), 27–28. On p. 29, Hetherington adds the proviso "if Wanley (an astute and generally meticulous scholar) has correctly identified the hand that assisted Joscelyn."

[12]The date stamps inside the back covers of the bindings record that MS Titus A. xv was rebound in May 1955, MS Titus A. xvi in December 1958.

leaves (the original seventh leaf having been excised during the process of production, perhaps after an error was made) and quire 4 (fols. 47–63) has seventeen leaves (the original sixteenth leaf having been excised, also during production); quire 15 (fols. 220–222 + five unnumbered leaves) has only eight leaves. Centered at the top of the first rectos of some quires of both manuscripts are quire signatures: for example, "e. 1" on fol. 94r of Titus A. xv, the first leaf of quire 7, the only quire containing entries beginning with *e*; "h. 3" on fol. 259r, the first leaf of quire 18, the third quire containing entries beginning with *h*; and "w. 3" on fol. 304r of MS Titus A. xvi, the first leaf of the third quire containing entries beginning with *w*. The script of some of the quire signatures is identifiable as Joscelyn's. The tops of several of the signatures have been trimmed away. Probably all the quires originally had such signatures, many having been lost completely as a result of trimming. Trimming has also reduced the outer edges of the leaves, as can be seen most easily in MS Titus A. xv, where on several leaves the binder has cut around entries that extend into the outer margin and has thereby preserved evidence of the formerly greater width of the leaves.

The division of the dictionary into two volumes goes back at least to Cotton's time and was probably effected by Joscelyn himself. Cotton described the dictionary as being in two volumes in his loan list mentioned above, and he entered his signature of ownership, "Robertus Cotton Bruceus," at the front of both volumes. There is also an early modern, probably seventeenth-century title at the beginning of each volume: "Dictionarium Saxonico-Latinum 1 p*ars*" in MS Titus A. xv, and "Dictionarium Saxonico-Latinum 2 p*ars*" in MS Titus A. xvi. The leaves of MS Titus A. xv are numbered "1" through "305" in a late nineteenth-century pencil foliation that supersedes various early modern ink foliations; in accordance with British Museum/British Library practice, the pencil foliation leaves blank leaves unnumbered. MS Titus A. xvi has only an early modern ink foliation from "1" through "308"; this foliation also does not number blank leaves. Blank leaves occur in several places, either within a quire, where Joscelyn or Parker left a single leaf blank between the end of the entries for one letter of the alphabet and the beginning of the entries for the next letter; or at the end of a quire, where the entries for one letter were completed a few leaves short of the quire-ending, and the entries for the new letter commenced with the next quire. For example, in quire 6 (fols. 80–93) of Titus A. xv, a single leaf is left blank between fols. 81 and 82, marking the transition between the entries for the letters c and d; the entries for d conclude on fol. 93, after which three blank leaves complete the quire, with the entries for e beginning on fol. 94, the first leaf of quire 7.

The entries are laid out in two columns and in fully alpha-betical order,[13] although with several errors in the sequence. For example, on fol. 88r of Titus A. xv, "Digolnyssa" preceded by the phrase "Ure digolnesse" appears out of sequence between "Diglice" and "Diglu," and on fol. 260v, "hromsa" and "hromsan crop" erroneously occur between "hrooc" and "hrorenlic." Fre-quently such errors are corrected by marks entered alongside the misordered entries.[14] Such marks occur in different versions, one of which consists of entering the letters b and a against con-secutive entries, to indicate that their order should be switched: thus on fol. 218r of Titus A. xv, b is entered next to "Growe," and a next to the following entry "Growað" (Fig. 1). The script and general aspect of the different types of marks indicate that they are the work of John Parker. Folio 181 of Titus A. xv is an added leaf of smaller size now mounted on a paper frame of the same dimensions as the other leaves of the manuscript. The added leaf supplies an omission: its recto carries, in John Parker's hand, a

---

[13]Hetherington (1980), 40, commented that Joscelyn "carried alphabetical order through the fourth letter of the word." My own examination of the dictionary indicates that it attempts a fully alphabetical ordering.

[14]See, for example, Titus A. xv, fols. 139r, 140v, 144r, 144v, 145v, 146v, and 147r.

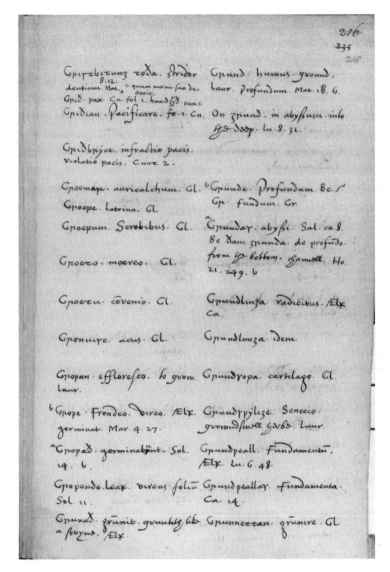

Figure 1. London, British Library, MS Cotton Titus A. xv, fol. 218r. Page in John Parker's hand from the Joscelyn-Parker Old English dictionary. The letters *b* and *a* entered next to "Growe" and "Growað" in the left column, and "Grunde" and "Grundas" in the right column, show that within each pair, the words should be switched to achieve correct alphabetical order.

sequence of entries from "Geomrunga" to "Geonet sped" that Parker had omitted from fol. 182r, where the sequence proceeds directly from "Geomrung" to "Geong."[15] Parker entered two alpha-shaped *signes-de-renvoi*, one before "Geomrunga" on fol. 181r and one after "Geong" on fol. 182r, to indicate where the entries on the added leaf should be inserted.

Throughout the dictionary, lemmata are given in inflected form, just as they occur in the original sources from which they derive. Not uncommonly, the lemma is a phrase rather than a single word, as with "weste hus" and "On weste stowe" on fol. 268r of Titus A. xvi, following the entry for "weste" itself. Frequently there are several entries for the same word, the different entries covering different inflections of the word, or variant spellings. Yet by contrast, a group of inflections or variant spellings sometimes occurs as a single entry: thus on fol. 240v of Titus A. xv, the inflected forms "heortan," "heortena," and "heortum" all occur within the same entry, while on fol. 128r of Titus A. xvi the variant spellings "Stale vel stæl" are combined in a single entry. Entries for adjectives may include the comparative and superlative forms, as with "hræd," "hrædre," and "hrædrest" [*sic*] within a single entry on fol. 266v of Titus A. xv, and "Smæl," "Smælra," and "Smælst" on fol. 116r of Titus A. xvi.[16] In writing the lemmata, both Joscelyn and Parker imitated Anglo-Saxon script, not only using the special Old English characters *æsc*, *eth*, *thorn*, and *wynn* but also imitating Anglo-Saxon forms of the letters **d**, **f**, **g**, **r**, **s**, **t**, and dotted **y**. (The font created ca. 1566, under Matthew Parker's sponsorship, for the printing of Old English texts similarly used Anglo-Saxon forms for these letters.)[17]

---

[15]See pp. 128–29 below for an explanation of why this omission occurred.

[16]See Hetherington (1980), 39–48, for a fuller description of the character of the lemmata.

[17]On this font, and the manuscript sources that inspired its forms, see Lucas (1997a).

The definitions that follow the lemmata are usually in Latin, sometimes in English, and sometimes in both languages. John Parker distinguished between Latin and English definitions by writing the former in italic, the latter in Secretary script; Joscelyn did not make a significant distinction of script for the two different languages. In many cases the definition is followed by an abbreviated reference to the source from which it derives, for example "Gr. Past." and "Reg. Ben." respectively for the Old English versions of Pope Gregory's *Regula pastoralis* and the *Rule* of St. Benedict, and "Pro. Sal." for the Old English gloss to the biblical book of Proverbs.[18] A range of abbreviations may be used for the same source, as with "Gloss. Cant.," "Gl. Cant.," "Gl. C.," and "Gl.," all of which refer to the ninth-century glossary from St. Augustine's Abbey, Canterbury, now CCCC MS 144; the unqualified "Gl.," however, is also used to refer to other glossaries.[19] Some references are unspecific, as with "Hom.," which occurs frequently, without further indication of the precise homily or homiliary referred to. Some references are erroneous, the result of confusion having occurred at an earlier stage in the accumulation of material for the dictionary (on which see below). Nonetheless, the references are of great importance in assisting the identification of the sources that lie behind the dictionary.

---

[18] On the source references, see Rosier (1960); and Hetherington (1980), 30–38 and Appendix 1.

[19] For example, the entry "Geðota. barritus. dissimilis. Gl." (Titus A. xv, fol. 201r) derives from the glossary in BL MS Harley 3376, where the equivalent entry occurs on fol. 3v (see Oliphant [1966], 25, entry B73). Some other entries derived from this glossary have no source cited, as with "Gesceot. cancelli. gradus ligneus" (Titus A. xv, fol. 188v; cf. Harley 3376, fol. 13r, and Oliphant [1966], 49, entry C200). Both *geðota* and *gesceot* occur in Joscelyn's list of words derived from Harley 3376 in Lambeth Palace Library, MS 692, fol. 34v. On the Lambeth word lists, see below.

The division of labor in the copying of the dictionary was uneven, the great majority of the work having been done by John Parker. In the first volume, Joscelyn wrote quires 1–4 (fols. 2–63), containing all the entries for the letter *a* and most of those for *b*, and also quires 7–9 (fols. 94–138), with all the entries for *e* and *f*. John Parker wrote quires 10–20 (fols. 139–304), with the entries from *g* to *l*.[20] In two quires they shared the work. In quire 5 (fols. 64–79), Joscelyn completed the *b*-entries on the first leaf (fol. 64). Parker then took over, beginning the *c*-entries at the top of the next leaf (fol. 65), continuing for ten leaves, and ending his stint at the bottom of column *a* of fol. 74v. Joscelyn returned at the top of column *b* and continued to the end of fol. 76. Parker wrote the last three leaves of the quire (fols. 77–79). In quire 6 (fols. 80–93), Parker completed the *c*-entries on fols. 80–81, and, after leaving a leaf blank, began the *d*-entries on fol. 82, continuing until fol. 90r, where he concluded about three-quarters of the way down column *a*. Joscelyn took up the work immediately below the point where Parker left off, reached the end of the *d*-entries on fol. 93v, and left the last three leaves of the quire blank. In the second volume, Joscelyn wrote only the first few leaves (fols. 1–5), with the first *m*-entries, and fols. 63–67, a block within the *o*-entries;[21] the rest is Parker's work, although there are occasional additions and corrections by Joscelyn within Parker's sections in both volumes. Altogether Parker was responsible for about eighty percent of the copying.[22] His hand is neater, more

---

[20]Within this span, however, there are a few references by Joscelyn on fols. 227r and 264rv.

[21]He ended his first stint about half-way down column *b* of fol. 5v. On fol. 63r, he took over from John Parker about three-quarters of the way down column *a*; he continued to the bottom of fol. 67v, with John Parker taking over at the top of fol. 68r.

[22]Rosier (1960), 28 n. 3, stated that "more than two thirds of the entries are in young Parker's hand." His figure underestimates John Parker's contribution and

easily legible, and of more professional appearance than Joscelyn's, and his sense of layout is better. It would appear that fairly early on the decision was taken to assign the bulk of the copying to him. Yet notwithstanding Parker's major role, it is with justice that the dictionary has traditionally been credited to Joscelyn for, as will become apparent below, most of the work that lay behind the dictionary was Joscelyn's.

The leaves copied by Joscelyn usually have between forty and fifty entries each, while those copied by Parker, using a more spacious script and layout, have approximately thirty entries each. Altogether, the 612 leaves of the two volumes must carry well over twenty thousand entries.[23] Notwithstanding that the same word, in different spellings or inflections, may span several entries, Joscelyn's is by far the largest dictionary of Old English produced in the sixteenth century. The only Old English word list to be published in the century was the glossary of certain terms found in the Anglo-Saxon law codes that William Lambarde included in his edition of the laws, *Archaionomia, sive de priscis Anglorum legibus libri*, published in 1568.[24] Only one sixteenth-century dictionary of Old English begins to approach Joscelyn's in scope: that compiled by Laurence Nowell before his departure to the Continent in 1567, when he left it, along with his other papers, in Lambarde's hands. Nowell's dictionary or *Vocabularium Saxonicum*, now Bodleian MS Selden supra 63, was published by Albert H. Marckwardt in 1952.[25] The entries span

---

is apparently based on an assessment of only the first volume of the dictionary ("Joscelyn was responsible for ff. 2^r–64^v, 74^v–76^v, 90^r–138^v, John Parker for 65^r–74^v, 77^r–90^r, 139^r–304^{v}").

[23]Rosier (1960), 29, estimated that there were approximately 22,500 entries.

[24]The glossary spans sigs. B.ii^v–D.iii^v. It is organized alphabetically by its Latin headwords; each of these is followed by its Old English equivalent and by a paragraph discussing the term.

[25]See Marckwardt (1952).

fols. 2–182 of the manuscript, with between thirty and forty entries per leaf. Altogether the *Vocabularium* must contain something over six thousand entries. Joscelyn made use of Nowell's dictionary—in MSS Titus A. xv and A. xvi borrowings therefrom are signaled with the source reference "Laur."[26]—but his own dictionary goes far beyond Nowell's by drawing upon a greater repertory of sources and by using the sources more extensively.

The dictionary was probably intended for publication. According to Matthew Parker's eighteenth-century biographer, John Strype, it was the archbishop who conceived the project and set Joscelyn to work on it, death alone having prevented Joscelyn from bringing it to completion:

> And that ingenious Men might be the more willing to engage in the Study of this [Saxon] Language, he [i.e., Parker] laboured to forward the Composing and Publishing of a Saxon Dictionary. There were two, that by their reading and converse in various Saxon MSS. had made good Store of Collections of Words. The one was Laurence Noel: and the other the Archbp.'s own Secretary, Joscelyn. Him the Archbp. earnestly excited to digest his Collections into a Lexicon for the publick Benefit. Which he accordingly intended to do, but was by Death prevented.[27]

There appears to be no surviving contemporary evidence attesting to Matthew Parker's involvement in the project, but, given his activity in publishing Old English texts, it is not unlikely that he encouraged it. There is also no direct evidence demonstrating the intention that the dictionary, once compiled, should be published. There is, however, some indirect evidence. MS Bodley 33, John Parker's index to Joscelyn's lost Old English grammar, shows clear signs that John Parker meant it to be

---

[26] Although not every entry labeled "Laur." derives from MS Selden supra 63. See below, pp. 106–07.

[27] Strype (1711), 536.

published. Folio 1r contains, in his hand, an elaborate title for the work, incorporating a lengthy description of it, in the manner common for sixteenth- and seventeenth-century title pages of published works.[28] The title includes several careful corrections. On the next page, fol. 1v, he has written a list of the letters of the alphabet, including Old English characters, in both upper- and lower-case forms; the list mirrors those included at the beginning or end of those of Matthew Parker's publications that use the special Anglo-Saxon font first created for *A Testimonie of Antiqvitie*, the aim of these lists being to familiarize readers with the Anglo-Saxon letter forms.[29] The next leaf, fol. 2a, carries John Parker's preface headed "Lectori benevolo." These are all signs that MS Bodley 33 was written as a fair copy to be passed to a printer for publication. If the index to Joscelyn's grammar was intended for publication, so also must have been the grammar itself. This renders it the more likely that plans were laid to publish the dictionary as well, so that through these editions scholars would be equipped with the essential tools required to understand Old English texts. Similarly, in the seventeenth century plans to publish an Old English dictionary usually went hand-in-hand with plans to publish a grammar,[30] and William Somner's dictionary of

---

[28]"DICTIONARIOLU*M*, sive index alphabeticus vocum Saxonicaru*m* (ni fallor) omnium, quas co*m*plectitur Gra*m*matica clarissimi viri D*o*mini Joa*n*nis Josselini: Item alius index alphabeticus, priorem illum subsequens, de o*m*nibus huius Gra*m*maticæ regulis; In eorum gra*ti*am, qui nostratis linguæ, veteris illius quidem, te*m*porum iniuria pæne extinctæ, iam tandem, & quasi sub desinentem diem studiosi fuerint: Opera Jo. P. collectus & dispositus vterq*ue*."

[29]See *A Testimonie of Antiqvitie*, sig. L.vii^v; *The Gospels of the Fower Euangelistes*, sig. A.i^v; and *Ælfredi regis res gestæ*, page facing p. 1. A similar list occurs on sig. B.ii^r of William Lambarde's *Archaionomia*, also printed by John Day.

[30]On Spelman's plans for an Old English dictionary and grammar, see p. 35 of the essay by Angelika Lutz in the present volume. On Sir Simonds D'Ewes's

1659—the first Old English dictionary to be published—included an edition of Ælfric's *Grammar and Glossary*.

Strype assumed that it was John Joscelyn's death that prevented his dictionary from being published. It is more likely that the significant factor was the death of Matthew Parker in 1575. Thereafter there was no full-scale publication in Old English until William L'Isle's *A Saxon Treatise Concerning the Old and New Testament* of 1623.[31] It would appear that without Parker's active patronage and financial support, Joscelyn and others lacked the means to bring their scholarly work on Old English to publication. While little is known of Joscelyn's personal circumstances between 1575 and his death in 1603, it is evident that John Parker experienced severe financial difficulties late in his life.[32] Nonetheless, much of the work on the dictionary may have been accomplished after Matthew Parker's death, as is suggested by an analysis of the watermarks of the leaves of MSS Titus A. xv and A. xvi.

Several different watermarks occur in the course of the two volumes. They include several varieties of fleur-de-lys watermarks that are difficult to identify precisely. Other marks, however, are more distinctive, and either match, or are closely similar to, examples illustrated by Briquet in his monumental survey of watermarks up to 1600.[33] The mark found on the first leaves of Titus A. xv, from fol. 5 to the first unnumbered leaf after fol. 31, depicts a shield surmounted by a crown, with the letters "IV" on a horizontal band within the shield. This matches Briquet 9546,

---

inclusion of a transcript of Ælfric's grammar in his dictionary, intended for publication, see Hetherington (1980), 102–04.

[31] See Adams (1917), 36–38 and 42–45. As Adams notes, in the intervening period there appeared only a few passages or extracts of Old English within larger publications.

[32] See Strongman (1977), 5.

[33] Briquet (1907).

dated 1581. The mark that occurs on fols. 32–79, which shows a six-petalled flower from the upper part of which issues a stem ending in an arrowhead motif, appears to match Briquet 6535, dated 1582. The mark on fols. 96–137, comprising a shield topped by a crown and bearing the initials "IP," is Briquet 9525, also dated 1582. In Titus A. xvi, the mark that occurs on leaves from fol. 184 to the second unnumbered leaf after fol. 216 consists of a stag's head with a fleur-de-lys between its horns; below the head is a panel containing the name "VIOCHE," "NOCHE," or "MOCHE." The mark is very similar to Briquet 15555, for which Briquet knew an example from the year 1595. Briquet emphasized that paper bearing a particular watermark might be used over a period of fifteen years or so; as a result, dated examples can provide only an approximate indication of the likely date of undated examples.[34] Nonetheless, because those watermarks in MSS Titus A. xv and A. xvi that are identifiable are known to occur in the early 1580s or later, it seems reasonable to conclude that much of the copying of the dictionary may have been carried out not before the 1580s. If this is correct, it provides the only evidence that has so far come to light that Joscelyn and John Parker continued to collaborate after the death of Archbishop Matthew Parker.

Although the dictionary was not published, it was consulted and utilized fruitfully by seventeenth-century lexicographers. The German philologist Friedrich Lindenbrog (1573–1628) made a transcript of part or all of it while visiting England early in the century.[35] A full transcript, now BL MSS Harley 8–9, was made by the antiquary Sir Simonds D'Ewes (1602–50). He and others added to this transcript further entries derived from other sources,

---

[34]Briquet (1907), I, pp. XVIII–XXI.

[35]See Ker (1957), 471 n. 1; and Hetherington (1980), 78–79. Lindenbrog's transcript, formerly Hamburg, Staats- und Universitätsbibliothek, MS germ. 22, was lost during World War II.

both manuscript and printed.[36] D'Ewes's plans to publish this expanded version of Joscelyn's dictionary were cut short by his early death. William Somner (1606–69) made a diligent study of MSS Harley 8 and 9 when preparing his own dictionary, published in 1659, and drew several entries from the Harley manuscripts.[37] Somner was aware that D'Ewes's dictionary had been transcribed from Joscelyn's and he had a high regard for the scope of Joscelyn's work, as he wrote in his preface. Joscelyn's dictionary thus contributed significantly to the first published Old English dictionary.

Whereas others were able to benefit from and draw upon his work for their own lexicography, Joscelyn lacked the support of a predecessor's work, with the exception of the more limited lexicographical collections of Laurence Nowell that were available to him. Joscelyn's primary method in compiling material for his dictionary was, perforce, to scrutinize the Anglo-Saxon manuscripts themselves and to draw most of his entries from them. Intermediate between his initial study of the manuscripts and the copying of the Titus dictionary came a stage of preparing lists of words derived from individual manuscripts, a stage attested by his surviving lists in London, Lambeth Palace Library, MS 692. The evidence (discussed below) of the watermarks in Lambeth 692 indicates that Joscelyn conducted these initial and intermediate phases of his lexicographical work in the 1560s, when he is known to have been studying manuscripts intensively in connection with his work for Parker.[38] Close examination of the manuscripts that he used, and of the Lambeth word lists, throws considerable light on his overall method for his pioneering work in Old English

---

[36]See Hetherington (1975), 77–86; and Hetherington (1980), 102–17.

[37]See Somner (1659), preface "Ad lectorem," paragraph 10, where Somner notes that he has marked with a *D* those entries in his dictionary that derive from D'Ewes's transcript of Joscelyn's dictionary.

[38]See below, pp. 124–26.

lexicography, allows a more precise appraisal of the different stages of the work, and explains some anomalies in the Titus dictionary.

Numerous Anglo-Saxon manuscripts carry evidence of Joscelyn's study of them by the presence on their leaves of notes in his small, somewhat cramped informal italic script. In several of these manuscripts, many Old English words have been underlined in ink.[39] This underlining evidently formed a preliminary phase of Joscelyn's lexicographical work, a phase in which he made his initial selection of words of lexicographical interest to him. That the underlining is indeed by Joscelyn is shown by the match between the ink of the underlining and that of Joscelyn's annotations in the manuscripts in question; and corroborative evidence is provided by the correlation between underlined words on the one hand, and entries in the Lambeth word lists and the Titus dictionary on the other. In some cases, as in CCCC MS 191 (a Latin and Old English copy of the enlarged version of Chrodegang's *Rule* for canons), pages 14, 19, and 20, underlined words also have Joscelyn's Latin glosses entered above them (Fig. 2). Even when a manuscript with underlinings has no glosses or other entries of words in Joscelyn's script, there can be grounds for assigning the underlining to him. For example, CCCC MS 144, a ninth-century glossary in which most of the Old English words have been underlined, has no notes by Joscelyn.[40] Yet the manuscript was exploited heavily by him for both the Lambeth word lists and the Titus dictionary, and it does include two examples of an unusual form of *nota bene* mark used by Joscelyn; these two

---

[39]For example, CUL MS Hh. 1. 10; CCCC MSS 41, 44, 144, 178, 191, 198, 201 Part II, and 265; BL MSS Cotton Nero A. i and Cotton Tiberius B. iv; Bodleian MSS Hatton 20 and Junius 121.

[40]For the underlinings in this manuscript, see the facsimile edition of Bischoff et al. (1988).

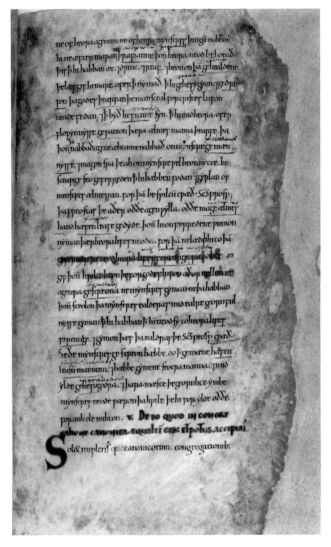

Figure 2. Cambridge, Corpus Christi College, MS 191, p. 19. The page carries the last portion of chapter IV of the Old English translation of the enlarged version of the *Rule* for canons by Chrodegang of Metz. Underlinings and interlinear Latin glosses are by John Joscelyn, who drew on this manuscript for his word lists in Lambeth Palace Library MS 692 and for his dictionary.

marks, which are surely Joscelyn's work, are in ink matching that of the adjacent underlinings.[41]

Another habit of Joscelyn's, less frequent than his underlining, was to enter numbers over selected Old English words.[42] Examples occur in CCCC MS 198 (fols. 1r, 7r–8r, 153r, and 160r–165v), BL MSS Cotton Tiberius B. iv (fols. 3rv and 26r–33r) and Cotton Nero A. i (fol. 110rv), and Bodleian MS Junius 121 (fols. 11r–14r, 59r–60r, and 101v–124r).[43] When using this method, he began a new sequence of numbers for each individual text that he numbered. For example, in Junius 121, words within the text *Be ðeodwitan* on fols. 11r–12v are numbered from 1 through 33, while a new sequence of numbers, running from 1 through 25, marks words in the next text, *Item de episcopis*, on fols. 12v–13v. Texts in which Joscelyn numbered words often also include underlinings by him, but there is only partial correlation between the two systems: that is, some words are both numbered and underlined, but some numbered words are not underlined, and some underlined words are not numbered. The numbering was evidently connected with Joscelyn's lexicographical work, as many (but by no means all) of the numbered words occur in the

---

[41]The mark takes the form of a squiggle at the left, similar in shape to a Greek ϵ, with a longer sinuous line at the right. Joscelyn used it frequently. The two examples in MS 144 occur on fol. 29r, in the intercolumn alongside line a23, and fol. 36v, in the inner margin alongside line b20; see the facsimile in Bischoff et al. (1988). For examples of Joscelyn's use of this mark in another manuscript that he studied closely, BL MS Cotton Nero A. i, see Loyn (1971), fols. 10v, 56v, 90r, 117r, and 143r.

[42]Joscelyn's numbering of words in Bodleian MS Junius 121 is also discussed in Schipper (1989), 85.

[43]Joscelyn also numbered words in his transcript, on fols. 1v–9v of BL MS Cotton Vitellius D. vii, of the copy of Ælfric's Second Pastoral Letter for Wulfstan that occurs on fols. 111r–124r of MS Junius 121: see Sanders Gale (1978), 84–103. The numbers in the transcript match those that Joscelyn entered in MS Junius 121 itself, that is, the same numbers are entered over the same words.

Titus dictionary. The numbers were intended to serve as a referencing system, as is shown by the occurrences in the Titus dictionary of entries derived from the copy of Ælfric's First Pastoral Letter for Wulfstan on fols. 101v–110v of Junius 121. For example, on fol. 102v of the latter, Joscelyn entered "10" above *geswican*; in the corresponding entry on fol. 195r of Titus A. xv, the source is cited as "Ælf. 1 ep. 10" (Fig. 3). Similarly, on fol. 104r of Junius 121, Joscelyn entered "52" above *gehadod*, and on fol. 164v of Titus A. xv, the source for this word is cited as "Ælf. 1 ep. 52." In several other cases, however, the reference numbers are omitted in the dictionary.

Many of the manuscripts in which Joscelyn's underlining occurs contain texts in both Latin and Old English versions, or texts that include a Latin component, or texts with extensive interlinear Latin glossing. For example, CCCC MSS 178 Part II, 191, and 201 Part II are respectively bilingual copies of the *Rules* of St. Benedict and of Chrodegang, and of the *Capitula* of Theodulf of Orléans. Joscelyn could therefore consult the Latin text to find definitions of the Old English words that interested him. In these cases, he used the manuscripts for a purpose opposite to that for which they had been created: the original intention had been that the Old English should assist those who found the Latin difficult. CCCC MS 144 is a glossary of Latin words in which many definitions are given in Old English; Joscelyn used the Latin lemmata to define the Old English words. CUL MS Hh. 1. 10 contains Ælfric's *Grammar*, in which Ælfric provides Old English definitions for the Latin words that he quotes; again, Joscelyn used the Latin to interpret the Old English. CCCC MS 198 and Bodleian MSS Hatton 20 and Junius 121 have all been extensively glossed by the thirteenth-century Tremulous Hand of Worcester. Joscelyn used his glosses to understand the Old English.

Joscelyn's habit of selecting Old English words by underlining or numbering was not, however, consistent. In CCCC MS 178 Part II, the bilingual *Rule* of St. Benedict, he underlined ten words occurring within Old English chapter 1 on pp. 291–92. Thereafter,

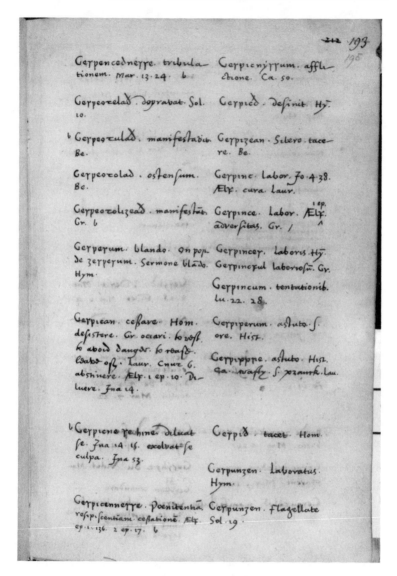

Figure 3. London, British Library, MS Cotton Titus A. xv, fol. 195r. Within the entry for *geswican*, the reference "Ælf. 1 ep. 10" corresponds with Joscelyn's entry of the number "10" above the occurrence of *geswican* in the copy of Ælfric's First Pastoral Letter for Wulfstan in Oxford, Bodleian Library, MS Junius 121, fol. 102v.

he made no further underlinings in the manuscript. Yet Joscelyn drew heavily on this manuscript both for his Lambeth word lists and for the Titus dictionary. Folios 17r–18r of Lambeth 692 contain 588 words drawn from chapters 1–8 and 31 of the copy of the *Rule* in MS 178,[44] and those words in the Titus dictionary whose source is cited as "Reg. Ben." derive from MS 178. In this manuscript, then, Joscelyn swiftly abandoned the practice of underlining but continued to study the manuscript lexicographically. Again, Bodleian MS Hatton 113, the first volume of a two-volume homiliary from Worcester, has just a few underlinings on fols. 131r–135v (and those underlinings may not be by Joscelyn). Yet the manuscript was exploited heavily by Joscelyn: fols. 38r–39v of Lambeth 692 are filled with more than twelve hundred words drawn from Hatton 113.[45]

The Lambeth word lists represent a stage in Joscelyn's work intermediate between his initial examination of the Anglo-Saxon manuscripts themselves and the production of the Titus dictionary. Lambeth 692 is a workbook of forty-three paper leaves within a limp vellum cover that consists of a single leaf (turned sideways) that has been removed from a fourteenth-century manuscript;[46] the quires are now sewn onto three modern vellum supports whose ends thread through the limp cover, and the whole manuscript is slipped into a removable modern buckram cover.

---

[44]These chapters are those numbered I–VII[b] and XXX in Schröer (1885–88).

[45]It is my assumption that all the words on these four pages of Lambeth 692 derive from Hatton 113, although I must admit to not having checked the Hatton manuscript for all the words. Joscelyn followed several of the entries on these pages of Lambeth 692 with a folio number, for reference purposes (e.g., Lambeth 692, fol. 39vc17: "mistlice diuersas. fol. 54"); these folio numbers certainly refer to Hatton 113, for the words in question occur on the appropriate leaves of that manuscript.

[46]The leaf contains a portion of Book II of St. Augustine's *Contra litteras Petiliani Donatistæ* (*Pat. Lat.*, XLIII, cols. 280/22–284/14).

Most of the leaves of Lambeth 692 measure ca. 308 × 207 mm; fols. 28 and 33, a bifolium, are somewhat smaller, at ca. 280 × 170 mm, and fols. 30 and 31, also a bifolium, measure only ca. 240 × 151 mm. On most leaves, Old English words are laid out in four columns and are arranged in alphabetical blocks according to the letter with which they begin (Figs. 4, 5). On the majority of these leaves the blocks are headed by the appropriate letter of the alphabet, and Joscelyn's first step as he wrote these pages was evidently to enter the alphabetical headings from *a* to *y*, leaving a suitable amount of space between each heading (he usually left more space under the *g*-heading to allow for the greater number of Old English words beginning with *g*); this can most easily be seen from fol. 12v, which has a full set of alphabetical headings but no entries, and fol. 18r, which has a full set of headings but only seven entries. Then, under the headings, Joscelyn entered Old English words beginning with the relevant letter. There is no attempt to organize alphabetically the words within each block. Alphabetization is by first letter only, and the order in which words are entered within each alphabetical block reflects in some way (sometimes straightforwardly, sometimes less so) the order in which the words occur in the manuscripts from which Joscelyn drew them. To the right of the word, Joscelyn usually provided a Latin definition, and very occasionally an English definition also; but some words remain without definition, presumably because Joscelyn had been unable to ascertain their meaning. For example, in column *b* of fol. 6v, the words *gierneð*, *geborgen*, *gitseden*, and *getyn* in lines 19, 41, 54, and 60 are left undefined. Sometimes Joscelyn ended by citing the chapter number or folio number from which the word was drawn. The folio numbers can help in identifying the source manuscripts, for potential source manuscripts can be examined to check whether the words in question occur on the cited leaves.

Most pages of Lambeth 692 contain words drawn from a single manuscript. Often several consecutive pages will contain words from the same manuscript, with each page in the sequence comprising a separate list in which all letters of the alphabet are represented. Thus fols. 4r–5r contain three lists compiled from the Old English glosses to the book of Proverbs in BL MS Cotton Vespasian D. vi. Each of the three lists includes words beginning with letters from *a* to *y* or *a* to *w*. Some pages of Lambeth 692 have a heading: for example, "Ex regula canonicoru*m*" on fol. 3r, and "ex prouerbia salomonis" on fol. 4r. When consecutive pages are drawn from the same manuscript, only the first page has a heading. Some first pages, however, have no heading, and in some cases it is possible that headings have been lost as a result of rubbing or of damage to the tops of the leaves.

Certain leaves of Lambeth 692 do not follow the general pattern. Folio 16v carries a single column of words with no attempt at alphabetical organization, not even by first letter (Fig. 6). Folio 30r—which, as noted above, forms part of a bifolium of much smaller dimensions than the other leaves— contains another single-column list with no alphabetization. The significance of these unalphabetized lists will be discussed below. Some pages of Lambeth 692 are blank, while others contain miscellaneous notes by Joscelyn, unrelated to his lexicographical work. Thus fol. 31v contains a set of sums (now turned upside down), and fol. 37r carries a brief text on tides, paraphrasing a sentence of chapter XXIX of Bede's *De temporum ratione*. Folios 29 and 32 are a bifolium written by Laurence Nowell. The two leaves contain some 530 Old English words drawn from two sources: the copy of the Old English version of Bede's *Historia ecclesiastica* in the now damaged BL MS Cotton Otho B. xi; and MS Cotton Vespasian D. xiv, a twelfth-century collection of homilies and other texts. Joscelyn must have obtained this bi-folium from Nowell (or perhaps from William Lambarde, in whose hands Nowell left his papers on his departure to the Continent in 1567[47]) and then combined it with his own lexicographical

---

[47]See Flower (1935), 59 (p. 13 in the reprint); Warnicke (1974); and Black (1977), 345–48.

material. Joscelyn evidently made use of the two leaves for his own dictionary, for certain words that occur on these leaves but that do not occur in Nowell's *Vocabularium Saxonicum* appear in the Titus dictionary with "Laur." cited as their source.[48]

Hitherto there has been no systematic account of the sources of the lists in Lambeth 692, the best information available being scattered through Neil Ker's *Catalogue of Manuscripts Containing Anglo-Saxon*, where Ker's descriptions of several manuscripts mention the presence in Lambeth 692 of lists derived from those manuscripts. However, often Ker does not indicate when Lambeth 692 contains more than one list for a particular manuscript. Further, the folio numbers of Lambeth 692 that he cites do not accord with the present foliation: most of his numbers are one short of the present numbers, which are entered in pencil in the top right-hand corners of the rectos. Again, the entry for Lambeth 692 in the manuscript bibliography at the end of Ker's *Catalogue* provides an only partly accurate guide to those of his descriptions that include references to Lambeth 692, for several of the descriptions there cited fail to contain any mention of the Lambeth word lists.[49] Since most of the manuscripts in question were indeed the

---

[48]Examples include five of the first eight entries in column *b* of fol. 29r of Lambeth 692: "Beladigen. excusare," "forgolden. restitutu*m*," "fode. alime*n*-tu*m*," "Brucan. comedere," and "ferde. bellu*m*." The equivalent entries occur on fols. 39r, 123v, 118r, 60r, and 113v of Titus A. xv. For all except the last of these entries, Joscelyn cites his source as "Laur. o." It is possible that the letter *o*, whose precise signification here is uncertain, was Joscelyn's means of indicating that his source was other than Nowell's *Vocabularium Saxonicum*.

[49]See Ker (1957), 509, entry for Lambeth 692, according to which Lambeth 692 should be mentioned in, among others, his descriptions of his nos. 36 (CCCC MS 144), 61 (CCCC MS 326), 107 (Durham, Dean and Chapter Library, MS B. III. 32), 164 (BL MS Cotton Nero A. i, fols. 70–177), 165 (BL MS Cotton Nero D. iv), 180 (BL MS Cotton Otho B. xi), and 207 (BL MS Cotton Vespasian D. vi). There is no reference to Lambeth 692 in the descriptions of these seven manuscripts.

source of lists in Lambeth 692, Ker evidently omitted the planned references to Lambeth 692 in his final version of his descriptions.

The table appended to this essay attempts a systematic identification of the sources of the lists in Lambeth 692. The table is based on detailed comparison of the entries in the lists with the source manuscripts themselves, and/or with the *Microfiche Concordance to Old English* and with printed editions that cite manuscript variants. As the table reveals, most pages in Lambeth 692 derive from a single source manuscript, but several pages combine entries drawn from different sources, sometimes in contradiction of the heading at the top of the page; these examples are discussed either in the text below or in the notes to the table. The table includes an indication of the date and provenance of the manuscripts used. It becomes apparent that Joscelyn's attention focused on manuscripts from Canterbury, Worcester, and Exeter (some of which he may have studied *in situ*, before they entered Parker's collection).[50] His lists were drawn from a total of nineteen or twenty manuscripts.

Close study of the lists in Lambeth 692 yields significant information both about the sixteenth-century state of some of the manuscripts used and about Joscelyn's methods of work. It is notable that fol. 3r (Fig. 4), with Joscelyn's heading "Ex regula canonicorum," includes words not only from CCCC MS 191, the enlarged version of the *Rule* for canons by Chrodegang of Metz, but also from CCCC MS 201 Part II, the *Capitula* of Theodulf of Orléans, in which Theodulf instructs the parish priests of his diocese in their pastoral duties. Each alphabetical block on fol. 3r

---

[50]See Ker (1957), lii, for the suggestion that Joscelyn carried out some of his work in the cathedral libraries of Exeter and Worcester. That Joscelyn knew the Worcester Cathedral Library at first hand is indicated, as has long been recognized, by his comment of 1565/6 re the Worcester copy (MS D) of the Anglo-Saxon Chronicle (now BL MS Cotton Tiberius B. iv), "Chronica Saxonica Wigorniensis ecclesiæ . . . est adhuc in bibliotheca ecclesiæ" (BL MS Cotton Nero C. iii, fol. 208r, quoted and discussed in, e.g., Atkins [1940], 25–26).

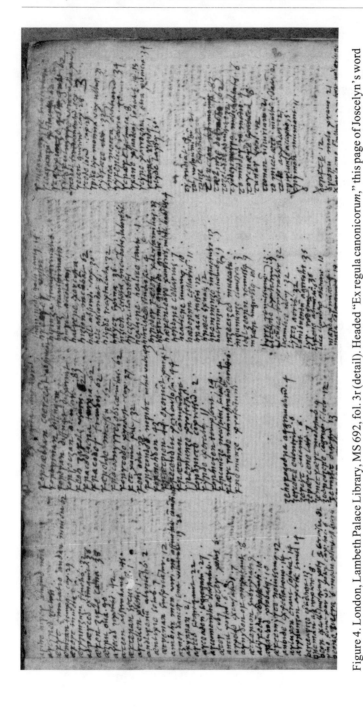

Figure 4. London, Lambeth Palace Library, MS 692, fol. 3r (detail). Headed "Ex regula canonicorum," this page of Joscelyn's word lists includes words from CCCC MS 191 (the *Rule* of Chrodegang) and CCCC MS 201 Part II (the *Capitula* of Theodulf of Orléans), which was formerly bound with MS 191.

includes words from both manuscripts. For example, within the block of words beginning with *l*, the first entry, "lysse remissione*m*," is from chapter 1 of the *Rule* of Chrodegang in MS 191; the next six entries, from "lictune sepulchru*m*" to "lys. redime," are from chapters 9, 32, 35, and 36 of the *Capitula Theodulfi* in MS 201 Part II; and the last two entries, "lifene alime*ntum*" and "luce claudere obserare," come from chapters 6 and 10 of the *Rule* of Chrodegang. Joscelyn gives no indication that his words derive from two separate manuscripts. MSS 191 and 201 Part II were written by the same Exeter scribe during the episcopate of Leofric (1050–72).[51] They were, moreover, joined within a single volume during the Middle Ages, as is shown by the entry encompassing both of them in the Exeter catalogue of 1327.[52] It was Matthew Parker who bound up the *Capitula* of Theodulf with CCCC MS 201 Part I, a manuscript of quite different content and provenance. Although (as will be discussed below) some of Joscelyn's lists in Lambeth 692 combine words from manuscripts that quite certainly were separate when he examined them, in the case of MSS 191 and 201 Part II it seems most reasonable to conclude that his listing on a single page of Lambeth 692 of entries that derive from both sources means that Parker had not yet separated the texts when Joscelyn examined them in connection with his lexicographical work. The list in Lambeth 692 would then provide the latest evidence for the continued existence of the two texts within a single volume.

For three manuscripts, Joscelyn's lists record portions that have subsequently been lost. Folios 4r–5r of Lambeth 692 contain over 1,190 words drawn from the glossed copy of the book of Proverbs on fols. 2–37 of BL MS Cotton Vespasian D. vi. The latter is a composite manuscript: fols. 2–77 come from St.

---

[51] That the two manuscripts are the work of the same scribe was first observed by Drage (1978), 151.

[52] See Ker (1957), 75.

Augustine's Abbey, Canterbury, while fols. 78–125, which contain an eleventh-century English copy of Stephen of Ripon's *Vita sancti Wilfridi*, are of uncertain provenance. The two parts were presumably combined by Cotton. The margins of both parts of the manuscript have been quite severely trimmed, probably at the time that the parts were bound together. Joscelyn's lists in Lambeth 692 preserve two glosses that have now been lost from above the first line of fols. 17v and 24v. The glosses occur on fols. 4vb27 and 4vd119 of Lambeth 692: "forni*m*ð," the gloss for *demolietur* (cf. Proverbs 15:25), and "weoli," the gloss for *diues* (cf. Proverbs 22:2).[53]

In other cases, the Lambeth word lists provide evidence for complete leaves that are now lost, as was first observed by Neil Ker.[54] Folios 9v–11v of Lambeth 692 are densely packed with words drawn from CUL MS Hh. 1. 10, a copy of Ælfric's *Grammar and Glossary* made at Exeter during the episcopate of Leofric. At the bottom of fol. 93v, the present last leaf of MS Hh. 1. 10, the text ends abruptly just a few lines into the *Glossary*.[55] The present last quire of the manuscript, fols. 88–93, has lost its last two leaves. Ronald Buckalew has calculated that those two leaves and one further quire would have sufficed to complete the text of the *Glossary*.[56] The two leaves that formerly followed fol. 93 still belonged to the manuscript when Joscelyn examined it for his word lists: on fols. 10rb55, 10rb101–12, 11ra53–57, and 11ra115–17 of Lambeth 692, Joscelyn recorded twenty-one words for which he

---

[53] In Joscelyn's dictionary, the equivalent entries occur on fol. 126v of MS Titus A. xv and fol. 262v of MS Titus A. xvi. It is worthwhile to point out that the spelling *weoli* is not listed in the *Microfiche Concordance to Old English* (which records five instances of the spelling *weolig*).

[54] Ker (1957), no. 17 (p. 22); and Ker (1956), 16.

[55] The last words on fol. 93v are "mentu*m*. cynn barba. beard." See Zupitza (1880), p. 298, line 7.

[56] I thank Prof. Buckalew for this information.

cited the source folio numbers as "94" and "95," and a comparison with Zupitza's edition confirms that those words should indeed have appeared on leaves immediately following fol. 93.[57] Joscelyn's failure to record any words from leaves after fol. "95" implies that the manuscript had already lost its last quire when he studied it. As for fols. 94 and 95, they were perhaps lost in connection with the theft of MS Hh. 1. 10 in the early seventeenth century. The manuscript was one of twenty-five given to Cambridge University Library by Matthew Parker in 1574. According to the list of Parker's gifts, the manuscript then contained 290 pages, i.e., 145 leaves, and included a "hist. Angliæ Saxon." as well as Ælfric's *Grammar and Glossary*.[58] The historical text need not have formed part of the original manuscript but could have been added by Parker himself; it has indeed been suggested that the text in question could have been BL MS Cotton Domitian A. viii, fols.

---

[57]The words listed by Joscelyn are "fot wilm. planta"; "gealla fel"; "gesinhiwan coniuges. co*n*iugales"; "gerefa comes"; "gisel obses"; "gebann edictu*m*"; "gegaderung co*n*gregatio"; "gemetung co*n*uentu*s* vel co*n*ue*n*tio"; "geongling iuuenis"; "gemot mann co*n*cionator"; "gligman poeta"; "geflitful contentios*us*"; "galere incantator"; "æddre vena"; "aðum gener"; "æðeling clito"; "angel ham*us*"; "ancer mann proreta"; "bymere tubicen"; "byme tuba"; and "bærnett arsura, vstulatio." See Zupitza (1880), p. 299, line 4; p. 298, line 8; p. 299, lines 16–17; p. 300, lines 15, 16, 19, 19–20, 20; p. 301, lines 10, 12–13; p. 302, lines 8–9; p. 303, lines 7, 9; p. 298, line 18; p. 300, lines 10–11, 15–16; p. 301, line 19; p. 302, lines 13, 5 (twice), 16–17. Joscelyn's entry "gligman poeta" suggests that the scribe of MS Hh. 1. 10 may have omitted some words at this point, for in Ælfric's text *gligmann* should define *mimus uel scurra*, not *poeta*. See Zupitza, p. 302, lines 8–9: "poeta sceop oððe leoðwyrhta. mimus uel scurra gligmann." On fol. 11ra118–19, Joscelyn lists two further words as occurring on fol. "95" of MS Hh. 1. 10: "bræwas palpebrę" and "ban os." However, these words in fact appear on fol. 93v (see Zupitza [1880], p. 298, lines 3–4 and 5).

[58]The list of Parker's gifts was appended to the "Catalogus Cancellariorum" that appears toward the end of those copies of Parker's *De antiquitate Britannicæ ecclesiæ* that were issued in 1574 (the book had first appeared in 1572; it was never fully published, but rather was privately printed and circulated).

30–70, the F-text of the Anglo-Saxon Chronicle,[59] although that is a bilingual rather than a purely Old English text. A note entered by Abraham Wheelock (University Librarian 1629–53) on fol. 1r of MS Hh. 1. 10 records that Wheelock restored the manuscript to the University Library after it had been stolen. By then it had lost its historical text, and it is possible that the two leaves formerly following fol. 93 were lost at the same time.[60]

Folios 6r–8r of Lambeth 692 contain five lists drawn from the copy of the Old English *Pastoral Care* in Bodleian MS Hatton 20, and again provide evidence for a leaf that is now missing from the manuscript. Within the five lists, Joscelyn frequently recorded the number of the chapter of the *Pastoral Care* from which he took his entries. That the entries derive from Hatton 20 rather than from another manuscript of the *Pastoral Care* is demonstrated both by Joscelyn's frequent underlinings in Hatton 20 and by the agreement in spelling between Joscelyn's entries and the text of Hatton 20; the spellings differ from those of CCCC MS 12, TCC MS R. 5. 22, CUL MS Ii. 2. 4, and BL MS Cotton Otho B. ii, which were also known to Joscelyn and the Parker circle.[61]

---

[59]The suggestion was made by Ker (1957), 22.

[60]Ronald Buckalew (personal communication) has noted that the requisite total of 145 leaves that the manuscript contained when given to the University Library could be reached if the manuscript then included the leaf now missing at the beginning of the first quire, the two leaves following fol. 93, the original last quire of Ælfric's text, and the forty-one leaves of MS F (1 + 93 + 2 + 8 + 41 = 145). He therefore inclines to believe that at the time of the gift, the original last quire of the *Glossary* was still present. That, however, would leave unexplained why Joscelyn's word lists cite no word from a leaf later than fol. "95." It is possible that Parker made good the loss of the original end of Ælfric's text by adding a quire containing a transcript of the missing text, just as he supplied a transcript to provide the missing beginning of another copy of the *Grammar and Glossary*, CCCC MS 449 (on which see Ker [1957], no. 71).

[61]On the acquaintance of Parker's circle with the manuscripts of the Old English *Pastoral Care*, see Page (1992).

Hatton 20 now lacks the leaf that originally followed fol. 41 and that would have carried a portion of chapter 33. In place of the lost leaf there now stands a transcript in the hand of Francis Junius (1591–1677). The original leaf must still have been present when Joscelyn examined the manuscript, for on fol. 8r of Lambeth 692, among the words and phrases derived from chapter 33 are thirty-three that would have appeared on the leaf.[62]

Folios 24r–25v of Lambeth 692 carry four lists derived from CCCC MS 198, an eleventh-century homiliary from Worcester, and Ker believed that here also Joscelyn recorded information from a lost leaf.[63] The present last leaf of MS 198, fol. 394, is the ninth leaf of its quire; it can be deduced that originally there would have been one more leaf in the quire, for the first leaf, fol. 386, now lacks a conjoint leaf at the end of the quire. The last five lines of fol. 394v contain the erased beginning of a homily, no doubt the homily *De virginitate* that is listed last in the sixteenth-century table of contents at the beginning of the manuscript. The homily would originally have continued on leaves following the present fol. 394: that is, on the conjectured original last leaf, now lost, of the present last quire, and, presumably, one more quire. It seems likely that the manuscript reached Matthew Parker in an incomplete state, for in other manuscripts Parker erased surviving portions of texts that lacked their beginning or ending.[64] Perhaps MS 198 had lost its original last quire when Parker acquired it, but still retained the last leaf of what is now the last quire; Parker might have decided to jettison that leaf for the same reason that he

---

[62]The words are listed in Ker (1956), 16 n. 19 (where Ker cites the page number of Lambeth 692 as "fo. 6").

[63]Ker (1957), no. 48 (p. 81).

[64]Examples include CCCC MSS 9 (fol. 9r), 44 (fol. 1r), 188 (p. 460), and 201 (p. 1). See also the discussion in Page (1993), 46–48.

erased the last lines of fol. 394v.[65] In Ker's view, Lambeth 692
provided evidence that when Joscelyn examined MS 198, it retained at least two more leaves than it now has. On fol. 24v of
Lambeth 692, three lines from the bottom of column *c*, is the entry
"sciccelse" with its definitions "polimita, chlamyde." A little to the
right, Joscelyn has written the number "396," which Ker interpreted as Joscelyn's citation of the number of the leaf on which the
word *sciccelse* occurred. But the somewhat tilted angle at which
"396" is written shows that Joscelyn did not enter this number on
the page at the same time as he wrote the *sciccelse* entry. Moreover, the word *sciccelse* occurs twice on fol. 164v of MS 198,
where Joscelyn has underlined it both times and where the
Tremulous Hand has both times supplied the gloss *polimita* that
Joscelyn used in Lambeth 692;[66] and the words that immediately
precede and succeed the *sciccelse* entry in Lambeth 692 are
themselves to be found on the neighboring leaves of MS 198,
which confirms that it is indeed the occurrences of *sciccelse* on fol.
164v that Joscelyn is here recording.[67] Therefore, "396" is not a
folio number. Rather, it is Joscelyn's rough total for the number of
entries he has written on fol. 24v of Lambeth 692. As such, it
parallels similar totals that he entered on a few other pages

---

[65]In the upper left corner of fol. 394v there is the offset of a sixteenth-century
folio number, probably "395," that must have been entered on a leaf that
followed fol. 394; however, it is not now possible to tell whether that leaf was
an original leaf or an added endleaf that was subsequently discarded. On this see
further Budny (1997), no. 36 (p. 563); and Graham (1997a), 43–44.

[66]Joscelyn took his other gloss, "chlamyde," from Matthew 27:28/31. (The
homily in which the word *sciccelse* occurs is on the Passion of Christ. The relevant portion of the homily describes how the soldiers stripped Jesus and clad
him in a scarlet robe to mock him.)

[67]The eight preceding entries in Lambeth 692, from "stængum" to "swutelað,"
are drawn from MS 198, fol. 162r, lines 3, 11, 13, 14, fol. 162v, line 22, and fol.
163r, lines 2, 3, 17; the succeeding entry, "swica," comes from fol. 166r, line 26.

(fols. 13rv and 24r). While it is possible that MS 198 retained into the sixteenth century at least one more of its original leaves than now survives, Lambeth 692 does not provide evidence for this.

The Lambeth word lists yield important insights into Joscelyn's methods in his lexicographical work and reveal that there must have been other stages in his work that are now hidden from view. Most of the lists derive from single manuscripts. There is clear evidence, however, that, with possible exceptions covered below, these were not the initial lists that Joscelyn compiled as he actually studied the manuscripts but rather that they represent a stage in which he had already progressed from an earlier stage of preliminary lists and had begun to organize his material in the form of partly alphabetized fair copies. As noted above, in most of the Lambeth lists words are grouped by first letter. If Joscelyn had been compiling these lists directly from their source manuscripts, he would have had to enter his chosen words now under one alphabetical heading, now under another, depending on the order in which the words occurred in the source manuscript and on the letter with which they began. The ductus of Joscelyn's script in most of the Lambeth lists is much too regular for this to have been his method of copying. He clearly copied the words by blocks, writing first a block beginning with *a*, then a block beginning with *b*, and so on. Having entered on a page one block beginning with each letter, he would then start again and enter further blocks, continuing until he filled up the page, and sometimes squeezing in some words in available space above his original alphabetical headings. A glance at certain pages of Lambeth 692 quickly reveals this method. On fol. 13r, for instance, Joscelyn first used a light brown ink to enter blocks of words under each letter, then switched to a darker ink and added further blocks; where darker-colored words within a particular alphabetical grouping occur above lighter-colored words, those darker-colored words were entered on the page later, in available space. Many other pages of the manuscript reveal the same method of copying.

That most of the Lambeth lists are based on now lost preliminary lists is demonstrated by two different types of error in Lambeth 692. Within the lists derived from CCCC MS 144 (the Corpus Glossary) on fols. 13r–14v, a group of six entries beginning with *w*, from "worhona fasianus" to "wulencu fastu," appears twice, on fols. 13vd101–06 and 14vd107–12.[68] In both cases the six entries appear in the same order and with the same Latin definitions. Similarly, a group of three entries beginning with *s*—"swæðila fasciaru*m*," "siðe falcis," and "sueðrað facessit"[69]—appears both on fol. 14rd6–8 and on fol. 14vd1–3, and one *r*-entry, "riftras falcis," occurs both on fol. 14rc86 and on fol. 14vc81.[70] Within MS 144, these ten Old English words beginning with *r*, *s*, and *w* all define Latin words that occur within the *fa* section of the glossary on fol. 28rb4–28vb8.[71] Ten other Old English words that occur within the same span of MS 144, and that begin with letters other than *r*, *s*, and *w*, appear only once in Lambeth 692.[72] If Joscelyn had been compiling fols. 13r–14v of Lambeth 692 directly from MS 144 and had accidentally covered this particular span of fol. 28 twice, he would have repeated all the Old English words within this span, not just those beginning with *r*, *s*, and *w*. His repetition of these specific groups of words

---

[68] In the edition of the Corpus Glossary by Lindsay (1921), the six entries are nos. F22, F23, F32/48, F37, F49, and F108.

[69] Lindsay (1921), entries F26, F32, and F100.

[70] Lindsay (1921), entry F32 (where *riftras* is grouped with *wudubil* and *siðe*, all three words defining *falcis*).

[71] See the facsimile in Bishcoff et al. (1988).

[72] In Lindsay's edition, these words occur at entries F25, F55, F61, F67, F83, F91, F99, F102, F104, and F107. In Lambeth 692 they are entered on fols. 14rc22 ("leasunge"), 14rc44 ("malscrung"), 14rd83 ("utgladius," a misunderstanding by Joscelyn of Latin *ut gladius*), 13va22 ("ægtero"), 13va123 ("faragem"), 13va122 ("foeða"), 13ra120 ("faag"), 13va23 ("acrummen"), 13va45 ("bean"), and 14ra67 ("cynedomas").

demonstrates that he must have been copying from his own preliminary lists in which these words had already been grouped together; he then mistakenly copied the grouping twice.

The second apparent anomaly occurs on fol. 21r of Lambeth 692, which Joscelyn headed "In ecclesiasticam historiam Bedæ interpretationes Saxonicorum verborum" (Fig. 5). Ostensibly, then, the page is given over to words derived from the Old English translation of Bede's *Ecclesiastical History*. The page includes 227 entries. In column *d*, next to the entry "to læne nimium laceratum," Joscelyn has added the note "this word is also in the epistle of Alfred before Gregorys pastorall." The note is misleading. The point is not that the phrase *to læne* occurs in the *Pastoral Care Preface* as well as in the Old English Bede, but that the entry in Lambeth 692 derives from the *Pastoral Care Preface* and not from the Old English Bede. The same is true of several other entries, for, despite Joscelyn's title, the page carries words derived from both these Old English texts, not just from the Old English Bede. Moreover, for both texts, the entries derive from two different manuscripts. Joscelyn drew upon the two Worcester copies of the *Pastoral Care*, Bodleian MS Hatton 20 and CCCC MS 12, as is shown by the spellings of the entries and by their Latin definitions. For example, in column b25 Joscelyn has written the double entry "giu quondam. gio. idem." *giu* is the form that occurs on fol. 1v, line 15 of Hatton 20, while *gio* is the version of CCCC 12, fol. 2r, line 20. Similarly, column c24–25 has the consecutive entries "mengeo turba" and "menigu idem." The first spelling is that of Hatton 20 (fol. 1v, line 6), the second that of CCCC 12 (fol. 2r, line 3). Joscelyn also exploited the Tremulous Hand's glosses in both manuscripts. In column b18 he has provided two Latin definitions for *geæmetige*: "vacas" and "vacetis." The first repeats the Tremulous Hand's gloss on fol. 1v, line 15 of CCCC 12, while the second is taken from fol. 1r, line 22 of Hatton 20. For those words on the page that derive from the Old English Bede, Joscelyn used the two copies of the work that came into Matthew Parker's hands, CCCC MS 41 and CUL MS Kk. 3. 18. It is again the occurrence of variant spellings that reveals

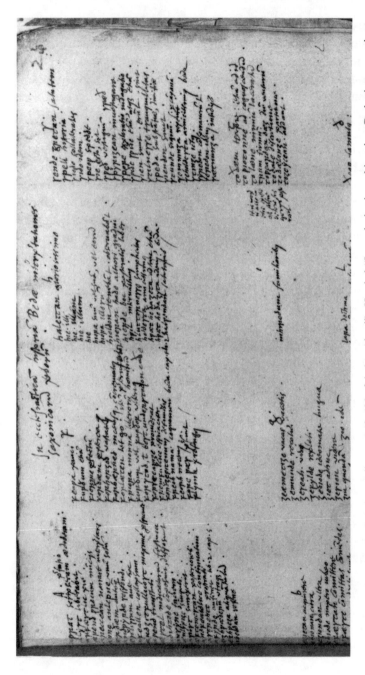

Figure 5. London, Lambeth Palace Library, MS 692, fol. 21r (detail). Headed "In ecclesiasticam historiam Bedæ interpretationes Saxonicorum verborum," the page includes words drawn from the *Pastoral Care Preface* as well as from the Old English Bede.

Joscelyn's use of two different manuscripts. The last two entries on column *a* of fol. 21r are "ealdor botl. villa regalis" and "ealdor bold idem." *ealdor botl* and *ealdor bold* are respectively the versions of MS Kk. 3. 18, p. 39, line 15 and MS 41, p. 97, line 22.[73] In column b51–52, the entries "geswiperu*m* astuto s*cilicet* ore" and "geswippre ide*m*" derive from MS 41, p. 97, line 24, and MS Kk. 3. 18, p. 39, line 16.[74] Joscelyn's combination on this page of words from two different texts, and from two different manuscripts of each of these texts (a combination that belies his title, which refers to just one text) is explicable only if the list on fol. 21r represents a stage of work separated by other stages from Joscelyn's initial examination of the manuscripts: by the time Joscelyn compiled this list, he was unaware that several of the words that he entered on the page derived from the *Pastoral Care Preface* rather than the Old English Bede.[75]

Two of Joscelyn's lists in Lambeth 692 provide insight into those earlier stages of Joscelyn's lexicographical work that are now largely hidden from view. Folios 30–31 are, as noted above, a bifolium of smaller dimensions than the other leaves of the manuscript. While the inner pages of the bifolium (fols. 30v–31r) are blank and the last page (fol. 31v) has Joscelyn's jottings of sums, the first page carries a list (in single-column format) of Old English words drawn from four charters in BL MS Additional

---

[73]See Miller (1890–98), I:1, 122 line 15, and the manuscript variants listed at II:1, 113.

[74]See Miller (1890–98), I:1, 122 line 16, and the manuscript variants listed at II:1, 113.

[75]It was in fact the words from the *Pastoral Care Preface* that Joscelyn entered on the page first: those words occur first in each alphabetical block, and they are in a browner ink than that used for the words derived from the Old English Bede. The ink of Joscelyn's title, which as noted refers to Bede, is of the same color as that of the words derived from the *Pastoral Care Preface*.

15350, a Winchester cartulary of the twelfth century.[76] Joscelyn has made no attempt to alphabetize the words, not even by first letter. Rather, the order in which he has entered them on the page matches, almost without exception, the order in which they occur in the cartulary, where they are to be found on fols. 8r, 10r, 24v, and 27v–28r. This list may therefore provide an example of the first written stage of Joscelyn's lexicographical work, when he moved from his initial study of a manuscript to write down those words of lexicographical interest to him.

Of somewhat similar character is the list on fol. 16v, which is again in single-column format and shows no alphabetization (Fig. 6). At the top of the page, using different ink and a broader nib than for the list itself, Joscelyn has added the title "verba hæc desumpta ex Aldelmo de virginitate." Most of the words on the page occur as glosses to the prose version of Aldhelm's *De virginitate* in CCCC MS 326, a late tenth-century copy of the work from Christ Church, Canterbury:[77] it is this manuscript that was Joscelyn's source for these words. The order in which the words occur in the list again reflects the order in which they appear in the manuscript, although in this case the manuscript order has been reversed; that is, the words that appear first in the list occur last in the manuscript, and vice versa. While the unalphabetized state of the list indicates that it represents an early stage in Joscelyn's work, it may not be a first stage, for other, non-Aldhelmian material has been integrated into the list. Alongside the

---

[76]In the order in which they are represented in Lambeth 692, the four charters are Sawyer (1968), nos. 1376, 817, 806, and 1819. MS Add. 15350 includes both Latin and Old English versions of the charters that it contains. Joscelyn used the Latin versions for his Latin definitions on fol. 30r of Lambeth 692. There are a few notes by Joscelyn in MS Add. 15350: in the outer margin of fols. 27v, 43v, and 50r. In the outer margin of fol. 59r he has entered his characteristic *nota bene* mark, described in n. 41 above.

[77]For the Old English glosses in the manuscript, see Napier (1900), 151–52.

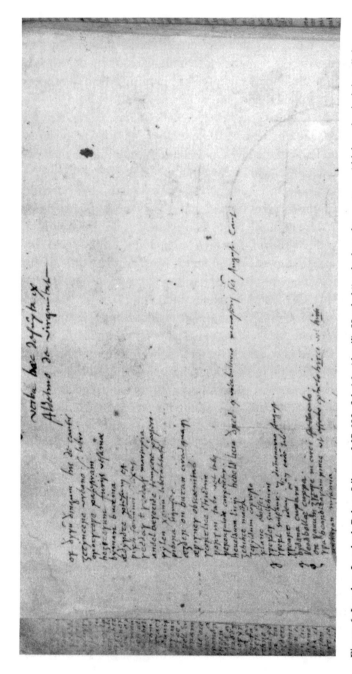

Figure 6. London, Lambeth Palace Library, MS 692, fol. 16v (detail). Headed "verba hæc desumpta ex Aldelmo de virginitate," the page includes, as well as glosses drawn from the copy of Aldhelm in CCCC MS 326, five entries drawn from the Corpus Glossary (CCCC MS 144).

seventeenth entry in the list, "heueldum liciis," Joscelyn has added a cognate entry drawn from another source: "hebeld licia ðred ex vocabulario monasterii s*ancti* Augus*tini* Cant*uariensis*." The reference is to the Corpus Glossary, CCCC MS 144 (a St. Augustine's manuscript), where *licia*, defined by the two Old English words listed by Joscelyn, occurs on fol. 38vb17.[78] Lower down on fol. 16v of Lambeth 692, Joscelyn has incorporated four further entries from CCCC MS 144 that provide either alternative forms or synonyms for words that appear among the Aldhelm glosses. In these four cases, Joscelyn did not add the words later but entered them as he wrote the list: the words occur in the same column as the Aldhelm glosses, not added at the side or squeezed between the lines (Fig. 6). That he combined in this list material drawn from two different sources, without apparent interruption to the rhythm of his script,[79] suggests that this list is already at one remove from an original, now lost list of words drawn from MS 326 (a list on which he could have entered the words drawn from MS 144 as additions). For three of the four words integrated into the column, Joscelyn indicated that their source was MS 144 by adding the source references "in dictionario August.," "in eode*m* lib*ro*," and "in vocabulario Cant."[80] At a later stage in his work these source citations were overlooked for two of the entries. The twenty-first

---

[78]See the facsimile in Bishcoff et al. (1988); and see also Lindsay (1921), 107 (L250).

[79]A group of three words in the middle of the list (two from MS 326, one from MS 144) are in lighter ink than the rest, which demonstrates that the list was not written in one uninterrupted session. My point is that Joscelyn's copying of those entries from MS 144 that are integrated into the column does not seem to have caused the sort of change in rhythm that would have resulted had he had to go hunting for those words in another list.

[80]For the entry "beodbollæ cuppa" (twenty-fifth in the list), Joscelyn did not indicate that the source was MS 144. The word occurs on fol. 20vb20 of MS 144: see Bischoff et al. (1988); and Lindsay (1921), 51 (C971).

entry in the Lambeth list is "swefles sulphuris," which derives from MS 326. Joscelyn followed this with the related entries "swefl sulphur" and "sweart idem," and noted that both of these derived from MS 144.[81] Yet on fols. 144r and 144v of MS Titus A. xvi, both words appear with "Ald. de virg." erroneously cited as one of their sources.[82]

Lambeth 692 preserves the record of important stages in Joscelyn's lexicographical work, steps along the path to the production of a fully alphabetized dictionary. It is somewhat curious that James L. Rosier, who published the first study devoted exclusively to Joscelyn's lexicography, believed that the Lambeth word lists postdated the Titus dictionary.[83] That the opposite is true is demonstrated not only by the consideration that a set of partly alphabetized lists compiled from individual manuscripts must surely represent an earlier phase of work than a dictionary that integrates and alphabetizes entries drawn from many different sources, but also by the evidence of the watermarks

---

[81]They occur on fol. 59rb31 of MS 144: see Bischoff et al. (1988); and Lindsay (1921), 171 (S683). Joscelyn has in fact misunderstood the compound adjective *sueflsueart*, which here defines Latin *sulforia*, i.e., *sulphurea*.

[82]Hetherington (1980), 245 n. 22, in reference to the "Sweart" entry of MS Titus A. xvi, noted that the word did not occur among published Aldhelm glosses and speculated, correctly, that "perhaps Joscelyn . . . included non-Aldhelm entries in a list from Aldhelm." Hetherington also suggested that the Titus dictionary wrongly ascribed to Aldhelm its entry "On wauum gestowe, in circi spectaculo." However, this entry is simply a mistranscription of the Aldhelm gloss "on wauung stowe" that occurs on p. 80 of CCCC MS 326 (see Napier [1900], 152, no. 59).

[83]See the two comments in Rosier (1960), 32 and 33. While the first comment could be interpreted otherwise, the second establishes clearly that Rosier believed Lambeth 692 to be the later work. Discussing the importance of the Old English *Pastoral Care* as a source for the Titus dictionary, Rosier observed that "since Joscelyn later used the Hatton manuscript for one of his glossaries in Lambeth 692, it is most likely that he also used that manuscript for the dictionary."

in the paper used by Joscelyn. As noted above, the identifiable watermarks in the Titus dictionary are mostly of types for which dated examples are known from the early 1580s. The watermarks in Lambeth 692 point to an earlier date. The two principal watermarks in the manuscript respectively show a left hand with a five-petalled flower above the middle finger, and a pot with one handle. The hand-and-flower mark occurs in several different versions, distinguished by the different combinations of initials at the bottom of the hand. The versions with the initials "GV" and "NI," found on fols. 17, 19, 20, and 39, are Briquet's nos. 11354 and 11360,[84] for which he cites examples dated to 1561, 1566, and 1568; the other versions are not listed by Briquet.[85] The watermark showing the pot with one handle, which occurs on eight leaves of Lambeth 692,[86] appears to match Briquet's no. 12557, for which he cites just one example, dated to 1564–65. Four other watermarks each occur once in Lambeth 692. That on fol. 42 is a variant of the pot with one handle; those on fols. 31 and 33 are not identifiable in Briquet; that on fol. 2, which shows the initials "PM" separated by a quatrefoil motif, is Briquet's no. 9634, for which his example is dated 1567, and for which he knew variant forms from the years 1568–1570.[87] The picture presented by the identifiable marks is thus consistent. Even allowing for the caution that must be exercised when using watermarks as evidence for

---

[84]The examples of no. 11360 in Lambeth 692 differ slightly from Briquet's illustration in that whereas the latter shows a hand of which the bottom is sharply curved in a crescent-like shape, in Lambeth 692 the curve at the bottom of the hand is much less pronounced.

[85]On fol. 16, the initials appear to be "BO"; on the unnumbered leaf following fol. 41, they are "IC." On fol. 3, the mark occurs with no accompanying initials.

[86]Folios 8, 11, 14, 21, 22, 23, 26, and 34.

[87]He also cites Likhachev's no. 3244, dated 1572 (for which see Simmons and Van Ginneken-van de Kasteele [1994], I, 288, and II, pl. 322), and a further variant from the years 1582–89.

dating, the occurrence in the manuscript of four marks known to occur on papers in use in the 1560s strongly implies that Joscelyn compiled the lists in Lambeth 692 during that decade (and perhaps the early 1570s also).

Clearly, the Lambeth word lists show Joscelyn at a relatively early stage of his work, still feeling his way toward the fully alphabetized dictionary. Most of the lists derive from single manuscripts. One or two are unalphabetized and reflect the order in which the listed words occur in their manuscripts; in most, Joscelyn has begun the task of alphabetization by grouping the words by first letter; in some he has begun to integrate by combining words from more than one source manuscript. Altogether the Lambeth word lists include approximately fifteen thousand entries by Joscelyn.[88] This represents a significant proportion— between two-thirds and three-quarters—of the total number of entries in the Titus dictionary. There are some important sources of the dictionary for which there are no lists in Lambeth 692, including the Old English translation of the Gospels,[89] the Old English law codes, the Anglo-Saxon Chronicle, and the Old English hymn glosses. Further, detailed analysis of Joscelyn's word lists for CCCC MS 144 in Lambeth 692, and of the entries derived from MS 144 in the Titus dictionary, shows that the relationship between the word lists and the dictionary is not straightforward. Joscelyn's lists on fols. 13r–14v of the Lambeth

---

[88]My attempt to count the number of entries in the manuscript produced a total of 14,953.

[89]Folio 12r of Lambeth 692 contains just twenty-two entries, all drawn from the Old English gloss to the Lindisfarne Gospels. These were not the source of the numerous entries derived from the Old English Gospels in the Titus dictionary. Those entries from fol. 21r that occur in the Titus dictionary are not there identified as coming from the Gospels; their source is cited sometimes as "Gl.," sometimes (curiously) as "Ælf."

manuscript do not include every Old English word in MS 144. For example, the lists omit all the Old English words that occur on fols. 60r–61r of MS 144. Most of these words have been under-lined in the manuscript, and most of them appear in the dictionary, with MS 144 cited as their source,[90] and with the Latin definitions that occur in MS 144. Again, the Lambeth lists omit a group of seven Old English words that have been underlined in the lower part of column *b* of fol. 61v of MS 144: *ðorhbrogden*, *auuel*, *meottoc*, *aespe*, *saes*, *scofl*, and *ðrifeoðor*.[91] All are listed in the dictionary, with MS 144 cited as their source.[92] These examples show that when Joscelyn and Parker incorporated into the Titus dictionary entries derived from MS 144, they cannot only have used the lists on fols. 13r–14v of Lambeth 692. Possibly they con-sulted the manuscript anew, but more likely they made use of other lists, now lost, in addition to or instead of those in Lambeth 692.

The surviving evidence for Joscelyn's lexicographical work thus both reveals and conceals. It demonstrates his basic working procedure but does not allow us to see every stage of the work. Two fragments of material provide an insight into how much has been lost even from late stages. Both fragments are found in BL MS Harley 6841, among a collection of papers that probably belonged to Sir Simonds D'Ewes.[93] Folios 98–125, written by Joscelyn, are an alphabetically organized list of words beginning

---

[90]As noted above, p. 91, Joscelyn and John Parker used various different ab-breviations to refer to MS 144 in the Titus dictionary.

[91]These words are not included in the lists derived from MS 144 on fols. 13r–14v of Lambeth 692, nor do they occur on any other page of the Lambeth manuscript.

[92]Two of the words are spelled differently in the dictionary: *ðorhbrogden* appears as "þrohbrogden" on fol. 208v of Titus A. xvi, and *scofl* as "sceofl" on fol. 94r. The Latin definitions of the words match those found in MS 144.

[93]See Wright (1972), where Wright indicates that fols. 57–172 of the manuscript may have belonged to D'Ewes.

with the letter g.[94] These leaves are of a size similar to those of the Titus dictionary; the layout is the same, with each page divided into two columns; and sources for the entries are cited in the same way as they are in the dictionary. The leaves are now out of order: fols. 112–25 should precede fols. 98–111. Comparison with MS Titus A. xv shows that these leaves are what John Parker copied when writing portions of the g-section of the Titus dictionary. Folios 112–25 contain words listed on fols. 141r–173r of Titus A. xv; fols. 98–111 words listed on fols. 177v–204v. In copying the Harley leaves, John Parker adjusted the alphabetical ordering when necessary. For example, on fol. 115v of Harley 6841, "gebrocen" follows rather than precedes "gebrocod" and "gebrocode"; on fol. 148v of Titus A. xv, Parker has listed the words in their correct order, although it is clear that he squeezed in the entry "Gebrocen" above that for "Gebrocod" only after he had first written the latter. Parker also integrated in their appropriate place on the Titus leaves those entries that Joscelyn added in the margins of the Harley leaves: thus Joscelyn's entry for "geweald," added in the margin of Harley 6841, fol. 111v, occurs in its proper place on fol. 204r of Titus A. xv. That John Parker was indeed copying from these very leaves of the Harley manuscript is further confirmed by a corrected error that occurs on fol. 177v of MS Titus A. xv, in the entry for "Gemindleas." Parker first wrote the incorrect Latin definition "impius," then crossed it out and entered the correct "imprudens." On fol. 98r of Harley 6841, Joscelyn divided the definition over two lines: "impru-/dens." John Parker's "impius" evidently resulted from his misreading of Joscelyn's "impru-"; he corrected the definition when he realized that the word continued on the next line. The Harley leaves also make it possible to understand why, in

---

[94]Mentioned in Hetherington (1980), 28.

MS Titus A. xv, the set of entries from "Geomrunga" to "Geonet sped" are on an added leaf (fol. 181), as has been noted above.[95] In Harley 6841, the equivalent entries fill column *b* of fol. 99v. Clearly, when John Parker copied this leaf, he at first omitted to copy this column, and proceeded instead from the bottom of column *a* to the top of fol. 100r. Later he realized his mistake and wrote out the omitted column of words on a smaller leaf that he inserted into MS Titus A. xv. The existence of fols. 98–125 of Harley 6841 suggests that there would have been similar drafts by Joscelyn for every portion of the Titus dictionary copied by Parker and strengthens the view that Parker's role was restricted to that of copyist.[96]

The other fragment in the Harley manuscript reveals a stage that is later than the Titus dictionary itself. Folios 131–32 of Harley 6841 are filled with certain of the *a*-entries that occur on fols. 5–17 of Titus A. xv. Hetherington believed the two leaves to be the work of William Dugdale (1605–86),[97] but they are in fact in the hand of John Parker. The script matches that of John Parker's sections of the dictionary and the two-column layout is the same as that of the dictionary (compare Fig. 7 with Figs. 1, 3, and 8). The stemless fleur-de-lys watermark on fol. 132 is somewhat similar to that on fols. 139–52 and 171–84 of MS Titus A. xv. That these two leaves of Harley 6841 were written later than those leaves of the Titus dictionary of which they repeat some of the entries is demonstrated by the fact that they include entries that Joscelyn added to the Titus leaves at some point after those leaves were first written. Further, at several points on the two Harley leaves Parker has entered reference numbers that cite the

---

[95]See above, pp. 88 and 90.

[96]Compare Rosier (1960), 28 n. 3; and Hetherington (1980), 28–29.

[97]Hetherington (1980), 95–96.

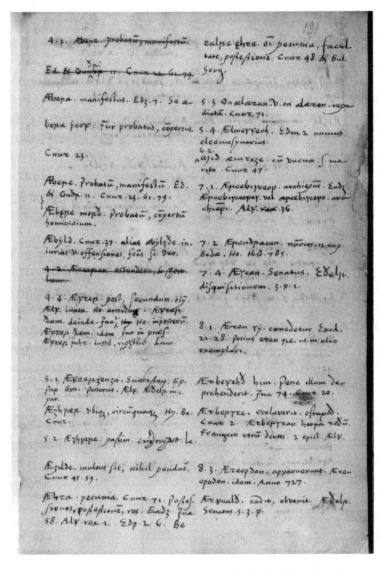

Figure 7. London, British Library, MS Harley 6841, fol. 131r. The reference numbers at the beginning of some entries refer to folio and column numbers in MS Titus A. xv, and show that the purpose of this page, which is in John Parker's hand, was to correct and clarify certain entries in the Titus dictionary (cf. Fig. 8).

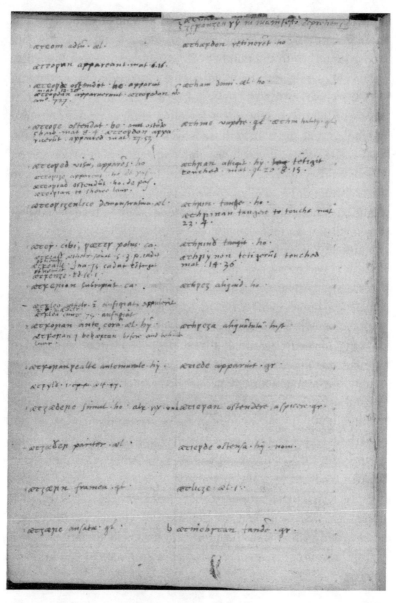

Figure 8. London, British Library, MS Cotton Titus A. xv, fol. 9v (formerly fol. 8v). The left column includes the entries for *æteowdan* and *ætfeald* to which the last two entries on fol. 131r of MS Harley 6841 refer (cf. Fig. 7).

relevant folio and column numbers of the Titus dictionary.[98] For example, on fol. 131r (Fig. 7), he precedes his entry "Æteowdan. apparuerunt" with the numbers "8. 3," indicating that this entry relates to one that can be found on the third column (i.e., column *a* of the verso) of fol. "8" (now fol. 9) of Titus A. xv (Fig. 8). Analysis of the two leaves in Harley 6841 shows that their purpose was to correct and clarify those leaves of the dictionary to which they relate. Where errors in the alphabetization of entries occur on the dictionary leaves, the two Harley leaves set those entries in their correct order; and where Joscelyn's entries and squeezed-in additions on the dictionary leaves are difficult to read because of the small size and the density of his script, the Harley leaves present the text in a clearly legible format. Thus on fol. 132r of Harley 6841, Parker's set of entries "Ahwæned," "Ahwær," "Ahwar," "Ahwear," "Ahwerf," "Ahyddan," and "Ahyddon" correct the alphabetical ordering of entries by Joscelyn that occur on fol. 14v of Titus A. xv while also incorporating into the sequence the entries for *ahyddan* and *ahyddon* that Joscelyn had added in the margin of Titus A. xv. It is possible that fols. 131–32 of Harley 6841 are the unique surviving record of a concerted campaign to "tidy up" the Titus dictionary. Their existence may indicate that plans to publish the dictionary had advanced far, for the intention may have been that these leaves and others like them would be given to the printer along with MSS Titus A. xv and A. xvi themselves, to guide the correct typesetting of the dictionary.

Yet the Titus dictionary, like Joscelyn's lost Old English grammar, was to remain unpublished. Nevertheless, Joscelyn's efforts had by no means been in vain, for his dictionary proved a fruitful resource for seventeenth-century scholars of Old English.

---

[98]Parker's folio numbers refer to a now partly trimmed ink foliation in John Joscelyn's hand on the first leaves of MS Titus A. xv. The numbers of that foliation are consistently one less than those of the modern pencil foliation.

The full range of the surviving evidence for Joscelyn's lexicographical activity reveals that the dictionary was the outcome of an extensive, long-term campaign of work that can now only partly be recovered, work that depended heavily on Joscelyn's firsthand study of the Anglo-Saxon manuscripts available to him. Anticipated in the field by Nowell, Joscelyn outstripped his contemporary by the larger scope of his efforts and succeeded in producing a dictionary that was fuller and more finished than Nowell's. Joscelyn's achievement and the labors underlying it establish him as the outstanding sixteenth-century pioneer of Old English lexicography.[99]

[99] I am very grateful to the British Academy for the award of a travel grant to attend the Twenty-Ninth International Congress on Medieval Studies at Western Michigan University (May 1994), at which I read a draft version of this paper. Warm thanks also to Vincent McCarren and Peter Lucas for reading and offering helpful comments on a near final version of the paper.

THE SOURCES OF JOSCELYN'S WORD LISTS
IN LONDON, LAMBETH PALACE LIBRARY, MS 692

Folio number(s)	Heading	Source manuscript(s) and comments
1rv	—	(Blank)[1]
2rv	(See next column)	(Blank apart from seventeenth-century title and note entered on the recto: "Collections in order to y^e making of a Saxon Dictionarie or Vocabularie. [Qu. whether they be Mr. Lisle's?]")[2]
3r	"Ex regula canonicorum"	1. CCCC MS 191 (Exeter, s. xi$^{3/4}$): bilingual copy of the enlarged version of the *Rule* of Chrodegang 2. CCCC MS 201 Part II (Exeter, s. xi$^{3/4}$): bilingual copy of the *Capitula* of Theodulf of Orléans[3]
3v	—	CCCC MS 191
4r–5r	"ex prouerbia salomonis" (on fol. 4r)	BL MS Cotton Vespasian D. vi (s. x^{med}, provenance St. Augustine's, Canterbury): glossed copy of the book of Proverbs
5v	—	(Blank)
6r–8r	"ex pastorale gregorii" (on fol. 6r)	Bodleian MS Hatton 20 (s. ix^{ex}, provenance Worcester): OE *Pastoral Care*
8v	—	(Blank)

Folio number(s)	Heading	Source manuscript(s) and comments
9r	—	Ælfric's *Grammar*[4]
9v–11v	"de pronomine," altered to "de verbo" (on fol. 10v, applying to the entries on that page, almost all of which are verbs)	CUL MS Hh. 1. 10 (Exeter, s. xi$^{3/4}$): Ælfric's *Grammar and Glossary*
12r	—	BL MS Cotton Nero D. iv (Lindisfarne, s. vii^{ex}, with OE additions of s. x^2): the Lindisfarne Gospels
12v	—	(Blank apart from Joscelyn's headings from *a* to *y*, distributed over the page)
13r–14v	Rubbed and damaged heading on fol. 13r, probably "ex glossa Cantuariensi"	CCCC MS 144 (s. ix^1, provenance St. Augustine's, Canterbury): glossary
15r–16r	—	(Blank)

(*Continued*)

Folio number(s)	Heading	Source manuscript(s) and comments
16v	"verba hæc desumpta ex Aldelmo de virginitate"	1. CCCC MS 326 (Christ Church, Canterbury, s. x^2): glossed copy of the prose version of Aldhelm's *De virginitate* 2. CCCC MS 144 (as for fols. 13r–14v)[5]
17r–18r	"ex regula Benedicti" (on fol. 17r)	CCCC MS 178 Part II (Worcester, s. xi^1): bilingual copy of the *Rule* of St. Benedict
18v–20v	—	(Blank apart from a note [now turned upside down] in the lower inner area of fol. 19v)
21r	"In ecclesiasticam historiam Bedæ interpretationes Saxonicorum verborum"	1. CCCC MS 41 (s. xi^1, provenance Exeter): OE version of Bede's *Ecclesiastical History* 2. CUL MS Kk. 3. 18 (Worcester, s. xi^2): OE version of Bede's *Ecclesiastical History* 3. CCCC MS 12 (s. x^2, provenance Worcester): OE *Pastoral Care* 4. Bodleian MS Hatton 20 (as for fols. 6r–8r)[6]
21v–23v	—	(Blank)
24r–25v	"homelię" (on fol. 24r)	CCCC MS 198 (Worcester, s. xi^{1-2}): homiliary glossed extensively by the Tremulous Hand of Worcester
26r–27v	—	(Blank)

Folio number(s)	Heading	Source manuscript(s) and comments
28r	—	Ælfric's *Grammar*[7]
28v	—	(Blank)
29r (in Nowell's hand)	—	1. BL MS Cotton Otho B. xi (Winchester, s. x[med]): OE version of Bede's *Ecclesiastical History* 2. BL MS Cotton Vespasian D. xiv, fols. 4–169 (Rochester or Canterbury, s. xii[med]): homiliary
29v (in Nowell's hand)	—	BL MS Cotton Vespasian D. xiv[8]
30r	—	BL MS Additional 15350 (Winchester, s. xii): the Winchester cartulary
30v–31v	—	(Blank apart from some sums and a Latin note based on Acts 13:20, all on fol. 31v)
32rv (in Nowell's hand)	—	BL MS Cotton Otho B. xi (as for fol. 29r)
33rv	—	(Blank)
34rv	—	BL MS Harley 3376 (?Worcester, s. x/xi): glossary[9]
35rv	—	(Blank)

(*Continued*)

Folio number(s)	Heading	Source manuscript(s) and comments
36r	—	1. CCCC MS 198 (as for fols. 24r–25v)
		2. Bodleian MS Hatton 114 (Worcester, s. xi$^{3/4}$): second volume of a two-volume homiliary (MSS Hatton 113–14) extensively glossed by the Tremulous Hand[10]
36v–37v	—	(Blank apart from a brief paraphrase on fol. 37r of a sentence of ch. XXIX of Bede's *De temporum ratione*)[11]
38r–39v	—	Bodleian MS Hatton 113 (Worcester, s. xi$^{3/4}$): first volume of the two-volume homiliary (cf. fol. 36r)
40r	—	1. Bodleian MS Junius 121 (Worcester, s. xi$^{3/4}$): collection of ecclesiastical institutes, homilies, and other texts, heavily glossed by the Tremulous Hand
		2. CCCC MS 41 (as for fol. 21r)
		3. CUL MS Kk. 3. 18 (as for fol. 21r)[12]
40v–41r	—	BL MS Cotton Nero A. i Part I (s. xi$^{3/4}$, provenance unknown): collection of Anglo-Saxon laws[13]
41v[14]	—	1. CCCC MS 41 (as for fol. 21r)
		2. CUL MS Kk. 3. 18 (as for fol. 21r)
		3. Bodleian MS Junius 121 (as for fol. 40r)[15]

Notes

[1]On fol. 1v there is offset from the text on the inside of the front cover of the manuscript. That the offset is on fol. 1v shows that the leaf has been reversed: the present verso must formerly have been the recto.

[2]The author of this note evidently thought that Lambeth 692 might be part of William L'Isle's lost lexicographical work, on which see n. 35 of the paper by Phillip Pulsiano in the present volume.

[3]For an explanation of why entries derived from two different manuscripts occur on this page, see above, pp. 108–10.

[4]The page is densely packed with some 405 entries, but Joscelyn cites no folio numbers that would help to identify the source manuscript (assuming that a single manuscript is the source). It might be worthwhile to check the entries on this page against the copy of Ælfric's *Grammar* in Durham, Dean and Chapter Library, MS B. III. 32 (?Canterbury, s. xi[1]), which Ker tentatively identified as a source for Lambeth 692 (see Ker [1957], 509, entry for Lambeth 692 in the manuscript bibliography). For example, Joscelyn's entry "niðer weard deorsum versum" corresponds with the Durham manuscript, but not with CUL MS Hh. 1. 10 (see Zupitza [1880], 238).

[5]For discussion of the occurrence on this page of words from CCCC MS 144, see above, pp. 121–24.

[6]For discussion of why the page includes entries derived from the Old English *Pastoral Care* as well as from the Old English Bede, see above, pp. 118–20.

[7]The page has just forty-five entries, most if not all of which come from Ælfric's *Grammar*. Joscelyn cites no folio numbers that might help to identify the source manuscript.

[8]In the bottom right area of the page, below the last entry, is the note "Mr Nowell," written twice.

[9]For a detailed study of the Harley glossary, see Cooke (1994), where evidence suggesting a Worcester origin is noted on pp. 28–29; Joscelyn's use of the manuscript is discussed on pp. 32–33.

[10]For four of the entries on fol. 36r Joscelyn cited folio numbers. These numbers enable the source of the four entries to be identified as CCCC MS 198, and comparison with that manuscript shows that several other entries on the page

derive from it. Other entries have been taken from MS Hatton 114. For example, the last ten entries in the g-block, from "geæswicod" to "getydeste," come from the homily *De nativitate Mariae* on fols. 201r–212r of Hatton 114.

[11]The text corresponds to Jones (1943), 234, ch. XXIX/41–42. Joscelyn's version is: "malinas estus maris crescentes, ledones estus maris decrescentes: beda de computo cap. 28. de concordia maris et lunę."

[12]The principal sources for the entries on this page are the ecclesiastical institutes on fols. 9r–31v of Junius 121, Ælfric's preface to his First Series of Catholic Homilies on fols. 154v–157r, the homily on the Assumption of the Virgin on fols. 157r–160r, and the homily for the First Sunday in Advent on fols. 138r–142r. For example, within the block of g-words, the first eleven come from Ælfric's preface, the next eleven from the Assumption homily, the next eighteen from the Advent homily, and the next eleven from the ecclesiastical institutes; I have not traced the source of the last eleven g-words. Within the a-block, all entries but one come from these texts in Junius 121; the exception is the entry for "ærend racan" with its variant "ærend wrecan," which, as Joscelyn notes, comes from Book I, chapter 12 of the Old English Bede (see Miller [1890–98], I:1, 50 line 26); the two spellings are respectively those of CCCC MS 41, p. 49, line 2, and CUL MS Kk. 3. 18, fol. 12v, line 7 (see Miller [1890–98], II:1, 24, where the variant spelling of CCCC 41 is noted).

[13]Joscelyn's entries are followed by folio references from "7" to "14"; these refer to fols. 51–58 of MS Nero A. i as now foliated.

[14]Folio 41v is followed by an unnumbered leaf. Both that and the following leaf, numbered "42," are blank. On fol. 42v is offset from the text on the inside of the back cover.

[15]The two principal sources of the entries on this page are (1) the chapter list of the Old English Bede (the variant spellings of Joscelyn's entries from which show that he used the two Cambridge manuscripts), and (2) the Old English Benedictine Office on fols. 42r–55r of MS Junius 121. For example, of the fifty-four entries in the g-block, the first forty, from "gesetnyss, gesetnes. situs" to "gewinne labore," are from the Bede chapter list, while the next twelve, from "gehremman impedire" to "gemet inuenerit," are from the Old English Benedictine Office. The source of the last two entries in the group, "gericena decentia" and "generige eripio," is as yet untraced.

THE ANGLO-SAXON PANTHEON
ACCORDING TO RICHARD VERSTEGEN
(1605)

Rolf H. Bremmer, Jr.

For T. A. Birrell

Anglo-Saxon paganism has exercised a strong fascination on generations of scholars, a fascination which is also shared by many students when they come to Old English literature.[1] The lasting interest may be illustrated by the fact that the most recent monograph on the subject, Gale Owen's *Rites and Religions of the Anglo-Saxons*,[2] has been twice reprinted since its appearance in 1981. One has the impression that scholarly curiosity concerning this aspect of Anglo-Saxon culture was aroused only with the Romantic Movement. At least, that is where Eric Stanley took the starting point for his exciting historiographical survey, *The Search for Anglo-Saxon Paganism*.[3] To be sure, a thorough and systematic study of Germanic mythology started only with Jacob Grimm's *Deutsche Mythologie*, first published in 1835. Yet the pursuit of Anglo-Saxon paganism dates back all the way to the infant years of Anglo-Saxon studies.

---

[1] I would like to thank Jan Bremmer and Bart Westerweel for their helpful comments on a draft of this essay.

[2] Owen (1981; repr. 1985 and 1996).

[3] Stanley (1975).

It was the former Oxonian Richard Verstegen (alias Verstegan alias Rowlands) who first extensively drew attention to the pre-Christian religion of the Anglo-Saxons in his *A Restitvtion of Decayed Intelligence in Antiquities. Concerning the Most Noble and Renovvmed* [*sic*] *English Nation*, printed at Antwerp by Robert Bruney in 1605. The title page also states that the book is to be sold "at London in Paules-Churchyeard, by Iohn Norton and Iohn Bill."[4] To the subject of the "idolatrie" of the Anglo-Saxons he devoted the greater part of chapter 3, entitled "Of the ancient manner of lyving of our Saxon anceters. Of the Idolles they adored whyle they were pagans . . ." (Table of Contents, p. [23]). Hitherto, Verstegen's *Restitvtion* has mainly received regard (and praise) amongst Anglo-Saxonists on account of his including an Old English glossary of well over nine hundred headwords; with the exception of the list of Old English legal terms appended to William Lambarde's *Archaionomia* of 1568, this was the first Old English glossary ever to be printed.[5] Verstegen has even been credited with having seen the importance of the Conquest in the field of literary history by separating such authors as Chaucer and Gower from the authors of the Anglo-Saxon period whose language was less corrupted by loanwords.[6] My paper seeks to redress this one-sided interest somewhat.

Who was the author of this successful book that saw reprints in 1628, 1634, 1652, 1655, and 1673,[7] as well as two facsimile

---

[4]These were also the publishers of books by other antiquaries, e.g., William Camden.

[5]On Verstegen's achievements as lexicographer, see Goepp (1949); Schäfer (1982); and Schäfer (1989), 52. For a recent assessment of *A Restitvtion* as a whole, see Clement (1998), which came to my attention too late to be taken into account.

[6]See Glass (1982), 99.

[7]See Pollard and Redgrave (1976–91), II, nos. 21361–63; and Wing (1972–88), III, V269–71.

reprints[8] in the seventies of our century? Richard Verstegen was born of mixed Dutch-English ancestry. His grandfather Theodore Rowlands Verstegen emigrated from Guelderland to England during the late years of Henry VII's reign, as Verstegen himself relates in the prefatory letter to the English nation.[9] The exact date of Verstegen's birth is not known but can be postulated at ca. 1550. In 1565 we find him as a sizar at Christ Church, Oxford. According to the eighteenth-century Roman Catholic historian Charles Dodd,[10] Verstegen devoted himself to the study of Anglo-Saxon and Gothic antiquities. Dodd's source of information in all likelihood was Anthony à Wood, who emphasized Verstegen's linguistic skills, calling him "a most admirable Critic in the *Saxon* and *Gothic* Languages."[11] Modern scholars concluded from such opinions that Verstegen studied Anglo-Saxon and Gothic while at Oxford,[12] but this is extremely unlikely. In 1565 not a letter of Gothic had been printed, and despite its many libraries, Oxford could not boast of possessing a single Gothic manuscript.[13] Moreover, Oxford is not the place where in the 1560s the first

---

[8]*English Recusant Literature*, no. 323 (Ilkley: Scolar Press, 1971) and *The English Experience*, no. 952 (New York: Da Capo Press, 1979), respectively.

[9]*Restitvtion*, sig. ††1[r]. The best book on Verstegen is still Rombauts (1933). For a succinct account, see the article by Anthony G. Petti in *The New Catholic Encyclopedia*, XIV (Washington, 1967), 627.

[10]See Dodd (1737–42), II, 428. Dodd is a pseudonym for Hugh Tootel.

[11]Wood (1721), I, 502.

[12]Thus, for example, Rombauts (1933), 25–26, and Blom (1979), 17.

[13]The Uppsala Codex Argenteus, the sumptuously executed sixth-century manuscript containing the Gospels in the Gothic language, was discovered only around 1555, and the first sample from it, the text of the Lord's Prayer, was printed by Johannes Goropius Becanus some ten years later. On the early years of Gothic studies, see Van de Velde (1966) and Dekker (1999). Wood obviously meant "Germanic" when he wrote "Gothic," cf. *Oxford English Dictionary*, s.v. *Gothic* (2).

steps were made on the path of Anglo-Saxon studies. Pioneers like Archbishop Matthew Parker and his secretary John Joscelyn, William Lambarde and Laurence Nowell—all were active in or around London. That is also where the first books with Anglo-Saxon texts were produced by the printer John Day, with the Anglo-Saxon type cast in bronze at the expense of Matthew Parker.[14]

What also speaks against Verstegen's alleged interest in Anglo-Saxon in those years is that the early study of the language was more or less a monopoly of Protestants, as appears from the publication of the Old English Gospels in 1571 and, slightly earlier in 1566, from Parker's tendentiously edited sermon by Ælfric on the significance of the Eucharist.[15] As a staunch Roman Catholic, Verstegen would probably have been forced to leave the university in 1570 through unwillingness to take the Oath of Supremacy. In any event, he did not finish his studies with a degree. Verstegen returned to his native London, became a goldsmith, and acquired great skill as an engraver. In 1580, he appears in Paris, with his wife, as an exile from England for his involvement in anti-Protestant propaganda. After prolonged stays in Paris and Rome, he eventually settled in Antwerp in the early 1590s. Antwerp would be his main domicile for the rest of his long life. Verstegen died in 1640 at the age of about ninety years.

During his life, Verstegen proved to be a very productive author. His entire oeuvre numbers well over thirty titles.[16] His first book was a kind of Baedeker guide to the major cities of Europe,

---

[14]See Adams (1917), esp. ch. 1 and Appendix III; Bromwich (1962); and Lucas (1997a) and (1999).

[15]See Leinbaugh (1982).

[16]Bibliographies are given by Rombauts (1933), 298–319, including a list of works erroneously attributed to Verstegen; and Petti (1963). The latter is supplemented with a few items in Allison and Rogers (1989–94), I, 169–72 and 290, restricting themselves to Verstegen's polemical works only.

which he translated from German and augmented with information on their antiquity and origin. The majority of his books, however, are of a less innocent nature, as they were all part of his ardent attempts to further the cause of the Counter-Reformation. Before the appearance of his *Restitvtion* he had published no fewer than twelve books and pamphlets, of which three were in Latin, one in French, and the remaining eight in English. In most of these he exposed the atrocities allegedly committed by the Protestant English against innocent Roman Catholics. Some books were of a devotional character, such as his English edition and translation of the *Primer or Office of the Blessed Virgin*, published in 1599. For over a hundred years this was *the* book for clandestine Marian devotion in England.[17]

In this context of Counter-Reformationist activities, Verstegen's *A Restitvtion of Decayed Intelligence in Antiquities* is the odd man out. The book was dedicated to "the King's most excellent maiestie, James by the grace of God, King of Great Britain, France, and Ireland: defender of the faith." It almost looks like an act of impertinence that Verstegen, jailed "ffor religion" at the Poultry Counter prison in London in 1577,[18] exiled from England around 1579 because of his Roman Catholic ideas, and the object of polemics by writers like Sir Francis Bacon,[19] should dedicate his book to the Calvinist that James I was. The pious conclusion to his dedicatory letter, expressing the desire for "Almightie God (as in my daylie prayers I hold my self obliged) to bee your

---

[17]Blom (1979), 16–19, 80–85, and passim.

[18]Rombauts (1933), 29 and n. 2.

[19]See Bacon's *Certain Observations Made upon a Libel Publishd This Present Year 1592 Entitled: A Declaration of the True Causes of the Great Troubles Presupposed to be Intended against the Realme of England* (London, 1592). Verstegen had (anonymously) published a pamphlet decrying the severe measures taken by Queen Elizabeth against the Roman Catholics; see Rombauts (1933), 84–89.

maiesties euer protector," looks downright hypocritical in the light of his other publications. What was Verstegen up to?

First of all, as Verstegen explains to the general reader, he had been moved to write his book by "the very naturall affection which generally is in all men to heare of the woorthynesse of their anceters, which they should in deed bee as desyrous to imitate, as delighted to vnderstand."[20] In other words, in holding up to the English nation a mirror in which they could see their distant past, Verstegen offered them an opportunity to reflect upon their present. In doing so the English might be able to improve whatever deviations they perceived from former laudable customs and usage of language.

Second, Verstegen explains, his book should be seen in a European perspective. Authors of many different countries had taken pains to describe the true origins of their nations, but for England such a study had yet to appear. In England the prevailing opinion still held that the English derived from the ancient British, i.e., Celts, and Verstegen makes abundantly clear, with some striking examples, to what misconceptions this error had led. Against these, Verstegen stated that the true descent of the English lay in Germany—to be precise, in Saxony. Indeed, Verstegen is the first in a line of historians whose aim it was to extol a Germanic England, contrasting it with an inferior Romanized Gaul. Tacitus, "a moste credit-woorthy wryter" (p. 40), is a crown witness in this new approach.[21]

To begin with, in chapters 1 and 2, Verstegen marshals the linguistic and historical evidence to bring out this point. Next, in chapter 3, he gives a detailed description of the way of life of the ancient Saxons, for example, how their society was divided into four classes, and how they used ordeals in their legal procedures. The remainder of this chapter is mainly taken up by a description of their pagan beliefs. In chapter 4, Verstegen deals with the

---

[20]*Restitvtion*, sig. †3[v].

[21]See Weinbrot (1993), 178.

history of Britain until the end of the Roman era, while in chapter 5 he treats of the coming of the Anglo-Saxons and their conversion to Christianity. Chapter 6 gives an account of the coming of the Danes and Normans, respectively. The remaining three chapters are taken up entirely by linguistic matter, such as extensive etymological glossaries of English personal names and place names, and the aforementioned Old English glossary. This brief sketch of the contents of the *Restitvtion* will have made it sufficiently clear that Verstegen's work is the first in a long series to present a survey of Anglo-Saxon England in its cultural and linguistic settings. In this approach Verstegen clearly belongs to a broader antiquarian current.[22]

Particularly interesting is what Verstegen has to say about the "idolatrie of the old pagan Saxons." In his account he first sets out to give a general characterization of their beliefs. In Verstegen's opinion, the ancient Saxons lived "according to the law of nature and reason," and through lack of knowledge of the true God, they worshipped idols. They were especially attentive to signs of nature before they went into battle, heeding, for example, the whinnying of horses and the flight of birds. As an illustration, Verstegen quotes on page 67 an incident from Flavius Josephus's *Anti-quitates Iudaeorum*, but he leaves unmentioned that his account on page 68 of the custom of casting lots was taken almost verbatim from Tacitus's *Germania*, chapter 10. Such an omission is in line with his methodological approach, which in its casualness is some-times irritating. Throughout his book, Verstegen is very generous with references to learned authors and their works. He often briefly indicates his debt by a marginal reference. Unfortunately, in doing so he rarely gives chapter and verse, which makes tracing his sources a cumbersome task. Tracking down copies of the books

---

[22]See Levine (1987), esp. ch. 3: "The Antiquarian Enterprise, 1500–1800."

he quotes is another obstacle,[23] although I cannot escape from the impression that Verstegen does not always quote directly from the works he mentions but regularly derives his knowledge from secondary sources.

Concerning the gods which they shared with the other Germanic nations (p. 39), Verstegen claims that the Saxons adored many idols, which were different from those the Romans worshipped. Yet, some authors would have it that these were the same as the Roman gods, albeit with different names. Verstegen is here confronted with the *interpretatio Romana*, the approach used by Roman authors to replace the name of a Germanic god with the nearest equivalent of one of their own deities. According to Verstegen, seven gods were worshipped in particular amongst the Saxons, whose names have been preserved in the days of the week. These gods "according to their cours and properties I wil heer to satisfy the curious reader descrybe, both in portrature and otherwise" (p. 68). We will see that in taking this approach, although on the right track, Verstegen was sometimes forced to make some curious assumptions with respect to the Anglo-Saxon pantheon. By presenting their portraiture, he flatly ignored Tacitus's information that the Germans "nec cohibere parietibus deos neque in ullam humani oris speciem adsimulare ex magnitudine caelestium arbitrantur" ("do not think it in keeping with the divine majesty to confine gods within the walls or to portray them in the likeness of any human countenance").[24] The temptation to enliven his account with pictures must have been too strong for Verstegen to resist.

---

[23]I realize I have merely scratched the surface of Verstegen's scholarly texture. I have used only the resources of the Leiden Universiteitsbibliotheek, the Koninklijke Bibliotheek in The Hague, and the Houghton Library, Harvard University.

[24]Winterbottom and Ogilvie (1975), 42 (*Germania* 9.3).

The first god, then, whom the ancient Saxons adored in particular, was the Sun, whose name has been preserved in "Sunday." His idol looked as follows (Fig. 9): his face was "as it

Figure 9. The idol of the Sun, from Richard Verstegen's *A Restitvtion of Decayed Intelligence in Antiquities* (1605), p. 69.

were, brightened with gleames of fyre," and he held "a burning wheel before his brest" (p. 69). The wheel, according to Verstegen, signifies the course that the sun runs around the world, and the fiery gleams, the light and heat with which he warms everything that lives and grows. Such an interpretation of the attributes of the gods, which makes up a significant component of Verstegen's account of the gods, betrays the fact that some of the accompanying engravings (which he made himself) were influenced by emblem literature, a genre becoming very fashionable in the Low Countries at the time. Verstegen was a skilled engraver, as we have noted above, and was also connected with contemporary emblem literature.[25] Though, in contrast to what is usual in emblem literature, Verstegen does not draw any moralistic conclusions from his illustrations, it is clear that they are charged with an allegorical symbolism that is also characteristic of emblem literature.

The Moon, he writes, was their second god, as the name "Monday," for "Moonday," makes clear. The form of this idol (see Fig. 10), according to Verstegen, "seemeth very strange and ridiculous," for "beeing made for a woman shee hath a short cote lyke a man" (p. 70). And he continues: "more strange it is to see her hood with such two long eares." She holds a mirror before her breast (as the sun god held a fiery wheel before his) to "expresse what shee is." In emblem literature, we regularly find the moon depicted as a mirror, to indicate it receiving its light from the sun.[26] Remarkably enough, Verstegen pretends to be unable to explain all her attributes, as he confesses to have been unsuccessful in finding the reason for the hood with long ears, the short coat, and the pointed shoes. It seems to me that Verstegen is here mystifying his account on purpose. His inability to give a meaning to these attributes only serves to enhance the veracity of the depiction. As a matter of fact, the pointedness of the shoes is totally irrelevant, as Woden, Thor, and Friga are likewise depicted with such shoes.

---

[25]Verstegen provided the English text for the Latin poems in Otto van Veen's *Amorum emblemata, figuris aeneis incisa studio Othonis Vaeni, Batavo-Lugdunensis. Emblemes of Love, with Verses in Latin, English, and Italian* (Antwerp, 1608). See Daly and Silcox (1990), 79–80, and Bath (1992), 35–36. On the collaboration between Van Veen and Verstegen, see also Porteman (1996), 7–9.

[26]See Henkel and Schöne (1967), I, 30–39 (moon), and II, 1350 (mirror with moon).

THE IDOL OF THE 𝕸𝕺𝕺𝕹.

Figure 10. The idol of the Moon, from Verstegen's
Restitvtion, p. 70.

Donkey's ears, though, signify folly and reflect the moon's lack of
constancy.[27]

The third god to make his appearance is Tuisco, "the moste
ancient and peculiar God of all the Germans" (p. 71), who gave his
name to Tuesday. This etymology of Tuesday, of course, is no
longer accepted, Verstegen being as yet ignorant of the existence
of the god Tiw. But as Tacitus had given such a prominent place

---

[27]For donkey's ears, see Henkel and Schöne (1967), II, 1605–06. Inconstancy is
one of the many notions the moon could represent: see, e.g., Ripa (1603), 225
(*Inconstanza*). Ripa links the moon with folly on p. 478 (*Stoltitia*). See also
Picinelli (1681), s.v. *luna*; Picinelli's index is reprinted in facsimile in Henkel
and Schöne (1967), II, 2113–96, where the entry for *luna* occurs in col. 2159.

to Tuisco/Tuysco (or Tuisto—there being some confusion about the correct version of the name), and as his name superficially resembles that of Tuesday, the equation was easily made. His picture (Fig. 11) receives little explanation. The only thing Verstegen remarks is that Tuisco is wearing a "garment of a skin, according to the moste ancient manner of the Germans clothing."

THE IDOL TUYSCO.

Figure 11. The god Tuisco, from Verstegen's *Restitvtion*, p. 71.

For this particular piece of information on their dress, Verstegen relies on Tacitus (*Germania*, ch. 17). The Tower of Babel, which can be discerned in the distance, is a silent reference to chapter 1 (pp. 9–13) of his book, in which Verstegen had extensively dealt with Tuisco. As Noah's great-great-grandson, the god had led the eponymous *Tuytsen* or Germans from Babel to Europe, as is also shown in the picture. The sceptre which Tuisco is wielding symbolizes his rulership. Verstegen's linking of the Tacitean Tuisco to the biblical story of Babel goes back to the Fleming Johannes Goropius Becanus, who in his *Origines Antwerpianae* (1569) devoted a good deal of attention to the etymology of *Teutsch* or *Dutch*, which he saw as a derivative of the name Tuisco,[28] a point on which Verstegen follows him. The linking of Tuisco to Noah—the urge to connect pagan ancestors with a biblical progenitor should not surprise Anglo-Saxonists—starts with Annius of Viterbo's *Commentaria super opera diversorum auctorum de antiquitatibus loquentium* ("Commentaries on the Works of Various Authors Discussing Antiquities"), an influential and brilliant forgery if ever there was one.[29]

With Woden, Verstegen arrives on more solid ground. This god, he says, was worshipped among the Saxons as their god of battle, as was Mars among the Romans. Woden's idol represents a man in full armour (Fig. 12). Verstegen gives a euhemeristic explanation of the god, saying that during his life he was "a most valiant and victorious Prince" (p. 72), but was after his death honored as a deity. The human sacrifices he mentions are silently lifted from Tacitus's *Germania*, chapter 9, where Tacitus notes that the Germans offered human sacrifices to Mercury, whom he describes as their most important god. Verstegen, however, rejects the view of some that Woden was the Germanic equivalent of Mercury, for "*Mercurie* among the Romans neuer was" a god of war (pp. 79–80). Verstegen remarks that the name Woden "signifieth fiers or furious" (which echoes Adam of Bremen's

---

[28]Becanus (1569), 460.

[29](Rome, 1498). See Grafton (1990); and Asher (1993), ch. 2. Annius makes Berosus the author of one of his major (fictitious) sources. Verstegen mentions Berosus as an authority on p. 11, albeit with some reservation: "if hee of some so called be the same, & so capable of credit."

remark "Wodan, id est furor"),[30] and he is the first to my knowledge to link the god's name with the English adjective *wood* ("insane"). "*Wedensday/* in steed of *wodensday*" still preserves the name of the god. Elsewhere in the *Restitvtion*, on page 81, Verstegen lists a number of English place names which contain the god's name as evidence of his worship: "*wodnesborough* in kent, *wodnesfeild* in Stafordshyre, *wodnesbeorgh* or *wannes-dytche* in

THE IDOL WODEN.

Figure 12. The god Woden, from Verstegen's *Restitvtion*, p. 72.

---

[30]Schmeidler (1917), 258.

wilshyre, &c." Using onomastics as a method to recover Anglo-Saxon pagan sanctuaries, so familiar to us now,[31] was certainly a novelty around 1600.

Thor (see Fig. 13) is identified as the most powerful of the gods, and the governor of the winds and the clouds, lightning and thunder. His idol is accordingly placed in a very large and spacious hall, where he sat "as yf he had reposed himself vpon a

Figure 13. The god Thor, from Verstegen's *Restitvtion*, p. 74.

---

[31]In our century, important contributions in this respect were made by Sir Frank Stenton, Bruce Dickins, Eilert Ekwall, and Margaret Gelling. For an account of the "state of the art," see Gelling (1973).

couered bed. On his head hee wore a crown of Gold," and around his head "were set or fixed twelue bright burnished golden starres. And in his right hand hee held a kingly septer" (p. 74). His name is preserved in "Thursday," which the Danes and Swedes still call *Thorsday*. In the Netherlands, according to Verstegen, it is called *Dundersdagh*, which corresponds to English "Thunders-day." From this Verstegen concludes (not surprisingly) that Thor was the god of thunder. As corroborative evidence he cites the form *Thunresdeag* [*sic*] as he had found it "in some of our old Saxon books." Unfortunately, he gives no more precise iden-tification of his source.

The next in line is the goddess Friga (Fig. 14). Curiously, Verstegen interprets her as a hermaphrodite, probably on account of her holding a sword in her right hand and a bow in her left. The two weapons, he says, signify that both women and men should be ready to fight in times of need. Her name is preserved in "Friday," which the Anglo-Saxons called *Frigedeag*.

Undoubtedly the most fanciful god is Seater (Fig. 15). His idol is placed on the sharp prickled back of a perch. In his right hand he holds a pail with flowers and fruits, signifying the fertility he was supposed to bring. The wheel in his left hand symbolizes "the knit vnitie and conioyned concord of the Saxons, and their concurring together in the running one cours" (p. 79). The girdle waving in the wind indicates the freedom of the Saxons. His name, unsurprisingly, is preserved in "Saturday."

Surveying Verstegen's discussion of what he took to be the seven most important gods, we can see how he proceeded. He structured his account on the names of the days of the week, which forced him to posit a god for each of these. Consequently, he had to invent at least three gods—the sun, the moon, and Seater—that we no longer recognize as Germanic gods.[32] They had their origin

---

[32]Despite the testimony of Caesar in his *De bello Gallico*, VI, 21 (Edwards [1917], 344–45), who claimed the celestial bodies as deities for the Germans. Verstegen would have been familiar with this report.

in the fact that some time before the close of the fourth century the Germans adopted the Roman names of the weekdays in a partly literally translated and partly adjusted form. Verstegen was probably not aware of this, and the ease with which he recreates this part of the Germanic past of the English sharply contrasts with his polemic tone in the introduction to his book and elsewhere, where he makes short shrift of all kinds of spurious and unfounded opinions of fellow historians.

Figure 14. The goddess Friga, from Verstegen's *Restitvtion*, p. 76.

His accounts of Woden, Thor, and Friga contain in embryonic form what we still know of them. The reason why Verstegen appears more knowledgeable about these gods is that he took most of his information directly from Olaus Magnus's impressive history of Scandinavia, *Historia de gentibus septentrionalibus*.[33] Not

Figure 15. The god Seater, from Verstegen's
Restitvtion, p. 78.

only does Verstegen adopt the description of the three gods, he also copies the etymologizing of the names of the weekdays. Olaus even provided inspiration for Verstegen's pictures of the gods, for, as a comparison with Olaus's illustration of the three shows (Fig. 16), Verstegen's portraits derive much of their iconography

---

[33](Rome, 1555), 100–01.

Figure 16. Friga, Thor, and Woden, from Olaus Magnus's
Historia de gentibus septentrionalibus (1555), p. 100.

from it.[34] Whereas Olaus had grouped all three gods together,
Verstegen gives each of them a separate picture, to accord with the
general set-up of his account.

    To be sure, from the point of view of our present state of
knowledge, Verstegen often erred in his analysis of the Saxon
gods. Yet we must give him credit for his innovative contribution
to the mythography of Anglo-Saxon paganism. No one before him
had devoted so much attention to Anglo-Saxon paganism. The
impact he made is almost immediately discernible. When William
Camden brought out the enlarged edition of his *Britannia* in 1607,
he had added a whole chapter on the Anglo-Saxons, including a
brief account of their pagan gods, which demonstrably contained
elements that he took from Verstegen although he did not

---

[34]The engraving in Olaus's book was copied from an earlier work. The picture
ultimately goes back to Hans Holbein the Younger; see Granlund (1976), I,
354–55.

acknowledge him.[35] Acknowledgment was made by John Speed in his *History of Great Britaine under the Conquests of the Romans, Saxons, Danes and Normans*, which appeared in 1611, and which includes a section on the pagan gods.[36] Even the great antiquary Sir Robert Bruce Cotton sent his "commendations" to Verstegen in Antwerp, an honor that Verstegen returned by sending Sir Robert a fossilized fish tongue found in Flemish soil.[37] Anthony à Wood, in his *Athenae Oxonienses*, adequately sums up the prevailing opinion of Verstegen in the seventeenth century when he says that he was "a great reviver of our *English* Antiquities."[38]

Verstegen was a shrewd man. In 1613 he published a book in Antwerp called *Nederlantsche Antiquiteiten*, that is, "Dutch Antiquities." In this slim volume he recycled large portions of his *Restitvtion of Decayed Intelligence*. This time it is not the Anglo-Saxons but the Dutch who are given the history of their origins. In his account of their conversion to Christianity by the English missionary St. Willibrord, Verstegen includes almost verbatim his discussion of the pagan Saxon gods, pictures and all. This book, however, was written with a purpose entirely different from that of its English predecessor. Whereas the *Restitvtion* of 1605 at first sight is a neutral, objective book, its Dutch remake of 1613 is outspokenly anti-Protestant in tone.[39] Following upon his account of the conversion, Verstegen embarks in chapter 6 on an extended lamentation over the religious convictions of the Dutch who have turned either Calvinist, Lutheran, or Mennonite, a passage that

---

[35]Camden (1607), esp. 96–97. There are also similarities between Verstegen's etymologies of "our Saxon proper names," listed in his eighth chapter, and Camden's "Anglo-Saxonum nomina" on pp. 99–101.

[36]Speed (1611), 200–04.

[37]Letter of 15 June 1609, BL MS Cotton Julius C. iii, item 47, fol. 376, printed in Petti (1959), 266; and Rombauts (1933), 327.

[38]Wood (1721), I, 502.

[39]See Buitendijk (1942), ch. 7: "Richard Verstegen," esp. 162–63.

reads as one long cry from the heart: "Oh, if only a new Willibrord would come to bring them back to the bosom of the Church!"

The Dutch version proved even more successful than the *Restitvtion*. It was reprinted in the Roman Catholic Southern Netherlands in 1631, 1646, and 1662. But even in the Northern Netherlands, people realized its intrinsic values. In 1700, an adapted version under the title *Antiquitates Belgicae of Neder-landsche Oudtheden: zijnde d'eerste opkomst van Holland, Zee-land, 't Sticht Utrecht* . . . was published in Amsterdam, stripped of its anti-Protestant passages, and brought up to date with the latest state of knowledge by the publisher-bookseller Jacob van Royen. The book contained very good copies of Verstegen's en-gravings of the gods and was further embellished with a number of engravings of various Germanic tribesmen and ruined medieval castles. Reprinted in 1701, it was succeeded by further reprints in 1705, 1714, 1725, 1733, and 1756. The 1756 reprint, again slightly updated, was furnished with some more illustrations. One of these, appearing between pages 114 and 115, is of a "Church Service of the Ancient Germans" (Fig. 17). Here we see Ver-stegen's representations of the sun god and the moon god in an imaginative context. The last dated edition, with an updated appendix but without illustrations, appeared in 1809,[40] while an undated edition, which stuck more closely to the text of the 1613 edition (without the anti-Protestant polemic, but with Roman Catholic devotional passages), came out around 1830.[41] It contains crude imitations of the original divine portrait gallery. In other words, Verstegen's work, if in slightly adapted versions, managed to bridge more than two hundred years. Generations of scholars and interested readers had imprinted upon their minds a textual

---

[40]Printed in Ghent by C. J. Fernand.

[41]Printed in Brussels by P. J. de Haas; see Petti (1963), item 14j.

and pictorial representation of the Anglo-Saxon/Germanic gods that was basically conceived in Verstegen's creative and learned imagination.

Figure 17. Scene illustrating a "Church Service of the Ancient Germans," from the 1756 reprint of *Antiquitates Belgicae*, between pp. 114 and 115.

The attraction of Verstegen's work lay partly in the illustrations with which he had furnished it. In the opinion of William Nicolson, bishop of Carlisle (1702–18), the *Restitvtion* "is handled so plausibly, and so well illustrated with handsome cuts, that the book has taken and sold very well."[42] The verbo-visual impact of the Dutch version is particularly apparent from engravings that

---

[42]Quoted after Dodd (1737–42), II, 428.

illustrate sections on paganism in later books, especially in the
Low Countries and Germany.[43] Thus in a book which deals with
the antiquities of Leiden, we find a long section on the pagan gods
accompanied by their images (Fig. 18).[44] A magnificent historical

Figure 18. The Germanic gods, from Simon van
Leeuwen's *Korte besgryving van het Lugdunum Batavorum nu Leyden* (1672), between pp. 250 and 251.

atlas in folio format, intended for a Francophone readership, reproduces yet another adaptation of Verstegen's pantheon (Fig. 19, a

---

[43]See Van de Waal (1952), I, 168–69 and 206, plus the relevant footnotes in
vol. II. I owe this reference to Paul Hoftijzer. Whether or not Verstegen's portraits of the gods had a similar iconographic influence in Britain I cannot say.

[44]Van Leeuwen (1672), 250–51 (plate). The verbal description of the gods on
pp. 246–55 is based almost word for word on Verstegen's 1613 Dutch remake
of the *Restitvtion*.

La Gaule Belgique assujettie à l'Empire Romain est en partie le païs que nous appelons aujourdhuy les Dix-Sept Provinces des Päis-Bas. Cesar qui les soumit fait remarquer dans ses commentaires l'estime toute particuliere que les Romains avoient pour ces peuples qui étoient affranchis de toute charge, et considérés plus comme un peuple libre, que sujet. Ils ne demeurèrent assujettis, ou plus tost alliez des Romains, que jusqu'à l'an 449: de l'Ere chrétienne, que Merovée Roy de France les assujetit a son Empire. Mais les Danois et les Normans en étant devenus les Maistres, desolèrent ces Provinces qui passèrent en suite soûs la domination des Ducs Forêtiers, et recouvrerent enfin leur liberté en 863, que Charles le Chauve Roy de France erigea la Hollande en comté, en faveur de Thierry, où Theodric, premier Comte de Holande, comme la branche Cronologique en à costé le fait voir et connoistre. Les autres Provinces avoient aussi des seigneurs particuliers, comme, Duc de Brabant et Comte de Flandre, dont nous donnons aussi la Cronologie cy jointe. Mais toutes les 17 Provinces furent reunies soûs le regne de Philippe le Bon, Duc de Bourgogne, et de Charles le Hardy son fils, qui fut tué devant Nancy, sa fille unique ayant epousé Maximilian d'Autriche: Par ce mariage les 17 Provinces ont été reduites soûs la domination d'Espagne. De Maximilian d'Autriche, et de Marie de Bourgogne vint Philippe premier marié a Jeanne de Castille, Doù nâquit Charles cinq. Roy d'Espagne et Empereur, et Ferdinant. Charles cinq. après avoir regné 38 ans quita l'Empire a Ferdinant son frere, et remit l'Esvani...

Figure 19a and b. The Germanic gods, from Henri Chatelain's *Atlas historique, ou nouvelle introduction à l'histoire, à la chronologie et*

à la géographie ancienne et moderne (1721), I, plate 42. The two parts of the figure show the upper and lower portions of a single page.

Figure 20. The god Crodo, from the second edition of Elias Schedius's *De diis Germanis* (1728), between pp. 736 and 737.

and b).[45] A curious wanderer is the engraving of Seater that emerges in the second edition of Elias Schedius's learned treatise on the Germanic gods (Fig. 20).[46] The first edition, which had

---

[45]Chatelain (1721), I, plate 42.

[46]Schedius (1728), 736–37.

appeared with Elzevier's in Amsterdam in 1648, had to do without such embellishments. In a chapter dealing with eight minor (now deemed spurious) gods, Schedius includes Crodo, whom he takes to be a version of Saturn. The description of his attributes and the explanation of them are a direct translation of Verstegen's account, without acknowledgment of the source. The last creative adaptation I have found was made by the prolific Dutch engraver Jacob Buys in an encyclopedic work on the history of the Netherlands.[47] The picture (Fig. 21) records St. Willibrord's destruction of a sanctuary dedicated to Woden, an episode found for the first time in Alcuin's *Vita sancti Willibrordi*, chapter 14,[48] but recounted numerous times in Dutch history books. In the foreground we see the missionary instructing a group of recent converts to demolish an idol of Woden which is a replica of Verstegen's engraving. One can hardly think of a better illustration of Richard Verstegen's long-lasting impact on the popular perception of Germanic paganism.

Verstegen's polemic Dutch remake of the *Restitvtion* in 1613 may give us a clue to the deeper motives that underlay the writing of this book. Is the *Restitvtion* really a non-religious work, as Petti wants us to believe?[49] Verstegen's prominent role in the Roman Catholic attempts to turn the tables in England to Rome's advantage should not be underestimated. By 1593 he had received special permission from the Jesuit headquarters in Rome to read "heretical books."[50] Verstegen knew all too well what to do with the fruit of his reading:

---

[47]Kok (1785–96), XXXIV, plate II, facing p. 112.

[48]See Krusch and Levison (1920), 128. Alcuin's original account speaks only of the destruction of an idol, without identifying it as an image of Woden.

[49]See Petti's *New Catholic Encyclopedia* article (cited in n. 9 above).

[50]See Rombauts (1933), 66–67.

HET AFGODSBEELD WODAN te WESTKAPPEL., door
WILLEBRORD, VERBRĲZELD.

Figure 21. St. Willibrord orders the destruction of an idol of Woden,
from Jacobus Kok's *Vaderlandsch Woordenboek* (1785–96), XXXIV,
plate II, facing p. 112.

me thinckes I could oute of sundry our late Englishe hereticall books (for I have licence to read them as also others) drawe foorthe very espetiall matter to move any indifferent Protestant to become doubtfull of the truthe in either the Puritane or Protestant religion.[51]

As I have now come to see it, the *Restitvtion* is a subtle attempt to show the English in 1605 that their Anglo-Saxon ancestors only gained happiness when they accepted the faith as it was preached by St. Augustine, the man sent by Pope Gregory the Great. Nowhere in the book is there one disparaging remark to be found on the Roman Catholic Church or its representatives. Admittedly, there is also no open praise for the contemporary Church of Rome. Occasionally, though, papal action is mentioned with barely concealed approval, as when Verstegen concludes his discussion of the legal custom of ordeals by having Pope Stephen II "vtterly" abolish "these tirrible kyndes of trials" which had "their beginnings in paganisme, and were not thought fit to bee continewed among Christians" (p. 67). And just as the conversion of the Anglo-Saxons is very much the substance of Bede's *Historia ecclesiastica*, likewise this episode in Anglo-Saxon history plays a pivotal part in chapter 7. Verstegen realized that he had to be brief in his account of the missionaries and their good message of salvation, so he concludes:

> Suche as are desyrous more particularly to vnderstand of the true manner and forme of the religion, and seruice wherevnto this our first christian English king and his people were conuerted, may for their further satisfaction therein haue recours vnto *Venerable Bede*, and all ancient authors that thereof haue written.[52]

---

[51]Letter of 30 April 1593 to Father Robert Persons, S. J., printed in Petti (1959), 142. Verstegen even used Chaucer for his polemics; see Petti (1959), 143 n. 3.

[52]*Restitvtion*, 145–46.

This is as close as Verstegen gets to saying "all these newfangled
Protestant ideas are wrong. Return to the doctrine of the Fathers.
Come back to Rome!" Slightly further down, a marginal summary
draws attention to "The frutes of the conuersion of our ancient
kings." What are these fruits? That "Churches Chappels and Monasteries were erected to the seruice of God," and that "they
buylded Colleges and Schooles for the encrease of learning."
Verstegen notes expressly on page 146 that charters were often
signed with a cross, in all likelihood a hidden allusion to the Act of
1571 which prohibited, on pain of forfeiture of property and exile,
the import of "any token or tokens, thing or things, called by the
name of *Agnus Dei*, or any crosses, pictures, beads, or suchlike vain
and superstitious things from the Bishop or See of Rome."[53] St.
Augustine's deliberations before King Æthelberht of Kent provided
Verstegen with a good excuse to depict monks in action, with
several attributes now banished from England such as a cross with
a banner depicting the crucified Christ flanked by two haloed
figures, most likely St. John and the Virgin Mary (Fig. 22).
Augustine's path to Æthelberht's heart had of course been somewhat paved by the king's Christian wife, who had with her "the
chaste and vertuous Bishop *Luidheard*" (p. 140). The bishop's
chastity, not mentioned by Bede, probably alludes to the state of
celibacy for clergymen, propagated by Rome but rejected by the
Protestants. Whenever Verstegen quotes from the Bible, he does
so in Latin in accordance with Roman Catholic practice; in fact
these are the only passages in that language in the entire book.[54]
No reference is made to the fact that at least the Gospels had been
translated into Anglo-Saxon, although Verstegen must have been
aware of John Foxe's edition of 1571. Such information

---

[53]See Tanner (1930), 149.

[54]Biblical quotations in Latin occur, e.g., on pp. 8, 95, and 96 and are sometimes
provided with a translation. The Roman Catholic Doway version of the Vulgate
had not yet appeared.

Figure 22. St. Augustine of Canterbury preaches
before King Æthelberht of Kent, from Verstegen's
Restitvtion, p. 144.

apparently had to be suppressed. And the only time Verstegen
mentions Martin Luther is to expose the Reformer's ignorance in
claiming that England was a part of Germany: "but heerof he
makes his own fancie his author, for other author of more
antiquitie then himself hee can fynd none" (p. 156).[55] So much for
Luther!

    In short, it is true that *A Restitvtion of Decayed Intelligence* is
Verstegen's only really scholarly work—indeed it displays his

---

[55]In the margin, Verstegen refers to "Io. Aurifaber in Luthers Tyschreden,"
undoubtedly one of the "heretical books" Verstegen was allowed to read, cf.
p. 167 and n. 50 above.

wide-ranging reading and critical attitude.[56] We sense in his account of the historical and linguistic past of Anglo-Saxon England an engagement with contemporary political and scholarly concerns that has long since disappeared from the discipline.[57] At the same time, the book reveals at another level a subtle discourse of Counter-Reformation propaganda. Strangely enough, this polemic aspect of the *Restitvtion* has been overlooked until now.[58] As a distant mirror, a reading of the book may help us to put the "objectivity" of our own work on Anglo-Saxon paganism into a proper perspective.

---

[56]That Verstegen contemplated an augmented second edition shows his continuing interest in the subject. He was eager to know what Sir Robert Cotton would think of such an undertaking; see his letter to Sir Robert of 6 October 1617, printed in Petti (1959), 268–69.

[57]Compare Frantzen (1990), ch. 2: "Origins, Orientalism, and Anglo-Saxonism in the Sixteenth and Nineteenth Centuries."

[58]The work is not listed by Allison and Rogers (1989–94).

WILLIAM L'ISLE AND THE EDITING OF OLD ENGLISH

Phillip Pulsiano (†)

William L'Isle (1569?–1637), one-time Fellow of King's College, Cambridge, and "Esquire to the King's Body" under James I, occupies a modest place in the history of antiquarian studies in England. His career as a scholar and writer reflects a diversity of interests and includes a partial translation of Salluste du Bartas's biblical epic *La Seconde Semaine* under the title *Babilon, a Part of the Seconde Weeke* (1596),[1] which was followed by the more extensive *Part of Dv Bartas* (1625),[2] a translation of Heliodorus's *Aethiopica* under the title *The Faire Æthiopian* (1631),[3] and a translation of Virgil's *Eclogues*

---

[1] *Babilon, a Part of the Seconde Weeke of Guillavme de Saluste Seignevr dv Bartas, with the Commentarie, and Marginall Notes of S. G. S., Englished by William L'Isle* (London, 1596). The work is a rendering of the story of Genesis 2–11, in which periods of scriptural history are treated as days.

[2] *Part of Dv Bartas, English and French, and in His Owne Kinde of Verse, So Neare the French Englished, As May Teach an English-Man French, or a French-Man English* (London, 1625). The edition was reissued in 1637 as a remainder under the title *Fovre Bookes of Du Bartas*.

[3] *The Faire Æthiopian. Dedicated to the King and Qveene* (London, 1631); reprinted under the title *The Famovs Historie of Heliodorvs. Amplified, Avgmented, and Delivered Paraphrastically in Verse* (London, 1638). The 1638 remainder issue (with an *imprimatur* of 30 January 1637, i.e., 1638 New Style)

173

(1628).[4] L'Isle was also the author of some second-rate verse, including "Nothing for a New-Yeares Gift"[5] and "The Effects Proceeding from Nothing," two Latin poems in Michael Dalton's

---

adds two pages of testimonies, a four-page summary of the work, and a four-page list of the contents of each of the ten books into which the work is divided; see Dickins (1947–48), 54. Earlier excerpts (six pages) in English by Abraham Fraunce were published under the title "The beginning of Heliodorus his Æthiopical History" as signature M of *The Countess of Pembrokes Yuychurch. Conteining the Affectionate Life, and Vnfortunate Death of Phillis and Amyntas: That in a Pastorall: This in a Funerall: Both in English Hexameters* (London, 1591); an English prose translation (perhaps by Thomas Underdowne) of the whole work was published in London in 1622 under the title *Heliodorvs His Æthiopian History*. In a letter of 16 March 1630 to Sir Robert Cotton (BL MS Cotton Julius C. iii, fol. 242r), L'Isle wrote: "The Faire Æthiopian, now almost ready for the presse, in forme of an Heroïck English poëme, longs to be lookt-vpon by the ladyes that readde her Historye with you in frenche prose. Such is my studye somtymes to refresh my sadder Muses: And this worke I know the printers will readily entertain, while the Saxon Bible & Chronicles lye dead by me." For references to L'Isle's letters and his connection with Cotton, see Sharpe (1979), 34–35, 58, 62, 75, and 219.

[4]*Virgils Eclogves Translated into English* (London, 1628). Here L'Isle states (p. 17) that "I used the freedome of a Translator, not tying my selfe to the tyranny of a Grammaticall Construction, but breaking the shell into many peeces, was onely carefull to preserue the kernell safe and whole, from the violence of a wrong, or wrested Interpretation." The translation incorporates words that L'Isle learned in the course of his study of Old English, for example: *Siker*, "an old *Saxon* word; as much as verily, or surely" (p. 16); *Sibb*, "an old *Saxon* word, as much as kinred or alliance: from hence coms our word Gossip; corruptly so written and spoken; it being indeede, God-sib: that is, a kinred in God . . ." (p. 17).

[5](London, 1603); also included (together with *The Effects Proceeding from Nothing*) in *Fugitive Tracts Written in Verse Which Illustrate the Condition of Religious and Political Feeling in England and the State of Society There during Two Centuries, Second Series: 1600–1700* (London, 1875), tract 5.

The Covntry Ivstice,[6] a number of dedicatory verses, and, least of all, a verse inscription on the tombstone of his cousin William Benson.[7] Anglo-Saxonists are perhaps most familiar with the work of L'Isle through his *A Saxon Treatise Concerning the Old and New Testament*,[8] in the preface of which he offers an absorbing account of his program of study for learning Old English, describing how he first immersed himself in works by Gavin Douglas, Marquard Freher, John Caius, John Foxe, William Camden, and others. The method outlined by L'Isle in this preface has often been cited as shedding light on antiquarian studies in the seventeenth century, but when it comes to tracing the application of this program in L'Isle's single publication in the field of Anglo-Saxon studies, the work and its preface prove less informative than one would like, so that for additional insights one must turn to L'Isle's unpublished transcripts and notes. One thus acknowledges the significance of his transcriptions in Bodleian MS Laud Misc.

---

[6]Michael Dalton, *The Country Ivstice, Containing the Practice of the Ivstices of the Peace out of Their Sessions. Gathered, for the Better Helpe of Such Iustices of Peace as Haue Not Been Much Conuersant in the Studie of the Lawes of This Realme* (London, 1618; rev. ed. 1619).

[7]See *DNB* s.n. "Lisle."

[8](London, 1623). In 1638 the book was printed as a remainder issue under the title *Divers Ancient Monvments in the Saxon Tongue: Written Seven Hundred Yeares Agoe. Shewing That Both in the Old and New Testament, the Lords Prayer, and the Creede, Were Then Used in the Mother Tongue: And Also, What Opinion was Then Held of the Sacrament of the Body and Blood of Christ* (London, 1638). L'Isle's Old English text and English translation of Ælfric's letter to Sigeweard on the Old and New Testaments are included in Crawford (1922), 15–75; but Crawford did not incorporate L'Isle's thirty-six stanza dedicatory poem "imitating the fourth [Eclogue] of Virgil," or his well-known preface to the book. Excerpts from the preface are printed in Appendix II of Adams (1917); and a passage from the preface is quoted in Murphy (1968), 346.

381,[9] or his notes interleaved in MS Laud Misc. 636 (the Peterborough Chronicle) and his annotations in BL MS Cotton Otho B. xi (which contains copies of the Old English Bede, the Anglo-Saxon Chronicle, and laws), although nowhere have these annotations been quoted or reproduced. Or, finally, one might light upon an unstudied, little known, edition and translation in his own hand of the Old English translation of the Psalms in the Eadwine Psalter (TCC MS R. 17. 1).[10] Completed in draft in 1630, and contained in Bodleian MS Laud Misc. 201, this stands as the first edition and translation of an Old English psalter to be produced—a full ten years before John Spelman's edition of BL MS Stowe 2[11]— and the first to collate a number of other glossed psalters. It contains as well a fair number of annotations that pertain to the translation itself or that supply commentary. The transcription and especially the translation show that the work proceeded through various stages before reaching completion. It thereby becomes possible to understand in greater detail L'Isle's methods of work, the types of problems that he faced, and the varieties of solutions at which he arrived. Method, then, only sketchily outlined in his *A Saxon Treatise*, is here accorded concrete application, and the result is a fuller and more interesting perspective on L'Isle's work as an Anglo-Saxonist.

---

[9]On which see the paper by Stuart Lee in the present volume.

[10]Notices of this edition are few. See Bennett (1938), Appendix A, 311–12; and Sisam and Sisam (1959), 1 n. 2. Adams (1917) lists the work along with L'Isle's other transcripts in a footnote (p. 46 n. 2); similar brief reference is made in the *DNB* entry on L'Isle. See also Pulsiano (1991), 89 and 92 n. 19; and Pulsiano (1989), 40. The most recent notice of L'Isle's edition appears in McKitterick (1992), 197–98. I am grateful to Prof. J. R. Hall for the reference to Bennett's dissertation.

[11]*Psalterium Davidis Latino-Saxonicum vetus* (London, 1640).

In his discussion of methods in the study of Old English in the sixteenth and seventeenth centuries, Michael Murphy referred briefly to the preface of *A Saxon Treatise* as providing an account of how "earlier students acquired their knowledge of the language."[12] This same view was earlier expressed by Eleanor Adams in her study *Old English Scholarship in England from 1566–1800*, where she wrote:

> [The preface] gives an account of how an early student gained some knowledge of the language without the aid of grammars or dictionaries. First he [i.e., L'Isle] acquainted himself with High and Low Dutch; then he began to read all the books and manuscripts he could find in archaic English, observing that the older they were, the nearer they seemed to approach the 'Saxon'. In the course of this reading he came upon Gavin Douglas' Scottish translation of Virgil. He found it very difficult, but mastered it by the help of the Latin. Next he read the work of Freher. So far, he had not attempted anything in the Anglo-Saxon character, of which he made some study before undertaking *A Testimonie*, the *Fower Gospels*, and such scraps of Old English as he could find in print, or in old charters and record-books. Being then able, as he says, 'to swim without bladders', he began to investigate the manuscript collections of Cotton, Spelman, and Cambridge University.[13]

L'Isle's own account is more detailed. He began, he says, with studying High and Low Dutch:

> But the Saxon, (as a bird, flying in the aire farther and farther, seemes lesse and lesse;) the older it was, became harder to bee vnderstood. At length I lighted on *Virgil* Scotished by the Reuerend *Gawin Dowglas* Bishop of *Dunkell*, and vncle to the Earle of *Angus*; the best translation of that Poet that euer I read: And though I found that dialect more hard than any of the former (as neerer the Saxon, because farther from the

---

[12]Murphy (1968), 347.

[13]Adams (1917), 46.

Norman) yet with helpe of the Latine I made shift to vnderstand it, and read the booke more than once from the beginning to the end. Wherby I must confesse I got more knowledge of that I sought than by any of the other. . . . Next then I read the decalogue &c. set out by *Fraerus* in common character, and so prepared came to the proper Saxon; which differeth but in seuen or eight letters from the Pica Roman: and therein reading certaine Sermons, and the foure Euangelists set out and Englished by M^r. *Fox*, so increased my skill, that at length (I thanke God) I found my selfe able (as it were to swimme without bladders) to vnderstand the vntranslated fragments of the tongue scattered in Master *Cambden* and others, by him some, and some by Sir *Henry Savill* set forth: as also those in *Tho:* of *Walsingham*, *Caius*, and *Lambard*; with certaine old charters that I met with among the Kings Records, and in the Coucher-bookes of Monasteries; Yet still ventring not far from the shore. At last waxing more able through vse, I tooke heart to put forth and diue into the deep among the meere Saxon monuments of my worthily respected kinsman Sir *H. Spelman*, my honorable friend Sir *Rob. Cotton*, & of our Libraries in Cambridge. So far about went I for want of a guide, who now (thanks be to God) am able to lead others a neerer way.[14]

L'Isle's course of study thus comprised, as he tells us, Gavin Douglas's translation of the *Aeneid*,[15] Marquard Freher's *Decalogi*,[16] John Foxe's edition of the Old English Gospels,[17]

---

[14]*A Saxon Treatise*, sigs. c4^v–d1^r.

[15]*The .XIII. Bukes of Eneados of the Famose Poete Virgill Translated out of Latyne Verses into Scottish Metir* (London, 1553).

[16]*Decalogi orationis symboli Saxonica versio vetustissima* ([Heidelberg,] 1610).

[17]*The Gospels of the Fower Euangelistes, Translated in the Old Saxons Tyme out of Latin into the Vulgare Toung of the Saxons, Newly Collected out of Auncient Monuments of the Sayd Saxons and Now Published for Testimonie of the Same* (London, 1571).

William Camden's *Remaines*,[18] Henry Savile's *Rervm Anglicarvm scriptores*,[19] Thomas Walsingham's *Historia breuis*,[20] John Caius's *De antiquitate Cantabrigiensis*,[21] and William Lambarde's *Archaionomia*,[22] ending up with Anglo-Saxon manuscripts owned

---

[18]*Remaines of a Greater Worke, Concerning Britaine, the Inhabitants Thereof, Their Languages, Names, Surnames, Empreses, Wise Speeches, Poësies, and Epitaphes* (London, 1605), which includes (pp. 15–16) an edition and translation into English of the Old English version of the Lord's Prayer, with notes. L'Isle may also have read Camden's *Britannia* . . . (London, 1586), but that work contains no Old English.

[19]*Rervm Anglicarvm scriptores post Bedam praecipvi ex vetvstissimis codicibus manvscriptis nvnc primvm in lvcem editi* (London, 1596). The work contains, e.g., chronicles of William of Malmesbury, Henry of Huntingdon, and Æthelweard.

[20]*Historia breuis Thomæ Walsingham, ab Edwardo primo, ad Henricum quintum* (London, 1574), published by Matthew Parker and bound with Parker's edition of Asser's life of King Alfred printed in Anglo-Saxon type. On pp. 41–44, following Asser's text, is an edition, with accompanying English and Latin translations, of the prose and verse prefaces to Alfred's Old English translation of the *Regula pastoralis* of Pope Gregory the Great. Asser's *Life* and the *Pastoral Care* material are reprinted in William Camden's *Anglica, Hibernica, Normannica, Cambrica, a veteribus scripta* (Frankfurt, 1602), although a running header (*Asservs de Ælfredi*) is added, and the book does not use an Anglo-Saxon typeface. The transcriptions of the Old English material are often botched, with letters misread (for example, "sitan" for "witan" of the 1574 edition), incorrect word separation (for example, "huge sæloglica"), and the transliteration of þ and ð by **th**.

[21]*De antiquitate Cantabrigiensis academiæ libri duo* (London, 1568), which contains scattered words and excerpts in Old English with Latin translations.

[22]*Archaionomia, sive de priscis Anglorum legibus libri, sermone Anglico, vetustate antiquissimo, aliquot abhinc seculis conscripti, atque nunc demum, magno iurisperitorum, & amantium antiquitatis omnium commodo, è tenebris in lucem vocati* (London, 1568); the edition contains the laws in Anglo-Saxon type with facing-page Latin translation. L'Isle would also have had access to Lambarde's *A Perambulation of Kent: Conteining the Description, Hystorie, and*

by his friends and contemporaries Henry Spelman and Robert Cotton, and by libraries at Cambridge University. L'Isle makes no specific mention of Matthew Parker's *A Testimonie of Antiqvitie*,[23] the first printed edition of Old English texts, but it is likely that his unspecific reference to "certaine Sermons" is an allusion to *A Testimonie*, in which the principal item is one of Ælfric's sermons for Easter Day. L'Isle included a complete reprint of *A Testimonie* at the end of his *A Saxon Treatise*.

To modern students of Old English, L'Isle's list of works may seem to be a hodgepodge. His twice-repeated thanks to God, however, may take on added force when we consider the tools his predecessors left him in the study of Old English. The *Aeneid* "Scotished" would have benefited L'Isle little, if at all, in his studies. Freher's *Decalogi* would have provided him with the Old English texts of the Ten Commandments, the Creed, and the Lord's Prayer, accompanied by twelve pages of Latin notes that include Latin equivalents of Old English terms (for example, "Wylne: Ancilla, serva"; "Cuma: Hospes, advena, peregrinus"); Caius's *De antiquitate Cantabrigiensis*, Camden's *Remaines*, Lambarde's *A Perambulation of Kent*, Savile's *Rervm Anglicarvm scriptores*, and Walsingham's *Historia breuis* would have provided only moderate instruction in the language, since in these works the Old English material is confined to scattered words and brief excerpts. However, following Asser's life of King Alfred bound with the Walsingham edition is the Old English preface to King Alfred's translation of Pope Gregory the Great's *Regula*

Customes of That Shyre (London, 1576), in which individual sections devoted to particular towns begin with a discussion of the place name, citing words and passages in Old English, with English translations.

[23]*A Testimonie of Antiqvitie, Shewing the Auncient Fayth in the Church of England Touching the Sacrament of the Body and Bloude of the Lord Here Publikely Preached, and Also Receaued in the Saxons Tyme, Aboue 600. Yeares Agoe* (London, 1566).

pastoralis, together with an interlinear English translation, and in Camden's *Remaines* is a fourteen-page section entitled "The Languages," in which the Old English version of the Lord's Prayer is given with an interlinear English translation. Lambarde's *Archaionomia* would certainly stand among the more immediately useful works L'Isle could have consulted in his study of the language, since it contains the laws with a facing-page Latin translation. More important, Foxe's edition of the Gospels would have provided a rich and instructive resource, not only for the study of Old English but also for Anglican polemic, which, as Theodore H. Leinbaugh has shown, informed the Parkerian translation of Ælfric's Easter Day sermon in Parker's *A Testimonie of Antiqvitie*.[24] Foxe would also have provided L'Isle with a clear rationale for the study of Old English. Foxe wrote in his preface:

> Some againe haue iudged our natiue tounge vnmeete to expresse Gods high secret mysteries, being so barbarous & imperfecte a language as they say it is. As though the holy spirite of truth mente by his appearing in clouen tounges, to debarre any nation, or any tounge, from vttering forth the magnificent maiestie of Gods miraculous workes. . . . Onely as touching this our Realme of *England*, if any shall doubt of the auncient vsage therof, whether they had the Scriptures in their language of old time, here he may haue a proofe of so much translated into our old *Englishe* tounge, the diuers translations wherof, and in diuers ages, be yet extant to be seene, as well long before the Conquest, as since, written and translated both of Kinges and Bishops, and so recorded in deedes of their donations amongest such bookes as they gaue to diuerse Churches. We haue in olde histories seene written before the Conquest that our countreyman *Bede* did translate the whole Bible in the *Saxon* tounge.[25]

---

[24] See Leinbaugh (1982).

[25] *The Gospels of the Fower Euangelistes*, sigs. Aii^v–Aiii^r.

And further:

> Albeit in some cases the same may serue to no small good steede,
> namely in courtes, & for them that be learned in the lawes, wherby
> they may more readily vnderstand many of their olde wordes &
> termes, also very many deedes and Charters of Princes giftes, and
> foundations geuen to the Church, and to Byshops Seas, and other
> ecclesiasticall foundations, wherin are to be seene and proued the old
> auncient boundes, & limites of townes, of commons, of woods, of
> riuers, of fieldes, & other such matters belonging to the same.[26]

The import of these two passages is reflected in L'Isle's own
preface to his *A Saxon Treatise*. In discussing the need to continue
in the study of Old English, he writes:

> If you aske mee to what purpose, I answer, first to know and make
> knowne to the world, that, howsoeuer the Scripture in vulgar hath
> beene since debarred; yet our Saxon Ancestors had both this and other
> bookes of Diuinity in the mother tongue; and to note in what sort it was
> then translated. Secondly, the memory and knowledge thereof serues
> well to finde out, when need is, the Etymologies and roots of our
> words and names now vsed. . . . A third vse of this knowledge is, to
> vnderstand the right meaning of our old lawes, which often giue light
> to the new. . . . A fourth vse thereof is that we may be able to declare
> vnto all men, whom it concernes, the true meaning of their titles,
> charters, priuiledges, territories and precincts, comparing with the
> nature of each thing, the name thereof so fitted, as the one to this day
> plainly points out the other.[27]

L'Isle's position, in fact, is announced formally in the full title to
his work:

---

[26] *The Gospels of the Fower Euangelistes*, sig. ¶ii[r].

[27] *A Saxon Treatise*, sigs. f1[v]–f2[r].

A Saxon Treatise Concerning the Old and New Testament. Written abovt the time of King Edgar (700 yeares agoe) by Ælfricvs Abbas, thought to be the same that was afterward Archbishop of Canterbvrie. Whereby appeares what was the Canon of holy Scripture here then receiued, and that the Church of England had it so long agoe in her Mother-tongue. Now first pvblished in print with English of our times, by William L'Isle of Wilbvrgham, Esquier for the Kings Bodie: The Originall remaining still to be seene in Sʳ Robert Cottons Librarie, at the end of his lesser Copie of the Saxon Pentatevch. And herevnto is added ovt of the Homilies and Epistles of the fore-said Ælfricvs, a second Edition of *A Testimonie of Antiqvitie, &c. touching the Sacrament of the Bodie and Bloud of the Lord, here publikely preached and receiued in the Saxons time, &c.*

And it is one that finds similar representation in the title that he wrote at the front of his edition of the Old English text of the Eadwine Psalter completed seven years later: "The Saxon-English Psalter, To preserue the memory of our mother Churche & Language, & to further the studye of our Antiquityes & Lawes."[28]

---

[28]Bodleian MS Laud Misc. 201, fol. 1r. The full title continues as follows: "Out of Manuscrpts most auncient remaining styll in the vniuersity-library, & that of Trinitye and Corpus Christi Colledge in Cambridge, Taken *and* fytted with the phrase of our tyme; not as a new English translation, but as the ouldest of all, to th'aforesaid end, renewed & made known." This title page bears the *imprimatur* of Henry Butts, Vice-Chancellor of Cambridge University, dated 3 December 1630. More pointed, perhaps, is the title page in Bodleian MS Laud Misc. 381, which contains L'Isle's transcriptions and translations of Old Testament material in Old English: "Saxon-english Remaines of the Pentateuch, Iosua, Iudges, &ct. Job &c out of Sʳ. Robert Cottons Manuscripts, of most reuerend antiquity now first new-englished & set-out by W. L." Various versions of a continuation of this title have been crossed out. Of these, the final version appears to have been: "To manifest unto the worlde how long since the Scriptures haue ben in English; and to preserue the memory of that ancient Dialect, which shewes the Roots & grounds of our ["now spoken English" crossed out] mother-toong." On the implications of this title page for L'Isle's intentions to publish, see the paper by Stuart Lee in the present volume.

While the works listed by L'Isle would have provided him with a sound enough course to follow in his studies—although the route outlined is certainly one that, by modern standards, is as arduous as it is circuitous—and while he made use of all the best published works available to him, the real test of his skill and his progress in the study of Old English came in his work directly based on original manuscripts, for it is in this area that his preparatory work, announced so concisely in his *A Saxon Treatise*, finds its challenge and its fullest application.

L'Isle's antiquarian and doctrinal interests led him to work directly with a range of original manuscripts, including BL MS Cotton Claudius B. iv and Bodleian MS Laud Misc. 509 for his projected edition of the Heptateuch;[29] BL MS Cotton Otho B. xi[30] and CCCC MS 173 (the Parker Chronicle), which L'Isle collated

---

[29]For L'Isle's work on these two manuscripts, see Graham (2000), 293–313. L'Isle's borrowing of the two manuscripts, which at the time both belonged to Cotton, and also of MS Cotton Otho B. xi, is recorded in Cotton's loan notes in BL MS Harley 6018, fol. 148v, within Cotton's "note of such Books as I hau befor this 23 Aprill 1621 lent out of my study": "Liber Genesis et pentatucha Saxonicæ bound with my armes and claspes in 4to" (= MS Laud Misc. 509); "Bedæ Historiæ et Chronicon Saxonice. bound in lether and clasps in Foll" (= MS Otho B. xi); "Genises [*sic*] Saxonicæ in picturis bound in lether and clasps Foll" (= MS Claudius B. iv). See also fol. 151r, where a list headed "The names of such as I hav lent books too" includes "Mr Leil of Cambridg Genesis. Beda. Saxon." References to other loans can be found in L'Isle's letters to Cotton contained in BL MS Cotton Julius C. iii, fols. 238, 239, 243, and 244, which offer a picture of active exchange between these two scholars. In one (damaged) letter of 1622 (fol. 240), L'Isle requests that Cotton give him a book: "Yet yf yt please you . . . bestow on me one of the book*es* I have, wherof you [h]ave another *and* fayrer Copy (else I would not desire yt [f]rom you) . . . I pray [y]ou, yf loving the Saxon as I doe, *and* having not a booke of myne owne, I make so bould a request . . . " (discussed further in Graham [2000], 289–90).

[30]This manuscript was badly damaged in the Cotton fire of 1731. Three of its leaves are now misplaced as MS Otho B. x, fols. 55, 58, and 62. A fourth leaf, removed before the fire, is now BL MS Add. 34652, fol. 2.

with Bodleian MS Laud Misc. 636 (the Peterborough Chronicle, which he owned), in connection with his studies of the Anglo-Saxon Chronicle;[31] TCC MS R. 17. 1 (the Eadwine Psalter), which he collated with BL MS Arundel 60 (the Arundel Psalter), MS Stowe 2 (the Stowe Psalter), and CUL MS Ff. 1. 23 (the Cambridge Psalter);[32] CCCC MS 402 (the *Ancrene Wisse*), passages of which L'Isle transcribed into MS Laud Misc. 381; and various manuscripts containing homilies in the Cambridge University Library and the libraries of Corpus Christi and Trinity Colleges in Cambridge, particularly CCCC MS 162, numerous extracts from which also appear in MS Laud Misc. 381.[33] The manuscript that was the source for L'Isle's transcription of the homily *Be Hester* on fols. 140v–147v of MS Laud Misc. 381 has apparently not survived.[34] Undoubtedly there were more manuscripts that L'Isle consulted, especially since he had evidently prepared an Old English lexicon, now lost, which, in a letter to Sir Simonds D'Ewes, Sir William Boswell mentions as being ready for publication.[35] L'Isle's letter to Henry Spelman dated 1 April

---

[31]In his notes in the Peterborough Chronicle, L'Isle identifies MS Otho B. xi and CCCC MS 173 respectively as "Cottonianus" and "Benet" or "Cantuariensis" ("Benet College" being a former alternative name for Corpus Christi College, and MS 173 being of Canterbury provenance).

[32]See also L'Isle's letter to Robert Cotton of 4 June 1622 (BL MS Cotton Julius C. iii, fol. 239r): "I can say no more yet, vntyll I see your psalmes; bycause I haue already taken the paines to compare foure or five such copies together; &, noting the diuers readings in margent, written-out the whole book with my own hand; & lastly so translated yt to the word; that, when yt comes foorth, yt may helpe well to, yf not stand instead-of a Saxon Dictionary."

[33]For more information about the homily manuscripts consulted by L'Isle for his transcriptions in MS Laud Misc. 381, see the paper by Stuart Lee below.

[34]The homily is edited in Assmann (1889), 92–101.

[35]"I should long ere this have sent you a Transcript of the Saxon Vocabularie, you had once of mee; but that it is collected only out of the four Evangelists, and one or two other small things, printed in that tongue; and farr short of a

1636 shows that L'Isle also had an interest in the laws; his mention of an earlier letter to Spelman, "enclosing those Saxon Lawes," may allude to work he had done on MS Otho B. xi, which includes a copy of the laws.[36] As his notes in the original manuscripts and as his transcriptions show, L'Isle engaged the texts as a serious editor, scholar, and translator. His transcriptions, in particular, provide valuable insight into his working methods.

Bodleian MS Laud Misc. 381 contains two principal sections following L'Isle's title page headed "Saxon-english Remaines of the Pentateuch, Iosua, Iudges, &ct."[37] The first section, fols. 2v–

Dictionarie with (our honorable frend) S[r] Thomas Cotton, made by Jocelinis . . . and one of another Dictionarie, which I did think Mr. Lisle of the Isle of Ely (whom I think you know to be extraordinarily skilfull in that language), would have printed long since, of his owne gathering." The letter, dated 18 December 1636, is printed in Ellis (1843), 152. In a letter to Robert Cotton of 16 March 1630 (BL MS Cotton Julius C. iii, fol. 242), L'Isle wrote, "Yet, for the Dictionarye of that Dialect; which you know how great & learned men desire me to set-out; that, which Archimedes did in prose, let me answer in verse. . . . A Dictionarye is a Theater of the whole worlde."

[36]The letter of 1 April 1636 is Bodleian MS Tanner 70, fol. 86rv. In it L'Isle discusses Spelman's translation, in material he had communicated to L'Isle, of *cwen* as *concubina*. L'Isle notes that "I nev*er* readde" the word "in so bad a sense." He suggests *uxor, matrona,* or *femina* as alternative meanings.

[37]The manuscript includes various foliations, four in ink by L'Isle applying to specific sections, and one in pencil (not by L'Isle, but in a hand that foliated other manuscripts in the Laudian collection in the Bodleian) spanning the whole manuscript. It is the latter foliation that is cited here. The first of L'Isle's foliations consists of the letters "A" through "C" entered in the top left corners of fols. 2–4, which carry his translation of Ælfric's *Preface to Genesis*. The second foliation, beginning with "1" entered centrally in the upper margin of fol. 4v, marks the page on which begins L'Isle's translation of the Old English Hexateuch and Ælfric's homily on Judges. This foliation continues on rectos until "113" on fol. 116r, on which ends L'Isle's translation of the Judges homily. The third foliation begins with "1" in the top corner of fol. 116v, on which begin L'Isle's excerpts from homilies. This foliation is entered consistently in the top

116r, comprises L'Isle's translation of Ælfric's *Preface to Genesis*, of the Old English version of the Hexateuch, and of Ælfric's homily on Judges.[38] The second section (fols. 116v–169r) includes L'Isle's transcriptions and facing-page translations of biblical material that he found in Old English homilies and in the Middle English *Ancrene Wisse*.[39] He provided this section with its own title on fol. 116v: "More of the Ould Testament quoted in the Saxon Homilies which are entitled in Latine Catholici Sermones: & Translated into this ould English by Ælfricus Abbas." The extracts that L'Isle compiled in this part of the manuscript vary greatly in length, from a single line or so in several cases to virtually complete transcripts of Ælfric's homilies on Esther (fols. 140v–147v) and Job (fols. 154r–159r). L'Isle's guiding principle for this section was to excerpt from the texts that he studied those portions that translated or paraphrased passages of the Old Testament.

It is L'Isle's handling of the material from the *Ancrene Wisse* that stands as most interesting with regard to assessing his work as an editor. L'Isle extracts forty-five passages from the Middle English work, usually giving an indication in the margin of the

---

left corners of versos up until "13" on fol. 128v. The numbers "14" through "19" are then entered on every second leaf (fols. 129–40), and thereafter L'Isle's numbering is only sporadic ("29" on fol. 150v, "32" on fol. 153v, and "38" on fol. 159v). A fourth foliation, consisting of the Greek letters "α" through "ε" entered in the top left corner of every second recto between fols. 160r and 168r, marks the section that L'Isle has entitled on fol. 159v, "Prophesies of Christe Applyed by The Saxon Homilist," this section again consisting of biblical excerpts from Old English homilies.

[38]For an edition of the Old English text translated by L'Isle, see Crawford (1922).

[39]L'Isle used the copy of the *Ancrene Wisse* in CCCC MS 402. The text of MS 402 is edited in Tolkien (1962), with an introduction by N. R. Ker. Neither Ker nor Tolkien was aware that many of the added markings throughout the manuscript are in L'Isle's hand.

biblical source (L'Isle typically provides a reference only to the particular book of the Bible, but in a number of citations also offers specific chapter numbers).[40] In nearly all cases, L'Isle's transcription shows minor, but not unimportant, variation, such as at fol. 135v5–6, where he writes "Aris up hihe þe heonewart Ᵹ cum to me my leofmon my culfre mine feire Ᵹ mine schene spuse," where the original manuscript reads "Aris up. hihe þe heonewart. Ᵹ cum to me mi leofmon. Mi culure. mi feire. Ᵹ mi schene spuse."[41] At fol. 136v13, L'Isle writes "Mine men sceallon eatan Ᵹ eow sceall æfre hingrian," where the manuscript reads "Mine men schulen eoten Ᵹ ow schal eauer hungrin."[42] Here and elsewhere, L'Isle was consciously revising his source text in the direction of Old English.

This process of revision can be examined most fully in a number of examples in which L'Isle departs from his manuscript source. At fol. 135v2–4, L'Isle transcribes a passage based on the Song of Solomon:

> Locað nu hu se leafdig godes deore spuse leareð eow by hire sahe hu ge sculen secgen. ic gehyre mine leof sprecende he cleopeð me. ic mot gan.

The source text offers a different version that incorporates part of the Latin text for reference:

[40]For a full listing of L'Isle's transcriptions from the *Ancrene Wisse*, see the table at the end of Stuart Lee's paper below.

[41]Tolkien (1962), 52 (fol. 25b/24–26): "Rise up, hurry from there, and come to me, my beloved, my dove, my fair one, my beautiful bride" (Song of Solomon 2:10). In his transcription, L'Isle first wrote "mi leofmon," then altered "mi" to "my."

[42]Tolkien (1962), 111 (fol. 58a/18–19): "My servants will eat, and you will always be hungry" (Isaiah 65:13).

Lokið nu hu propreliche þe leafdi i canticis godes deore spuse leareð
ow bi hire sahe hu ge schule seggen. En dilectus meus loquitur michi.
Surge propera amica mea ꝉ cetera. low ha seið hercne. Ic ihere mi leof
speoken. he cleopeð me ich mot gan.[43]

Here, in addition to modifying the language, L'Isle edits the text,
deleting "propreliche," the Latin text, and the introductory remark
"low ha seið hercne." In the following excerpt from fols. 136v32–
137v4, L'Isle's facility with rendering the Middle English text into
Old English is apparent. The text of the *Ancrene Wisse* reads:

> Ne beo ge nawt offearede. ne drede ge ham nawiht þah ha beon stronge
> ꝉ monie; þe feht is min; nawt ower. Sulement stondeð sikerliche ꝉ ge
> schulen mí sucurs. habbeð ane to me trusti bileaue; ꝉ ge beoð al
> sikere.[44]

In sharp contrast, L'Isle renders the passage as:

> ne beo ge nawht afearede. ne drede ge þam nawht. þeah hi beon strong
> ꝉ monige. se feoht is min. nawht eowres. stondaþ ge sicerlice ꝉ ge
> sceallen min fultum habban. ane to me trust ge. geleafe ge ꝉ ge beoð
> eall sikere.

An additional example in which L'Isle shows his editorial
method is found at fol. 135v21–23, where he heavily abbreviates

---

[43]Tolkien (1962), 52 (fol. 25b/16–20): "See now how fittingly the lady in the
Song of Solomon, God's dear bride, teaches you by her words how you should
speak. 'En dilectus meus loquitur michi. Surge propera amica mea,' etc. [Song
of Solomon 2:10]. 'Hark!' she says, 'listen! I hear my beloved speak. He calls
me, I must go.'"

[44]Tolkien (1962), 137 (fol. 72b/21–25): "Do not be frightened, do not be in any
way afraid of them though they are strong and many. The battle is mine, not
yours. Just stand with full certainty and you will have my help. Only have firm
faith in me, and you will be completely safe" (cf. 2 Chronicles 20:15–17).

the corresponding passage in the source. The manuscript source reads:

> þe eadi Ieremie seið he sit ane. ⁊ seið þe reisun for hwi. Quia comminatione tua replesti me. Vre lauerd hefde ifullet him of his þrea-tunge. Godes þreatunge is wontreaðe ⁊ weane i licome ⁊ i sawle. worlt buten ende. þe were of þis þreatunge as he wes wel ifullet; nere þer nan empti stude i þe heorte to underfon fleschliche lahtren. for þi he bed wealle of teares. Quis dabit michi fontem lacrimarum? þæt ha ne adruhede neauer namare þen wealle forte biwepe slei folc.[45]

L'Isle's version is:

> Eadig Ieremias segð he sit ane ⁊ secgð for hwi. drihten hæfð gefylled hine of his þreatunge. forþy he bed wealle of teares. þæt heo ne adrywode næfre na mare.

Throughout his transcriptions from the *Ancrene Wisse*, two main principles were at work. L'Isle's interest was specifically in vernacular citations of the Old Testament. He therefore excluded the Latin versions of the scriptural passages, along with most of the accompanying comment by the author of the *Ancrene Wisse*. And he adjusted the language of his Middle English source in an attempt to make it appear more like Old English. All this was in line with his overall purpose in the second main section of MS Laud Misc. 381, which was to compile an anthology of Old Testament quotations in Old English. The facility with Old English that his work

---

[45]Tolkien (1962), 81 (fol. 42a/21–42b/1): "The blessed Jeremiah says that he sits alone, and tells the reason why: 'Quia comminatione tua replesti me' [Jeremiah 15:17]. Our Lord had filled him with his threats. God's threats are misery and grief in body and soul, world without end. If a person were filled with these threats, as he was, he would have no empty place in the heart to receive fleshly laughter; therefore he prayed for a fountain of tears: 'Quis dabit michi fontem lacrimarum?' [Jeremiah 9:1]—that it might nevermore dry up, any more than a well does, so as to weep for those who had been killed."

on the *Ancrene Wisse* reveals suggests that L'Isle may even have developed the ability to compose in Old English.[46]

Elsewhere in MS Laud Misc. 381, L'Isle sprinkles his text with editorial comments. On the first page of his transcription and translation of Ælfric's homily on Job (fols. 153v–159r), for example, he has entered in the margin the comment "Added by the Homilist" alongside a passage of his translation beginning "So stood the devil in gods sight, as doth a blinde man in the su*n*ne. . . ." L'Isle's point is that there is no source for this passage in the biblical book of Job, but that it is Ælfric's interpolation. Further up the page, L'Isle has written the marginal comment "*x*vna translatio dicit filii dei et altera translatio dicit Angeli dei," referring to a marked and underlined word in his translation, "Yt befell one day when gods *x*Angells came *and* stood. . . ." In this case, his comment simply repeats what he found in his source manuscript, CUL MS Gg. 3. 28 (fol. 223v);[47] he incorporates the same comment in his transcription on the facing page (fol. 154r), where he has drawn a box around it, adding the observation "In margi*n*e" and linking it by a pair of crosses to the underlined word "englas" in the next line. On a page containing the text "Be Ionas" (fol. 168r)—text that L'Isle crosses out with a large "X" across the

---

[46]See also the further evidence for this revealed by L'Isle's work in MSS Cotton Claudius B. iv and Laud Misc. 509, discussed in Graham (2000), 296–300.

[47]See Godden (1979), 260, no. XXX, line 19. The comment "Una translatio . . ." does not occur in any other copy of the homily (cf. Godden's apparatus). In MS Gg. 3. 28, it occurs in the main text, not in the margin (where it would more appropriately belong). L'Isle's own note "In margi*n*e" may mean either that he added this note to his transcription later, when he did not have MS Gg. 3. 28 in front of him and was of the erroneous opinion that he must have found the comment in the margin rather than in the main text; or else that his note was an instruction to himself, or his prospective printer, to place the comment in the margin in the edition of the Bible in Old English that he planned.

page, writing "habet*ur* alibi" in the top right margin[48]—he adds variants in the margin to the Old English text: in line 6 he underlines "reohnesse" and writes "unwyder" in the margin, while nine lines further down the page he underlines "seo reohnes" and writes "þæt unwyder." L'Isle, certainly, was not an unthinking copyist, and he was generally interested to compare versions of texts at what he considered significant points. That he occasionally canceled passages and whole texts shows that he subjected his work to review, and that he made adjustments here and there to his translation demonstrates that he conceived of his work as a book in process and perhaps nearing completion, as his title page and the changes he made to it also suggest.

Bodleian MS Laud Misc. 636, the Peterborough version of the Anglo-Saxon Chronicle, contains extensive notes written by L'Isle on paper leaves that he inserted between the original vellum leaves of the manuscript. In the main, the notes collate the Peterborough version with that contained in CCCC MS 173, the Parker copy of the Chronicle, but they also include occasional comments approximating a modest textual apparatus. Thus, in the annal for 855 (fol. 29v), L'Isle underlines and marks with an "X" the name "ecgbrihting"—which identifies Ecgbriht/Egbert as the father of King Æthelwulf of Wessex—and at the end of the annal he adds this comment (preceded by a matching "X"): "the pedegree of this Ecgbriht is drawn vp to hrawra [libro Cottoniano] who is there said to be the sonne of Noe, borne in the Arke." His reference is to the version of the annal in the now mostly destroyed MS Cotton Otho B. xi (which still retains a few scattered notes by L'Isle in its margins). L'Isle also adds on the paper leaf inserted at this point in the Peterborough Chronicle, "this pedegree is also in Benet

---

[48]He presumably crossed out the text when he realized that he had already transcribed another version of the Jonah story (the version of CCCC MS 162, representing the Vercelli Book tradition rather than that of Ælfric) on fols. 120v–121v of MS Laud Misc. 381.

Coll: booke" (a reference to CCCC MS 173), and he corrects the end of the 855 annal—which refers to the rule of two of Æthelwulf's sons—by adding in the interline the names of Æthelberht and Æthelbald, which he has drawn from one of the two other manuscripts. Extended comments by L'Isle, however, are few in number; most notes simply draw attention to divergences between the manuscripts or supply variants, such as at the annal for 894 (fol. 34v), "Liber Cottonian*us* \et Benet/[49] multa hab*en*t de hoc Anno et reliquis," or the annal for 644 (fol. 13v), against which L'Isle writes on the adjacent paper leaf, "Benet 645 *and* so dyffering in others." His last entry in the main body of the manuscript occurs on the paper leaf adjacent to fol. 59v, where, alongside the annal for 1070, he transcribes the complete annal for this year from the Parker Chronicle, following it with the comment "Here endes the Saxon of Canterbury book, in Benet Coll. at Cambridge." From this point onwards, neither CCCC MS 173 nor MS Otho B. xi (in which the text ended at 1001) furnished him with material with which to compare the Peterborough Chronicle, which itself continues to 1154.

There is, however, further work by L'Isle on a group of thirteen paper leaves (numbered "1" through "13" by him in the lower right area of their rectos) that he added at the back of the manuscript, and that now constitute fols. 92–102 in the continuous foliation.[50] Folios 92r–97r contain L'Isle's extensive transcriptions of certain passages that occur in the Parker but not the Peterborough Chronicle, beginning with the annal for 894 and ending with that for 975. He wrote the last three entries, for 973–75, at a different time from the others, as is shown by a change in the color of his ink and in the thickness of his nib. On fol. 96rv is his

---

[49]"et Benet" is added by L'Isle in the interline. The addition shows that he consulted MS Otho B. xi first, CCCC MS 173 later.

[50]Two of the leaves are blank and so have not been assigned numbers in the continuous foliation.

transcription of the Parker Chronicle's annal for 937, the Chronicle poem known as *The Battle of Brunanburh*. Although he did not specifically identify it as a poem, he sensed its poetical quality, for he headed his transcription "This is mysticall *and* written in a poeticall vaine obscurely of purpose to avoid the daun*ger* of those tymes *and* needs dechyphring." L'Isle's transcription of the *Brunanburh* entry is mostly accurate, although he at times expands silently, substitutes the manuscript's þ with ð and vice versa, and consistently omits accents. He occasionally emends silently, as at verse lines 8 "hi" > "hie," 16 "oð" > "oððe," and 26 "þæ" > "þe."[51] Word separation is editorial and for the most part accurate, although, for example, at line 21 L'Isle reads "ond longne" where "ondlongne" is correct; at line 24, he first writes "myrcne," combining two words, but realizes his error and inserts an *e* interlinearly, thus giving correctly "myrce ne"; at line 25, "hæleþa" is divided as "hæle þa"; at line 44, "gelpan ne" is transcribed as "gelpanne"; at line 72, "weealles" is transcribed as two words, "we ealles." Occasionally, L'Isle miscopies, as at line 30 "aswefede," given as "aswesed." L'Isle takes care to supply pointing in his transcription, following the manuscript. What he meant by his supplied editorial comment at the head of the poem with regard to its purposeful obscurity in order to avoid dangers remains obscure, although it does tantalize in suggesting that L'Isle did have an interpretive view of the poem, having understood something of its "mystical" meaning (in the sense of not being apparent or obvious).

L'Isle also transcribed the annal for 941, containing *The Capture of the Five Boroughs* (fol. 96v). While he again senses the poetical qualities of the annal (as intimated by his comment at the head of the annal, "This is also mysticall"), he nevertheless does

---

[51]For a facsimile of *The Battle of Brunanburh* as it occurs in the Parker Chronicle, see Flower and Smith (1941), fols. 26r–27r. The edition to which the line numbers refer is that of Dobbie (1942), 16–20.

not divide its poetic portion from its prose portion. The end of the annal posed problems for him, for the original last words "bisceopes handa" are followed in CCCC MS 173 by an addition in a post-Conquest hand, the first part of this addition having been subsequently erased and partly overwritten with the word "arcebisceop" by a second post-Conquest hand, while the last part stands next to the originally barren annal number 943.[52] The addition, as reconstructed by Plummer, probably originally read as "[Her Eadmund cing S. Dunstane Glæs]tingeberig betæhte ðær he syððan ærest abbud wearð."[53] The text now visible in the Parker Chronicle appears as follows (colons indicate erasures; the original text is here displayed in normal font, the surviving portion of the addition by the first post-Conquest hand in bold, the addition by the second hand in italics):[54]

bisceopes handa : : : : : : : : : *arcebisceop.*
: : : : : : : : : : :
.an. dcccc. xliii. **tinge berig be tæhte ðær he syððan ærest abbud wearð**

The situation clearly perplexed L'Isle, who tried unsuccessfully to make sense of it by ending the annal for 941 with "bisceopes handa   tingeberig betæhte" (leaving a gap to take account of the erasure) and by then creating a brief annal for 943: "her he syððan ærest abbud wearð arcebisceop." One can understand his difficulties with the text at this point. L'Isle also transcribes the Chronicle poems *The Coronation of Edgar* (fol. 97r) and *The Death of Edgar* (fol. 97r). To the first he adds the comment "This is also mysticall," and to the second "And this." But he also divides the latter poem midway at line 16 ("Ða

---

[52]On the erasure and the puzzling addition of "arcebisceop," see Dumville (1983), 50.

[53]See Plummer (1892–99), I, 110; and see also Bately (1986), 73. "In this year King Edmund entrusted Glastonbury to St. Dunstan, where he afterwards first became abbot."

[54]Facsimile in Flower and Smith (1941), fol. 27v.

wæs on myrceon"), providing this section with the comment "And this," thus suggesting that he recognized it as constituting a separate text. Since this section of the poem begins with its own large initial at the top of fol. 29r of CCCC MS 173, it is easy to see how L'Isle came to his opinion, even though he recognizes that both items come within the annal for 975.

The last item in Old English transcribed by L'Isle is found at fol. 98r, headed "The Pedegree of Woden," drawn from the Parker Chronicle's annal for 855, which reads as follows (fol. 13r):

> woden friþowalding friþuwald freawining frealaf friþuwulfing friþu-
> wulf finning fin godwulfing godwulf geating geat tętwaing tętwa
> beawing beaw sceldwaing sceldwea heremoding heremod itermoning
> Itermon hrawraing se wæs geboren in þære earce noe lamach. . . .

L'Isle's text remains close to that of the manuscript, but with the addition of "freawin frealafing" in the first line:

> woden friþuwalding friðuwald freawining freawin frealafing frealaf
> friþuwulfing friþuwulf finning fin godwulfing godwulf geating geat
> tętwaing tęwa [*sic*] beawing beaw sceldwaing sceldwea heremoding
> heremod Itermoning Itermon hrawraing se wæs geboren In þære earce.
> noe lamach &ct. l. Cant. dccclv.[55]

The addition is evidently L'Isle's own interpolation, to make sense of a clear error in the sequence of the genealogy in his manuscript source. He did not draw the addition from MS Otho B. xi, the other Chronicle manuscript that he is known to have consulted, for there the sequence was ". . . freawining freawine [corrected to "frealaf"] frithuwulfing. . . ."[56] Nor does the sequence "freawining freawin frealafing frealaf" occur in any other manuscript of the

---

[55] A letter *n* is crossed out after the second *e* of "heremoding," and "hrawra" is cancelled after "hrawraing."

[56] See Lutz (1981), 43 and 177.

Anglo-Saxon Chronicle.[57] L'Isle's emendation, based on his understanding of the structure of the genealogy, marks him as a critical editor whose methodology might well be regarded as approaching modern principles of editing.[58]

Following this leaf, and concluding the manuscript, is a batch of seven pages (fols. 99r–102v, with fol. 101v left blank) on which L'Isle copied the contents lists of ten Old English homiliaries, nine of them in the library of Corpus Christi College and the other at Trinity College, Cambridge. All ten homiliaries had belonged to Matthew Parker, who had numbered them from one to ten and had had them supplied with contents lists. L'Isle's lists simply copy the Parkerian ones and provide no additional information about the contents. At the bottom of his first list (fol. 99r) he adds this note: "Decem Libri Homiliarum Saxonicarum fuerunt; sed Nonus ex isto numero desideratur: Reliquæ compinguntur octo voluminibus; & in Collegio Benett (præter 10 Librum) conservantur. . . " ("There were ten books of Saxon homilies, but the ninth of them is missing; the rest are contained in eight books preserved at Benet College, except for the tenth book"). Some time after writing the note, he must have discovered Parker's ninth book (CCCC MS 303), for he includes its contents list, headed "Catalogus Homiliarum Libri noni in Coll. Benet," on fol. 101r. L'Isle's wish to record the contents of the homiliaries is explained by the fact that he consulted the manuscripts extensively for his transcriptions of Old English scriptural quotations in MS Laud Misc. 381. Of some interest are three glossary entries from the homilies that he wrote at the bottom of his first list on fol. 99r but then crossed out. These entries may perhaps have been used in the preparation of

---

[57]See Thorpe (1861), 126–27.

[58]Thorpe (1861), 126, emends the text by altering "freawining" to "frealafing," a more expedient solution to the problem of the sequence.

L'Isle's lost lexicon. The entries are: "gyfernysse. gula"; "syfernysse. sobrietas"; "eawfæstnysse. religio."[59]

A final manuscript to be considered is Bodleian MS Laud Misc. 201, which comprises L'Isle's edition and translation of the Old English text of the Eadwine Psalter, including the canticles, to which L'Isle appended (fols. 264r–266r) "Certaine prayers of the Saxon times taken out of the Nunnes Rule of Saint James order in Bennet Coll. library."[60] The manuscript is arranged so that the Old English text (with numbered psalm verses) faces its English translation. The leaves with the Old English text are slightly smaller than those with the translation (ca. 203 × 150 mm as opposed to ca. 212 × 160 mm), and it is only the smaller leaves that carry L'Isle's ink foliation. Evidently L'Isle first made his transcription on gatherings of these smaller leaves, then interleaved them with the larger leaves on which he entered his translation. (Later, the whole manuscript was given a continuous pencil foliation by the same hand as foliated MS Laud Misc. 381 and other manuscripts in the Laudian collection.) L'Isle used the margins of the pages containing his transcription to enter numerous variant readings from the other Old English psalters he consulted, along with sporadic notes and comments. He linked the variants and notes to the relevant point in the text by underlining

---

[59]It is interesting to note in this connection that on fol. 2r of London, Lambeth Palace Library, MS 692, which contains John Joscelyn's collection of Old English word lists, is a note in a later seventeenth- or early eighteenth-century hand querying whether the lists might be L'Isle's work: "Collections in order to ye making of a Saxon Dictionarie or Vocabularie [Qu. whether they be M^r. L'Isle's?]." I am grateful to Timothy Graham for bringing this note to my attention and for supplying me with a photocopy of the page.

[60]He excerpted these prayers from the *Ancrene Wisse* in CCCC MS 402, altering the language to make it appear more like Old English, just as he had done with his excerpts from MS 402 in MS Laud Misc. 381. His reference to "Saint James Order" is explained by the fact that MS 402 had belonged to the church of St. James at Wigmore, Herefordshire.

within the text the word or words to which they related, and
sometimes also by adding a matching pair of crosses or other
symbols, one at the appropriate point in the text and the other at
the beginning of his marginal note. His English translation shows
numerous layers of translation attempts, with words and lines
crossed through and alternative translations interlined. At fols.
161v–162r, for example, L'Isle was faced by a particularly
complicated passage in his rendering of Psalm 101:7. He originally
transcribed the Old English text as it stood in the manuscript:
"gelic geworden ic eom felle hundes onlicnesse. geworden eom
swæ nihtrefne on husehere" ("I have become as the likeness of the
skin of a dog, I have become like a night raven on the dwelling
place"), but, against the authority of the manuscript, he crosses out
"felle hundes onlicnesse" ("likeness of the skin of a dog") and
writes above the line "þam fugele westnes" ("to the bird of the
wilderness"), the reading of the Stowe Psalter. The mistranslation
of "pellicano in solitudine" as "felle hundes onlicnesse" in the
Eadwine Psalter is well known, but what is not known is that it
was L'Isle who first recognized the error. He writes in the margin
alongside the Old English text, "felle hundes. a pelle & cane.
stangillan. the stonegull."[61] Evidently, L'Isle's collation with
Stowe 2 brought him to reconsider the gloss and to correct the
error in his own edition. The same process caused him to alter his

---

[61]The Eadwine Psalter reads (fol. 178r): "Similis / factus sum pelli/cano in
solitudine. factus sum / sicut nocticorax in domici/lio" (that is, "I am become like
the pelican in the wilderness; I am like a night raven on the housetop"). The
glossator adds "uel nic" above "nocticorax" (> "nicticorax"). The error in the Old
English translation seems to have originated with the Eadwine glossator and to
have been caused by the splitting of the word *pellicano* over two lines, which
suggests two words, *pelli* and *cano*, which he glossed accordingly. The gloss
"Gelic" begins with a capital in the manuscript but is trancribed as "gelic" by
L'Isle, a minor departure from the original. Of interest in connection with the
translation of *pellicano* as "stonegull" is Bierbaumer (1985), 70–71 and 74 n. 41.
See also Lendinara (1992), 228–30.

translation, in which his rendering of the original reading of the Eadwine Psalter is rejected in favor of that in the Stowe Psalter:

the foule of the desert
I am become lyke ^an Image of dog skynne;

a   to watche   toppe
I am become as ^ nyght-raven ^on the house toppe;

on the house-toppe
^to watche yt in a houshould overwatched; and

lonely
and become I am as a ^ sparrow vpo*n* ye buylding.

At Psalm 28:7, L'Isle first records the Old English as "stefn drihtnes hrysiendis on westen ꝥ astyred drihten onwendeþ westen gefeællende" (fol. 39v) as a rendering of "uox domini concutientis solitudinem et commouebit dominus desertum cades" ("the voice of the Lord striking the wilderness, and the Lord will shake the wilderness of Kadesh"),[62] but, realizing that "onwendeþ" is redundant, he crosses it out in order to bring sense to the passage. Although L'Isle translates the passage in agreement with his revision of the manuscript reading, he adds a note to his translation of "westen gefeællende" (where the Old English glossator has rendered the proper name "Cades" as though it were the present participle of *cado*) as "the falling wyldernesse": "so the Saxo*n* turnes p*r*oper names, to ye latin sound: Cades." The kinds of changes reflected in the text and translation in these two examples are mirrored throughout the entire edition. What they show is that L'Isle was a keen editor who understood the problems posed by the text as well as the difficulties in rendering the Old English into a modern translation. And he understood as well some of the failings of his Anglo-Saxon predecessors in translating the psalms.

---

[62]Folio 48v in the Eadwine Psalter.

If L'Isle's alterations in these passages show him to have been a serious editor and translator, his notes scattered throughout the psalms further reveal his understanding of Old English and his interest in "the Roots & grounds of our mother-toong." The notes variously provide the original Latin words that lie behind the variant readings that he records from other Old English glossed psalters, supply English translations for the variants, discuss etymologies and Old English grammatical forms, and the like. At fol. 88v, L'Isle adds a note to explain the Eadwine glossator's translation of certain proper nouns in Psalm 59:9–10, which in the Romanum version reads "[9] Meus est Galaad, et meus est Manasses; Et Effrem fortitudo capitis mei. Iuda rex meus; [10] Moab olla spei meae. In Idumaeam extendam calciamentum meum: mihi allophili subditi sunt" ("Galaad is mine, and Manasses is mine; and Ephraim is the strength of my head. Judah is my king. Moab is the pot of my hope. In Idumaea I will stretch out my shoe: to me the foreigners are made subject").[63] The glossator of the Eadwine Psalter provides translations of the proper nouns; thus "Galaad" is rendered as "helm," "Manasses" as "to wunienne," "Effrem" as "to onfonne," and "Idumaea" as "fnestum him"; "Moab olla" is combined into a single word, "moabolla," and tagged simply as "næmæ" ("name"), as also is "allophili."[64] Rather than translating the proper names, L'Isle retains the Old English translations (underlined) in his modern English rendering in order to call attention to them. On the word "helm," he

---

[63] I use the text of the Romanum as prepared by Weber (1953), p. 134; the punctuation is supplied. The Old English gloss in the Eadwine Psalter is to the Romanum.

[64] Harsley (1889), 101. Readers may wish to refer to the facsimile edition with introduction, James (1935), fol. 104rv. Harsley divides "moabolla" into two words; although there is space between the *b* and the *o* in the manuscript, the gloss, "næmæ," clearly extends across both words, thus indicating that it was understood as a single term.

comments, "bycause galaad is lyke galea" (fol. 88v), thus noting the link between Latin *galea* ("helmet") and Old English *helm*, even though the proper noun derives from the Hebrew word meaning "rocky," referring to the mountainous region along the east bank of the Jordan.[65] Of the translation of "Manasses" as "to wunienne," L'Isle writes: "bycause Manasses sound*es* as yf yt came of manare" (fol. 88v).[66] With his note on the translation of "Effrem" as "to onfonne" (= "to take"), L'Isle expresses what might be taken as mild exasperation at the glossator's rendering of proper names: "bycause Effrē (as yt is heere wrytten) sound*es* like Efferre. In these dayes were men so ignorant of the hebrue *and* greeke that they translated most p*roper* names according to their latin-seemyng sound. as may appeere by many not vnlyke these. this I thought good to note once for all" (fol. 88v). With regard to "Moabolla," he observes simply, "for Moab olla w*hi*ch not vnderstood is taken for one woord" (fol. 90r); of "fnestum him," he writes: "for Idumea as yf it were of Idus *and* Ea" (fol. 90r); and, finally, in a note on his rendering of "allophili" as "straunge names," L'Isle ascribes to the Eadwine glossator more credit than is deserved. In the Eadwine Psalter, the glossator simply wrote "næmæ" above "allophili" to indicate that it is a proper name, but the word remains untranslated. L'Isle's knowledge of Greek and Latin brings him to combine the Old English gloss with the meaning of *allophili* ("foreign"), yielding "strange names." He

---

[65]Britt (1928), 109.

[66]Here, L'Isle has misunderstood the meaning of *to wunienne* ("to dwell, remain"), as is shown by the fact that above the term he has written "to spring." He therefore erroneously links the Old English gloss to the glossator's perception of a correspondence between "Manasses" and Latin first conjugation *mano, -are* instead of second conjugation *maneo, -ere*. The text of Psalm 59:9–10 is repeated at Psalm 107:9, where the Old English gloss to "Manasses" is "wuniende"; on this occasion L'Isle's marginal note related the Old English gloss to the correct Latin verb: "Manasses. as of maneo" (fol. 181r).

comments: "heer the Saxon vseth latin as yᵉ Latin hath don greeke. ἀλλόφυλι allophyli" (fol. 90r). L'Isle's learning perhaps got the better of him in this instance.

L'Isle's interest in the grammar of Old English and in etymology is also reflected in his notes. In a comment on the Eadwine glossator's translation of "synagoga deorum" as "gemot-stowe be hira" at Psalm 81:1, L'Isle writes, "the Saxon vnwilling to make a plural of god for Deorum giues a translation as yt were of Eorum. nere in sound but far of in sense" (fol. 134r). Perhaps as he continued in his collation of the psalters against his base text, L'Isle realized that his initial perception of the explanation for the Old English gloss was mistaken (the Cambridge Psalter, for example, records the genitive plural "goda," as do the Stowe and Arundel Psalters), for he crosses out the note, and one can only assume that he recognized the reading in Eadwine as a random error. Unwilling to retain the error in his edition of the Old English text, he crosses out "be hira" and writes "goda" above the line. At Psalm 67:7, where Eadwine has "anmode" as a gloss on "unanimes," L'Isle writes: "aliás. anemode-þeawes id est unius-modi moris. the termination of the substantive serves also for the adiective. as yf it were anesmodes-þeawes" (fol. 97v). In his comment on "gehyðlic" ("favorable") as a gloss on "oportuno" at Psalm 144:15, L'Isle notes the relationship between the gloss and "hyð" ("port"): "As the latin opportunus comes of portus a haven so this saxon of hythe. which is the same" (fol. 233r). On an earlier page, regarding the Eadwine gloss "gætum" for "portum" in Psalm 106:30, he notes next to his transcription that "other copyes have hyðe id est haven. and that is better" (fol. 179r); in a corresponding note to his translation, he observes that the source of the erroneous gloss in Eadwine lay in the glossator's confusion of Latin *portus, -um* ("port, harbor") with *porta, -am* ("gate"): "though the latin hath portum, not portam" (fol. 178v).

L'Isle often calls attention to such errors in the Old English rendition of the Latin. In addition to the example above, he notes the mistranslation of "Non est occultatum os meum" ("My bone is not hidden") as "Ne is bedigled muð min" ("My mouth is not hidden") in Psalm 138:15. The confusion of *os, oris* ("mouth") for *os, ossis* ("bone") is fairly commonplace in the psalms, and L'Isle succinctly notes the error ("os oris for os ossis"; fol. 224v), but retains the incorrect Old English rendering in his translation: "My <u>mouth</u> is not hydden." Interestingly, L'Isle's attention was not focused solely on the Old English in this instance, for he writes on fol. 225r: "so hath ye french here ma buche." Although the note is crossed out, it shows that L'Isle also consulted on occasion the Anglo-Norman gloss in the Eadwine Psalter. At Psalm 106:3, the Eadwine glossator renders "ab aquilone" as "fro*m* eæstdæle," where all other glossed psalters render the Latin with forms of *norðdæl*.[67] L'Isle retains the translation of "eæstdæle" as "from east" (fol. 176v) but adds, "the latin hath ab Aquilone. nordæle" (fol. 177r). At times, however, L'Isle's comments may hit slightly off the mark. In a note on Psalm 113:12,[68] where the Latin "simulachra" has the Old English gloss "diobolgield," which he (correctly) translates as "Idolls," he writes: "the saxo*n* word signyfies: shrines of deuils.[69] yet the ould latine manuscript*es* haue Idola. Sculptilia & Simulacra. in this *and* the like places" (fol. 188v). Yet the Old English gloss is correct in this instance:

---

[67]The other psalters' readings are: "norðdęle" (A), "norðdæle" (BCGHIK), "norþdæle" (DJ), "nordæle" (F). A = the Vespasian Psalter, for which see Kuhn (1965); B = the Junius Psalter (see Brenner [1908]); C = the Cambridge Psalter (see Wildhagen [1910]); D = the Royal Psalter (see Roeder [1904]); F = the Stowe Psalter (see Kimmens [1979]); G = the Vitellius Psalter (see Rosier [1962]); H = the Tiberius Psalter (see Campbell [1974]); I = the Lambeth Psalter (see Lindelöf [1909]); J = the Arundel Psalter (see Oess [1910]); K = the Salisbury Psalter (see Sisam and Sisam [1959]).

[68]Psalm 113B:4 in modern editions.

[69]L'Isle originally wrote "signyfies: guild devils," but then crossed out "guild" and added in "shrines of."

diobolgield/deofolgyld is frequently attested with the meaning "idol."[70]

In the examples discussed above, and elsewhere throughout his text, L'Isle demonstrates more than casual familiarity with the text of the Eadwine Psalter and with Old English broadly.[71] His unpublished edition, with its extensive revisions to the translation and with its wide range of notes, stands as a valuable document not only in the study of the early history of editorial work on the Eadwine Psalter, but also because it allows us a glimpse of a scholar at work honing his translation, consulting other texts, and applying his command of Old English, strengthened by his knowledge of Latin, Greek, and Hebrew and of the Bible. As a translator of Old English, L'Isle seems to have remained true to his statement made earlier in *A Saxon Treatise*,[72] in which he derides "some late translators" who "are faine to stuffe the text with such fustian, such inkehorne termes, as may seeme to fauour their parts; or darken at least the true meaning of holy Scripture." As Allen J. Frantzen notes in a brief comment on L'Isle, he combined "a passion for classical antiquity" with "a linguistic focus unlike that of the earlier polemicists."[73] L'Isle's progress from his somewhat wayward beginnings with Virgil's *Aeneid* "Scotished" to his more mature work as editor in Bodleian MSS Laud Misc. 201 and 381 stands as a noteworthy achievement, although, if his preface to *A Saxon Treatise* is any indication, it is an achievement tempered by modesty: "Lo here in this field of learning, this orchard of the old English Church, haue I set my selfe on worke, where though

---

[70]See *DOE*, entry for *dēofol-gyld*.

[71]L'Isle did not recognize that Psalms 90:16–95:2 are written in verse, although his work on the Chronicle shows that he had some sensitivity to Old English poetry; see pp. 194–96 above.

[72]Sig. e3[r].

[73]Frantzen (1990), 163. Frantzen mistakenly attributes *A Saxon Treatise* to a "John L'Isle" at pp. 161 and 246 n. 104.

I plant not a new, I may saue at least a good old tree or two, that were like to be lost."[74] Although his work would be superseded, and although subsequent generations of scholars would pass him over even in discussions of doctrinal polemic in the sixteenth and seventeenth centuries, L'Isle's transcripts nevertheless reward study, particularly as they provide an intimate view of his method of work and the broad range of skills he applied in his role as editor and translator.[75]

---

[74] *A Saxon Treatise*, sig. b4ʳ.

[75] I wish to thank Carl Berkhout for supplying me with a copy of Laurence Nowell's transcript of BL MS Cotton Otho B. xi in BL MS Additional 43703 and George Hardin Brown for supplying me Abraham Wheelock's edition of the same (Cambridge, 1643; reissued 1644). I would also like to express my deep appreciation to Timothy Graham for his comments on and meticulous corrections to an earlier draft of this paper.

OXFORD, BODLEIAN LIBRARY, MS LAUD MISC. 381: WILLIAM L'ISLE, ÆLFRIC, AND THE *ANCRENE WISSE*[1]

Stuart Lee

For Barbara Raw

William L'Isle (1569?–1637) has a mixed reputation as an Anglo-Saxonist.[2] His work on Ælfric's *Letter to Sigeweard* published in *A Saxon Treatise Concerning the Old and New Testament*,[3] and his diligence with the Eadwine Psalter, draw praise from such scholars as Eleanor N. Adams, who considered him "the first Old English editor of the [seventeenth] century,"[4] while Dorothy Whitelock described him as "one of the keenest

---

[1]I am indebted to Prof. Jane Roberts of King's College, London, for providing comments and suggestions during the composition of this essay.

[2]That his contemporaries viewed his work with high regard is clear from a letter of Sir William Boswell to Sir Simonds D'Ewes of 18 December 1636 in which Boswell described L'Isle as "extraordinarily skilfull" in the Old English language (see Whitelock [1954], 24; ultimately taken from Letter LIII in Ellis [1843], 152).

[3]Printed in London, 1623, and reprinted fifteen years later under the title *Divers Ancient Monuments in the Saxon Tongue* (London, 1638). The text of the *Letter to Sigeweard* is reprinted in Crawford (1922), 15–75.

[4]Adams (1917), 45. Adams draws attention to L'Isle and the 1623 publication of *A Saxon Treatise*, and notes that the latter was the first publication in Old English in the seventeenth century.

Saxon scholars of his day."[5] More recently, David McKitterick has noted that if L'Isle had fulfilled his intention of publishing his transcription and translation of the Old English text of the Eadwine Psalter, "his edition would have been the first book to have been printed in Anglo-Saxon type at Cambridge."[6] Significantly, L'Isle's preface to *A Saxon Treatise* provides a firsthand account of how a scholar learned Old English before the days of primers and textbooks.[7] Had L'Isle succeeded in publishing his proposed editions of the Anglo-Saxon Chronicle and of those portions of the Bible that existed in Old English translation, the esteem accorded him might have risen still further.[8] Yet, at the same time, a cloud hangs over L'Isle because of his alleged habit, in some of his transcriptions, of tampering with the text of his originals, so that Fred C. Robinson, for example, has noted "his facility at recreating Old English texts."[9] The present essay has two purposes: first, to reassess the reputation of L'Isle as a

---

[5]Whitelock (1954), 24.

[6]McKitterick (1992), 197. For L'Isle's transcription of the passage on fol. 10r of the Eadwine Psalter describing a comet, see Lee (1993).

[7]For a description of L'Isle's preface and its significance, see the essay by Phillip Pulsiano in the present volume. For other studies of L'Isle's work, see Bennett (1938), 9 and 311–12; Tuve (1939), 169–71, 176–77, and 182; Murphy (1968), 346–47; and Graham (2000), 287–313.

[8]L'Isle alluded to the difficulties impeding these editions in a letter to Sir Robert Cotton of 16 March 1631 (BL MS Cotton Julius C. iii, fol. 242r): referring to his *The Faire Æthiopian*, published later in the same year, L'Isle commented that "this worke I know the printers will readily entertain, while the Saxon Bible and Chronicles lye dead by me." Apparently commercial considerations obstructed the further publication of Old English material.

[9]Robinson (1993), 280. Citing Kenneth Sisam's *Studies in the History of Old English Literature* (Oxford, 1953), 234, Robinson associates L'Isle with other antiquaries, for example Laurence Nowell, who archaized texts in order to produce "Old English."

collector and transcriber of Old English material by examining in detail hitherto undiscussed examples of his work in Bodleian MS Laud Misc. 381; and second, to address the tarnishing of L'Isle's reputation by examining one of his more infamous "forgeries" in the light of material previously overlooked in this context.

MS Laud Misc. 381 (hereafter Laud 381) is notable not only for being one of the five manuscripts in which we can clearly see L'Isle's working method in some detail,[10] but more famously for preserving Ælfric's homily on the Old Testament book of Esther,[11] which is not now to be found in any surviving medieval manuscript. Laud 381 thus acquires special status as the source for over three hundred lines of Ælfrician prose, and it adds to the canon of Ælfric's Old Testament translations.[12] Its position as the unique surviving copy caused L'Isle's transcription to be listed in Neil Ker's *Catalogue of Manuscripts Containing Anglo-Saxon*, in a section devoted to early modern copies made from lost and untraced manuscripts, where Ker noted that "Lisle gives no indication of the source from which he obtained his text."[13] As his interest was restricted to the Esther transcription, however, Ker did not provide an account of the manuscript as a whole.

---

[10]The other four are: Bodleian MSS Laud Misc. 201 (his transcription and translation of the Old English text of the Eadwine Psalter), Laud Misc. 636 (the Peterborough Chronicle, which L'Isle interleaved with pages of his own notes), and Laud Misc. 509 (the Old English Hexateuch + Ælfric's homily on Judges); and BL MS Cotton Claudius B. iv (the Old English illustrated Hexateuch). L'Isle collated the two Hexateuch manuscripts against one another, entered the variant readings of the one into the other, and made use of them both for his *A Saxon Treatise* of 1623.

[11]Edited in Assmann (1886) and Assmann (1889), 92–101. The homily has been re-edited in Lee (1992), 202–12.

[12]A complete list of Ælfric's Old Testament works is given in Pope (1967–68), I, 143.

[13]Ker (1957), no. 410.

Laud 381 still retains the seventeenth-century brown leather-over-pasteboard binding given it by William Laud, archbishop of Canterbury (1633–45), whose arms, in gold, are positioned centrally on the front and back covers. Within the binding, the manuscript comprises 174 paper leaves, foliated i, ii, 1(a), 1(b), and 2–171. Folios i–ii and 170–71 are flyleaves, for the most part blank. Folio 1(a)r carries titles by L'Isle, described below, while fol. 1(b) is blank. On fol. 2r is an ownership inscription entered by Laud, who acquired the manuscript (and others that had belonged to L'Isle)[14] in 1638, shortly after L'Isle's death. The inscription reads: "Liber Guill*elmi* Laud Archiep*iscop*i Cant*uariensis* et Cancellar*ii* Uniuersit*atis* Oxon*iensis* 1638." The main text occupies fols. 2v–169r. The leaves of the manuscript measure at the most ca. 230 × 180 mm. The written space measures ca. 180–200 × 145–150 mm. On fols. 1(a)–127 there are no rulings. On fols. 128–69, L'Isle has ruled a frame around each page. This frame comprises a single horizontal ruling in the upper margin, a single vertical ruling in the outer margin, and two horizontal rulings in the lower part of the page. The frame served as a rough guide for entering the text on these pages. Usually L'Isle began writing directly below the top horizontal ruling, but sometimes he entered the first line of text above the ruling. The two lower rulings have text entered between them, frequently as many as five or six lines; occasionally there is an overspill of text below the bottom ruling, but otherwise that area is reserved for L'Isle's catchwords, which provide the word(s) with which the next page begins.

A detailed description of the contents of Laud 381 is to be found in Humfrey Wanley's *Librorum veterum septentrionalium . . . catalogus historico-criticus* of 1705. Referring to the manuscript by its former pressmark, Laud E. 33, and making use

---

[14]See Ker (1957), no. 344 (p. 424) and no. 346 (p. 426).

of L'Isle's titles within the manuscript itself, Wanley divided its contents into six sections:[15]

> Laud. E. 33. I. Saxon-English Remains of the Pentateuch, Josua, Judges, Job, &c. Out of Sr. Robert Cotton's Manuscripts of most reverend Antiquity, now first new Englished and set out by W. L. (i.e. *Will. L'isle.*)
>
>> John 6.12. Gather up the fragments that remain, that nothing be lost.
>>
>> *Codex autem hic continet translationem Pentateuchi Anglo-Saxonici (qui in bibliotheca Cottoniana inscribitur* CLAVDIVS B.4.*) in linguam Anglicanam, per* Will. L'isle.
>
> II. More of the ould Testament quoted in the Saxon Homilies which are entitled in Latine *Catholici Sermones* and Translated into the ould English by Aelfricus Abbas.
>
>> *Continet hic tractatus plurima loca veteris Testamenti, Saxonicè & Anglicè.*
>
> III. fol. 19.[16]   B E H E S T E R.
>
>> *Incip.* Iu on ealdum dagum wæs sum rice cyning nam cuð on worulde Asuerus gehaten. ꝺ se hefde cynerice east fram Indian oð Eþiopian lande þæt is fram easte-weardan þissere worulde ꝺ suþ-weardan oð to þam Silhearwum.
>>
>> *Expl.* ofer swilcne anweald. ꝺ he wæs rihtwis. ꝺ rædfæst on weorcum. ꝺ he hæfde oþerne naman artarxerses. Sy wuldor ꝺ lof þam welwillendan gode. Se þe æfre rixaþ on ecnesse. AMEN.
>>
>> *Haec narratio, seu potius Homilia, scripta est Saxonicè & Anglice.*

---

[15]Wanley (1705), 99–100. In listing the contents by sections, Wanley mistakenly used the section number "III" twice.

[16]Wanley is here citing an intermittent and somewhat erratic foliation by L'Isle that begins on fol. 116v. L'Isle used another foliation sequence for fols. 2v–116r. After L'Isle had entered his own foliations, another hand foliated the whole manuscript in one continuous sequence. For a fuller description of the foliations in the manuscript, see n. 37 of the essay by Phillip Pulsiano above.

III. *De Templo Hierosolymitano, Saxonicè & Anglicè.*

Incip. Dauid se mæra cyning hæfde gemynt *þæt* he wolde *þæt* tempel
aræran þam ælmihtigan gode to wurðmynte. ac he him sæde þurh
his witegan Naþan *þæt* his sunu sceolde þæt tempel areran ꝸ he
wolde him beon for fæder ꝸ him mid mildheortnysse gyrde styran
gif he ahwar unrihtlice dyde.

IV. fol. 32.[17]   B E   I O B.

Incip. Sum wer wæs geseten on þam lande þe is gehaten Hus. his nama
wæs Iob.

Expl. ꝸ geseah his bearna bearn oð ða feorðan mægðe. on eallum his
life he leofode twa hund geara ꝸ eahta ꝸ feowertig geara he wæs
se fifta man æfter abrahame þam heahfædere.

Tractatulus sive Homilia habetur Saxonice & Anglice.

Saxonicum ex hoc Apographo edidit Edwardus Thwaites
cum Heptateucho suo, Oxon. *1699.*

V. *Prophetiæ per Homilistam Saxonicum ad Christum applicatæ,
Saxonicè & Anglicè*

Incip. Se ælmihtiga god behet gefyrne worulde Abrahame *þæt* on his
cynne sceolde beon eal mancynn gebletsod. ꝸ him eac swa galæste
[*sic*].

  Omnia manu propria Gulielmi L'isle.

Wanley's description, although detailed, is nonetheless far
from complete and does not sufficiently indicate the precise character of the manuscript. Analysis of Laud 381 must therefore be
preceded by an accurate account of its nature and contents. For
L'Isle the manuscript appears to have served as a workbook in
which he included translations and transcriptions of Old English
material, his underlying principle of choice being the representation of the Old Testament. He evidently intended eventually to
publish the material. Folio 1(a)r contains two titles by L'Isle that
relate only in part to the contents of Laud 381; their format and
wording indicate that they are trial title pages for planned publications. The two trials were written by L'Isle at different times and

---

[17]See previous note.

include his alterations. The upper portion of the leaf has been cut away, removing at least one line of text of which only the bottoms of a few letters remain. The surviving part of the leaf begins with the title reported for the most part accurately by Wanley:

> Saxon-english / Remaines of the Pentateuch, / Iosua, Iudges, &ct. / out of S^r. Robert Cottons / Manuscripts, of most reuerend antiquity / now first new-englished & set-out / by W. L.[18]

The words "by W. L." have been crossed out. Then follows a statement of purpose that has also been crossed out, after having already undergone several alterations. Its final form before L'Isle canceled it appears to have been:

> To manifest unto the worlde / how long since the Scriptures haue ben in English;[19] / and to preserue the memory of that ancient / Dialect, wch shewes the Roots & grounds / of our mother-toong.[20]

Below this, not crossed out, is the quotation from John 6:12 noted by Wanley.

This portion of the page, apparently all written with the same pen, forms L'Isle's first trial title page. Below, he has made an

---

[18] After "Iosua," "&c" has been crossed out. After "Iudges, &ct." has been added, perhaps by L'Isle at a later time, "Job &c." L'Isle originally wrote "Sr Robert Cottons most ancient Manuscripts," then crossed out "most ancient." For a reproduction of this page, see Graham (2000), fig. 31.

[19] L'Isle first wrote "Not so much for matter of Religion, as to preserue the memory. . . ." Then, after "matter of Religion," he added "more then to shew how long since the Scriptures haue ben in English." Then, he added at the beginning "To manifest unto the worlde," crossed out the following text, and changed "as to preserue" to "and to preserue."

[20] L'Isle first wrote "of our now-spoken English," then crossed out "now-spoken English" and substituted "mother-toong."

addition, evidently written at a later time and using a different pen
with a narrower nib. The addition, which also includes several
alterations, is as follows:

> Remaines of the Saxon English Bible / wherin the psalmes & Four
> Euangelists (except / names of Genealogie Luk. 3.) are whole / &
> perfect; Now first all published & counterpaged / wth answerable
> english of our tyme, by W.L. / To shew th'antiquity & perspicuous
> manner of translation / into our then mother toong. as appears by the
> sundry / faire ould Manuscripts yet in th'Vniuersities of England / &
> those of Cathedrall Churches & late Abbyes there; now gathered / into
> S[r] Ro: Cottons Librarye.

Both versions show that L'Isle planned an edition of the
Scriptures in Old English, accompanied by a translation into the
English of his own day. The first version mentions by name only
the books of the Heptateuch, but L'Isle's unspecific "&ct." might
refer to the miscellaneous passages of additional Old Testament
material (described below) that he assembled in Laud 381. The
second version, which refers to the Psalms and Gospels, might
indicate that L'Isle planned to publish the Psalms and Gospels in
a separate volume that would follow up the other. L'Isle's work on
the Old English Psalter is contained in MS Laud Misc. 201.[21] He
is, however, not known to have transcribed or translated the Old
English Gospels, and it is possible that for this portion of his
planned publication he would have used the edition and translation
of the Gospels published in 1571 under the editorship of John
Foxe and through the sponsorship of Matthew Parker; L'Isle had,
after all, included a reissue of another of Parker's publications,
A Testimonie of Antiqvitie, in his *A Saxon Treatise* of 1623. The
trial title pages on fol. 1(a)r of Laud 381 throw important light on
L'Isle's plans for his work on the Scriptures in Old English and
help to explicate the unspecific allusion, in his letter to Cotton of

---

[21]On which see the paper by Phillip Pulsiano above.

16 March 1631, to his wish to publish the "Saxon Bible."[22]

Following the blank fols. 1(a)v–1(b)v, and fol. 2r which is blank apart from Laud's added ownership inscription, the first section of Laud 381 spans fols. 2v–116r. The section presents L'Isle's translations into seventeenth-century English of Ælfric's *Preface to Genesis* (fols. 2v–4v/16) and of the Old English versions of the first six books of the Bible and Ælfric's homily on the seventh: Genesis (fols. 4v/17–39v/26), Exodus (fols. 39v/27–68r/14), Leviticus (fols. 68r/15–74v/3), Numbers (fols. 74v/4–85r/2), Deuteronomy (fols. 85r/3–101r/13), Joshua (fols. 101r/14–109v, followed by the blank fol. 110r), and the homily on Judges (fols. 110v–116r). The Judges translation ends with L'Isle's comment "much wanting," in recognition that his Old English source (which is a paraphrase of portions of Judges) does not continue to the end of the biblical book. This first section is the portion of Laud 381 subsumed under Wanley's section I, which Wanley stated derived from MS Cotton Claudius B. iv. In fact, L'Isle had access not only to Claudius B. iv, the illustrated copy of the Old English Hexateuch, but also to Cotton's other copy, now Bodleian MS Laud Misc. 509. L'Isle's borrowing of both manuscripts is recorded in a list of loans made by Cotton from his library before 23 April 1621:[23]

---

[22]See n. 8 above. A further trial title page by L'Isle occurs on fol. iii[r] of Laud Misc. 201: "Remaines of the Saxon-English Bible / accosted with aunswerable English / of our times, / By Will: L'isle. / Augustin*us* de Doctrina Christiana / 2. 12. / Diuersitas exemplarior*um* & interpretatio*n*um / plus adiuuit intelligentia*m*, q*uam* impedivit; / simodo legentes no*n* sint negligentes: na*m* no*n*-/nullas obscuriores sententias pluriu*m* Codicum / sæpe manifestavit inspectio." The next leaf of Laud Misc. 201 (fol. 1r) bears L'Isle's title page for his planned edition of the "Saxon-English Psalter," with the *imprimatur*, dated 3 December 1630, of the Vice-Chancellor of Cambridge University; this title page is described by McKitterick (1992), 197–98.

[23]BL MS Harley 6018, fol. 148v. I am indebted to Dr. Colin Tite for drawing these loan notes to my attention.

Liber Genesis et pentatucha Saxonicæ bound with my armes and claspes in 4to	Mr Lyll of Cambrig
Genises [sic] Saxonicæ in picturis bound in lether and clasps Foll	Mr Lyll of Cambridg

The quarto-sized "Genesis et pentatucha" to which Cotton here refers is Laud Misc. 509, while the folio-sized "Genises . . . in picturis" is the illustrated Claudius B. iv. L'Isle studied both manuscripts in detail, collating the one against the other and annotating them in his own hand.[24] Despite Wanley's belief, Laud Misc. 509 is more likely to have been the principal source for L'Isle's translations on fols. 2v–116r of Laud 381.[25] Only Laud Misc. 509 could have provided the source for the translation of the homily on Judges, for the Judges text does not occur in Claudius B. iv. Further, L'Isle evidently retained Laud 509 in his hands for much longer than he did Claudius B. iv; presumably he still had it at his death in 1637, as that would explain how it came into William Laud's possession, along with others of L'Isle's manuscripts, in 1638.

This first section of Laud 381 comprises only English translations, without the accompanying Old English text, presumably because for his planned edition L'Isle would have made direct use of one or both of the surviving Anglo-Saxon manuscripts for the Old English: it would have been unnecessary labor to transcribe the Old English. At fol. 116v there comes a

---

[24]For L'Isle's annotations in the two manuscripts, see Crawford (1922), 2–4; Dodwell and Clemoes (1974), 13; and Graham (2000), 293–302.

[25]Wanley could have been influenced by the reference, in L'Isle's title on fol. 1(a)r, to "S^r. Robert Cottons Manuscripts of most reuerend antiquity"; this might have caused him to identify the Cottonian MS Claudius B. iv as L'Isle's source for his translation in the first section of Laud 381, although Wanley was in fact aware that Laud Misc. 509 had formerly also been in the Cottonian library (see Wanley [1705], 69, at the end of his description of Laud Misc. 509).

change in the character of Laud 381. From this point onwards, L'Isle provides both transcriptions of Old English material and, on facing pages, English translations of the material. There is a shift in L'Isle's mode of presentation at fol. 150. Up to this point, on fols. 116v–149r, the Old English transcriptions are on the verso of each leaf, with L'Isle's rather idiosyncratic translations on the facing rectos (within this span, fols. 138v–139r are blank). From fol. 150r onwards, by contrast, the Old English transcriptions occur on the rectos, with the translations on the facing versos. There is no translation on fol. 149v or at the top of fol. 150v because the passage that L'Isle transcribed on fol. 150r and in the first eleven lines of fol. 151r mostly duplicated material that he had already transcribed and translated on fols. 122v–124r: he evidently realized his mistake before translating the duplicated material, which he has crossed out, adding the marginal comment "habetur supra" ("occurs above").[26] In similar fashion, fol. 167v and the top of fol. 168v contain no translation because L'Isle has crossed out the Old English transcription on fols. 168r–169r/3, adding the comment "habet*ur* alibi" ("occurs elsewhere").

The material assembled by L'Isle on fols. 116v–169r is consistent in character. The nature of the material is indicated by L'Isle's title at the top of fol. 116v, a title quoted for the most part accurately by Wanley at the beginning of his section II: "More of the ould Testament quoted in the Saxon Homilies wch are entitled in Latine Catholici Sermones: & Translated into this ould English by Ælfricus Abbas."[27] In effect, this title applies to all the material

---

[26]Various indications show that L'Isle supplied the translations some time after making his transcriptions. For example, on fols. 119v and 120v, L'Isle added Old English material in the lower margin of the first page and the upper margin of the second; his translation on fols. 120r and 121r takes account of this added material, so must have been written after the addition.

[27]L'Isle added the words "into this ould English" in the interline, indicating with a caret the point where they should be inserted.

on fols. 116v–169r, although there are additional titles, corresponding with Wanley's sections III–V, at the head of the group of longer transcriptions/translations that occur on fols. 140v–148r, 150v–153r, 153v–159r, and 159v–165r. The transcriptions that L'Isle made in this part of Laud 381 are of Old English translations or paraphrases of passages of the Old Testament.[28] In most cases, L'Isle supplied in the margin an identification of the biblical source of the passage, sometimes citing only the relevant book, sometimes providing the relevant chapter number and occasionally also the verse number. L'Isle drew his material from a large number of Old English homilies. Contrary to the claim of his title on fol. 116v, not all these homilies are by Ælfric: several are pre-Ælfrician, although L'Isle came upon these in manuscripts that predominantly contain material by Ælfric; one or two are Wulfstanian. L'Isle's method was evidently to work his way through the various homiliaries that were available to him, hunting for any Old English versions of scriptural texts and noting these texts down when he came upon them, later adding his translation on the facing page. The work would have formed part of his plan, evidenced by the trial title pages on fol. 1(a)r, of publishing as much of the Bible in Old English as he could find. The order in which the transcriptions occur in Laud 381 bears no relation to the order of the books of the Bible. For example, on fol. 122v there occur passages from Daniel, Ezekiel, Lamentations, and Jeremiah, in that order, whereas in the Old Testament the order is Jeremiah, Lamentations, Ezekiel, Daniel. L'Isle's order resulted simply from the order in which he found the passages in the manuscripts that he studied; presumably, had his plans for publication advanced more fruitfully, he would have arranged the passages in their proper biblical order. The title

---

[28]A very few passages are of New Testament material: fols. 116v/8–9, 116v/22, and 139v/2–4. L'Isle crossed out these passages, presumably after realizing that they derived from the New Testament.

on fol. 116v gives no indication of which manuscripts he used, but internal evidence within his transcriptions, detailed below, shows that all the identifiable manuscripts were in Cambridge libraries.

While all early transcriptions of original Old English material have their particular interest, L'Isle's transcriptions in Laud 381 are of especial note because of their extent and because of their inclusion, on fols. 140v–147v, of material transcribed from a source now lost, Ælfric's homily on Esther. The character of L'Isle's transcriptions was determined by his purpose of collecting biblical material. As a result, on some occasions he copied only one or two lines from a homily, whereas at other times he copied a much more substantial portion of material. For example, following L'Isle's title in the first four lines of the page, fol. 116v contains twenty-three lines of Old English, drawn from four different homilies. Lines 5–9 derive from Clemoes XIX; lines 10–14, from the homily *Be þam drihtenlican sunnandæg folces lar*; lines 15–23 from Godden XIX; and lines 24–27 from *Lives of Saints* XIII.[29] By contrast, fols. 131v/1–134v/12 contain a lengthy, continuous transcription from *De falsis deis*, corresponding to lines 210–99 of Pope XXI, and apparently deriving from CCCC MS 178. The Esther homily is a further example of an extensive transcription.

I have undertaken a close examination of L'Isle's transcriptions with a twofold aim: first, to identify (using modern editions) the homilies from which the extracts derive; and second, to identify the manuscripts used by L'Isle in making his transcriptions. Several difficulties presented themselves. L'Isle himself provided no identifications of the manuscripts that he used. Further, with a few exceptions, most of his extracts are short, frequently only one or two lines, so that there is little material on

---

[29]For the editions here cited, see the list of Works Cited at the end of the present volume. The homily *Be þam drihtenlican sunnandæg folces lar* is edited in Napier (1901). *Lives of Saints* = Skeat (1881–1900).

which to base an identification, a problem exacerbated by the possibility that L'Isle did not always transcribe accurately. In addition, we know that L'Isle had access to at least one manuscript that no longer survives, and this opens the possibility that other transcriptions as well as the homily on Esther may derive from a source now lost. Nonetheless, it has been possible to compile a list of likely source homilies and manuscripts, and the results are displayed in the table at the end of this paper. It should, however, be borne in mind that in some cases the texts and manuscripts listed are only the "most probable" sources in the light of current evidence. The manuscripts were identified by checking L'Isle's transcriptions against manuscript variants recorded in modern editions and to some extent against the manuscripts themselves, taking into account the order in which L'Isle's transcriptions occur in relation to the order of the respective homilies in the manuscripts. In several cases the passages selected for transcription by L'Isle have been marked in the manuscripts themselves, these markings being attributable to L'Isle.[30]

The table reveals how for the work on fols. 116v–169r of Laud 381, L'Isle shifted his attention away from manuscripts borrowed from the Cotton collection to manuscripts in Cambridge, above all at Corpus Christi College. All the Cambridge manuscripts had already arrived there by the time that L'Isle worked on them. Those at Corpus Christi had been entrusted to the college by Matthew Parker, archbishop of Canterbury (1559–75), through a

---

[30]The marks, most frequently in pencil, include underlining of passages within the text, and crosses and vertical wavy lines entered in the outer margin; very occasionally a word is entered in the margin. Such marks occur, e.g., in CCCC MSS 188, 303, and 421, and TCC MS B. 15. 34. It has not previously been realized that these markings are by L'Isle. That they are his is indicated by the character of their script (when they include words), and by the correlation between the passages that they mark and L'Isle's transcriptions in Laud 381.

quadripartite indenture drawn up in the year of Parker's death.[31] Cambridge University Library MS Gg. 3. 28 had reached the library by 1600.[32] Trinity College MS B. 15. 34 was bequeathed to the college by John Whitgift, archbishop of Canterbury (1583–1604).[33] In several cases, L'Isle made transcriptions from two different copies of the same homily, found in two different manuscripts; sometimes he transcribed the very same passage, although in most cases where he did so, he subsequently realized this and crossed out the duplicate transcription. Altogether, L'Isle's transcriptions derive from fifty-nine surviving homilies and the lost *Esther*. Of the fifty-nine surviving homilies, twenty-one are edited in Clemoes, sixteen in Godden, seven in Pope, three in Assmann, three in Scragg, three in Skeat, and six in various other collections.

Because his interest was selectively focused on biblical material within the homilies, L'Isle frequently extracted from a single homily a series of passages of such material, omitting the intervening passages that were not biblical. In some cases he indicated an omission by entering "&ct." at the point where the omission begins, as he did on fol. 152r/29. Here, within the lengthy passage on the Temple of Jerusalem in the homily *In dedicatione ecclesiae*, he omitted Ælfric's interjection "Us is langsum to gereccene ealle ða bletsunga and ðancunga þe salomon ða gode sæde on his folces gesihðe" ("It will be long-winded for us to relate all the blessings and thanks that Solomon then uttered to God in sight of his people"), corresponding to Godden XL/70–71. Unfortunately,

---

[31] See Dickins (1972), 26.

[32] Although Anglo-Saxon scholars have believed that MS Gg. 3. 28 was the gift of James Pilkington, bishop of Durham, in 1574 (see Sisam [1953b], 168 n. 2; and Ker [1957], 21), Oates has shown that the manuscript had evidently not reached the University Library by 1583. Its presence there by 1600 is assured by its being listed in Thomas James's catalogue of that year (see Oates [1986], 100–01).

[33] As is noted by Ker (1957), 132.

however, L'Isle did not always indicate his omissions. For example, on fol. 159r, in the middle of a substantial series of transcriptions from the homily *Dominica I in mense Septembri* (Godden XXX), he omitted two portions of material without indication. At line 12 on the page, where his transcription reads "þingrædene forgeaf. Drihten eac," he omitted thirty words that follow the word *forgeaf* in the source manuscript, CUL MS Gg. 3. 28:

> . . . ðingrædene forgeaf; Ðeah þe iobes ansyn wære atelice toswollen. and his lic eal maðan weolle. swa þeah is awriten þæt se ælmihtiga underfeng his ansyne. þa þa he for his freondum gebæd; Drihten eac. . . .[34]

Similarly, at lines 14–15 on the page, L'Isle's transcription reads "be twyfealdum. Iob hæfde," with no indication that a substantial portion of text has been omitted after "twyfealdum":

> . . . be twyfealdum; Be ðisum is to understandenne. þæt se ðe for oðrum gebit fremað him sylfum micclum. swa swa þæt halige gewrit segð. þæt ða ða Iob for his freondum gebæd. þa gecyrde god to his behreowsunge. and swa eaðelice hine eft gehælde. swa he hine ær geuntrumode; Iob hæfde. . . .[35]

---

[34]Godden XXX/193–96: "through his [Job's] intercession [the Lord] forgave [their sin]. Although Job's countenance was swollen foully, and all his body swarmed with worms, yet it is written that the Almighty accepted his countenance when he prayed for his friends. The Lord also [then took pity on Job]."

[35]Godden XXX/198–204: "[God repaid him all his possessions] twofold. By this one is to understand that he who prays for others benefits himself greatly, just as the holy Scripture says that when Job prayed for his friends, then God took pity on him, and healed him as easily as he had previously afflicted him. Job had [before his sickness seven thousand sheep . . .]."

Like the extracts themselves, the omissions vary in length. The two examples cited above constitute only a few lines of text each, but between the bottom of fol. 152r and the top of fol. 153r of Laud 381, within the excerpts from *In dedicatione ecclesiae*, there is an omission of a substantial portion of text corresponding to seventy-four lines of the printed text (Godden XL/73–147: "Ðeos racu hæfð . . . him to clipigendum"). The omitted lines provide a lengthy explication by Ælfric of the typological relationship of Solomon to Christ and the significance of Solomon's building of the Temple.

This tendency to omit material, and more significantly L'Isle's inconsistency in indicating omissions, has important implications for our perception of Ælfric's paraphrase of the Old Testament book of Esther. As it stands in L'Isle's transcription, the homily on Esther is rather barren, containing none of the usual digressions or explanations common in other homilies by Ælfric. At first sight this might be taken as a sign of lack of interest on Ælfric's part, and, as Ælfric's writings are one of the best indicators we have of Anglo-Saxon attitudes at the turn of the millennium, this might also imply that the book of Esther was not regarded with such high esteem as, for example, the book of Judith: in his homily on Judith, Ælfric incorporated lengthy digressions and explanations within his paraphrase of the book.[36] However, given L'Isle's purpose of seeking biblical material and his habit of silent omission, it is reasonable to assume that originally Ælfric included some digressions within his paraphrase of Esther, and that these were omitted by L'Isle without indication.[37] It is also possible that material was omitted from the beginning and ending of the homily. Although in the upper margin of fol. 140v L'Isle entered the title *Be Hester*, seemingly indicating

---

[36]The homily on Judith is edited in Assmann (1889), 102–16, and re-edited in Lee (1992), 186–201.

[37]There is no occurrence of "&ct." or any other indication of omitted material throughout L'Isle's Esther transcription.

that this is the beginning of the homily, the case of his transcription of Ælfric's homily on Job, which begins on fol. 154r with the title *Be Iob*, provides a warning. This homily survives in four manuscripts, all of which have the following introductory section:

> Mine gebroðra. We rædað nu æt godes ðenungum be ðan eadigan were IOB. nu wille we eow hwæt lytles be him gereccan. for ðan þe seo deopnys ðære race oferstihð ure andgit. and eac swiðor þære ungelæredra; Man sceal læwedum mannum secgan be heora andgites mæðe. swa þæt hi ne beon ðurh ða deopnysse ærmode. ne ðurh ða langsumnysse geæðrytte;[38]

L'Isle chose to omit all of this introduction, without indicating that he was doing so, and started his transcription with the words "Sum wer wæs geseten" ("A certain man was settled") which follow immediately afterwards in the original homily. Had L'Isle been our only witness to Ælfric's homily on Job, readers might never have questioned whether the text originally contained an opening prefatory section or not. It seems not unlikely that *Be Hester* also originally had some opening comments by Ælfric to explain the importance of the story.

L'Isle's transcription of *Be Hester* ends on fol. 147v with the words "æfre rixað on ecnysse. AMEN" ("reigns forever and ever. Amen"). Comparison with the homily on Judith suggests that this phrase might not have been the true ending of Ælfric's homily. At line 423 of Assmann's edition of *Judith* there is a similar "closing" statement: "Þam sy a wurðmynt to worulde! Amen" ("To whom be glory forever! Amen").[39] There then follows both a lengthy

---

[38]Godden XXX/1–6: "My brothers, we read now at God's service about the blessed man Job. We will now relate to you a little about him, for the depth of the narrative surpasses our understanding, and the more so that of the unlearned. One should speak to laymen according to the measure of their understanding, so that they are not discouraged through the deepness, nor wearied by the length."

[39]Assmann (1889), 115.

explanation of the importance of Judith as a role model for nuns and an incomplete life of St. Malchus (lines 424–52). In its original form, the homily on Esther may well have ended with some concluding comments by Ælfric.

Knowledge of L'Isle's methods of transcription throughout Laud 381 thus suggests that the version we have of Ælfric's homily on the book of Esther may not be complete. On the one hand, examples found elsewhere in the Laud manuscript show that L'Isle freely omitted material from the beginning and middle of his other lengthy transcriptions. On the other hand, comparison of the Esther narrative with another similar text by Ælfric suggests that the last line of the transcription need not necessarily be a closing declaration. Indeed, if L'Isle's transcription of *Be Hester* were a complete version of the original homily, it would be unique within Laud 381, for none of L'Isle's other transcriptions in the manuscript presents a complete text of any work by Ælfric.

There are further important discoveries to be made within Laud 381. Folios 134v/27–139v/7 contain a set of transcriptions of Old Testament material whose source I have labeled in the table as "pseudo-*Ancrene Wisse*." These passages need to be considered in conjunction with a set of transcriptions at the end of MS Laud Misc. 201, which contains L'Isle's transcription and translation of the Old English text of the Eadwine Psalter. On fols. 264r–266r of Laud Misc. 201 is a set of six Old English prayers described by L'Isle's title on fol. 263v as "taken out of the Nunnes Rule of S^{nt} James order in Bennet Coll. library." In 1907, Heuser identified these texts as deriving from the Middle English *Ancrene Riwle*.[40] Because L'Isle's transcriptions display letter forms and spellings characteristic of Old rather than Middle English,[41] Heuser argued

---

[40]See Heuser (1907).

[41]Heuser (1907), 111–12: "Das alter unserer excerpte wird bewiesen durch die fast ganz ags. schriftzeichen. . . . Das alter der excerpte wird ferner bewiesen durch den noch fast altenglischen stand der sprache mit erhaltenem *æ*, *y*, *ea*, *eo*. . . ."

that L'Isle was using a twelfth-century version of the *Ancrene Riwle* which has since been lost. In 1909, Napier effectively quashed Heuser's suggestion.[42] Napier stated that the prayers transcribed by L'Isle were in fact extracts from CCCC MS 402 and that L'Isle deliberately archaized them to make them look more like Old English. CCCC 402 contains a thirteenth-century copy of the *Ancrene Riwle*; on the authority of the original title in the manuscript itself, its version is normally known as the *Ancrene Wisse*.[43] That L'Isle's extracts derive from a Corpus Christi College manuscript is indicated by his reference to "Bennet College," this being an alternative name for the college that was frequently used in the seventeenth and eighteenth centuries and that was derived from the dedication of the college's chapel, the parish church of St. Benet. Napier's arguments rested on three points: first, that L'Isle was sufficiently familiar with Old English to be capable of archaizing a text; second, that it is highly unlikely that, had Corpus Christi College ever possessed two copies of the *Ancrene Riwle*, it would have lost one of them; and finally, that two of L'Isle's extracts include textual features that occur only in CCCC 402, and thus confirm his use of that manuscript.

All these arguments are valid, and in particular the second, given the impeccable record of Corpus Christi College in preserving its manuscripts.[44] The extracts on fols. 134v–139v of

---

[42]Napier (1908–09). That Napier's conclusions remain in force is clear from Robinson (1993), 280–81. Referring to the six prayers transcribed by L'Isle in Laud Misc. 201, Robinson writes, "When he made his transcript . . . of some prayers from the *Ancrene Riwle*, he archaized the language of the latter texts, transforming the early Middle English of the *Ancrene Riwle* back into a form of Old English. . . . The restoration of older forms is imperfectly executed, but L'Isle's intention is clear: he wanted to construct an Old English text of the *Ancrene Riwle*."

[43]Edited in Tolkien (1962).

[44]See Page and Bushnell (1975), 7–8.

Laud 381 furnish further material to illuminate the issue, as they also come from an archaized version of the *Ancrene Wisse*. In total, they constitute a further ninety-nine lines of text. Neither Heuser nor Napier appears to have been aware of these extracts. They require careful analysis to see whether they might vindicate Heuser's theory that L'Isle had access to a now lost twelfth-century version of the *Ancrene Riwle*, or alternatively, whether they confirm Napier's conclusion. Study of the rest of L'Isle's transcriptions in Laud 381 shows that, omissions aside, he provided reasonably accurate transcriptions when dealing with known homilies. Further, the presence of his transcription of the homily on Esther shows that he had access to at least one manuscript that no longer survives. Again, the extracts from the pseudo-*Ancrene Wisse* in Laud 381 show little sign of the kind of reworking that one might expect from someone attempting to archaize a lengthy sequence of passages of Middle English.

An example will show the differences between L'Isle's transcriptions and the text of the *Ancrene Wisse* as it occurs in CCCC 402. On fol. 136v/27–32 of Laud 381, L'Isle provided the following transcription of a passage of text based on 2 Chronicles 20:12:

> In us nis na deorewurþ hlaford swa micel strengð *þæt* we magon wiðstonden se deofles fyerde þe is swa strong upon us. ah hwen we beoð swa bisteadet. swa strong bistonden. *þæt* we mid ealle na read ne cunnen bi us sylfu*m*. þis an we mage don. heouen ehnen up to þe mildfulle hlaford. þu send us fultum. þu to dreaf ure foen. for to þe we locað.

The equivalent passage in CCCC 402 is as follows:

> In us nis nawt deorewurðe lauerd swa muchel strengðe. *þæt* we mahen wiðstonden þe deofles ferd þe is se strong up on us. Ah hwen we swa beoð bisteaðet. swa stronge bistonden. *þæt* we mid alle na read ne cunnen bi us seoluen: þis an we mahe don. heouen ehnen up to þe

mildfule lauerd. þu send us sucurs. þu todreaf ure fan: for to þe we lokið.[45]

The differences between the two versions include the use of recognizably Old English forms in L'Isle's transcription: *hlaford* rather than *lauerd*, *magon* rather than *mahen*, *ealle* rather than *alle*, and so on, as well as the use of *fultum* in place of *sucurs*. L'Isle's other extracts on fols. 134v–139v show similar differences from the version of the *Ancrene Wisse* in CCCC 402.[46]

Despite these differences, there appears to be clear proof that L'Isle's source was in fact CCCC 402. That manuscript includes various early modern markings that Ker noted in his introduction to Tolkien's edition of the *Ancrene Wisse*:

> The *Ancrene Wisse* was read again carefully in the sixteenth century. The many crosses in the margins and the marking of passages in the text by underlining and side-scoring in pale ink are of this date, as appears from the script and the ink of words which in four places accompany these marks (f. 44.16 *Eccl'*; f. 63.27 *Cantic'*; f. 70.7 *þreagendes*; f. 72b.1 *Josaphat*).[47]

The marginal crosses and the "underlining and side-scoring" mentioned by Ker call to mind similar marks made in two other manuscripts known to have been used extensively by L'Isle, both now in the Bodleian Library: MS Laud Misc. 636, the Peterborough copy of the Anglo-Saxon Chronicle, and MS Laud Misc. 509, the copy of the Hexateuch borrowed by L'Isle from Cotton

---

[45]Tolkien (1962), f. 72b/8–14: "In us, dear Lord, there is not sufficient strength to withstand the devil's army which is so strong against us. But when we are so placed, so severely beset that we cannot even devise a plan for ourselves, this one thing we can do: lift our eyes to you, merciful Lord. You send us help, you drive away our foes, for to you we look."

[46]See the examples quoted in the paper by Phillip Pulsiano, above.

[47]Tolkien (1962), xviii.

for such a lengthy period. Dorothy Whitelock, in her facsimile edition of the Peterborough Chronicle, commented that L'Isle was responsible for entering in that manuscript "many ink under-linings, and . . . various crosses, trefoils, triangles and squares as caret marks."[48] Laud Misc. 509 includes, in addition to numerous notes by L'Isle (as on fol. 24rv), several underlinings of words within the text, with accompanying crosses in the margin. Similar marks occur in several other manuscripts and can be attributed to L'Isle.[49] It seems likely, then, that the marks in CCCC 402 may also be by L'Isle, and may not belong to the sixteenth century as Ker believed.

A study of the correlation between L'Isle's transcriptions and the marks in CCCC 402 confirms this. The first underlining in CCCC 402 occurs on fol. 23v/3–4 and 7–8, marking Latin and Middle English versions of Zechariah 8:2, the Middle English being "Ich am gelus of þe Syon mi leofmon wið muche gelusie" ("I am jealous of you, Sion, my beloved, with great jealousy"). This corresponds with the first extract from the pseudo-*Ancrene Wisse* in Laud 381 (fol. 134v/27): "Ic eom gelous of þe Sion myne leofman." Two further passages are underlined on fol. 23v of CCCC 402 but have no corresponding transcriptions in Laud 381. L'Isle's next transcription occurs at the top of fol. 135v of Laud 381; it consists of a single line that L'Isle crossed through after realizing that its text pertained to the New rather than the Old Testament (Revelation 2:17): "Hit is an dearne healewi[50] þe nan mon ne cnaweþ þæt næueð hit gesmacd."[51] This corresponds with an underlined passage on fol. 24v/4–5 of CCCC 402: "Hit is a dearne healewi þæt na mon ne cnaweð þæt naueð hit ismecchet" ("It is a secret healing liquid that no one knows who has not tasted

---

[48]Whitelock (1954), 24.

[49]See n. 30 above.

[50]Above *healewi* L'Isle has written the gloss "nomen."

[51]The final *d* is partly hidden in the gutter of the leaf.

it"). The next text underlined in MS 402 occurs on fol. 25v/16–20, and corresponds to Laud 381, fol. 135v/2–4. Indeed, for every transcription in Laud 381 from the pseudo-*Ancrene Wisse*, the corresponding lines in MS 402 are underlined. The reverse is not true: there are several underlined passages in MS 402 for which there is no corresponding transcription in Laud 381. Nonetheless, the evidence is strong enough to indicate that the marks in MS 402 were made by L'Isle to draw attention to passages of interest to him, some of which he then transcribed into Laud 381, archaizing them into "Old English" in the process.[52] Further, while most of L'Isle's transcriptions from the *Ancrene Wisse* fail to betray that he was modifying the text as he went along, two errors in his transcription on fol. 135v/24 reveal his process of "translation" and furnish additional confirmation that his source was MS 402. Folio 42v/14–15 of the Corpus Christi College manuscript provides a Middle English version of Lamentations 3:26: "God hit is i silence ikepen godes grace" ("It is good to await God's grace in silence"). L'Isle's transcription, in its corrected form, reads "God hit is on stilnesse gecepen godes hal." But before writing "stilnesse," L'Isle first wrote "silen," beginning the word "silence" that occurs in MS 402. Realizing that this was not an Old English word, he crossed it out and substituted "stilnesse." Again, before writing "hal," L'Isle first wrote "gyfe." He was evidently struggling to find the best Old English equivalent to the Middle English *grace*; his second version was closer to the word *salutare* that

---

[52] It is worth noting that L'Isle was not the only one to produce altered versions of the text in CCCC 402, although others directed their efforts at modernizing rather than archaizing the original. As Ker noted (Tolkien [1962], xviii), "one of Parker's expert scribes wrote on the flyleaf, f. iib, and also filled two inserted parchment leaves (ff. iii, iv) with a modernized version of the text on ff. 2.20–3b.1"; see further Wada (1994), xlvi and n. 5. Tolkien himself remarked on a "late 14th-century hand" which on fols. 1r, 2r, and 3r "began an attempt to modernize the text" by sporadically erasing and replacing obsolete letter forms (Tolkien [1962], 5, within the critical apparatus).

occurs in the Latin Vulgate version of the text that is cited in MS 402. L'Isle made both corrections as he wrote his transcription: the corrections occur within the line, alongside the words they replace, and are not later additions in the interline. L'Isle's transcriptions on fols. 134v–139v of Laud 381 therefore reinforce Napier's original conclusion that the six prayers at the end of Laud Misc. 201 were archaized from the text in CCCC 402; they confirm that L'Isle was capable of manipulating Middle English to make it appear to be Old English.

Close study of Laud 381 thus reveals much about L'Isle's intentions, methods, and abilities in the field of Anglo-Saxon studies. From the trial title pages at the beginning of the manuscript we learn of his plan to publish as much as he could of the Bible in Old English, a plan to which he alluded in his correspondence with Cotton.[53] The texts that he assembled in Laud 381 attest to his diligent examination of several manuscripts as he hunted for material to fulfill his purpose. The motto from St. John's Gospel that he included in one of his trial titles—"Gather up the fragments that remain, that nothing be lost"—is especially relevant to L'Isle's achievement in this manuscript, given that it includes, in his transcription of *Be Hester*, an Old English text of which no other copy now survives. Yet, as his work with the *Ancrene Wisse* shows, L'Isle was capable not only of preserving but also of transforming his sources.

---

[53] See n. 8 above.

THE SOURCES FOR THE TRANSCRIPTIONS
ON FOLIOS 116v–169r OF LAUD 381

The three columns of the table provide: (1) the folio and line numbers on which L'Isle's transcriptions occur in Laud 381; (2) references to the modern printed editions in which the texts transcribed by L'Isle may be found; (3) indications of the manuscript sources, or likely sources, from which L'Isle made his transcriptions. The editions to which reference is made are listed in the bibliography at the end of this volume (*LS*, i.e., Ælfric's *Lives of Saints*, appears in the bibliography as Skeat [1881–1900]). Where appropriate, the homilies listed in the table are cited by their item numbers (in upper-case Roman) within the modern editions. In all cases I have noted the line numbers within the editions where the passages transcribed by L'Isle may be found. For this, I have adopted the line-numbering conventions used within the editions, where in most cases individual items have a line numbering that continues throughout the item. In the right-hand column of the table, the item numbers that specify individual homilies within the source manuscripts are those of Ker's *Catalogue*.

Folio and lines	Source homily	Source MS and item number
116v/5–9	Clemoes XIX/55, 56–57, 89–90, 237–38	CCCC 162, art. 2
116v/10–14	Napier (1901), p. 361/1–5	CCCC 162, art. 4
116v/15–23	Godden XIX/149–52, 192–95, 247, 257–58	CCCC 162, art. 5
116v/24–117v/27	*LS* XIII/241b–267, 314–24	CCCC 162, art. 6
118v/1–18	Godden IV/182–97	CCCC 162, art. 9

Folio and lines	Source homily	Source MS and item number
118v/19–20	MacLean, lines 343–44, 408–09	CCCC 162, pp. 139–60[1]
118v/21–22	Godden V/254–55	CCCC 162, art. 11
118v/23–119v/5	*LS* XII/152–56	CCCC 162, art. 14
119v/6–10	Godden VII/61–64	CCCC 162, art. 16
119v/11–12	Scragg III/50, 130–31	CCCC 162, art. 19
119v/13–22	Pope III/65–79	CCCC 162, art. 20
119v/23–120v/5	Clemoes, Appendix B, no. 3/8–20, 21–26[2]	CCCC 188, art. 18
120v/6–15	Clemoes XVII/60–68	CCCC 162, art. 34
120v/16–121v/26	Scragg XIX/109–46	CCCC 162, art. 35
122v/1–6	Clemoes XXIV/158–60, 194–97	CCCC 162, art. 43
122v/7–8	Godden XXV/106–07	CCCC 162, art. 44
122v/9–14	Clemoes XXVIII/65–66, 129–30, 130–32	CCCC 162, art. 46
122v/15–124v/14	Godden XXVIII/64–69, 104–32, 134–59	CCCC 162, art. 47
124v/15	Clemoes XXXIII/52–53	CCCC 162, art. 50
124v/16–21	Clemoes XXXV/30–31, 137–39, 204–06	CCCC 162, art. 51

(*Continued*)

Folio and lines	Source homily	Source MS and item number
124v/22–28	Clemoes XXXIX/79–80, 81–85	CCCC 162, art. 53
125v/1	Scragg V/44–45	CCCC 198, art. 1
125v/2–3	Clemoes V/64–66	CCCC 198, art. 4
125v/4	Clemoes VII/233	CCCC 198, art. 6
125v/5	Godden IX/147–49	CCCC 198, art. 11
125v/6–12	Clemoes XIII/25–30	CCCC 198, art. 14
125v/13–15	Godden VII/13–16	CCCC 198, art. 18
125v/16–19	Scragg III/66–68, 137–39	CCCC 198, art. 19
125v/20–31	Assmann (1889), XI/9–11, 16–17, 27–29, 90–91, 93–95	CCCC 198, art. 20
126v/1–4	Belfour VI, p. 50/26–29; p. 52/5	CCCC 198, art. 21
126v/5–7	Assmann (1889), XII/99–102	CCCC 198, art. 22
126v/8–10	Godden XXXVII/125, 126–27	CCCC 198, art. 49
126v/11–13	Godden XXXVIII/84–85, 217–19	CCCC 198, art. 50
126v/14	Clemoes XXI/91	CCCC 198, art. 33
126v/15–17	Clemoes XXII/60–62	CCCC 198, art. 34

Folio and lines	Source homily	Source MS and item number
126v/18–22	Clemoes XXV/212–13, 186–89	CCCC 198, art. 38
126v/23–26	Clemoes XXVI/40–43	CCCC 198, art. 41
126v/27	Pope XVIII/176	CCCC 178, art. 9?[3]
126v/28–127v/15	Clemoes XXVII/228–47	CCCC 198, art. 43
127v/16–17[4]	Clemoes XXIV/194–97	CCCC 178, art. 4
127v/19–20	*LS* XV/116–18	CCCC 198, art. 59
127v/21	Clemoes XXXII/218–19	CCCC 188, art. 34
127v/22–129v/23	Clemoes XXXVII/154–202	CCCC 188, art. 41
129v/24–27	Clemoes XXXVIII/22–24, 138–39	CCCC 188, art. 42
130v/1–4	Clemoes XL/168–72	CCCC 188, art. 44
130v/5–13	Morris, Appendix II, p. 303/8–10, 24–30	CCCC 178, art. 7
130v/14–30	Pope XXIX/37–49, 55–59, 90–95	CCCC 178, art. 8
131v/1–134v/12	Pope XXI/210–99	CCCC 178, art. 18
134v/13–14	Bethurum Xc/190–91	CCCC 419, art. 9
134v/15–16[5]	Assmann (1889), XI/93–95	CCCC 419, art. 14
134v/17–19	Pope XXX/21–24	CCCC 419, art. 15

(*Continued*)

Folio and lines	Source homily	Source MS and item number
134v/20	Godden XXXV/91	CCCC 421, art. 2
134v/21–22[6]	Godden XXXVII/126–27	CCCC 421, art. 3
134v/23–24	Napier (1883), XLII, p. 198/21–23	CCCC 419, art. 1
134v/25–26	Godden XXXVII/153–54	CCCC 421, art. 3
134v/27	Pseudo-*Ancrene Wisse*: cf. Tolkien, f. 23b/27	CCCC 402
135v/1	cf. Tolkien, f. 24b/4–5	
135v/2–6	cf. Tolkien, f. 25b/16–18, 19–20, 24–26	
135v/7–9	cf. Tolkien, f. 26a/21–24	
135v/10	cf. Tolkien, f. 27a/14–15	
135v/11–12	cf. Tolkien, f. 28b/22–23	
135v13–15	cf. Tolkien, f. 29a/25–28	
135v/16	cf. Tolkien, f. 37b/14–15	
135v/17–20	cf. Tolkien, f. 40b/16–19	
135v/21–23	cf. Tolkien, f. 42a/22, 23–24, 27, 28	
135v/24–27	cf. Tolkien, f. 42b/14–16, 22–24	

Folio and lines	Source homily	Source MS and item number
136v/1	cf. Tolkien, f. 45b/15–16	CCCC 402 (*cont.*)
136v/2	cf. Tolkien, f. 44a/17–18	
136v/3–6	cf. Tolkien, f. 45b/25, 27–28	
136v/7–9	cf. Tolkien, f. 51a/3–6	
136v/10–12	cf. Tolkien, f. 51b/24–26	
136v/13–14	cf. Tolkien, f. 58a/18–19, 24	
136v/15	cf. Tolkien, f. 59b/23–24	
136v/16–22	cf. Tolkien, f. 60a/1–3, 4–5, 8–9, 18–19	
136v/23	cf. Tolkien, f. 62b/27	
136v/24	cf. Tolkien, f. 63a/25–26	
136v/25–26	cf. Tolkien, f. 70a/8–9	
136v/27	cf. Tolkien, f. 72a/16	
136v/28–137v/4	cf. Tolkien, f. 72b/8–14, 21–25	
137v/5	cf. Tolkien, f. 73a/1–2	
137v/6–9	cf. Tolkien, f. 74a/11–14	
137v/10–12	cf. Tolkien, f. 78a/5–8	
137v/13–16	cf. Tolkien, f. 79b/15, 24–26	

(*Continued*)

Folio and lines	Source homily	Source MS and item number
137v/17–18	cf. Tolkien, f. 80a/1–3	CCCC 402 (*cont.*)
137v/19–20	cf. Tolkien, f. 80b/12–13	
137v/21–22	cf. Tolkien, f. 82a/18–20	
137v/23–24	cf. Tolkien, f. 83b/25–26	
137v/25–27	cf. Tolkien, f. 84b/4–6, 25–26	
137v/28	cf. Tolkien, f. 96b/23–24	
137v/29	cf. Tolkien, f. 98a/21–22	
137v/30–31	cf. Tolkien, f. 99a/17–18	
137v/32	cf. Tolkien, f. 102a/7–8	
138v	[Page Blank]	
139v/1 and 5[7]	cf. Tolkien, f. 109b/12–13, 16–17	
139v/2–4	cf. Tolkien, f. 103a/25–27	
139v/6–7	cf. Tolkien, f. 110b/13–14	
139v/8	Napier (1883), XLVIII, p. 246/11, 8–9	CCCC 421, art. 8
139v/9–14	Clemoes XXXIV/264–69	CCCC 303, art. 29
139v/15–17	Assmann (1889), III/276–78	CCCC 188, art. 35[8]
140v–147v	Ælfric's homily on Esther	[Source lost]

Folio and lines	Source homily	Source MS and item number
148v/1–3	Clemoes, Appendix B, no. 3/95–97, 180–81	TCC B. 15. 34, art. 5
149v	[Page blank]	
150r/1–151r/11[9]	Godden XXVIII/98–139	CUL Gg. 3. 28, art. 77
151r/12–153r/25	Godden XL/10–70, 71–73, 147–75	CUL Gg. 3. 28, art. 91
154r/1–159r/33	Godden XXX/7–176, 179–87, 190–93, 196–98, 204–25	CUL Gg. 3. 28, art. 79
160r/1–164r/31	Godden I/127–272	CUL Gg. 3. 28, art. 44
165r/1–6	Godden XVI/58–63	CUL Gg. 3. 28, art. 59
166r/1–15	Godden IV/211–26	CUL Gg. 3. 28, art. 47
166r/16–17	Godden XII/252–53	CUL Gg. 3. 28, art. 55
166r/18–167r/11	Godden XIX/137–52, 200–04, 277–81	CUL Gg. 3. 28, art. 65
167r/12–16	Godden XXV/105–09	CUL Gg. 3. 28, art. 73

(*Continued*)

Folio and lines	Source homily	Source MS and item number
167r/17–21	Godden XXXV/59–62, 90–91	CUL Gg. 3. 28, art. 86
167r/22–30	Godden XXXVI/124–28, 44–48	CUL Gg. 3. 28, art. 87
168r/1–169r/3[10]	Clemoes XVIII/14–38	TCC B. 15. 34, art. 9
169r/4	Clemoes XXI/91	TCC B. 15. 34, art. 12
169r/5	Pope XI/107–08	TCC B. 15. 34, art. 17
169r/6–7	Pope XVI/117–18	TCC B. 15. 34, art. 27
169r/8–11[11]	Clemoes XXVIII/129–30, 130–32	TCC B. 15. 34, art. 28

Notes

[1]The text of the *Interrogationes Sigeuulfi* from which L'Isle was here transcribing was originally in CCCC 178 (as its third item), but was moved to CCCC 162 by Matthew Parker: see Ker (1957), 60, and Page (1993), 54.

[2]L'Isle crowded this transcription into the lower margin of fol. 119v and the upper margin of fol. 120v sometime after he had written the transcription on fol. 120v/6–15. The latter transcription is of a portion of Ezekiel 34 that L'Isle derived from the copy of Ælfric's homily *Dominica II post Pasca* (Clemoes XVII) in CCCC 162. As Ker notes (1957, no. 43, art. 18), a variant version of this homily, with a lengthy continuation, occurs in five manuscripts. The continuation, printed

by Clemoes in his Appendix B, includes an Old English version of another portion of Ezekiel 34. L'Isle evidently came upon the variant version of the homily at some point after making the transcription on fol. 120v/6–15, and added from the variant version its additional material from Ezekiel 34. His addition corresponds to CCCC 188, p. 177/14–p. 178/10; there are pencil markings attributable to L'Isle next to the opening of this passage on p. 177.

[3]L'Isle's transcription on fol. 126v/27 is of a translation of Isaiah 56:10: "Hi synd dumban hundan. ꝸ hi ne magon gebeorcan" ("They are mute dogs, unable to bark"). According to Cook (1898–1903), I, 25, and II, 51 and 73, this text occurs three times in Old English prose. Of these three occurrences, the most relevant is that in Ælfric's *Sermo de die iudicii* (Pope XVIII/176). This homily is not to be found in CCCC 198, but it does occur in CCCC 178, which was the source for some of L'Isle's transcriptions on later pages of Laud 381. Probably CCCC 178 was the source for this line. The line appears to be a later insertion by L'Isle; this might explain the apparent skip from one source manuscript to another.

[4]Lines 16–17 are crowded into the space between lines 15 and 18 on fol. 127v, and are a later addition to the page by L'Isle. This increases the difficulty of identifying the manuscript from which he derived these lines. Manuscripts consulted by L'Isle that contain this homily include CCCC 178 (art. 4), CCCC 188 (art. 25), and TCC B. 15. 34 (art. 21). Among these three manuscripts, the precise wording of L'Isle's transcription agrees only with CCCC 178, art. 4. L'Isle made no markings next to this passage in MS 178; he did, however, mark the equivalent passage in TCC B. 15. 34. Having added lines 16–17 to this page of Laud 381, L'Isle subsequently crossed out this transcription when he realized that he had already transcribed the same text on fol. 122v/3–6. He also crossed out line 18, which contains not a transcription but his comment "against Images. Deut. 12. 30, 31."

[5]L'Isle crossed out these two lines after realizing that he had already transcribed the same text on fol. 125v/30–31.

[6]L'Isle crossed out these two lines after realizing that he had already transcribed the same text on fol. 126v/9–10.

[7]This transcription is split between lines 1 and 5 because L'Isle wrote it after crossing out the transcription in lines 2–4; he began the new transcription in the line above the crossed-out text and completed it in the line below. He did not

wish to retain the text of lines 2–4 because it comprised New Testament material that he did not require for his purpose.

[8]The brevity of L'Isle's transcription makes it difficult to identify his source; however, among surviving manuscripts at Cambridge, this homily occurs only in CCCC 188 and 303. The wording of L'Isle's transcription agrees with CCCC 188, in which he has marked the passage in question.

[9]L'Isle crossed out this transcription and added the comment "habetur supra" after realizing that he had already transcribed an equivalent passage on fols. 122v/21–123v/25.

[10]L'Isle crossed out this transcription and added the comment "habetur alibi," presumably after realizing that he had transcribed an alternative version of the story of Jonah on fols. 120v/16–121v/26.

[11]L'Isle crossed out these four lines with the comment "habetur supra," after realizing that he had already transcribed the same text on fol. 122v/11–14.

THE CONSTRUCTION OF STRUCTURE
IN THE EARLIEST EDITIONS
OF OLD ENGLISH POETRY

Danielle Cunniff Plumer

The earliest printing of Old English poetry is now believed to have occurred in 1574 with the publication of Matthew Parker's edition of *Ælfredi regis res gestæ*, which includes Alfred's *Metrical Preface* to his translation of Pope Gregory the Great's *Regula pastoralis.*[1] Since that time, all known surviving Old English poetry has been translated from a manuscript context to a print context, from script to print. The change in context is not merely one of method of production. It also involves changes in expectation, in audience, in meaning. These changes are realized and made visible in the editions themselves, through the formats they use.

The differences between Old English poems in their manuscript contexts and those same poems as they are printed in modern editions are most visible when the two forms are presented side by side. The changes in visual formatting that such a comparison reveals did not come about instantaneously. They arose during the course of three hundred years of printing and editing Old English poetry; they represent responses to audience and

---

[1] Lucas (1995), 44. I am grateful to Prof. Lucas for bringing his article to my attention and for offering his comments on this paper.

editorial expectations of what it means for something to be an Old English poem. In the very earliest editions of Old English poetry, developments in format were in part designed to answer critics of Anglo-Saxon studies who held the language to be a "vulgar Tongue, so barren and so barbarous."[2] In short, changes in the presentation of Old English poetry were designed to bring about changes in its reception and to increase the acceptance of Old English studies themselves.

The most visible of these changes in presentation is lineation, that is, presentation in verse lines, which governs the shape of the text. In its manuscript context, Old English poetry is unlineated. The poetry is written continuously across lines, like prose, frequently with no indication that it is to be read as poetry.[3] This manuscript presentation is abandoned in modern editions, yielding texts like the following:

> HWÆT, WĒ GĀR-DEna in gēardagum,
> þēodcyninga þrym gefrūnon,
> hū ðā æþelingas ellen fremedon!

These famous lines, which open *Beowulf*, are here reprinted as they appear in Frederick Klaeber's edition, the standard critical

---

[2]Jonathan Swift, *A Proposal for Correcting, Improving, and Ascertaining the English Tongue* (London, 1712), 40.

[3]This is true of almost all Old English poems. Two Old English poems do appear to be lineated: the *Gloria II* (BL MS Cotton Titus D. xxvii, fol. 56v) and the *Leiden Riddle* (Leiden, Universiteitsbibliotheek, MS Vossianus lat. 4° 106, fol. 25v). The evidence for lineation in the *Gloria II* is fairly unambiguous, but not all scholars believe that the *Leiden Riddle* is lineated or derived from a lineated exemplar. For more discussion, see my M.A. thesis, "Lineation and Meter in Old English Poetry" (Univ. of California, Davis, 1994), which traces the lineation of Old English poetry and the evolution of theories of Old English meter from the manuscript presentations to modern editions.

edition of the poem.[4] Compare them to a transcription of the same lines, taken from the Nowell Codex, BL MS Cotton Vitellius A. xv, fol. 132r:[5]

HPÆT ÞE GARDE
na ingear dagum · þeod cyninga
þrym ge frunon huða æþelingas ellen
fre medon·

The differences between these forms of presentation are visually unmistakable and critically suspect. The capitalized words in the first line, which are given a whole line in the manuscript, lose their "space" in Klaeber's edition; the edition also regularizes the word breaks and spacing. But most important for the poem as a whole, the edited version presents a collection of half-lines, dividing the poem into short metrical units. This form of presentation erases a major difference between Old English and more modern poetry, that difference being, of course, spatial shape. The lineation of Old English poems encourages us, the readers, to read those poems as if they were modern poems, as objects with an inherent and visible structure.

The first editions of Old English poetry did not use lineation. This was largely due to the fact that the earliest editors of Old English poetry did not realize that they were editing poems. Matthew Parker's 1574 publication of Alfred's prefaces to his Old English *Regula pastoralis* included the text known today as the *Metrical Preface*, but the presentation offers no hint that Parker considered it to be poetical. The poem, which is given the heading "Liber loquitur," is not lineated by any metrical principles,

---

[4]Klaeber (1950), lines 1–3.

[5]For a facsimile of the poem, see Malone (1963).

although it is printed in the shape of a cup.[6] When William Camden reprinted the *Metrical Preface* in 1603 in his *Anglica, Normannica, Hibernica, Cambrica, a veteribus scripta*, he discarded even the shape and printed the preface as ordinary prose.

Other Old English poems made it into print purely as the result of accident. In 1605, the short *Proverb from Winfred's Time* was printed in a collection of the letters of St. Boniface (Winfrith/ Winfred), although not as a result of any intrinsic interest of its own. The two-line poem appears as a quotation in a letter written by one anonymous ecclesiastic to another who was about to begin a journey. The writer reminds his correspondent (I here quote the version of the 1605 edition): "Memento Saxonicum verbum: 'Ost daed lata domæ foreldit sigi sithagahuem suurltit thiana.'"[7] In this case, it seems questionable whether Serarius, the seventeenth-century German editor, realized—or could have realized—that this was a piece of Old English poetry. It appeared in his edition virtually by coincidence and only because it occurred in an anonymous letter that was included in a manuscript that contained the letters of St. Boniface that were the focus of Serarius's interest.

This is typical of the circumstances in which Old English poetry was published in the early seventeenth century. Much of the

---

[6]Lucas (1995), 44 n. 8, notes that other books of the period include this feature and that there is no evidence to indicate that the shape is copied from a manuscript exemplar.

[7]Serarius (1605), 73. The spelling of the proverb is continental because of its occurrence in a letter written on the Continent. Serarius's edition includes the errors "Ost" for *Oft* and "suurltit" for *suuyltit*, and some faulty word division: compare plate 1 in Robinson and Stanley (1991) and the edition in Dobbie (1942), 57. The precise meaning of the proverb is difficult to ascertain. Dobbie (p. 177) suggested "Often a sluggard delays in his [pursuit of] glory, in each of victorious undertakings; therefore he dies alone." See the Appendix at the end of the present paper for a chronological bibliography of the early editions of Old English poetry, 1574–1799.

interest in Old English at this time had a religious and polemical orientation. Early Old English scholars were primarily interested in the doctrinal support that Old English religious texts could provide the still fledgling Anglican Church. Among those scholars were Matthew Parker, archbishop of Canterbury (1559–75), and his followers, including John Foxe, author of the *Actes and Monuments* or *Book of Martyrs*. For Parker and his "school," the value of Anglo-Saxon studies was that they showed "how much this our Church, by the Encroachments of the Papacy, had deviated from its antient Doctrines and Practices."[8] Another group of antiquaries focused their studies on Anglo-Saxon law in order to bring early precedents to bear on English common law and its reform. The first and most important of these scholars was Laurence Nowell, who transcribed a substantial collection of Anglo-Saxon laws. Following Nowell's departure from England in 1567, the laws were published by his associate William Lambarde in 1568, accompanied by a Latin translation and by a glossary of legal terms that drew on the extensive Old English dictionary, the *Vocabularium Saxonicum*, that Nowell had compiled in manuscript.[9]

---

[8]These are the words of Parker's early eighteenth-century biographer John Strype, quoted in Tuve (1939), 166. For the early history of Old English studies, see also Petheram (1840), chs. II–VI; Adams (1917); Bennett (1938); Douglas (1951), chs. III–V; Levine (1987), 88–89 and 174–77; and Frantzen (1990), among others.

[9]William Lambarde, *Archaionomia, sive de priscis Anglorum legibus* (London, 1568). For more information about the legal aspect of early Anglo-Saxon studies, see Adams (1917), 27–28; and Schoeck (1958). The manuscript of Nowell's *Vocabularium Saxonicum* was used by successive Anglo-Saxonists, including John Selden and William Somner. It was finally published in 1952: see Marckwardt (1952). The fullest account of Nowell's work is still Flower (1935). Flower's erroneous belief that Laurence Nowell the dean of Lichfield and Laurence Nowell the antiquary were one and the same person was corrected by

The early polemicists, then, made enormous contributions to the study of Anglo-Saxon ecclesiastical and legal history but had little or no interest in Anglo-Saxon literature and art. It is therefore not surprising that when Old English poetry made its way into their editions, as with the *Metrical Preface* and the *Proverb from Winfred's Time*, they should ignore it or possibly fail to recognize its poetic nature. The next Old English poem in print, *Thureth*, also illustrates this. It was printed in Sir Henry Spelman's *Concilia, decreta, leges, constitutiones, in re ecclesiarum orbis Britannici*, published in 1639. Spelman had been a founding member of the Elizabethan Society of Antiquaries and was one of the leading antiquaries of his time.[10] His goal, comparable to that of Parker, Foxe, Nowell, and Lambarde, was to illustrate contemporary English civil and ecclesiastical law through a study of their Anglo-Saxon origins. His first work, the *Archæologus*, was a glossary of Old English and Latin legal terms.[11] Spelman was also interested in church history and founded the first Anglo-Saxon lectureship, at Cambridge, which was designed to provide a "Lecture of domestique Antiquities touching our Church and reviving the Saxon tongue."[12] The *Concilia* was Spelman's second major work, and it should not be surprising that it is a compilation of English church councils, decrees, laws, and constitutions.

Retha M. Warnicke in 1974, and a series of subsequent articles by various scholars has clarified the details of the antiquary's career: see, e.g., Berkhout (1985) and Berkhout (1998).

[10]For details of Spelman's biography, see the "Life of Sir Henry Spelman" in Gibson (1698). See also *DNB* s.n. The *DNB* contains biographies of most of the scholars mentioned in this paper.

[11](London, 1626). See the comments on the *Archæologus* and the history of its publication in the paper by Angelika Lutz in the present volume.

[12]Henry Spelman to Abraham Wheelock, 28 September 1638. Quoted in Adams (1917), 52.

On the face of it, it is somewhat surprising that *Thureth* should be included in Spelman's *Concilia*. The poem praises and intercedes for Thureth, the layman who paid for the binding of the *halgungboc* at whose beginning the poem was originally inscribed. That *halgungboc* principally contains pontifical and benedictional material, that is, texts for liturgical rites and benedictions that could be performed only by a bishop or archbishop.[13] It also includes a record in Latin and Old English of the proceedings of a synod held at Eanham (Hampshire) between 1008 and 1011. It was this synodal record that was the focus of Spelman's interest: he printed it on pages 511–29 of his *Concilia*. In the manuscript, *Thureth* faces the opening page of the account of the synod, and it may have been largely for this reason that Spelman included it in his compilation. Spelman's treatment of the poem, however, seems to indicate that he regarded it as being of some importance in and of itself. He edited it with some attempt at visual formatting, and accompanied it with a Latin translation so that it could be understood by those who did not know Old English:

Ego sum liber administratio-	Ic eom halgung boc healde hine
num sacrarum, propitius sit	dryhten þeme fægere þus
Dominus ei precor, qui me	frætewum be lægde þureð to
tam pulchrè ornatum posuit,	þance þus het mewyrcean to loue
piæ memoriæ ðureð sic me	ꓶ to wurðe þam þe leoht gesceop.
jussit concinnari, amoris & eo-	gemyndi ishe mihta gehwylcne
rum causâ qui luminis emendi	þas þe he onfoldan gefremian
sunt memores: multum valet	mæg ꓶ hunge þancie þeoda wal-
is qui me rectè explicare pote-	dend þæs þe he on gemynde mad-
rit, & retribuet ei Rector nati-	ma manega wyle gemearcian
onum quòd fuerit solicitus	metode tolace. ꓶ he sceal

---

[13] *Thureth* occurs in a composite manuscript presumed to have been assembled into its present form by Sir Robert Cotton: BL MS Cotton Claudius A. iii. The original manuscript to which *Thureth* belongs comprises the present fols. 31–86 and 106–50. See Ker (1957), no. 141; and Turner (1971), v–vii.

multas mihi pretiosas res of-   exelean ealle findan þæs
ferre, & mercedem inte-   þe he onfoldan
gram accipiet rectæ   fræmaþ to
suæ ac fructuosę   ryhte;[14]
explicati-
onis.

Spelman's formatting, however distinctive, is nonetheless by itself no indication that he was consciously editing *Thureth* as a poem, nor even that he realized that it was indeed poetry. His triangular tapering of the last lines mimics the manuscript layout of the original, there being six tapered lines in both the manuscript and the printed versions (although Spelman's version does not attempt to match the line-by-line layout of the original text, with the result that throughout the poem, line breaks occur at different points in the two versions).[15] In his introductory comments, Spelman described *Thureth* as an *elogium*, by which he probably meant an inscription. He noted that it was written "dialecto sanè insueta" ("in a highly unusual dialect"), but gave no hint that he recognized it as a poem. The inclusion of *Thureth* in Spelman's *Concilia* is perhaps an indication of a broadening base for Anglo-Saxon studies, a base that addressed a sincere interest in the materials themselves as well as in their contribution toward polemical debate and specific antiquarian interests, but it does not indicate that Spelman was the first editor of Old English literature as such.

The first scholar who seems to have made some real attempt to understand the nature of Old English poetry was Abraham

---

[14]Spelman (1639), 510–11. There are several errors of word separation and spelling in Spelman's edition of the Old English, as noted by Woolf (1953), 114 n. 9. Spelman's use of "exelean" where the manuscript has "ęcelean" resulted from his misunderstanding of *e*-caudata.

[15]For a reproduction of the original, see Robinson and Stanley (1991), plate 10.

Wheelock, the recipient of Spelman's Cambridge lectureship in Anglo-Saxon. Spelman first encouraged Wheelock to take up the study of Old English after visiting Cambridge in the mid-1630s in search of materials for his *Concilia*, a visit that caused him to decide that he needed a permanent helper in Cambridge to provide him with transcriptions of Old English texts. Wheelock was already University Librarian (and lecturer in Arabic), with privileged access to manuscripts, one of his tasks as librarian being to act as amanuensis for the copying of texts. The plan for the lectureship was conceived in December 1637, although Spelman did not disclose it to the university authorities until 1640. His death in 1641 prevented the lectureship from becoming the permanent post that he had envisaged, but under the patronage of Spelman's son and grandson, Wheelock continued to engage in Old English studies until his own death in 1653.[16] By 1641, Wheelock knew enough Old English to produce an admittedly idiosyncratic Old English version of a Hebrew poem he had written. Both the Hebrew poem and its Old English translation appeared in the collection *Irenodia Cantabrigiensis*, published in Cambridge in 1641 and commemorating the return of Charles I from a mission to Scotland in that year.[17] Wheelock's poem provides an interesting view of what Anglo-Saxon scholars thought that an Old English poem should be:

---

[16]On the history of the creation of the Cambridge Anglo-Saxon lectureship and on Wheelock's relationship with the Spelmans, see Adams (1917), 51–55; and Oates (1986), 185–88. For an account of how scholars of this period managed to learn Old English despite the shortage of printed texts and dictionaries, see Murphy (1968).

[17]*Irenodia Cantabrigiensis: ob paciferum serenissimi regis Caroli è Scotia reditum mense Novembri 1641* (Cambridge, 1641), sigs. A3^v–A4^r. Wheelock's Old English poem is transcribed, with translation and discussion, in Utley (1942). See also Murphy (1982a), 27–28.

Eadem Anglo- & Scoto-Saxonicé.

Scotland buton feohte
Ongel lond geswiþ'de.
Iacobus gryp'd hire ho's
Ond æfter his Carlos.
Eala Huntingdon hwære
Is þine dryman ðæt ðære
From Norþ dæl ure freondas
Woldon don ure feondas
Ond Breoton gehergian
Ðurh wordum to flitan·
Leasan wordas syndon.
Is þine heafod comon
Eadig Ceorl's Salome's
Sunu· sunu sibbes.
Na Dauides sunu.
Uncer Dauid eart þu
Ban ond flesc we beoþ
Ðine. on þe we ðeoþ
We ðine ðeod trywan
Unc ðin saul on gyman⁊

Francis Utley, whose study of this poem remains the fullest in print, claimed that Wheelock used Old English poetry as a model for his attempt and excused the weaknesses of the poem on the grounds that few models of Old English poetry were available for study.[18] Despite Utley's views, I believe that this poem of Wheelock's is based more on wishful thinking than on actual study of Old English poetry. The use of a trochaic rhythm does not imply that Wheelock had "some feeling for an unusually strong accentual principle in Old English verse," as Utley claimed.[19] William Retchford, who also contributed an Old

---

[18]Utley (1942), 258–60.

[19]Utley (1942), 259.

English poem to the *Irenodia*, wrote his in iambic tetrameter.[20] If, as Utley believed, Retchford was Wheelock's student, then it would be logical to suppose that Retchford would have followed his teacher's model if there were any reason to think it to be the more authentic. That Retchford did not copy Wheelock's example suggests that the choice of meter was arbitrary. Furthermore, the most distinguishing feature of Wheelock's poem is its use of rhyming couplets. Retchford's poem also uses rhyming couplets, as did a third Old English poem printed in a 1654 miscellany.[21] This use of rhyme could not be based on any models of Old English poetry (except for the *Riming Poem*, which there is no evidence Wheelock ever saw).[22] It seems likely that Wheelock and Retchford were simply inventing verse forms for Old English that had no connection with actual Anglo-Saxon poetry. They were creating Old English verse in the image of the poetry of their own time.

Even in the work for which Wheelock is most famous, his bilingual Latin–Old English edition of Bede's *Historiæ ecclesiasticæ gentis Anglorum libri V*,[23] in which he included an edition of the Anglo-Saxon Chronicle, there is no evidence that Wheelock had connected his conception of Anglo-Saxon poetry to actual Old

---

[20]Retchford's poem appears on sig. G4ʳ of *Irenodia Cantabrigiensis* and is reprinted in Utley (1942), 253, with discussion on pp. 254–60.

[21]Joseph Williamson, *On thære sibbe betweox Breotone & Holland*, in *Musarum Oxoniensium elaiophoria* (Oxford, 1654). A transcription and study of this poem can be found in Turner (1948), 389–93.

[22]The *Riming Poem* occurs on fols. 94r–95v of the Exeter Book (Exeter Cathedral Library, MS 3501). Wheelock's knowledge of Anglo-Saxon manuscripts appears to have been restricted to those in Cambridge and in the Cotton collection.

[23](Cambridge, 1643). Reprinted in 1644 with an augmented edition of Lambarde's *Archaionomia* appended.

English poems. In fact, the manner of presentation of those Old English poems that occur within Wheelock's edition suggests that he did not recognize the nature of Old English poetry as it was preserved in manuscript. Wheelock based his text of the Anglo-Saxon Chronicle on MS G (BL MS Cotton Otho B. xi), subsequently reduced to a fragment in the Cotton fire of 1731, and compared it with MS A (CCCC MS 173, Part I). Both manuscripts use verse for their annals for the years 938 (937 in MS A), 942 (941 in MS A), 973, and 975: these are the four poems now known as *The Battle of Brunanburh*, *The Capture of the Five Boroughs*, *The Coronation of Edgar*, and *The Death of Edgar*.[24] Wheelock was aware that there was something unusual about these passages. In editing the annal for 938—*The Battle of Brunanburh*—Wheelock noted in the margin of his edition, "Idioma, hîc & ad annum 942. & 975. perantiquum, & horridum" ("The idiom, here and at the years 942 and 975, [is] very ancient and rough").[25] That Wheelock recognized a difference in the style of these passages is significant. Yet he evidently did not recognize them as verse. Wheelock was not alone in this. John Milton also commented on the *Brunanburh* passage, observing that "the Saxon Annalist wont to be sober and succinct . . . now labouring under the weight of his Argument, and overcharg'd, runs on a sudden into such extravagant fansies and metaphors, as bare him quite beside the scope of being understood."[26]

Wheelock's failure to recognize the Chronicle poems as poetry—a failure paralleled by his apparent innocence of the

---

[24]For which see Dobbie (1942), 16–24.

[25]Wheelock (1643), 555.

[26]John Milton, *The History of Britain*, in Fogle (1971), 308–09; cited in Murphy (1982b), 15–16 n. 12. As Fogle points out (308 n. 65), Milton did not know Old English and gained his knowledge of the passage from Wheelock's Latin translation and that of the twelfth-century historian Henry of Huntingdon.

poetic nature of *Cædmon's Hymn* within the Old English text of the *Historia ecclesiastica*—is more understandable when the circumstances behind his edition are taken into account. His motives for publishing the *Historia ecclesiastica* were hardly unbiased. In his prefatory epistle addressed to the Chancellor, Vice-Chancellor, Masters of Colleges, and teachers of Cambridge University, he noted that the supplementary material with which he accompanied his edition of Bede, and which consisted of texts drawn from Anglo-Saxon manuscripts, "vobis præstabunt antiquitatem quæ crimen novitatis eluet: præstabunt veritatem, si accusatores sibi constare velint, hæresis expultricem: præstabunt consensum, quæ nostram cum grandæva matre *Ecclesia* communionem prolixè monstrant" ("will show you the antiquity [of current Anglican doctrine] which will remove the accusation of novelty; will show truth (if the accusers wish to be self-consistent) as the expeller of heresy; will show harmony, by amply demonstrating our communion with the ancient mother Church").[27] In this, Wheelock was largely carrying out Sir Henry Spelman's wishes; Spelman had requested Wheelock to "applie your self to the antientest Authors of our Church and Church History."[28] It is not surprising, then, that Wheelock had neither the time nor the inclination to evaluate more precisely the "perantiquum, & horridum" style of the Chronicle poems.

Other scholars were more persistent and, fortunately for modern readers, lacked Wheelock's polemical handicaps.[29] The first scholar to make an attempt fully to understand Old English

---

[27]Preface, sig. A3[r].

[28]Spelman to Wheelock, 28 September 1638; cited in Adams (1917), 53.

[29]One who shared those handicaps was Sir Roger Twysden, who published *Durham*, without lineation, in his *Historiæ Anglicanæ scriptores X* (London, 1652), 76, and (in a corrected version) on an unnumbered page following the *Glossarium* toward the end of the book.

poetry was undoubtedly the Dutchman Francis Junius, who worked in England as librarian to the earl of Arundel from 1621 to 1651. He devoted himself to studying Old English, a task for which his prior study of German and other northern languages had prepared him.[30] Unlike earlier scholars, such as Spelman and Wheelock, Junius's interest in Old English was primarily philological and not based on legal or ecclesiastical leanings. He worked regularly on an Old English dictionary, which was never published,[31] and transcribed many manuscripts containing Old English. His efforts bore fruit in two Old English publications: an edition of "Cædmon's Metrical Paraphrase,"[32] as it was known for centuries, and, in collaboration with the Oxford scholar Thomas Marshall, an edition of the Gothic and Anglo-Saxon Gospels.[33]

It is especially in his transcriptions, both published and unpublished, that Junius's awareness of the nature of Old English poetry becomes apparent. In his edition of the so-called Cædmon Manuscript—Bodleian MS Junius 11, now generally called the Junius Manuscript, acquired by Junius from Archbishop James Ussher—Junius made the metrical nature of the poems visible by a system of pointing. The manuscript itself is unique among the major codices of Old English verse for the heaviness and

---

[30]*DNB* s.n., p. 1116.

[31]A dictionary based on Junius's materials and compiled by Edward Lye was published by Owen Manning in 1772; in 1743 Lye had published Junius's *Etymologicum Anglicanum*. For a detailed consideration of Junius's manuscript Old English dictionary, see the study by Kees Dekker in the present volume.

[32]*Cædmonis monachi paraphrasis poetica Genesios ac præcipuarum sacræ paginæ historiarum, abhinc annos M. LXX. Anglo-Saxonicè conscripta, & nunc primùm edita* (Amsterdam, 1655).

[33]*Quatuor D. N. Jesu Christi euangeliorum versiones perantiquæ duæ, Gothica scil. et Anglo-Saxonica* (Dordrecht, 1665).

regularity of its metrical pointing.[34] Throughout most of the manuscript, the scribe used medial points to mark the end of each verse half-line.[35] The presence of these points may well have helped Junius to become aware of the poetic nature of the texts. In his edition, however, Junius did not simply reproduce the pointing of the manuscript. He introduced points where they had been omitted by the scribe. He also used a stronger form of punctuation to indicate the close of sense units. This can be seen from a comparison of the opening of *Genesis* as it appears in MS Junius 11 with Junius's published version of the same text. The manuscript version is as follows:

US IS RIHT MICEL ÐÆT
we rodera weard · wereda wuldor cining ·
wordum herigen · modum lufien · he is mægna
sped · heafod ealra heah gesceafta · frea ælmihtig ·[36]

Junius reproduced the text thus:

Us is riht micel. ðæt we rodera weard. wereda wuldor
cining. wordum herigen. modum lufien: he is mægna sped. heafod ealra heah gesceafta. frea ælmihtig:·[37]

The only end of a half-line that Junius failed to signal in this passage occurs after "heafod ealra," where his text runs on to "heah gesceafta," following the example of the manuscript. In

---

[34]See Krapp (1931), xxii–xxiv; Ker (1957), 408; and O'Keeffe (1990), 182–86.

[35]As has been noted by Ker (1957), 408, and O'Keeffe (1990), 182, some of the original punctuation was altered by a corrector who converted some of the points to *punctus versi* or *punctus elevati* by adding strokes.

[36]See Gollancz (1927), p. 1.

[37]Junius (1655b), 1.

contrast to this, Junius inserted a point not present in the manuscript version, to indicate the end of the first half-line after "micel." He used a set of three points in triangular formation to establish the end of sense units at "lufien" and "ælmihtig." His entire edition continues with the same degree of regularity of pointing, presenting an almost fully verse-delimited text. Small wonder that Junius was sure enough of his analysis to title his edition *Cædmonis monachi paraphrasis poetica*.

Another of Junius's transcriptions, this one in manuscript, more dramatically shows his use of the point to delimit verses of Old English poetry. Junius transcribed the *Meters of Boethius* from BL MS Cotton Otho A. vi before that manuscript was damaged in the Cotton library fire of 1731. For the most part, the manuscript lacks pointing, as can be seen in the following passage from the end of *Meter 24* on fol. 88v (asterisks indicate portions of the manuscript now illegible due to fire damage):

> ðe þis we
> **** folc wyrst tuciað *þæt* hi symle
> **** swiðe earme unmehtige ælces
> ****es emne ða ilcan þe þis earme folc
> **** hwile nu swiðost ondrædæð ·,·

Junius's transcription, found in Bodleian MS Junius 12, fol. 62f ^{r},[38] adds points throughout this passage:

> þe ðis werige folc .
> wyrst tuciað . *þæt* he symle bioð . swiðe earme . unmehtige .
> ælces ðinges . emne þa ilcan . þe ðis earme folc . sume
> hwile nu . swiðost ondrædeð .

By visually delimiting poetic half-lines, Junius's points make it clear that this is in fact poetry. His use of points to achieve this

---

[38]There are facsimile reproductions of MS Otho A. vi, fol. 88v, and MS Junius 12, fol. 62f ^{r}, in Robinson and Stanley (1991), plates 5.25.3.1–2.

enabled him to remain faithful to manuscript methods of presentation while still giving his audience, composed primarily of Old English scholars,[39] the means to identify Old English poetry on sight. By making verse lines visible, Junius revolutionized the study of Old English poetry.

The influence of Junius's system of pointing can be seen in Edmund Gibson's 1692 edition of the Anglo-Saxon Chronicle. Gibson's edition was based on Wheelock's, to which he added material from the Peterborough Chronicle and two other recensions of the Chronicle.[40] Gibson undertook to correct Wheelock's text of the Chronicle and to provide a new Latin translation. He also brought the knowledge provided by Junius's system of pointing to his edition. Although Wheelock's and Gibson's editions of *Brunanburh*, the annal for the year 938, give precisely the same text, the effect of Gibson's edition is totally changed by his treatment of the poem in his notes. Gibson's note on the 938 annal first quotes Wheelock's statement: "Idioma hîc, & ad An. 942. & 975. perantiquum & horridum." Gibson then adds his own comment on the style: "Perantiquum proculdubio; horridum interim haud dicendum: quippe quod stylum Cædmonianum, elegantissimum plane, & in quo Ducum res gestæ ob ejus sublimitatem decantari antiquitus solebant, aliquatenus saltem referat" ("undoubtedly very ancient, but it should in no way be called rough, for it reproduces, to some extent at least, the Cædmonian style, of great elegance; in olden times the deeds of the leaders were customarily recited in this style, because of its loftiness").[41] With this knowledge provided, the annal resolves itself into a poem based on the points

---

[39]The question of whether or not Milton had read or heard the "Cædmonian" poems before writing *Paradise Lost* has occupied Old English scholars for years. Modern opinion suggests that he probably had not, but it remains a tantalizing possibility.

[40]Douglas (1951), 70.

[41]Gibson (1692), 112 n. *d*.

already incorporated into it. Though Wheelock's text is virtually the same, with points in almost all the same places,[42] their effect was not understood by him. The interpretation of pointing offered by Junius shed new light on the structure of this and other Old English poems and enabled Gibson's recognition of *Brunanburh* as a passage in elevated, poetic style.

With the metrical structure of Old English poems rendered visible through pointing, the next step was to make this structure available to the average reader. The earlier editions of Anglo-Saxon materials had been predominantly targeted at antiquaries and polemicists. Junius's edition of the "Cædmon poems," which identified for the first time a purely literary element in Anglo-Saxon studies, did not sell well; Junius in fact had to keep most of the unbound printing of it in his own possession, though obviously antiquaries like Gibson were aware of it.[43] More drastic measures were needed to "popularize" Old English poetry. A movement grew up, composed of members of Oxford's Queen's and University Colleges, which aimed to acquire a complete understanding of all branches of Anglo-Saxon studies. These "Saxonists," as they were called, were led by Edward Thwaites and, most important, George Hickes.

Hickes began his Oxford career at St. John's College in 1659, soon transferred to Magdalen College where he was servitor to Henry Yerbury, and was elected a Fellow of Lincoln College in 1664. He was a student of Thomas Marshall, himself a friend and student of Francis Junius. Hickes was therefore well aware of Junius's work and indeed of all the work that had been done in the field of Anglo-Saxon studies. Hickes held the position of Dean of Worcester Cathedral from 1683 to 1689, when his refusal to take the oath of allegiance to William of Orange forced him into

---

[42]Gibson's text includes points in twelve places where Wheelock's has none, while Wheelock's text has six points not in Gibson.

[43]See Birrell (1966), 111.

hiding.[44] In 1689, he published *Institutiones grammaticæ Anglo-Saxonicæ, et Moeso-Gothicæ*. In this work, which does not deal with poetry directly, Hickes nevertheless managed to address Old English poetical style in a comment on the Chronicle poems:

> Non horrida hæc [quamvis perantiqua] ut *Whelocus* autumat, sed Poëtica, sed *Cædmoniana*. Ast excusandus erat vir Clarissimus, utpote cui nondum in manus inciderat ineditus liber Poëticus, quem *F. Junius* F.F. meritò vocat reconditæ antiquitatis Thesaurum.[45]

> (These [words] are (although very ancient) not rough, as Wheelock avers, but rather poetic, Cædmonian. Yet that eminent man was to be excused as being one into whose hands had not yet fallen the then unpublished poetic codex that F. Junius justly calls a treasure-house of hidden antiquity.)

After the publication of the *Institutiones*, Hickes conceived the idea of publishing a second, expanded, edition of that work. This idea grew out of letters between Hickes, Arthur Charlett, William Nicolson, and Edmund Gibson, as well as the young Humfrey Wanley, then at the beginning of his career as a paleographer. Later, Edward Thwaites was recruited to join the project. The idea of a second edition of the *Institutiones* was eventually abandoned, and a new work, which would become the *Linguarum vett. septentrionalium thesaurus grammatico-criticus et archæologicus*, was planned, although it was not published until 1703–05.[46] According to William Gardner, work on the *Thesaurus* began as

---

[44]*DNB* s.n., p. 802. For another, fuller, account of Hickes's life and work, see Harris (1992), Introduction, pp. 3–125.

[45]Hickes (1689), 74, asterisked note at the foot of the page. The initials "F.F." that follow Junius's name in Hickes's Latin stand for "Francisci Filius."

[46]See Harris (1992), 39–107. See also Bennett (1948).

early as September 1696;[47] and in some memoranda that he entered
at the back of a pocket almanac, Edward Thwaites noted on 28
July 1698 that "This evening, Dr. Hickes, the great restorer of our
Saxon learning, was pleased to give me leave to wait upon him,
shewing me his two chapters, of ye dialects one; y^t concerning the
poetry of ye old Saxon being the other."[48]

Printing of the *Thesaurus* could not begin immediately, since
Oxford had only one set of Anglo-Saxon types, the Junian types
created by Francis Junius. Hickes was therefore obliged to wait
until the completion of the printing of Thwaites's *Heptateuchus*
and of Christopher Rawlinson's edition of the Alfredian version of
Boethius's *Consolatio philosophiæ*.[49] Rawlinson printed as his
main text Alfred's initial, prose translation of the *Consolatio*, but
he provided in an appendix Alfred's later poetic version of the
metra of Boethius's text (now known as the *Meters of Boethius*).
Rawlinson set out to make the poetic nature of the *Meters* visible
and, with help from Thwaites, was able to put into practice some
of the ideas Hickes and his collaborators had formulated. In a letter
to Hickes dated 22 February 1698, Thwaites noted that Rawlinson
was "very desirous to have some account of the *Poeticall part
from* you. if you can conveniently let him have any small account
either out of the chapter you designe for the Poetic Part of the
tongue, or any other way you shall think proper, you will find him
very gratefull."[50] Whether or not Rawlinson received this material
is not clear, but Hickes's ideas must already have been communicated to Rawlinson by Thwaites.

---

[47]Gardner (1955), 199.

[48]Quoted in Petheram (1840), 75.

[49]Bennett (1948), 32. Thwaites's *Heptateuchus* included an edition of the Old
English poem *Judith* in which there is neither pointing nor any other indication
that it is poetry. This illustrates the continuing difficulty over the identification
of Old English poetry.

[50]Quoted in Harris (1992), 200–01.

Rawlinson was undoubtedly further assisted by the fact that he used as his base manuscript for the *Meters* not the tenth-century MS Cotton Otho A. vi, the only surviving medieval manuscript to contain the poetic Old English version of the *metra*, but Junius's transcript of the Old English *Consolatio*, Bodleian MS Junius 12. This is not apparent from the title to Rawlinson's appendix on page 150: "VERSIONES POETICÆ è Codice Cottoniano desumptæ." Rawlinson's title page for the whole volume, however, states that his edition was made "Ad apographum JUNIANUM." Further, in his preface to the reader,[51] Rawlinson recorded how, having first become acquainted with Bodleian MS Bodley 180— the other medieval manuscript of the Old English *Consolatio*, in which the *metra* are rendered in prose—he subsequently discovered Junius's transcript which included in the margins the variants of the Cotton manuscript. Rawlinson also noted that in his manuscript exemplar for the *Meters*, the verses were indicated by metrical pointing. We have already seen that Junius's transcript of MS Otho A. vi introduced metrical pointing not in the original manuscript. Rawlinson's exemplar for the *Meters* must therefore have been MS Junius 12. Rawlinson's debt to Junius was noted by William Nicolson in a letter to Ralph Thoresby of 22 October 1698, in which Nicolson drew attention to Rawlinson's edition and noted that it was done "from a fair Copy that Junius left behind him."[52]

Rawlinson went beyond Junius in that he not only included Junius's metrical pointing in his edition, he also took the further step of setting the text in verse lines. In his preface, he noted that he had laid out the poetic version of the *metra*:

---

[51] Adams (1917), 80, stated that this preface was "probably by Thwaites, so that Rawlinson was practically little more than an amanuensis for the edition." The preface is, however, signed by the initials "C. R."

[52] Harris (1992), 249.

ita quidem, ut Anglo-Saxonicæ poeseos ratio, ut ita dicam, ac forma, quoad ejus fieri poterat, exhiberetur; divisis scilicet ac distinctis singulis versibus, qui in exemplari MS continuâ scripturâ, posita licet ad singulos versus interpunctione, repræsentantur.[53]

(in such a way that the mode, as I may say, and the form of the Anglo-Saxon poetry might as far as was possible be displayed; namely with the individual verses divided and distinguished, which in the manuscript exemplar are formatted in continuous writing, although with points marking the individual verses.)

Rawlinson's appendix thus presents a series of lineated poems, the first lineated Old English poetry in print. The *Meters* appear as single lineated verses, two columns per page. Each verse, or half-line in modern terms, is concluded by a point. The opening of *Meter 1*, for example, is as follows:

> Hit wæs geara iu.
> ðætte Gotan.
> eastan of Sciþþia.
> sceldas læddon.
> ðreate geþrungon.
> ðeod lond monig.[54]

Rawlinson's edition thus moves one step beyond Junius's system, in that it incorporates a fully visual system of delimiting verses which eliminates the possibility of misreading Old English poems as straightforward prose. Indeed, in Rawlinson's system the points marking the verse ends have become redundant. Had he realized that they did not occur in the Cotton manuscript itself, he might not have retained them.

---

[53]Rawlinson (1698), sig. a2ᵛ.

[54]Rawlinson (1698), 150.

Rawlinson's visual presentation of Old English verse links well with the ideas that Hickes put forward in his *Thesaurus*. Presumably the section on Old English poetry, one of the first completed, was one of the first printed. This section shows how much the understanding of Old English poetry had progressed since Hickes's *Institutiones* were published, and it makes explicit some of the principles of lineation that in Rawlinson's *Boethius* were only implicit. In the chapter entitled "De poetica Anglo-Saxonum" in his *Thesaurus*,[55] Hickes begins by remarking that Old English poetry needs to be considered from the standpoint of diction, meter, and rhythm, and he discusses these in order. In considering meter, he notes the quantitative nature of the poetry. Observing that its individual verses (i.e., half-lines) can contain anything between three and eight syllables, and occasionally more, he contrasts it with the poetry of his own day, in which lines contain an equal number of syllables.[56] The variation of the number of syllables in the verses of Old English poetry, and the lack of rhyme, prove to Hickes that the poetry is genuinely metrical, but he acknowledges that the meter is frequently difficult to identify because of current ignorance of the quantitative value of individual syllables. He notes that verses most frequently contain four, five, or six syllables comprising two or three spondees, or a combination of spondee and dactyl.[57] The way in which feet are combined constitutes rhythm, and rhythm, in Hickes's view, is the "soul" of meter, enabling the life of the poem to manifest itself so that the poem can move its audience.[58] All in all, Hickes's review of Old English metrics suggests that he did not perfectly understand Old English poetry, and he admits that Old

---

[55]Hickes (1703–05), Part I, 177–221.

[56]Hickes (1703–05), Part I, 180–81.

[57]Hickes (1703–05), Part I, 180 and 186–89.

[58]Hickes (1703–05), Part I, 188.

English poetry is "spinosa" ("thorny") and difficult to understand,[59] though he still recommends the study of Old English poetry as a pleasant and useful activity.[60]

Daniel Calder has suggested that Hickes was attempting to base Old English metrics on a foundation of Greek and Latin prosody,[61] and this classical orientation was undoubtedly responsible for many of Hickes's misconceptions about Old English poetry. Hickes in fact traces some similarities between Greek and Latin poets, including Pindar, Homer, Catullus, and Virgil, and such Anglo-Saxon poets as Cædmon. One of the similarities Hickes notes is the use of alliteration. Hickes compares the alliteration of Virgil's "Mæonia mentum mitra crinemque madentem" (*Aeneid* IV, 216) to Cædmon's "Metodes mihte ꝺ his mod geðanc" (*Cædmon's Hymn* 2).[62] Essentially, Hickes suggests that alliteration in Old English poetry is similar to that in Greek and Latin poetry, and to that used by more modern English poets such as Donne and Dryden; he suggests, in other words, that alliteration in Old English poetry is ornamental instead of structural.

As Rawlinson had done with the *Meters of Boethius*, Hickes lineates a number of Old English poems in his chapter on Anglo-Saxon poetry, basing his lineation on his notions of quantitative rhythm. He admits that it can be difficult to tell where one line ends and another begins because it is impossible to know how many syllables should be in each line, what the quantity of those syllables is, and how diphthongs should be treated.[63] As a result of his guesswork approach, Hickes's lineation is sometimes inaccurate, as his treatment of *Brunanburh* shows:

---

[59]Hickes (1703–05), Part I, 177.

[60]Hickes (1703–05), Part I, 203.

[61]Calder (1982), 203.

[62]Hickes (1703–05), Part I, 196–97.

[63]See Hickes (1703–05), Part I, 181.

Her Æþelstan cyning.
Eorla drihten.
Beorna beah-gyfa.
And his broðor eac Eadmund æþeling.
Ealdor langne tyr.
Geslohgon æt secce.
Sweorda ecgum.
Ymbe brunan-burh.[64]

This example does more than illustrate the problems of Hickes's metrical theory. It also shows to what degree Hickes's actual lineation was based on the practical use of manuscript pointing. The opening of *Brunanburh* in Gibson's *Chronicon Saxonicum* appears as follows:

An. DCCCCXXXVIII. Her Æðel-
stan cyning. eorla Drihten. beorna
beah-gyfa. ꝛ his broðor eac Eadmund
æðeling. ealdor langne tyr. geslohgon æt secce. sweorda ecgum. ymbe
Brunan-burh.[65]

Hickes's edition of *Brunanburh* is pointed exactly as Gibson's is. Gibson does not have a point between "broðor" and "eac Edmund" and neither does Hickes. The result of this missing point is a line that is obviously too long in Hickes's edition. Hickes's metrical theory was not capable of picking up where his practical guide, pointing, left off.

Hickes often admits the utility of manuscript pointing, even providing, in one section, a guide to some different types of points

---

[64]Hickes (1703–05), Part I, 181.

[65]Gibson (1692), 112.

used in manuscripts.[66] However, Hickes seems to treat points as essentially equivalent to but less useful than lineation. He occasionally leaves a poem, such as *Cædmon's Hymn*, without lineation, furnishing it with enough pointing to make the verse divisions clear,[67] but he does this only after he has lineated enough poems to establish the poetic nature of his texts. Like Rawlinson, Hickes retains points at the ends of lines, although in Hickes these strongly resemble stops more than the metrical markers of the manuscripts. He does not attempt to explain why the Old English poems were unlineated in their manuscripts, but it is clear that he regards lineation as a vast improvement over the manuscript system.

One other significant feature of Hickes's texts is his use of capitalization. Hickes edits Old English poems with a capital beginning each new line. Other editors had not adopted this practice. Even Christopher Rawlinson followed manuscript capitalization when he edited the *Meters of Boethius*. Hickes, while acknowledging Rawlinson's edition, edits the *Meters* more freely, as is shown by his version of the opening of *Meter 3*:

> Ææla [*sic*] on hu grimmum
> And hu grundleasum.
> Seaðe swinceð.
> Ðæt sweorcende mod.
> Ðonne hit ða strongan.
> Stormas beatað.[68]

Hickes's edition, in fact, presents Old English poems according to the standards of poetic presentation common in his own time, complete with initial capitals and end-stopped lines. He therefore

---

[66]Hickes (1703–05), Part I, 203.

[67]Hickes (1703–05), Part I, 198.

[68]Hickes (1703–05), Part I, 177.

completes the circle begun by Wheelock in his *Eadem Anglo- & Scoto-Saxonicé*. Wheelock created a new type of Old English poetry that resembled the poetry of his own time, while Hickes transformed authentic Old English poetry so that it resembled the poem composed by Wheelock.

It should be noted that Hickes's approach to lineation was not the definitive word on the subject in the eighteenth century. John Smith, whose Latin and Old English edition of Bede's *Historia ecclesiastica* was completed by his son George and published in 1722, chose not to edit *Cædmon's Hymn* into a lineated poem, but to present it in long lines like the surrounding prose, as it occurs in the manuscripts of the Old English Bede (although he did assign it its own paragraph).[69] He did this despite the fact that *Cædmon's Hymn* is lineated both in the *Thesaurus* and in Humfrey Wanley's *Librorum vett. septentrionalium . . . catalogus historico-criticus* (1705), which forms the second volume of the *Thesaurus*.[70] While working on his edition, Smith had in fact received from Wanley a letter that included a discussion of *Cædmon's Hymn* and its manuscript context. Writing on 28 August 1703 on the subject of the Moore Bede (now CUL MS Kk. 5. 16), a copy of the Latin *Historia ecclesiastica* written within a few years of Bede's death in which the Old English *Cædmon's Hymn* occurs as a contemporary addition,[71] Wanley informed Smith:

> One thing more I take the liberty of acquainting you with; that this Book, confirm's a most ingenious Conjecture of Dr Hickes, who reading over the Saxon Version (or Paraphrase) of Bede, in *Lib*. IV. *Cap*. 24. observed the Song of Caedmon, to be in *Verse*, & answering to Bedes *Latin* Words, which made him ghess, that K. Ælfred when he came to that place, did not translate Bede, but put in Caedmons own

---

[69]Smith (1722), 597.

[70]Hickes (1703–05), 187, and Wanley (1705), 287.

[71]See Ker (1957), no. 25.

Words, which were then extant. . . . So, the Dr ha's printed this Song,
in his Grammars now in the Press, mending some faults therein: and I
in this MS. upon the same leaf of Parchment with the abovewritten List
& Notes, *but before them*, and (I verily think) by the same hand (tho'
in lesser characters) was glad to find the same, with Caedmons name
to it, in the following words, which being, as the rest, written A.D. 737
I take to be one of the most antient Specimens of our language any
where extant. Nu scylun hergan. hefaen ricaes uard. metudaes maecti.
end his mod gidanc. uerc uuldur fadur. sue he uundra gihuaes. eci
drictin. ora stelidae; He aerist scopa. elda barnum. heben til-hrofe.
haleg scepen. tha middun geard. moncynnaes uard. eci dryctin. aefter
tiadae. firu[m] foldu. frea allmectig; Primo cantauit Caedmon istud
carmen.

These words are thus written in the MS. afte[r] the old Orthography, but I add the distinguishing points which are not in the MS. The
Orthography of all living Languages does change in tract of time; and
. . . these said words, would have been differently written 200 years
after. . . .[72]

When Wanley edited this poem for his *Catalogus*, he lineated
it (while noting that in its manuscript it was written "perpetua . . .
scriptione").[73] By contrast, and despite having been informed by
Wanley that *Cædmon's Hymn* was a verse composition, Smith
showed greater editorial conservatism by sticking more closely to
the manuscript format for both the West Saxon version in his main
text and the Northumbrian version which he placed in a note.[74]

---

[72]Heyworth (1989), 225. For more information on Wanley, see Wright (1960).

[73]Wanley (1705), 287.

[74]It is interesting to note that Smith's manner of editing *Cædmon's Hymn* has
remained the *de facto* standard for editing this poem in the context of Bede's
Historia ecclesiastica. Outside of the context of the *Historia* as a whole,
however, *Cædmon's Hymn* is almost universally lineated. Even when it is
presented in the context of the "Story of Cædmon," in anthologies and Old
English readers, for example, the poem itself is lineated. A similar situation

The modernization effected by Hickes and other Anglo-Saxonists was unsuccessful in at least one other sense. Their efforts did not legitimize Anglo-Saxon studies in any real way, at least not as far as audiences were concerned. Hickes's *Thesaurus*, published by subscription, even so did not do well, and on Hickes's death twenty unbound copies were still in his possession.[75] Rawlinson's edition of Boethius was limited to 250 copies, printed apparently at Rawlinson's expense, and most of these were given away rather than sold.[76] Even Junius's edition of the "Cædmon poems" did not become popular until long after his death.[77]

The fortunes of Anglo-Saxon studies perhaps reached their nadir in 1712, when Jonathan Swift published his *Proposal for Correcting, Improving, and Ascertaining the English Tongue.* Swift referred to antiquarians as "laborious Men of low Genius" and took a contemptuous stance toward the studies of "the vulgar Tongue."[78] His remarks were quickly answered by Elizabeth Elstob, one of Hickes's adherents and an Anglo-Saxonist in her own right,[79] but Swift's comments seem to have been typical of the times. Although a number of studies of Old English were published during the eighteenth century—Hickes's *Thesaurus* alone was adapted six times[80]—there was little emphasis on Old English poetry, and only one edition of an Old English poem was

---

exists for the poems of the Anglo-Saxon Chronicle. See Kiernan (1990) for a discussion of the manuscript and modern contexts of *Cædmon's Hymn*.

[75]Bennett (1948), 44.

[76]Petheram (1840), 73.

[77]Birrell (1966), 111.

[78]Swift (1712), 40.

[79]See the *Apology for the Study of Northern Antiquities* in Elstob (1715). For more information on the scholarly activities of Elizabeth Elstob and her brother William, see Collins (1982) and Sutherland (1998).

[80]For a listing of these adaptations, see Adams (1917), 91–92.

printed in England, Thomas Hearne's 1726 edition of *The Battle of Maldon*, which was inserted into his *Johannis confratris et monachi Glastoniensis chronica sive historia de rebus Glastoniensibus*.[81] Some poetry did get published in the course of editing histories or the Anglo-Saxon laws, and Johann Adelung and Anthony Willich included Hickes's versions of *Cædmon's Hymn* and *Durham* in their philological treatises, but other proposed editions of Old English poetry failed for lack of funds. When Daines Barrington printed the Old English version of Orosius's *Historiae adversum paganos*—a prose text—in 1773, he wrote in his preface that "There are so few who concern themselves about Anglo-Saxon literature that I have printed the work chiefly for my own amusement, and that of a few antiquarian friends."[82]

The early editors of Old English poetry, then, failed to popularize Old English poetry and the study of Anglo-Saxon despite their "modernization" of Old English poems. It is surprising that their failure did not lead to a rejection of their methods of visual formatting, but it did not. Instead, during the nineteenth century, which witnessed the next great revival of Anglo-Saxon scholarship, editorial emendation of Old English poems, particularly in the realm of emendation *metri causa* and lineation, became more and more silent, more and more unacknowledged, until even the foremost editions of our day do not explain their lineation or the reason for it. In Klaeber's edition of *Beowulf*, with which I began this paper, Klaeber mentions only once that the manuscript itself is unlineated, when he notes that "In accordance with the regular practice of the period, the Old English text [in the manuscript] is written continuously like prose";[83] he never mentions his own lineation or the basis of it. A study of the evolution of lineation in

---

[81] *The Battle of Maldon* appears in vol. II, 570–77.

[82] Quoted in Adams (1917), 106.

[83] Klaeber (1950), xcvi.

the first two centuries of editing Anglo-Saxon poetry should remind us that lineation is not an intrinsic part of Old English poetry, as it is of modern poetry, but extrinsic. Lineation in Old English poetry is an evolved artifact, a response to audience expectations that poems, all poems, are lineated, and to a desire to shape the future of Anglo-Saxon studies by shaping the poems themselves to suit modern taste.

APPENDIX

PRINTED EDITIONS OF OLD ENGLISH POETRY 1574–1799[84]

1574   Parker, Matthew, ed. *Ælfredi regis res gestæ* (London). Includes Alfred's *Metrical Preface* to his translation of Pope Gregory the Great's *Regula pastoralis* on sig. F.ii^v.

1603   Camden, William. *Anglica, Normannica, Hibernica, Cambrica, a veteribus scripta* (Frankfurt). Includes Parker's edition of Alfred's *Metrical Preface* to the *Regula pastoralis* on p. 27.

1605   Serarius, Nicolaus, ed. *Epistolæ s. Bonifacii martyris, primi Moguntini archiepiscopi, Germanorum apostoli: pluriumque pontificum, regum, & aliorum* (Mainz). Includes *A Proverb from Winfred's Time* as no. LXI, p. 73. See Woolf (1953), 115, for a transcription.

1639   Spelman, Henry. *Concilia, decreta, leges, constitutiones, in re ecclesiarum orbis Britannici*, I (London). Includes *Thureth* (p. 510) in an unlineated but formatted version with a parallel Latin translation. See Woolf (1953), 114, for a transcription.

1643   Wheelock, Abraham, ed. *Historiæ ecclesiasticæ gentis Anglorum libri V a venerabili Beda presbytero scripti* (Cambridge). Parallel Old English and Latin texts for Bede. *Cædmon's Hymn* appears on p. 328. An edition of the Anglo-Saxon Chronicle, based on MS G (BL MS Cotton Otho B. xi) and including its poems, follows Bede. None of the poems is lineated or separated from the surrounding texts in any way, although a note by Wheelock to the poem for 938, *The Battle of Brunanburh*, observes that "Idioma, hîc & ad annum 942. & 975. perantiquum, & horridum, Lectoris candorem, & diligentiam desiderat" (p. 555).

---

[84]I want to thank Timothy Graham for his help in compiling and correcting the information in this Appendix.

1652   Twysden, Roger, ed. *Historiæ Anglicanæ scriptores X* (London). A collection of Latin historical texts. The Old English *Durham* appears twice: once in col. 76, with the heading "De situ Dunelmi, & de sanctorum reliquiis quæ ibidem continentur carmen compositum," and again following the glossary toward the end of the book, with the heading "Scriptura Saxonica, de Dunelmensis urbis situ, &c. ad fidem codicis MS. Simeonis, loci monachi, col. 76. exhibita, hîc denuò recognita, gravioribus à mendis repurgata, & (ad verbum) Latinè reddita." Both versions are unlineated.

1655   Junius, Franciscus. *Cædmonis monachi paraphrasis poetica Genesios ac præcipuarum sacræ paginæ historiarum, abhinc annos M.LXX. Anglo-Saxonicè conscripta* (Amsterdam). Contains the four major "Cædmonian" paraphrases (*Genesis A* and *B*, *Exodus*, *Daniel*, and *Christ and Satan*) along with the metrical *Prayer* (pp. 110–11) of BL MS Cotton Julius A. ii, fols. 136r–137r. All poems are unlineated.

1692   Gibson, Edmund, ed. *Chronicon Saxonicum* (Oxford). Based on Wheelock's edition, supplemented by passages from other manuscripts. Includes the Chronicle poems, although these are not separated from the surrounding text or lineated. Adds to Wheelock's note on the poems for the years 938, 942, and 975 the following comment (p. 112 n. *d*): "Perantiquum proculdubio; horridum interim haud dicendum: quippe quod stylum Cædmonianum, elegantissimum plane, & in quo Ducum res gestæ ob ejus sublimitatem decantari antiquitus solebant, aliquatenus saltem referat."

1698   Rawlinson, Christopher, ed. *An. Manl. Sever. Boethii Consolationis philosophiæ libri V. Anglo-Saxonice redditi ab Alfredo, inclyto Anglo-Saxonum rege* (Oxford). Includes the *Meters of Boethius*, beginning on p. 150, taken from Junius's transcript (Bodleian MS Junius 12) of BL MS Cotton Otho A. vi. The poetry is lineated on the half-line, two columns per page, making this, to my knowledge, the first lineated Anglo-Saxon verse.

1698   Thwaites, Edward, ed. *Heptateuchus, liber Job, et evangelium Nicodemi; Anglo-Saxonice. Historiæ Judith fragmentum; Dano-Saxonice* (Oxford). Includes *Judith*, without lineation or any indication that it is poetry.

1703–05   Hickes, George, and Humfrey Wanley. *Antiquæ literaturæ septentrionalis libri duo*, 2 vols. (Oxford). The first major compilation of Old English poetry is found in vol. I of this work, Hickes's *Linguarum vett. septentrionalium thesaurus grammatico-criticus et archæologicus*. Hickes edits, and lineates, the following poems: Meters 2, 3, 4, 6, 9, and 20 (lines 210b–224a) of the *Meters of Boethius* (Part I, pp. 177, 178, 182, 183, 184, and 185; following Rawlinson); *Durham* (pp. 178–79; with parallel Latin translation); lines 1–50 of *Gloria I* (pp. 179–80); a portion of *Judith* (p. 180); *Brunanburh* (pp. 181–82); portions of *Genesis* (pp. 182–83, 184–85, 187, 188, and 189); portions of *Exodus* (pp. 180 and 187); *The Death of Edgar* (pp. 185–86); the West Saxon version of *Cædmon's Hymn* (p. 187); *Finnsburh* (pp. 192–93); and a complete edition of the *Menologium* and *Maxims II* (pp. 203–08). All these poems are lineated on the half-line according to Hickes's notions of meter. Hickes also publishes some poems and passages of poetry in unlineated format. These include the *Rune Poem* (Part I, p. 135), and *Cædmon's Hymn* and passages of *Genesis, Exodus, Judith*, and *The Death of Edgar* that he cites when discussing peculiarities of word order and poetic construction (Part I, pp. 198–202). In the second volume of the work, Humfrey Wanley's *Librorum vett. septentrionalium . . . catalogus historico-criticus*, *Cædmon's Hymn* is edited again, this time from the Northumbrian version (p. 287). This version is also lineated by half-line. Wanley also edits the Anglo-Saxon *Lord's Prayer III* and the *Creed* (pp. 48–49), and *Thureth* (pp. 225–26), all without lineation.

1708   Wotton, William. *Linguarum vett. septentrionalium thesauri grammatico-critici, & archæologici, auctore Georgio Hickesio, conspectus brevis* (London).

1721   Wilkins, David. *Leges Anglo-Saxonicæ ecclesiasticæ &
        civiles* (London). Contains *Thureth* (p. 119).

1722   Smith, John, ed. *Historiae ecclesiasticae gentis Anglorum
        libri quinque, auctore sancto & venerabili Baeda presbytero
        Anglo-Saxone* (Cambridge). Contains *Cædmon's Hymn* (West
        Saxon version) on p. 597 and provides the Northumbrian
        version in a footnote. The Latin version occurs on p. 171.
        None of the versions is lineated, although the Latin version
        is marked as speech through quotation marks at the beginning
        of each (prose) line.

1726   Hearne, Thomas, ed. *Johannis, confratris et monachi
        Glastoniensis, chronica sive historia de rebus Glas-
        toniensibus*, 2 vols. (Oxford). The first edition of *The Battle
        of Maldon* (vol. II, pp. 570–77).

1735   Shelton, Maurice, trans. *Wotton's Short View of George
        Hickes's Grammatico-Critical and Archeological Treasury
        of the Ancient Northern Languages* (London). Includes
        Cædmon's Hymn in a lineated version (p. 19).

1737   Wilkins, David. *Concilia magnae Britanniae et Hiberniae, a
        synodo Verolamiensi A. D. CCCCXLVI ad Londinensem
        A. D. MDCCXVII*, 4 vols. (London). Contains *Thureth* in an
        unlineated version (vol. I, pp. 285–86).

1763   Grupen, Christian Ulrich. *Observationes rerum et anti-
        quitatum Germanicarum et Romanarum* (Halle). Prints
        Cædmon's Hymn in both the West Saxon and Northumbrian
        versions, following Hickes and Wanley (p. X); includes
        Hickes's "unscrambled" version (pp. X–XI).

1773   Langebek, Jacobus, ed. *Scriptores rerum Danicarum medii
        ævi*, II (Copenhagen). Includes an edition of *The Battle of
        Brunanburh* (pp. 413–19).

1776   Michaeler, Karl. *Tabulae parallelae antiquissimarum
        Teutonicae linguae dialectorum, Moeso-Gothicae, Franco-
        Theotiscae, Anglo-Saxonicae, runicae, et Islandicae*

(Innsbruck). Contains editions of the West Saxon and Northumbrian versions of *Cædmon's Hymn* (Part III [*Monimenta veteris linguae Teutonica selectiora*], pp. 154–55), *Brunanburh* (Part III, pp. 227–40), and *Durham* (Part III, pp. 241–44). The poems are lineated on the half-line. The two versions of *Cædmon's Hymn* are preceded by Bede's Latin account and followed by an "unscrambled" version of the Old English. *Brunanburh* and *Durham* are provided with parallel Latin translations.

1777   Strutt, Joseph. *The Chronicle of England*, 2 vols. (London). Prints in an appendix a lineated version of *Cædmon's Hymn* (vol. II, p. 282).

1783   Adelung, Johann Christoph. *Neues grammatisch-kritisches Wörterbuch der englischen Sprache für die Deutschen; vornehmlich aus dem grössem englischen Werke des Hrn. Samuel Johnson nach dessen vierten Ausgabe gezogen, und mit vielen Wörtern, Bedeutungen und Beispielen vermehrt*, I (Leipzig). Contains *Cædmon's Hymn* in both West Saxon and Northumbrian versions on p. XV, after Hickes and Wanley. Contains *Durham* on p. XXIV, after Hickes.

1787   Suhm, Peter Frederik. *Symbolæ ad literaturam Teutonicam antiquiorem ex codicibus manu exaratis, qui Havniæ asservantur, editæ* (Copenhagen). Contains on pp. 147–50 an unlineated version of the metrical charm *For Unfruitful Land*.

1789   Würdtwein, Stephan Alexander, ed. *Epistolae s. Bonifacii archiepiscopi Magontini et martyris ordine chronologico dispositae* (Mainz). Prints *A Proverb from Winfred's Time* as no. CLII, p. 352.

1798   Oelrichs, Johann. *Angelsächsische Chrestomathie oder Sammlung merkwürdiger Stücke aus den Schriften der Angelsachsen, einer uralten deutschen Nation* (Hamburg). Contains *Durham* on pp. 49–51. The poem is lineated on the half-line.

1798   Willich, Anthony F. M. *Three Philological Essays, Chiefly Translated from the German of John Christopher Adelung* (London). Contains *Cædmon's Hymn* (Essay 1, p. viii) in parallel-column reprints of the editions by Hickes and Wanley; mentions Wheelock's edition but concludes that his text does not seem as authentic. Gives English and German translations below the Old English text. *Durham* appears with a parallel English translation and with a German translation below (Essay 1, pp. xviii–xix). The editions are lineated on the half-line.

"THE ORACLE OF HIS COUNTREY"? WILLIAM SOMNER, *GAVELKIND*, AND LEXICOGRAPHY IN THE SEVENTEENTH AND EIGHTEENTH CENTURIES

Kathryn A. Lowe

William Somner (1606–69)[1] is best known as the scholar who produced the *Dictionarium Saxonico-Latino-Anglicum* (1659), the first Old English dictionary to be published. The importance of the *Dictionarium* for the development of the study of Old English during the period was immense, and studies of Somner have concentrated on this aspect of his accomplishment.[2] In this essay, however, I wish to consider the use made of Somner's works by scholars in the wider field of modern English lexicography at a time when derivations of words regularly began to be included in

---

[1] For Somner's correct date of birth, see Urry (1977), vi–vii.

[2] See, e.g., Hetherington (1982); and the chapter "William Somner's *Dictionarium*" in Hetherington (1980), 125–82. Douglas (1951), 55–57, places Somner in the context of English medieval scholarship during the period. The origins of Somner's work are considered in Lutz (1988). The only full-length study of Somner's *Dictionarium* is the unpublished doctoral dissertation by Joan K. Cook, "Developing Techniques in Anglo-Saxon Scholarship in the Seventeenth Century: As They Appear in the *Dictionarium Saxonico-Latino-Anglicum* of William Somner" (University of Toronto, 1962).

English dictionaries. In particular, I focus on the etymology of one word, *gavelkind*, on which Somner worked in detail and which can be seen as representative of his interests.

Although Somner's other works are today generally forgotten, the *Dictionarium* in fact emerged as an offshoot of his major interest, the history of Kent. Somner's first work, *The Antiquities of Canterbury* (1640), dealt only with post-Conquest material in Latin. His eventual aim (which was never realized) was to write a work on the history of the antiquities of Kent, and he was aware that Celtic and Old English would be necessary for this project. Somner's biographer, White Kennett (1660–1728), eloquently explained the difficulties of such an enterprise:

> To acquire the first, there were rules of Grammar, explication of words, and other sufficient Memoirs, beside the living Dialect, to guide a man of industry and resolution. But the Saxon language was extinct, and the monuments of it so few and so latent, that it requir'd infinite courage and patience, to attempt and prosecute the knowledge of it.[3]

Somner was taught the basics of Old English by Meric Casaubon and quickly became an authority on the subject, producing a very well-received glossary to Twysden's *Historiae Anglicanae scriptores X* (1652) and contributing translations of Old English material in Dugdale's *Monasticon Anglicanum* (1655–73). His newly acquired knowledge enabled him to study the customs and tenures of Kent using pre-Conquest material. This led to the publication of *A Treatise of Gavelkind*, finished in 1647 but unpublished until 1660. At the same time, Somner worked on his *Dictionarium*. The importance of his work to the development of the subject was recognized and the annual stipend of the Lectureship in Anglo-Saxon at the University of Cambridge was

---

[3]White Kennett, "The Life of Mr. Somner," in Somner (1726), 27.

eventually diverted to allow him to complete the project which "would more improve that tongue than bare Academic Lectures."[4]

In 1659 the *Dictionarium* was published in Oxford with the help of public and private subscriptions. Although it was an essential tool for scholars and students, initially supply appeared to

---

[4]Somner (1726), 88. White Kennett here renders part of the dedicatory preface to the *Dictionarium* in which Somner explains how he came to be appointed to the lectureship: "Eodem itaque *Abrahamo Wheloco* defuncto, meque deinceps viri cujusdam amplissimi literis & testimonio Dominationi tuæ commendato, (*Saxonici* mei de quo supra instituti intuitu, quo multo magis quam Academicâ prælectione, ut verisimile fuit linguam essem promoturus:) eidem in stipendii quadam parte qui succederem non indignus judicatus sum. Hoc autem non sine illius assensu & consensu, (Quod absque debitâ erudito ingenuo viro, ob ipsius erga me benevolentiam, gratiarum actione, non omnino memorandum:) quem nullâ hactenus de me Dom. tuæ factâ mentione, eidem *Abr. Wheloco* successurum designaveras" ("And so, after Abraham Wheelock had died, and I had thereafter been commended to your lordship by the letters and the testimony of a certain most renowned man—prompted by the sight of my Saxon dictionary mentioned above, through which it seemed that I was much more likely to promote the tongue than through academic lectures—I was judged not unworthy to succeed him in a certain portion of the stipend. But this was not without the assent and agreement of him whom, before my name had been mentioned to you, you had designated to succeed the same Abraham Wheelock; an agreement in no way to be recalled without rendering due thanks to the learned and liberal man for his goodwill toward me"). A printed marginal note identifies Somner's farsighted benefactor as the archbishop of Armagh. James Ussher (1581–1656) was primarily a theologian and biblical scholar, but was himself deeply interested in early British history. He is known to have corresponded with Sir Henry Spelman about the study of Old English (Hetherington [1980], 61) and had helped to set up the Anglo-Saxon lectureship with him. Abraham Wheelock had been the first incumbent of the lectureship. After Wheelock's death in 1657, Roger Spelman (Henry's grandson and heir) had planned to give it to the "eruditus ingenuus vir" of the extract, Samuel Foster, a clergyman, before Ussher interceded on Somner's behalf ("The Life of Mr. Somner," in Somner [1726], 88). Somner appropriately chose to dedicate his work to Roger Spelman.

outweigh demand. A year after publication, Dugdale noted in his diary that the bookbinder "piled up the Saxon Dictionaries in my upper chamber, wch were in number 514 perfect, and six imperfect."[5] A year later, Hamper notes, Dugdale "left Ten Copies of Somner's Saxon Dictionary with Booksellers, 'to trye if they can sell them.'"[6] Yet, as Hetherington observes, within thirty years Somner's *Dictionarium* was almost impossible to obtain. In 1699 Edward Thwaites, who had begun to teach Old English at Queen's College, Oxford, declared, "We want Saxon Lexicons. I have fifteen young students and but one Somner for them all."[7] In 1701 a condensed version (*Vocabularium Anglo-Saxonicum*) was made to enable students to buy the work. This version was published under the name of Thomas Benson, one of Thwaites's younger colleagues. It seems likely, however, that Thwaites lent considerably more than the inspiration to the project, and his contribution may indeed have been greater than that of the named author.[8]

The interest of Somner's work to general lexicography lay in his contribution to etymology. To that extent, the publication of the *Dictionarium* was well timed, for it was during this period that English dictionaries began to include etymologies on a regular basis and (occasionally) to give the root form of words derived from Old English.[9] Hayashi considers the rise of Old English scholarship during the sixteenth and seventeenth centuries to have

---

[5]Hamper (1827), 107.

[6]Hamper (1827), 107.

[7]Nichols (1812–15), IV, 141. Hetherington (1980), 177, notes that the young Humfrey Wanley laboriously transcribed Charles King's copy of Somner's *Dictionarium* for his own use.

[8]See Douglas (1951), 66; and Adams (1917), 78.

[9]Starnes and Noyes (1946), 46, credit Thomas Blount as the first lexicographer of a purely English dictionary to attempt the etymology of words. Blount's *Glossographia* (on which see below, pp. 288–89) appeared in 1656.

been a major factor contributing to this development.[10] Early interest in Anglo-Saxon studies, as will be seen below, resulted in the publication of a number of works of use to the would-be etymologist well before the publication of Somner's *Dictionarium*. Somner himself relied heavily on such material in the preparation of the *Dictionarium*, as well as on several Old English dictionaries in manuscript form.[11] It is therefore often impossible to determine the exact source for the derivation of a particular word, so that any investigation of Somner's influence on modern English lexicography of the period must be based on work that he is known to have developed himself and where his research challenges a previously accepted etymology.

Somner had learned Old English in order to be able to read pre-Conquest charters relating to the history of Kent. His main interest lay in this legal material, and this was where he was able to make his most substantial and original contribution to learning. His understanding of Old English together with his wide knowledge of both pre- and post-Conquest material relating to Kent allowed him to dispute and refine current theories on a type of land tenure largely peculiar to Kent, that of gavelkind. Most important for our purposes, Somner spent some forty pages of *A Treatise of Gavelkind* discussing the etymology of the term itself. Previously held opinion derived the term from three Old English words, *gife*, *eal*, and *cyn* (together interpreted as "given to all the kin"), with

---

[10]Hayashi (1978), 50.

[11]The unpublished dictionaries or glossaries of Nowell, D'Ewes, and Dugdale were made available for Somner's use (see Hetherington [1980], 144). Printed sources of the *Dictionarium* included Lambarde's *Perambulation of Kent* (1576), Camden's *Britannia* (1586), and Verstegen's *Restitvtion of Decayed Intelligence* (1605). A list of published material to which Somner referred in his *Dictionarium* is given as Appendix 4 in Hetherington (1980), 209–21, reproduced from Cook's dissertation. Other unpublished material that Somner is known to have used is considered in Hetherington (1980), 145–52. See also Lutz (1988).

scant regard for inflexional endings. This derivation, advanced by scholars such as Lambarde, Camden, Verstegen, and Spelman, arose largely as a result of the observation that the principal distinguishing feature of this type of land tenure appeared to be that, on the tenant's death, land was to be equally divided among the tenant's sons or children. Lambarde is accredited by Somner as the first scholar to offer the etymology,[12] which appeared in his *Archaionomia* of 1568: "Gauelkyn, *quasi* gife eal cyn, *id est, omnibus cognatione proximis data.*"[13] Lambarde was also the first (and apparently the only authority before Somner) to inject a note of caution. His later work, *A Perambulation of Kent* (1576), offered an alternative explanation:

> Two coniectures I haue of the reason of this name, the one grounded vpon the nature of the discent, and inheritance of these landes themselves: the other founded vpon the manner of the duetie and seruices, that they yeald: bothe whiche I will not sticke to recite, and yet leaue to eache man free choice, to receaue either, or to refuse both; as it shall best lyke him. . . . Nowe, for as muche as all the nexte of the kinred did this inherite together, I coniecture, that therfore the land was called, eyther *Gauelkyn*, in meaning, *Giue all kyn*, bycause it was giuen to all the nexte in one line of kinred: or *Giue all kynd*, that is, to all the male children: for *kynd*, in Dutche, signifieth yet a male childe. . . .
>
> My other coniecture, is raysed vpon the consideration of the rent and seruices going out of these landes. . . . This rent, and customarie payment of works, the Saxons called, *gafol*, and therof (as I think) they named the lande that yealded it, *gafolette*, of *gafolcynd*. that is to saye, lande *Letten for rent*, or of the kinde to yealde rent.[14]

---

[12]Somner (1660), 3.

[13]Lambarde (1568), sig. D.ii^r.

[14]Lambarde (1576), 388–89.

Somner disposed of the *gife eal cyn* theory with a thoroughness typical of his work. Illustrating his argument with quotations from charters, he showed that the etymology, although superficially plausible, had little to recommend it. He succeeded in demonstrating that this type of land tenure could be alienable outside the male line, and, indeed, outside the immediate family, thus challenging the derivation of the second element from *cyn*. He also pointed to the existence of related compounds such as *gavelcorn* and *gaveldung*, where the first element, in his words, "will not bear the derivation of it from *Gife-eal*, without absurdity."[15] He concluded unambiguously (and not without a certain sense of triumph):

> And now to wind up all (concerning this first Proposition) and not to enlarge with any further instances (wherein I might be infinite) for asserting this truth of our *Gavelkynds* derivation: *Gavelkynd*, we see, is the lands right name, whose Etymologie was never wrested to *Gife-eal-cyn*, whose signification of Censual, Rented, land, or Rent-service land, was never questioned till that within our fathers memories, one and all, by a kind of errour, *jure veluti successionis*, transmitted to them, run a head in a wrong and mistaken derivation.[16]

Instead, Somner showed that the term derived from OE *gafol* ("tribute, rent") and *gecynd* ("nature, custom"). The results of his research were published in the *Dictionarium*:

> Gafel. Tributum, census, vectigal, pensio, redditus. tribute, tol, custome: a subsidy: yearly rent, payment or revenew. Barbarè, *gabella*. Hinc nostratium Gavel-kind, & Gavelkind-land, *i.e.* terra vel fundus sui natura tributarius. de quo nos pluribus, in voce *gablum*, in Glossario.

---

[15]Somner (1660), 11.

[16]Somner (1660), 41.

The reference "in Glossario" is to Somner's glossary attached to Twysden's *Historiæ Anglicanæ scriptores X*, where the relevant portion of the entry for *Gablum* reads:

> . . . Gavelkynd, *quod fundum signat, non (quomodo Lambardo, &*
> *sequacibus ejus expositum) omnibus cognatione proximis datum,*
> *q.* gife-eal-cyn: *sed censualem, tributarium, reditui annuo, cæterisque*
> *plebeiorum prædiorum servitutibus & oneribus obnoxium.* . . . *Fusiùs*
> *autem de hoc Tractatu nostro de* Gavelkynd, *cap.* I. *Plura etiam apud*
> *Spelmann. in voce Gabella.*[17]

Although the *Treatise of Gavelkind*, mentioned here, was not published until 1660, it was finished by 1647 and it is natural that Somner should have referred to it. Somner's disagreement with the etymology traditionally given for *gavelkind* first appeared in print, then, with the publication of Twysden's work in 1652.

The publication of Somner's *Dictionarium* seems to have been eagerly anticipated by others outside the sphere of Anglo-Saxon studies. The lexicographer Thomas Blount mentioned it in his address "To the Reader" in his *Glossographia* (1656):

> I have likewise in a great measure, shun'd the old *Saxon Words*; as
> finding them growing every day more obsolete then other. Besides
> there is an excellent *Dictionary* thereof shortly expected from the
> learned Mr. *Somner.*[18]

---

[17]Twysden (1652), s.v. *Gablum* (Somner's glossary appears on unnumbered leaves toward the end of the book): ". . . Gavelkind, which signifies an estate, not (as explained by Lambarde and his followers) given to all those related by kinship, as if it were 'gife-eal-cyn,' but one that is censual and tributary, liable to rent and the other dues and burdens of the common people's estates. This is covered more fully in our *Treatise of Gavelkind*, ch. I. More also in Spelman, s.v. *Gabella*."

[18]Blount (1656), sig. A3ᵛ.

It is unfortunate that the notice of the imminent arrival of the *Dictionarium* seems largely to have served as an excuse to dispense with obsolete Old English words in general English dictionaries, a practice, of course, still followed today. Blount's etymology for *gavelkind* is a summary of Lambarde's discussion of the word in the *Perambulation*, admitting two possible derivations:

> Gavelkind . . . is derived of three Saxon words, gife, eal, cyn, that is, given to all the kin. . . . Or rather from gafel i. *sensus, tributum, pensio,* and cynd *natura, genus, conditio.*

This careful approach can be contrasted with that of Edward Phillips, the first edition of whose *The New World of English Words* appeared in 1658, a year before the publication of the *Dictionarium*. Phillips had pretensions to learning. The frontispiece of his dictionary had engravings of famous antiquaries and literary figures associated with Oxford and Cambridge: Spenser, Chaucer, Lambarde, Camden, Spelman, and Selden. As Blount was to point out acidly in his 1673 pamphlet *A World of Errors Discovered in the New World of Words*, this "pompous Frontispiece" lent a false sense of authority and scholarship to the work. Blount similarly attacked as highly misleading the catalogue of present-day scholars "Eminent in, or Contributory to, any of those Arts, Sciences or Faculties contained in the following Work"[19] which Phillips prefixed to the dictionary. In Blount's view, by including this list at the beginning of the dictionary "the Author would at least obscurely insinuate, that those Learned Persons had contributed to or assisted him in it, thereby to advance its

---

[19]This quotation is from the third (1671) edition of *A New World of English Words*. As Starnes and Noyes observe (1946, p. 54), the parallel phrase in the first edition is the unambiguous "The names of those learned Gentlemen and artists, as also of those Arts and Sciences, to which they contributed their assistance."

reputation; but I believe nothing less, having heard some of the chief of them utterly disown both the Author and his Work."[20] Blount was quite right, for there is no evidence at all that these scholars either contributed to the dictionary or that Phillips used their works. In fact, the majority of the definitions in *The New World of English Words* are demonstrably borrowed directly from *Glossographia*, although Phillips himself was dismissive of Blount's work and methods in his "Advertisement to the Reader" prefixed to his dictionary:

> the Saxon words, as in reference to our Lawes, cannot be accounted so obsolete as some would have them. For my own part, I have made it my businesse with my greatest care and diligence to consult with ancient Manuscripts; nor have I wanted in these scrutinizings the assistance of Grand Persons.

These "Grand Persons" apparently did not include Somner, nor indeed Lambarde, for the etymological entry under *gavelkind* reads simply: "*Gavelkind*, from the three Saxon words, *Gife*, *Eal*, *Cyn*, i.e. given to all the kind." Further, despite the publication of Somner's *Dictionarium* almost half a century before, this etymology of *gavelkind* remained in the revised edition of Phillips's work, John Kersey's *The New World of Words* (1706). Notwithstanding the similarity of title, Kersey's revision is considered so thoroughgoing as to constitute a new work in itself.[21]

Nathan Bailey's *Universal Etymological English Dictionary* (1721) was a work that enjoyed considerable popularity and ran through thirty editions, the last of which appeared in 1802. The emphasis placed on word derivation is evident from the title of the work. The Preface to the first edition shows that Bailey was aware of Somner's importance:

---

[20]Preface to *A World of Errors* as quoted by Starnes and Noyes (1946), 52.

[21]Starnes and Noyes (1946), 84.

> And besides, very few of the Etymological Words are my own, but I
> have generally the suffrage of *Somner, Camden, Verstegan, Spelman,*
> *Casaubon,* Dr. *Th. Henshaw, Skinner, Junius, Menagius, Minshew,* and
> other Great Names and approved Etymologists to bear me out.

Indeed, Bailey's dictionary is the only one of the period to provide
Somner's etymology as the sole and standard explanation of the
term: "Gavel-kind, [of Gafel Tribute, and Cind Nature, *Sax.*]." It
is surprising, however, that the traditional etymology was given in
Bailey's folio *Dictionarium Britannicum* (1730): "*Gavel-kind* [of
gife eal cyn, Sax. i.e. given to all the kin]."[22]

Fourteen years after the first publication of the *Dictionarium*
Britannicum, Benjamin Martin's *Lingua Britannica reformata*
appeared. It gave no etymology for *gavelkind.*[23] This type of
omission is apparently a characteristic feature of Martin's work
and is especially prevalent with words of Germanic origin.[24] Perhaps more surprising, however, is the fact that Samuel Johnson's
famous *Dictionary of the English Language* (1755) also failed to
offer an etymology for *gavelkind.* Johnson knew comparatively
little about the historical study of the language and is known to
have relied heavily on authorities such as the Saxonist Edward Lye
(with whom he corresponded) for his information about the
subject.[25] At this time Lye was preparing his *Dictionarium*
Saxonico et Gothico-Latinum (1772), which effectively replaced
Somner's own *Dictionarium.*[26] Among the subscribers to the work
was Johnson himself.

---

[22]The assistance of the etymologist Thomas Lediard in the second (1736) edition
of the *Dictionarium Britannicum* did not lead to a revision of the etymology.

[23]I am grateful to Dr. Graham Woan for checking this work for me.

[24]See Starnes and Noyes (1946), 159.

[25]See Reddick (1990), 74–75.

[26]There is no entry for *gavelkind* in Lye's dictionary, perhaps because the
compound does not in fact appear in surviving pre-Conquest material. The
Middle English Dictionary records its first occurrence in a document of 1199.

Almost a century after the publication of Somner's *Dictionarium*, then, we find that only two dictionaries published during the period offer the etymology for *gavelkind* that Somner proposed. The first occurrence, in Blount's *Glossographia*, appeared three years before the publication of Somner's *Dictionarium* and is not therefore attributable to the reputation of Somner's scholarship; indeed, Blount's citation of the elements *gafel* and *cynd* occurs within the context of an entry that summarizes Lambarde. The other occurrence, in Nathan Bailey's *Universal Etymological English Dictionary*, was replaced in his later work, *Dictionarium Britannicum*, by the traditional etymology advanced first by Lambarde in his *Archaionomia* of 1568. Despite the popularity of the *Archaionomia*, it is, of course, most unlikely that an eighteenth-century dictionary would have prepared an entry making direct use of a work written a century and a half previously. To an extent, the perpetuation of this false etymology can be explained by the well-documented interdependence of dictionaries during this period.[27] Yet it is also clear that English lexicographers did not depend principally for information about such technical vocabulary on specialist works dealing with specific subjects, such as those by Lambarde, Camden, or (demonstrably, it appears) Somner, nor even on other general English dictionaries. Instead they derived their material from the variety of law dictionaries available at the time.

One of the most popular of these was John Rastell's *Expositiones terminorum legum Anglorum* (1527), an Anglo-Norman text accompanied by an English translation. It passed through at least twenty-nine editions under various editors, last

---

[27]For this reason, highly derivative works such as Coles's *An English Dictionary* (1676; based largely on Phillips) and *Cocker's English Dictionary* (1704; based on Coles and Phillips) have been excluded from the discussion. These dictionaries, and those of other lexicographers not considered here, are discussed by Starnes and Noyes (1946).

appearing in 1819.[28] As Cowley notes, the first four editions of *Expositiones* (1527, after 1530, 1563, and 1572) were issued apparently without change.[29] Gavelkind is not mentioned in any of these editions. The fifth (1579) edition is considerably extended and was the first to contain the *Consuetudines Kanciae*, printed from Lambarde's text in his *Perambulation*, which had appeared three years earlier. The reference to gavelkind reveals the extent of its reliance on Lambarde's etymology:

> Gauelkind . . . is thought by ye skilfull in Antiquities, to be called Gauelkind, of Giue al kin, y^t is to say, to all the kindred in one line, according as it is vsed among the Germans, from whom we Englishmen, and chiefly of Kent come. Or els it is called Gauelkind of gyue al kinde, that is to say, to all the male children; for kinde in Dutch signifyeth a male childe. And dyuers other like coniectures are made by them, of the name (Gauelkind), which I omit of purpose for shortnes sake.[30]

The editor seems to have grown tired of Lambarde's etymological speculations. Later editions of *Expositiones* (or *Les Termes de la Ley* as it became known after 1624)[31] explicitly refer the reader to the *Perambulation*, again without rehearsing the rest of Lambarde's argument: ". . . And Divers other Customes are used in Kent of the Lands in Gavel-kinde, for which see Lambert's Perambulation of Kent."[32] Somner's work is not mentioned in editions published after the appearance of *A Treatise of Gavelkind*.

---

[28]The last enlarged edition (the twenty-sixth) was that of 1721, reprinted in 1742 and reproduced in later American editions (see Cowley [1932], lxxxiv).

[29]Cowley (1932), lxxxiii and n. 2.

[30]*Expositiones* (1579), fols. 100v–101r.

[31]Rastell's dictionary and its various editions are discussed by Cowley (1932), lxxxi–lxxxiv.

[32]*Les Termes de la Ley* (22nd edn., 1667), 394. I should like to thank Timothy Graham for checking this reference for me.

The inherent sense of fatigue with etymological speculation is, indeed, a feature of many discussions on the subject. For example, Charles Sandys' *History of Gavelkind*, very much a product of the mid-nineteenth-century era in which it was published, summarizes Lambarde's argument thus:

> If . . . we have regard to the nature of the lands in point of *discent*, then Gavelkind is derived from the Saxon Gif eal cyn, because the lands descend to all the male children equally, and not to the eldest son by right of primogeniture. But if we have respect to the *rent* and services issuing out of lands of Gavelkind tenure, then the derivation of the word is from Gafol, which in Saxon signifies rent or payment, and therefore called Gafol-cynd, Gavelkind, or land yielding rent. Somner has very learnedly established this latter to be the correct etymology of the word.[33]

The author rather detracts from this endorsement of Somner's work by observing that Sir Edward Coke in his 1628 *Institutes* had adopted the *gife eal cyn* etymology. Sandys then adds this tart footnote:

> This, amongst innumerable other instances, shows the fallacy of attempting to ascertain the nature and quality of things from mere etymology. Upon no other subject has so much learned ink been so

---

[33]Sandys (1851), 52. The peculiar quality of this work is best transmitted by a quotation from its triumphal conclusion (p. 307): "Thus have we adventured into the wide field of 'hoar antiquitie.' . . . And thus have we attempted to pourtray, in vivid contrast, the conflicting elements of Saxon liberty and Norman despotism. And this we have done with a heart glowing with the same aspirations which animated the Saxon mother, when she presented her child at the shrine of the immortal Alfred. There he bowed his youthful head, and bade the 'Father of his Country' Hail! There the ardent boy drank deeply of the gushing tide of patriotism! And there, upon the Altar of his Country, the Saxon Hannibal proclaimed eternal hatred to the Norman!"

unnecessarily wasted. Antiquaries too frequently indulge in these fruitless speculations.[34]

Another extremely influential work known to have been used by the early lexicographers was the law dictionary by John Cowell, known as *The Interpreter*, first published in 1607. After a troubled start, culminating in the suppression of the work by proclamation in 1610,[35] it was eventually to pass through eight editions, the last of which appeared in 1727.[36] The first edition naturally bases its entry upon Lambarde and Verstegen:

> *Gavelkind*, is, by *M. Lamberd* in his Exposition of Saxon words, *verbo. Terra ex scripto*, compounded of three Saxon words, *gyfe*, *eal*, *cin*: *omnibus cognatione proximis data*. But *M. Verstegan* in his restitution of decayed intelligence, *cap. 3.* calleth it (*Gavelkind*) *quasi*, giue all kind, that is, giue to each child his part.

Subsequent revisers, however, did not update the information. The one other law dictionary of note to appear during this period was Giles Jacob's *A New Law-Dictionary*, first published in 1729. This enjoyed considerable popularity, and ran through eleven editions before reaching America, where it was last reissued in 1838.[37] Jacob's dictionary was rather different from its predecessors, with the emphasis strongly on the statement of the law, abandoning many words of purely antiquarian interest. This is made clear in the Preface to the first edition:

---

[34]Sandys (1851), 52 n. 31.

[35]See Cowley (1932), lxxxvi.

[36]Cowley (1932), lxxxviii and 216. The importance of Cowell's work to general lexicographers is illustrated by the fact that Johnson cites Cowell's *Interpreter* as the direct source for his definition of *gavelkind*.

[37]Cowley (1932), xci.

> although I have the Interpretation of Words, to give it the Title of a
> *Dictionary*, yet my Scheme is very different from the other Law-
> Dictionaries. . . . As for the *other Dictionaries*, let who will for the
> Future Enlarge them, it must always be confess'd, that it was I who
> first attempted a Body of the Law, and the Practise of it, in any Law-
> Dictionary.[38]

It is unsurprising, given Jacob's professed lack of interest in matters antiquarian, that the etymology owes a considerable debt to the latest edition of Cowell's *Interpreter* without the supporting bibliographical references.

The reliance that modern English lexicographers placed on law dictionaries for this type of information can thus be seen to account for all the etymologies cited above with the exception of the ones appearing in Bailey's *Universal Etymological English Dictionary* (1721) and Blount's *Glossographia* (1656), the earliest English dictionary considered in this essay. Rather than using the basic *Archaionomia* etymology adopted by the law dictionary makers, Blount had summarized Lambarde's discussion of the term in his *Perambulation of Kent*, thus admitting two possible derivations of the word. Blount's comparative success is easily explained, for he himself was a barrister of the Inner Temple (although, as a Roman Catholic, he was not allowed to practice) and, unlike Phillips, he had genuine antiquarian interests. He knew William Dugdale (whom he consulted about land tenures), corrected proof sheets of Dugdale's *Monasticon*, and consulted manuscripts in Cotton's library. This background enabled Blount to identify what he considered to be etymological shortcomings in existing law dictionaries. In 1670 his own *Law-Dictionary* appeared, fourteen years after the publication of the *Glossographia* and ten years after *A Treatise of Gavelkind*. In the Preface to the dictionary, Blount voiced his principal complaint against Cowell's *Interpreter*:

---

[38]Quotation taken from Cowley (1932), xc.

he directly mistakes the meanings of some Words, and derivation of others. . . . He is sometimes too prolix in the derivation of a Word, setting down several Authors Opinions, without categorically determining which is the true . . . lastly, [he] gives us divers bare Words without explication . . . which I have supply'd; Not but that I have left some *quære's* too but those in Words of greater difficulty.[39]

Recent advances in scholarship had allowed Blount to rectify these deficiencies:

it will abate the wonder, that I, who *inter doctos me non effero*, should yet not onely assume the liberty in many places to correct those learned *Authors* . . . if it be consider'd, That they wanted those Helps I have had, *viz.* That incomparable *Glossarium Archaiologicum* of Sir *Henry Spelman*; The elaborate *Institutes* of Sir *Edward Coke*; That excellent *Dictionarium Saxonico-Latino-Anglicum* of Mr. *Somner*; The Learned Works of Mr. *William Dugdale*, Mr. *Fabian Philips*, and others, publish'd since those *Authors* wrote.[40]

Blount's etymology in his *Law-Dictionary* took full account of Somner's work:

Gavelkind, (from the Sax Gafel. i. *Census*, *tributum*, and cynd, *Natura*, *Genus*.) But Doctor *Powel* in his *Additaments* to the *Cambrian History*, and from him *Taylor* in his History of *Gavelkind*, *fol.* 26. wou'd have it deriv'd from the British word, Gavel, importing a Hold, or Tenure. . . . See *Lamberts Perambulation* of *Kent*, and *Sumners* learned Discourse on this Subject.[41]

---

[39]Blount (1670), sig. a1[r].

[40]Blount (1670), sigs. a1[v]–a2[r].

[41]As the *Oxford English Dictionary* notes (s.v. *gavelkind*), the notion that the word was of Celtic derivation, from *gafael* "take" and *cenedl* "race/family," resulted from the application of the term to the Welsh and Irish system of succession. This etymology was current in the sixteenth and seventeenth centuries.

Blount's interest in the subject remained keen, for in 1679 he published a work entitled *Ancient Tenures of Land*. Yet, as we have seen, the 1667 (the twenty-second) edition of *Les Termes de la Ley*, for which Blount was responsible, and which was reprinted in 1671 and 1685, disappointingly failed to revise the entry for *gavelkind* in the light of Somner's work.

Blount had criticized Cowell's *Interpreter* for its lack of attention to etymological detail. This was exactly the same charge leveled against his own work by William Nelson, the reviser of the third edition (1717) of the *Law-Dictionary*. Once again Somner's work is mentioned:

> AND because we have the Opinion of another great Lawyer, Sir *John Dodridge*, in his *English Lawyer, fol* 75, that *Etymologies, if they be rightly used, and drawn from the Final Cause, or from the Effect, do not only yield an Argument of good Consequence, but also afford Illustration and Delight*; and knowing that many of our Laws and Customs proceed from a *Saxon* Original, I have carefully examined every Word which is derived from thence, either by Mr. *Somner's Lexicon*, or by Mr. *Benson's Thesaurus Saxonicus* lately published, and haue corrected those Mistakes which are in the former Editions; so that according to the Opinion of that Lawyer, I have made this Edition not only necessary but delightful.[42]

The quotation from the popular *English Lawyer* by John Doddridge (1631) appears to have been taken from the first edition of the *Law-Dictionary*, where it was used by Blount as a pretext for including a greater amount of etymological information. Here

---

[42]Nelson appears here to refer to Benson's dictionary under a different title. A proposed digest of Somner with the title *Thesaurus linguae Anglo-Saxonicae dictionario Gul. Somneri quoad numerum vocum auctior* (1690) never made it past a specimen printed page and was superseded by Benson's *Vocabularium Anglo-Saxonicum, lexico Gul. Somneri magna parte auctius* (discussed above, p. 284) (Douglas [1951], 56; Greenfield and Robinson [1980], no. 56).

Nelson neatly turns the same passage against Blount's own efforts, arguing that a new edition of the law dictionary could be justified since revision of its etymological content was necessary.

By the time that Benson's digest of Somner's *Dictionarium* had been published, Cowell's *Interpreter*, the more popular rival to Blount's *Law-Dictionary*, had gone through six editions. By 1701, the reference to *gavelkind* had been extended, mostly by citation of sources. Somner's work is mentioned, but apparently not used:

> Gavel-kind, Is by Mr. *Lambert* in his *Exposition of Saxon words*, verbo *Terra & Scripto*, compounded of three Saxon words, *Gyfe, Eal, Cyn*; *Omnibus cognatione proximis data.* But *Verstegan* in his *Restitution of decayed Intelligence*, cap. 3 Calls it *Gavel-kind, quasi, give all kind*, that is, give to each Child his part. But *Taylor* in his *History of Gavel-kind*, would derive it from the Brittish *Gafael*, a Hold or Tenure, and *Cennee* or *Cennedh, Generatio aut familia*, and so *Gavel cenedh* might signifie *Tenura generationis, pag.* 92 & 132. But whatever is the true Etymology, it signifies in Law a Custome. . . . See *Lamberts Perambulation* of *Kent, Sumners* Discourse on this Subject, [*Taylors* History of *Gavel-kind*.]. *Vide etiam Termes de Ley.*

The terse tone of "whatever is the true Etymology" suggests some impatience with the subject, and the reviser is apparently aware of Somner's *Treatise of Gavelkind* only to the extent that the work existed. This is indeed ironic, as the 1701 editor of *The Interpreter* was Bishop White Kennett, Somner's biographer.[43] Kennett's

---

[43]Cowley (1932), lxxxvii, notes that the edition is assigned to Kennett on the authority of Bishop Thomas Tanner's note in his annotated copy in the Bodleian: "Ex dono doctissimi viri mihique amicissimi R. White Kennet S. Th. Pr. qui hanc Editionem nova praefatione additionibusque quamplurimis ornavit" ("By the gift of the most learned man my good friend the Reverend White Kennett, Professor of Sacred Theology, who adorned this edition with a new preface and very many additions").

account of his life appeared first in Somner's posthumously published *Treatise of the Roman Ports and Forts in Kent* (1693).[44] In the "revised and much enlarged" version of the biography attached to the second (1726) edition of *A Treatise of Gavelkind*, Kennett remarked that "upon the great questions in descent of families, tenure of estates, dedication of Churches, right of tithes, and all the history of use and custom, he was consulted as a *Druid* or a *Bard*."[45] Somner, he added, was "The Oracle of his Countrey." However, although Somner's works were considered important enough to be cited both in the general English dictionaries and specialist law works of the period covered here, it seems that they were only occasionally read or used. Although this judgment has been reached on an examination of only one word, *gavelkind*, it would be hard to find a term more obviously reflecting Somner's life interests, given that the term is concerned with the land tenure of Kent and has a history (and etymology) deriving from the Anglo-Saxon period. In each of these fields Somner's reputation was that of a great authority. Here, if anywhere, we might expect to find some evidence that Somner's work was actually used. We are forced to conclude that (to extend Kennett's own metaphor) if Somner was an oracle, he was one rarely consulted by lexicographers in the hundred years before his greatest work, the *Dictionarium Saxonico-Latino-Anglicum*, was finally superseded.[46]

---

[44]In Greenfield and Robinson (1980), no. 801A, the biography is mistakenly attributed to James Brome, to whom the work is addressed. The error is duplicated by Stanley (1981), 235. Neither work mentions the expanded version of the biography in the second edition of *A Treatise of Gavelkind*, where Kennett signals additions to the original account by the use of square brackets.

[45]"Life of Mr. Somner," in Somner (1726), 12.

[46]I should like to acknowledge the financial assistance of the British Academy which supported my attendance at theTwenty-Ninth International Congress on Medieval Studies at Kalamazoo in May 1994.

"THAT MOST ELABORATE ONE OF FR. JUNIUS": AN INVESTIGATION OF FRANCIS JUNIUS'S MANUSCRIPT OLD ENGLISH DICTIONARY[1]

Kees Dekker

I. Introduction

When, in 1696, William Nicolson (1655–1727), later bishop of Carlisle, gave a brief description of the history of Old English lexicography, he left no doubt as to the work he considered the paragon of the then existing dictionaries of Old English. Pride of place went to:

> That most elaborate one of *Fr. Junius*,[2] who has infinitely outdone all that went before him. His large Glossary or Lexicon of the five old Northern Languages (whereof the *Saxon* has the preference) may be seen in the Author's own MS. in *Bodley*'s Library; and a fair

[1] I am indebted to Sophie van Romburgh for allowing me to use her transcripts and translations of the correspondence of Francis Junius, to Philippus H. Breuker for his notes on Bodleian MSS Fell 8–18, and to Rolf Bremmer, Colin Ewen, and Angelika Lutz for their helpful suggestions. This study resulted from a research project funded by the Netherlands Organization for Scientific Research (NWO).

[2] Francis Junius, alias du Jon (Heidelberg 1591–Windsor 1677). For an up-to-date view of various aspects of Junius's life and work, see Bremmer (1998a).

Transcript of it (in Eleven Volumes, at the charge of the late pious Bishop *Fell*) in the *Musæum Ashmoleanum*.[3]

Nicolson's knowledge of Junius's Old English–Latin dictionary, now Bodleian MSS Junius 2 and 3,[4] was based on his own involvement in one of the unsuccessful plans to publish these manuscripts in the late seventeenth and eighteenth centuries. After the eighteenth century, interest in the dictionary waned. J. A. W. Bennett was the first to describe in any detail the history of the attempts to publish these manuscripts, and he gave an outline analysis of Junius's method.[5] In this paper I will survey the history of MSS Jun. 2 and 3, and describe Junius's sources and method of compilation. I have taken into account Bennett's analysis, some of which, however, should not be followed uncritically as I shall show below.[6]

MSS Jun. 2 and 3 were presented to the Bodleian Library in Oxford by their compiler, the Dutch philologist Francis Junius. The books formed part of a bequest made by Junius toward the end of his life that stipulated that the most important part of his library, including his medieval manuscripts, his autograph manuscripts, and a number of printed books of which most carried his annotations, were to go to the Bodleian Library. The notion that Junius bequeathed his entire library to the Bodleian now seems to be contradicted by the number of books with Junius's autograph

---

[3]Nicolson (1696–99), I, 104. In the second edition of 1714, Fell's transcripts are said to be not in the Ashmolean but "in the same place," i.e., the Bodleian.

[4]Following Junius's own practice, I shall refer to the work as his Old English–Latin dictionary. For the sake of brevity, all further references to the Junius manuscripts will be in the form "MS Jun."

[5]See Bennett (1938), viii, 22–49, 218–19, 315–19, 363–69, and 374.

[6]My own observations are based on personal inspection of the manuscripts and a microfilm copy.

annotations found among the books of Junius's cousin Isaac Vossius in Leiden University Library. These suggest that some of Junius's books were inherited by Vossius.[7] Apart from books and manuscripts, Junius's special types cut for publishing his works also formed part of the Oxford bequest, for the latter had been made on the understanding that the university would undertake the publication of a number of Junius's manuscripts that he had not managed to publish during his lifetime.[8] Despite efforts made by the university, very little came of Junius's wishes: only MSS Jun. 4 and 5, the *Etymologicum Anglicanum*, were eventually published.[9] The rest of Junius's manuscripts remained unpublished, although they were frequently consulted by eighteenth-century scholars, and many were to form the basis for later publications.[10]

---

[7]See Bremmer (1998b), 232–34.

[8]See Hetherington (1980), 231; and Bennett (1938), 316. Junius was slow to publish his works. Of all his projects on Old Germanic languages, he only published: *Observationes in Willerami abbatis Francicam paraphrasin Cantici canticorum* (Amsterdam, 1655); *Cædmonis monachi paraphrasis poetica Genesios* (Amsterdam, 1655); *Quatuor D. N. Jesu Christi evangeliorum versiones perantiquæ duæ, Gothica scilicet et Anglosaxonica* (in collaboration with Thomas Marshall; Dordrecht, 1665); and *Gothicum glossarium quo pleraque argentei codicis vocabula explicantur et illustrantur, atque ex linguis cognatis illustrantur* (Dordrecht, 1665). That these publications represented only part of his plans can be deduced from the *Observationes*, in which his many references to his Old High German glossaries and to his annotations to Tatianus's *Harmonia evangelica* imply that he intended to publish those works. On p. 302 he describes how he was temporarily diverted from his labors on Tatianus by a request from friends to work on Willeramus.

[9]Edward Lye, ed., *Francisci Junii Francisci filii Etymologicum Anglicanum* (Oxford, 1743).

[10]See Bennett (1938), 344–45, for a list of eighteenth-century projects.

II. METHOD OF COMPILATION

In the Bodleian Library's *Summary Catalogue of Western Manuscripts*, MSS Jun. 2 and 3 are assigned the numbers 5114 and 5115 and are described together in a single entry as:

> In Old English and Latin, &c., on paper: written in the third quarter of the 17th cent. by Francis Junius: $13^1/_5 \times 8^1/_2$ in. (5114) and $17^1/_2 \times 12^1/_2$ in. (5115), xxv + 590 (5114) and 498 leaves (5115) in double columns. The Old English–Latin dictionary of Francis Junius, in two volumes arranged alphabetically (5114 contains B–T), preceded (fol. vii) by additional alphabetical notes.[11]

Six more lines of text supply additional information but tell us no more about the actual manuscripts. Apart from being brief, the description in the *Summary Catalogue* is inaccurate, and in some respects wrong.[12] A correct inventory of the contents of both volumes is, therefore, indispensable.

MSS Jun. 2 and 3 are gathered in eighteenth-century bindings, respectively containing xxv + 590 leaves and 498 leaves. The contents of MS Jun. 2 are as follows:

> **fol. i:** a fly-leaf.
>
> **fol. ii:** a doubled leaf comprising two leaves pasted together, with the letter *a* written in the top left corner of the recto of the upper leaf.
>
> **fols. iii–vi:** a single leaf that has been folded to make four leaves; on fol. vi^v, the capital letters of the alphabet are written, using Anglo-Saxon letter forms, in a vertical column. The letters *G, I, K, T, Þ,* and *Y* are indented toward the right, and have next to them,

---

[11]Madan et al. (1937), 964.

[12]The inaccuracy of the *Summary Catalogue*'s descriptions of the Junius manuscripts as a whole (see Madan et al. [1937], 962–90) has been noticed by E. G. Stanley, who has made many valuable corrections, emendations, and additions, especially with respect to the printed books. See Stanley (1998).

written in a cursive hand, the entries: "Mr Redman. returned."
(*G*), "Mr Evans. returned." (*I* and *K*), "Mr Nicholson Returned"
(*T*), and "Mr. Todd." (*Þ* and *Y*).

fols. vii–xxii: sixteen leaves, most of which contain jottings that are in
an eighteenth-century hand and that derive from different sections
of the manuscript. On fols. vii^v and ix are philological notes on
Gothic words; these notes seem unrelated to the rest.

fols. xxiii–xxv: three rotographs (i.e., black-and-white photographs
with reverse polarity) of BL MS Add. 4720 (the first volume of
a three-volume eighteenth-century transcript of MSS Jun. 2
and 3), showing the opening of the missing *A* section of the dictionary.[13] The rotographs were received by the Bodleian Library
in 1916 and have been tipped into the manuscript.

fols. 1–588: the *B* to *T* sections of the Old English–Latin dictionary in
the hand of Francis Junius. The sections are alphabetically
ordered, and the first leaf of each section is a doubled leaf
comprising two leaves pasted together, with the letter of the
section written in minuscule in the top left corner of the recto of
the upper leaf.[14] The span of the sections is as follows: *B*: fols.
1–42; *C*: fols. 43–62; *D*: fols. 63–79; *E*: fols. 80–108; *F*: fols.
109–58; *G*: fols. 159–248; *H*: fols. 249–92; *I*: fols. 293–303; *K*:
fols. 305–11;[15] *L*: fols. 313–33; *M*: fols. 334–56; *N*: fols. 357–74;
O: fols. 376–425; *P*: fols. 426–37; *Q*: fols. 439–44; *R*: fols.
446–67; *S*: fols. 478–550; *T*: fols. 551–83.[16]

---

[13]See note 20 below.

[14]In each case the letter of the section was also entered in the top left corner of
the recto of the lower leaf, before the two leaves were pasted together. This was
also the case with the *a* heading on fol. ii.

[15]Folio 304, another doubled leaf, is blank, as are fols. 312, 375, 438, and 445
(all of these being doubled).

[16]Folios 584–88 are blank. A twentieth-century pencil note on the recto of the last
leaf (fol. 588r) reads: "[Really XXV + 590 leaves, for 5 is double and 9 is
double]." The note refers to the fact that two consecutive leaves are numbered "5"
and two consecutive leaves are numbered "9." Folios 468–77 contain a glossary
of "Runic" words. Folios 552–56 are from the *T* section of MS Jun. 115a.

MS Jun. 3 is a combination of the remainder of Junius's dictionary and later attempts at editing it. The material from Junius's dictionary forms only a small part of the volume: Þ: fols. 2–23; W: fols. 141–84; U: fols. 373–407; Y: fols. 464–81. Apart from some miscellaneous writings in the hand of Francis Junius,[17] the remaining parts of the book consist of transcripts in eighteenth-century hands of Junius's Old English entries, in alphabetical order, without the Gothic and Runic material.[18] The four sections of Junius's dictionary are compiled in the same way as those in MS Jun. 2, i.e., with a doubled leaf acting as cover for each section and in alphabetical order.

From the eighteenth-century transcripts bound in with Junius's material it appears that the dictionary was not bound until well after Junius's death.[19] The vertical list of capital letters on fol. vi[v] of MS Jun. 2 clearly represents the order of the covers before they were bound. Here, the final sequence is listed in the order T, Ð, U, W, Y, whereas in the bound version, W precedes U. The names entered next to the indented letters in the list indicate that several sections were lent out to different people, possibly even at the same time. Unfortunately, these notes give no clue as to what happened to the A section that is missing from the beginning of the dictionary.[20] It is evident, then, that Junius kept his Old English

---

[17]Folios 360–72 contain a short Old High German–Latin lexicon and some miscellaneous notes by Junius. Folios 450–63 contain another small glossary by Junius, mainly Old High German–Latin but also with some references to Old Frisian.

[18]I use the term *Runic* to distinguish the entries in runes from the Icelandic additions in Roman script. The eighteenth-century transcripts are grouped as follows: Ð: fols. 24–66; W: fols. 67–140; S: fols. 186–300; T: fols. 301–48; U: fols. 408–49; Y: fols. 482–96.

[19]As was also observed by Bennett (1938), 28 n. 1.

[20]The transcripts of the dictionary in Bodleian MSS Fell 8–18 and BL MSS Add. 4720–4722 both contain the A section. Macray (1890), 147, mentions that the F

dictionary in the form of unbound sheets with separate covers, rather than in the form of a book.

The separate sections of the dictionary consist mainly of leaves of two distinctly different sizes, which may be classified as folio-sized and quarto-sized.[21] There are clear differences between the two types. The majority of the quarto-sized leaves (hereafter referred to as Type 1 leaves) are of a somewhat browner hue than the folio-sized leaves (hereafter, Type 2 leaves) and the remaining portion of quarto-sized leaves (hereafter, Type 3 leaves). These Type 3 leaves are, in general, slightly smaller than the Type 1 leaves. The Type 1 leaves display, on average, the highest density of entries, whereas leaves of Types 2 and 3 are less full. The addition of Gothic and Runic words is mostly restricted to the Type 2 leaves. There is no clear continuing line discernible in the alphabetical order of the entries if the three types of leaves are considered together, for if we take the first and last words of all leaves of a section and look at the alphabetical order, there is considerable overlap among the leaves. When, on the basis of this observation, the Type 1 and Type 2 leaves are considered separately, there appears to be a more transparent order in both series.[22]

---

and *S* sections were restored by Johannes Eckard in 1720, after they had been stolen by an unnamed Dane.

[21] The eighteenth-century transcripts in MS Jun. 3 are on leaves of large folio size; hence the difference in the dimensions of MSS Jun. 2 and 3 noted in the *Summary Catalogue*'s description quoted above.

[22] In my survey of the *E* section of MS Jun. 2, this gives the following results for the Type 1 leaves: "ea"–"eaxla" (fol. 83), "ece drihten"–"euorfearn" (fol. 86), "efne"–"ehtan" (fol. 89), "ehtan"–"elriord" (fol. 92), "eldo"–"embe" (fol. 95), "embesmeagung"–"emlicnes" (fol. 99), "emnreðe"–"eowan" (fol. 101), "eowd"–"eswicnis" (fol. 103), "eð"–"eðle" (fol. 105), "etnehstan"–"exla" (fol. 107). The Type 2 leaves show a less fixed order: "ea"–"eall" (fol. 82), "eadige"–"eallic geleafa" (fol. 81), "eala"–"edneowe fyr" (fol. 85), "ealdan"–"eawfæst" (fol. 84), "edstaðelung"–"eglan" (fol. 87), "egor"–"ehtnysse" (fol. 90), "eisile"–

It seems, therefore, that Junius started by compiling his dictionary on the Type 1 leaves. In each section, the first of the Type 1 leaves has the letter of the section in the top left-hand corner. Subsequently, when he ran out of space, he continued working on the Type 2 leaves. The Type 3 leaves, which often contain Icelandic, were probably working sheets of a preliminary kind, intended for later re-working into a bigger glossary. I shall refer to occasional small notes pasted in as Type 4 leaves.

We know that expanding the dictionary with Gothic and Runic entries was not part of the original plan, as such entries are rare on the Type 1 leaves but frequent on the Type 2 leaves, which contain the bulk of these words; occasionally pages contain only Gothic and Runic. To distinguish among the various languages used in the dictionary, Junius employed five types of script: (1) his book-hand for Latin; (2) a minuscule script that incorporated Anglo-Saxon letter forms for Old English; (3) uncials that imitated Wulfila's alphabet for Gothic; (4) runes for words derived from the works of Olaus Wormius; and (5) Greek characters, to give the Greek renderings of Gothic words. Other hands than Junius's occur only very rarely.[23]

The basic construction of Junius's Old English entries is remarkably regular, although the length of the entries varies. Junius's standard entry consists of an Old English word or short

---

"embhæmbendne" (fol. 98), "elcur"–"ellenlæca" (fol. 93), "embefær"–"egor" (fol. 96), "emertung"–"eom" (fol. 100), "eoredmen"–"ern" (fol. 102), "escesdun"–"eðhelde" (fol. 104), "eðiende"–"ettan" (fol. 106), "Exancestre" (fol. 108). There are three Type 3 leaves in the *E* section, of which one contains Old English, "efter onfonde"–"eftswellung" (fol. 88), and the other two only Runes and Icelandic (fols. 91 and 97). One small Type 4 leaf has a note on *elys* (fol. 94).

[23]On fol. 33r of MS Jun. 2, a different hand wrote "V. beran" below the entry "bord, mensa."

phrase followed by a Latin gloss, which, in turn, is followed by a reference to the source, for example, "flæsc, Caro; Ælfr. gloss. 2 & 21" (MS Jun. 2, fol. 122v). Subsequent information, if any, consists of Old English quotations in which the headword features. These are then followed by a Latin gloss, and by a reference to the source. Junius is remarkably consistent in his punctuation of the entries. The Old English headword always begins with a lower-case letter, but the Latin gloss usually begins with a capital letter.[24] The Latin gloss is followed by a full stop if another quotation follows immediately afterwards, but by a semicolon if the next item is the reference to the source. The same pattern is maintained in further quotations, glosses, and source references. Additional information is situated immediately underneath the entry to which it belongs, and is indented, which makes the layout of the entries very clear.

The basic principle behind Junius's dictionary is that different meanings, often reflected by a different contemporary Latin gloss, are assigned different entries. Junius's distribution of entries is entirely based on this principle, which, as will become clear, sometimes leads to multiple occurrences of the same word on various pages (for example, "brædan handa" on fol. 34v and "brædan" on fol. 35r of MS Jun. 2), due to the fact that on many occasions he came across the same forms, but with a different meaning or translation. A single entry is not glossed by words carrying different meanings. At most, it may be glossed by nearly synonymous words, as is shown by these three examples, all on fol. 110v of MS Jun. 2: (1) "fæst, Firmus, munitus"; (2) "fæsten, Murus, munimentum"; (3) "fadian, Ordinare, disponere, dividere." One or more attestations of the meaning expressed in the first

---

[24]Regarding the capitalization of the first letter of the Latin glosses, there is a distinct difference between the Type 1 leaves, where this occasionally occurs, and the Type 2 leaves, where it seems to be the rule.

gloss are often found in the immediately following quotations, producing entries such as:

esne, Adolescens. C. Matth. XIX,20.
    esne. ðe ic cuoeðo. aris. Adolescens, tibi dico, surge; C. Luc. VII,14.
    ging esne sum, Adolescens quidam; C & R. Marc. XIV,51. XVI,5.[25]

The entry for "esne, Adolescens" is then followed by two subsequent entries featuring the same Old English word but with a different meaning: "esne, Juvenis" and "esne, Servus." An additional entry, with three attestations in each of which *esne* is glossed as "Vir," is found on fol. 104r.

Entries containing more than one Old English word are not frequent, and, when they occur, they always contain words which in Junius's opinion had the same meaning. These mostly concern spelling variants of the same word. In rare instances, morphological variants are listed under one entry, for example "bye *vel* bying" (MS Jun. 2, fol. 18v), or forms with and without a prefix, for example "bylgean. abylgean" (fol. 23r) and "eowan. oðeowan" (fol. 101v). The verb forms "began. begangan" (MS Jun. 2, fol. 8r) are also listed together. Two totally unrelated words may be presented together in a single entry when they are copied verbatim from a medieval glossary, for example "bigegnes *vel* smeagung, Studium; Gloss. R. pag. 90." (MS Jun. 2, fol. 21r). This illustrates again that for Junius the meaning of the word was the basis for the entry.

The contents of the entries together with the additional quotations give an idea of Junius's method and lexicographical principles, and, at the same time, may reveal something of the scope of the dictionary and the extent of Junius's knowledge. Apart from the basic entry described above, in the additional

---

[25]MS Jun. 2, fol. 103v. For the meaning of the abbreviations "C." and "R." preceding the Gospel references, see below, p. 312.

quotations he attempted to provide a variety of uses of the word in the Old English language, illustrated by quotations and glosses. At the same time he tried to restrict himself to the meaning of the word as given in the entry and the principal gloss. A typical entry with its gloss, source references, and additional information will make this clear:

> degullice, occulte. C. R. Matth. I,19. XVII,19. XX,17.
>> deagolnesse heortan, Latebrae cordis; Beda IV,27.
>> in degulnisse, in abscondito. C. R. Matth. VI,4 & 6.
>> in degolnisse, in absconso. R. Luc. XI,33 – Joh. VII,10.
>> on degolnesse, In abscondito. V. Ps. LXXX,7.
>> in degle *vel* in deigelnise, In occulto; C. Joh. VII,4.
>> of degolnessum, De recessibus; gl. Cott. 69.[26]

A closer look at the contents of the entries shows the various types of information that Junius provided or omitted.

In many instances Junius attempted to combine spelling variants in clusters, for example "beran. bæran. beoran" (MS Jun. 2, fol. 13r), "eorre. yrre" (fol. 101v), "erian. erigan. erigean" (fol. 102v), "feran. færan. faran. foeran" (fol. 118v), and "losnian. hlosnian" (fol. 332r). Some clusters like "heg. hieg. hig" occur more than once in different orders (MS Jun. 2, fols. 259v, 266v, and 272r), each time with a different form first. The extent of Junius's research becomes apparent in entries such as "mænigeo" (MS Jun. 2, fol. 341r), to which he added "menigeo," "menegeo," "mænigo," "menego," "mænio," "menio," "menego,"[27] "menegu," and "menigu." Sometimes the alphabetical order was disregarded in order to combine spelling variants. Thus, the entry on *gehwearf* follows that on *gehwyrfednes* (MS Jun. 2, fol. 230r). Variations of spelling in unstressed syllables, such as *-on*, *-an*, and *-un* endings,

---

[26]MS Jun. 2, fol. 65v.

[27]Junius listed *menego* twice with exactly the same attestations.

or variations between -*u* and -*o*, are systematically grouped under the same entry.[28]

The dictionary provides ample evidence of Junius's collations of different copies of the same text. The most noticeable case of this concerns the Lindisfarne and Rushworth Gospels,[29] respectively referred to as "C." or "Cott." and "R."; examples such as "metebælg, Pera; R. Luc. XXII,35. ubi Cott. metbælig" (MS Jun. 2, fol. 4v) frequently occur. There are also collations of other texts, for example "eldung, Mora; Boëth. XXXVIII,3. ubi tamen in codice Cottoniano est eldcung" (MS Jun. 2, fol. 92v), and "pin — dægmæles pin, Gnomon; Ælfr. gloss. 27. ita codex D'Eusianus habet pro dægmæles pil;" (fol. 429v). Junius's collations sometimes display a critical eye for misconceptions on the part of medieval scribes. For example, he voiced his doubts about an unusual meaning for the word *nu* listed in the Cotton glossary:[30] "nu *v*el ær, Dudum; gl. Cott. 67. Nisi forte ibi legendum putes iu. Passim enim apud Bedam iu ær & iu geara ponuntur pro Dudum, quondam" (MS Jun. 2, fol. 373r). With his superior knowledge of both Old English and Latin, he corrected a scribe of the Old English Psalter glosses in his entry "oneled. ascensiones. Ps. 83,6" (MS Jun. 2, fol. 398v). Knowing that *onælan* means "to set fire to,"[31] he added: "pro Ascensione *v*el ascensus Glossator videtur legisse Accensus & oneled vertisse."

The dictionary does not substantiate the assumption that Junius sometimes tried to regularize the Old English language by silently altering forms,[32] for he seems to have collected as many different

[28] For example, *gearu* and *gearo* are in the same entry (MS Jun. 2, fol. 173r). See also my quotation above of the entry for *degullice*.

[29] BL MS Cotton Nero D. iv and Bodleian MS Auct. D. 2. 19.

[30] BL MS Cotton Cleopatra A. iii.

[31] See MS Jun. 2, fol. 394v, where this word is listed.

[32] Compare Logeman (1888), xxxii. Logeman did not refer here to Junius's lexicographical work but to his editorial principles, which were also reviewed by

forms as possible. But the texts were not sacrosanct to him, as appears from his abridging the quotations, a not uncommon feature in the dictionary. After all, quotations only served to illustrate the meaning of the word under investigation and to give a faithful record of its spelling. A complete presentation of the text was not the object, and it was therefore justifiable to omit superfluous information. In the quotation "bed him gestreht ꝺwel gestreht,"[33] for example, Junius (MS Jun. 2, fol. 8r) left out the word *him*. A more substantial simplification occurred in the case of a passage excerpted from Cnut's laws: "And gyf man gehadodne mid fæhðe belecge ꝺsecge, þæt he wære dædbana oððe rædbana. . . ."[34] Junius altered this to "gif man secge *þæt* he wære dædbana oððe rædbana" (MS Jun. 2, fol. 5b[r]). In a long quotation from Ælfric's *Grammar* (MS Jun. 2, fol. 289r), the beginning is altered from "Sume þas habbað ðryfealde getacnung"[35] to "hit hæð ðryfealde getacnung," to allow the quotation to conform logically to the headword, which is a singular form. That Junius's alterations could lead to mistakes is shown here by *hæð* ("has"), which is a form that does not occur in Old English[36] but which is evidently Junius's own back-formation from seventeenth-century *hath*.

Junius restricted grammatical information in the entries mostly to details. Parts of speech are not identified separately, and there is evidence that he was not really concerned with this aspect of Old English grammar. Under the entry on *lustfullian* (MS Jun. 2,

---

Bennett (1938), 341–44, who praised Junius for his collations and emendations of the text. For an evaluation of Junius's editorial principles, see Dekker (2000).

[33] From *De somniorum diversitate* in BL MS Cotton Tiberius A. iii. Compare Förster (1910), 60.

[34] Compare Liebermann (1903–16), I, 286.

[35] Compare Zupitza (1880), 231.

[36] See Venezky and Healey (1980).

fol. 333r), Junius listed, apart from an attestation of the headword itself and of the word *lust*, a quotation with the adjective *lustfull* and one featuring the noun *lustfulnes*. He saw no need to make explicit distinctions between the verbal and the nominal forms. Case forms of nouns and adjectives are sometimes translated by their correct Latin counterparts, which gives some insight into Junius's knowledge of case endings. To the noun "eage, Oculus" (MS Jun. 2, fol. 81v) Junius added "egna, Ocellorum" and "eagan, Oculi." The adjective *eall* was illustrated by the inflections *ealle*, *ealra*, and *eallum* (MS Jun. 2, fol. 82v). Declined forms may appear as separate entries, for example accusative masculine *bradne* (MS Jun. 2, fol. 33v), which Junius glossed with the nominative "Latus," leaving it uncertain whether he recognized the accusative form. Despite the fact that his translations are on the whole grammatically correct, there is no discernible conscious attempt to list, let alone explain,[37] separate forms from the nominal, adjectival, or pronominal paradigms.[38]

Entries for verbs are generally more elaborate than those for nouns, because Junius tended to list more verb forms and because nominal forms related to verbs were sometimes also listed under the same entry. In the indented information under "gnornian, murmurare; Ps. 58, 17." (MS Jun. 2, fol. 343v), he not only listed the forms *gnornadun*, *gnorniende*, and *gnornodon* but also

---

[37]*bec* is entered under *boc*, without an explanation for the mutated form (MS Jun. 2, fol. 29v).

[38]Hetherington (1980), 167, mentions the fact that John Joscelyn (1529–1603) and Sir Simonds D'Ewes (1602–50), each of whom compiled a manuscript dictionary of Old English, reproduced paradigms from Ælfric's *Grammar*. Although Junius frequently used the *Grammar* as a source for words and often cited it, such paradigms do not occur in his dictionary. He did not even add the oblique forms to pronouns such as *ic* (MS Jun. 2, fol. 299r). Instead, he merely remarked, "declinatur per omnes utriusque numeri casus" ("it is declined through all cases, singular and plural").

gnornung, gnorninga, and even *gnornword.* As with nouns, there is no conscious attempt to reconstruct the paradigm, but sometimes Junius goes a long way in that direction. The Class 3 weak verb *libban* and its Late West Saxon derivation *leofian* are presented under one entry, with a considerable number of forms (MS Jun. 2, fol. 322r). A clear error is the inclusion of forms of *eacnian* under *ican* (MS Jun. 2, fol. 299r), where the two synonyms seem to have fooled even Junius.[39] This is exceptional, however. The entry on *don,* which commences on a Type 1 leaf (MS Jun. 2, fol. 73r), reaches considerable size in its continuation on the preceding Type 2 leaf (fol. 72r). Eleven attestations are listed in the first entry, and no fewer than forty-five in the continuation.

Affixing, a phenomenon that was no doubt very familiar to Junius as a result of his Dutch background, was given considerable attention. Entries that represented formative elements of adjectives or nouns, such as *-dom* and *-ful,* were frequently supplied with a list of formations.[40] The infinitive ending *-lǣcan* was provided with eighteen examples.[41] Similarly, words that are frequently compounded, such as *crǣft* (MS Jun. 2, fol. 57r) and *hus* (fol. 286r), were richly illustrated. Lexicographically, such forms were important to Junius, for—much more than grammatical or orthographical variants—they enlarged the lexicon he was trying to represent.

---

[39]His entry lists the forms "geice," "icton," "togeyc," "geeacnige," "geeacnode," "geicte," "geichte," and "æce."

[40]Thus "arful," "earful," "deoreful," "estful," "fremful," "hlisful," "hogful," "mæðful," "modful," "niðful," "reafful," "sacful," "sandfull," "ðancfull," "sideful," "synful," "slacful," "teamful," "teonful," "tungful," "ðeostorful," "weorðfull," "wlitefull," and "wohfull" (MS Jun. 2, fol. 157v).

[41]"æfenlǣcan," "efenlǣcend," "ic geanlǣce," "geedlǣcan," "geferlǣcean," "gelǣccan," "wiðerlecan," "gelomlǣcing," "gerihtlǣcan," "geswǣslǣcan," "geþǣslǣcan," "geðristlǣcean," "geweredlǣht beon," "gewistlǣcan," "gewundorlǣcan," "nealǣcean," "olǣcan," "twyferlǣcan" (MS Jun. 2, fol. 314r).

Even though Junius made Gothic, Runic, and Icelandic additions to the manuscript—additions to which I shall return— etymology and comparative language studies do not play a role in the dictionary. Naturally, this does not imply that Junius was not interested in this aspect of Old English studies; in fact, the contrary is true. The study of the etymology of the Germanic languages was, in all probability, the overall objective of his work. In this dictionary, however, Junius clearly aimed at describing the Old English lexicon as he found it in his sources, without investigating the possible origin of words and writing extensively on Germanic cognates. The occasional slip of the pen—after all, blood is thicker than water—provides a glimpse of the great etymologist he was. After providing an attestation for the verb *clumian* (MS Jun. 2, fol. 52v), he wrote: "Danis klemmer, Belgis klemmen est Arctare, stringere, arcte comprimere. iisdem quoque Belgis in de klem brengen, Ad angustias redigere. Danis klempt inde, Ad incitas reductus." Similarly, he could not resist adding to the entry for *embe utan* (MS Jun. 2, fol. 95v) that Modern English *about* appeared to descend from it. He gave a reference to the *Gothicum glossarium* for *eadig* (MS Jun. 2, fol. 81v), and he also referred to his *Observationes in Willerami . . . paraphrasin* (fol. 100r). A number of small notes or Type 4 leaves, which may have lain loose between the pages of the unbound dictionary, are now bound into MS Jun. 2 (fols. 94, 117, 279, 314 *bis*) and give etymological information that seems irrelevant to this dictionary. An unnumbered Type 4 leaf (MS Jun. 2, between fols. 332 and 333) contains etymological information on two modern English words, "lure" and "lushious," which Edward Lye added to the *Etymologicum Anglicanum*.[42] Apart from these incidental exceptions, which may have been the product of work done by Junius after he had completed the dictionary itself, etymology does not form part of the material presented.

---

[42]See Lye (1743), sig. Ttt. 1ᵛ.

So far, I have discussed the structure and contents of single entries in Junius's Old English–Latin dictionary, but it is only when we look at a succession of entries on cognate forms that we get a complete picture of the nature of the dictionary. By way of example I have chosen a series of entries related to the modern English word *day*. Junius started on a Type 1 leaf (MS Jun. 2, fol. 65r) with "dæg, dies," which he illustrated with citations from the Psalms, the Gospels, and Bede.[43] In a long block of indented information he then gave: "dægred," "dæghwamlice," "dægsteorre," "dægredlice," "dagung," "on dagung," "dagian," "dæghwamlic," "ðis wæs his dæghwamlice weorc," "dæghuæm mið iuwih ic sæt," "dægmæl," "dægmæles pil," "dægmæls pilu," and "gewisse dægmæl," each with a Latin gloss and one or more source references. In order to make room for all these entries, he crossed out some entries for other words that he had already written on the page. He even added another example above the first: "dæg, Dies; Ælfr. gloss. 10, Gloss. R. p. 94." He then continued on fol. 64r, a Type 2 leaf, with a repetition of the entry "dæg, Dies," and referred to Ælfric's *Grammar* for a complete declension of the word. This is then followed by eleven related examples, of which four are provided with indented information: (1) "dæghwamlice," to which he added "God dæghwamlice us deð ure neode"; (2) "dæghwamlic leoht"; (3) "ænes dæges weorc"; (4) "ærran dæge"; (5) "anum dæge ær"; (6) "æren dæg," to which he added "to dæg" and "ofer ðrige"; (7) "æron dæg"; (8) "georsten dæg," to which he added "gyrstan dæg," "ondæg," "to dæg," and "heo dæg"; (9) "dægræd"; (10) "dægrima"; (11) "dægwæccan," to which he added "dægweard," "nihtwæccan," "dægwine" (twice), "dægwine *vel* andliofen," "geheald dagas *vel* halige dagas," "ceapdagas," "restedæg," "swæsingdagas," "symbeldæg," "smolte dæge," and "sumorlic dæg." Again all entries are followed by a

---

[43] For the sake of brevity, I have refrained from including the citations with their Latin glosses and source references.

Latin gloss and one or more source references. This block of information is immediately followed by Gothic and Runic cognates, which I shall list below. On fol. 64v, however, Junius continued his work on *dæg*, but with a different gloss: "dæg, Tempus vitæ humanæ. Ælfr. can. 28. Oros. VI,30." This is also followed by a block of quotations, each followed by a Latin gloss and one or more source references. The quotations include spelling variants from non-West Saxon dialects and instances of the cognate form *dogor*: (1) "on dæge ꝺ æfter dæge"; (2) "ðu scealt greot etan þine lifdagas"; (3) "ær his swylt dæge"; (4) "ðrio dogor gee derhuunas mec mið"; (5) "oðero þonne doege"; (6) "gewarð halig doeg *vel* sunna doeg"; (7) "heonu ge ðrio doger gebidas mec"; (8) "feower dogor is"; (9) "his þara nyhstana dogora gemyndig"; (10) "þa he þa to ðam ytemestan dogore becom." Junius concluded the list with a number of shorter entries: "dægeseage," to which he added "dægesege," "dægmel sceawere" (which is entered twice, with different glosses), "dægmete," and "dægþern," to which he added "tyslian hi mid dægþernum gescyum." Although *dæg* is a frequently occurring word in Old English, the entries give a clear image of the exhaustiveness of Junius's work, which is only limited by his selection of sources.

In addition to Old English, Junius added Gothic, Runic, and Icelandic to the dictionary. In a letter of 28 January 1656 to William Dugdale, Junius stated: "I keep my selfe in the meane while busie with referring the most antient Gothike dialect, occurring in the Codex Argenteus, to that collection of an Anglo-Saxonike Dictionarie I have bene long gathering for mine owne private use."[44] Gothic cognates, with Greek translations and references to the Gospels, were added directly underneath the Old English entries if there was sufficient room. If not, and this was often the case on the Type 1 leaves, separate blocks, columns, or even pages were filled with Gothic entries. To the above entry on

---

[44]Hamper (1827), 301. This passage is also quoted by Bennett (1938), 29 n. 1.

dæg, Junius added (fol. 64r): (1) "dags. Joh. IX,4."; (2) "in daga stauos Matth. XI,24."; (3) "himma daga. Matth. VI,11 & 30."; (4) "gistradagis. Matth. VI,30."; (5) "iftumin daga. Matth. XXVII,62. Marc. XI,12."; (6) "und hina dag. Matth. XI,23. XXVII,7."; (7) "fidurdogs ist. Joh. XI,39."; (8) "daga hwammeh. Marc. XIV,49. Luc. XIX,47. XVI,19."; (9) "daghwanoh. Luc. IX,23." Junius provided all of these with Greek glosses. Longer Gothic quotations are rare.

Runes form the third component in the dictionary. Junius, who based his study of runes mainly on the works of the Danish polyhistor Olaus Wormius, was of the opinion that Runic was the original Norse language, which had been written in the characteristic Runic script,[45] in the same way as Gothic and Old English had their own alphabets. The addition of Runic words follows predominantly the same pattern as that of Gothic, but translations are always in Latin. Where Runic cognates are joined with Gothic words, they are invariably placed underneath their Gothic counterparts, which indicates that they were included later. Junius's sources for his Runic additions were all works by Olaus Wormius, his complete works in the field of runes. Junius's source reference "Monumenta Danica" refers to MS Jun. 8, his copy of Wormius's *Danicorum monumentorum libri VI* (Copenhagen, 1643); "Fasti Danici" to MS Jun. 14, Wormius's *Fasti Danici universam tempora computandi . . .* (Copenhagen, 1643); "Lex. Runicum" to Wormius's *Specimen lexici runici . . .* (Copenhagen, 1650); and "Literatura Runica," "Epicedium R. Lodbrog," and "Wormius ad Egilli Skallagrini" all to Wormius's *RUNER, seu Danica literatura antiquissima* (Copenhagen, 1636), reprinted in 1651 together with the *Specimen lexici runici*.[46] It seems likely that Junius used, and

---

[45]See Bennett (1950–51), 271.

[46]The final part of Wormius's *RUNER* consists of a treatise on Old Icelandic poetry, followed by *De prisca Danorum dissertatio*, a transliteration into runes of two Old Norse poems. The first is the skaldic poem *Krákumál*, which is part

perhaps owned, the 1651 edition, although it is not now among his manuscripts.[47] Junius's Runic additions to the entry on *dæg* are:[48] (1) "ÞAG SETT ER. Dies occidit."; (2) "ÞAG SETUR, Diei occasus."; (3) "I ÞAG, Hodie; Lex. Runicum in IA."; (4) "EIN ÞAG, Certo aliquo tempore, aliquando."; (5) "VAR EIN ÞAG VEÞUR BAEÞE HUAST AG KALLT, Erat aliquand [*sic*] aër tempestuosus & frigidus; Lex. Runicum in KALNAR."

The fourth language that Junius added to his dictionary was Icelandic, which he believed to be different from the Runic language described in the works of Olaus Wormius.[49] There is no question of systematic addition of Icelandic cognates; the number of Icelandic words is in no way comparable to that of Gothic or Runic, and they occur only at irregular intervals. Sometimes, Icelandic words are added immediately underneath Old English

---

of the twelfth-century *Ragnars saga Loðbrókar* and consists of twenty-nine stanzas of ten lines each. The second poem is the *Hǫfuðlausn* from the thirteenth-century *Egils saga Skallagrímssonar*. Bennett (1938), 221, observed Junius's remarks on these poems in the preface of the *Gothicum glossarium* but did not give the source of the material.

[47] Junius mentioned the work in *Gothicum glossarium*, sig. ***4ᵛ.

[48] For the rest of this paragraph, words that I have rendered in capitals are written in runes in Junius's dictionary. (Similarly, in the title of Wormius's book cited above, the word *RUNER* is written in runes.)

[49] See Bennett (1938), 219. Bennett made some contradictory observations on the presence of Icelandic in MSS Jun. 2 and 3. He stated on p. 40: "Junius had left the dictionary as a huge mass of entries in four languages—Anglo-Saxon, Old High German, Gothic, and 'Runic'. . . . Indeed, the fact that Icelandic words are not given in Junius's own manuscript seems not to have been noticed hitherto," to which he added on p. 219: "In MSS Junius 2 and 3 Icelandic words are rare. They are usually taken from 'gr. Islandica'; sometimes they are quoted as parallels to Anglo-Saxon or Runic forms." One page earlier, Bennett had commented on Junius's glossary (MS Jun. 36) compiled from the Icelandic grammar by Runólfur Jónsson: "It was not used [by Junius] in his enormous glossary of the five Northern languages. . . ."

entries. With respect to Icelandic there is no difference between the Type 1 and Type 2 leaves.[50] There are two pages on Type 3 leaves that exclusively contain Icelandic words.[51] The hand in which the Icelandic words were added is rather tall and unsteady, and it stands out among the rest of the entries in the dictionary.[52] Nevertheless, it is clearly Junius's hand, perhaps dating from a later period. Junius indicated his source of Icelandic as "grammatica Islandica," which refers to MS Jun. 36, fols. 4–79, his Icelandic-Latin vocabulary compiled from Runólfur Jónsson's Icelandic grammar, which thus indirectly formed the source for Junius's additions.

Bennett's claim that MSS Jun. 2 and 3 include "Franconian (Old High German)" as one of their five basic languages is totally unfounded.[53] When an Old High German cognate occurs[54]—and this happens very rarely indeed—it forms part of an etymological remark. These remarks may be regarded as asides and do not form

---

[50]See, for example, MS Jun. 2, fols. 429 (Type 2) and 430 (Type 1), which both contain Icelandic additions.

[51]See MS Jun. 2, fols. 97r and 541r.

[52]Some of the entries derived from Laurence Nowell's *Vocabularium Saxonicum* are in the same hand.

[53]Bennett (1938), 28. Bennett's use of the term "Franconian" goes back directly to Nicolson, and it would appear that Bennett's views of Junius's dictionary were sometimes influenced by Nicolson's transcripts of MSS Jun. 2 and 3 rather than by the original manuscripts. Bennett first claimed that Junius had written his dictionary in four languages, to which he added on p. 40: "Who decided that Icelandic words were to be added, thus making it a 'Glossarium quinque Linguarum Septentrionalium,' we cannot say." On pp. 217–18 Bennett speaks of Junius's "glossary of the five northern languages," after which he again mentions only four languages on p. 367. It was in fact William Nicolson who referred to MSS Jun. 2 and 3 as a "Glossary or Lexicon of the five old Northern Languages" (cf. my quotation at the beginning of this paper), and in writing this he must have had in mind his own transcripts of MSS Jun. 2 and 3.

[54]For example, MS Jun. 2, fol. 408r: "Anolkiu, Integra. vide Keronem in Integra."

part of the original design of the dictionary. Apart from a sporadic Old High German cognate, Junius at times also added Dutch,[55] Danish,[56] and contemporary English[57] in such etymologies.

III. Sources

Junius conscientiously aimed at providing all Old English words and phrases that he entered in his dictionary with exact references to their sources, and virtually succeeded in this. The number of words without a reference is negligible. All sources are indicated by abbreviations, which, while including some slight variation, are recognizably similar throughout the entire work. Furthermore, Junius's source references include citations of chapters, verses, or other subdivisions of the text, which enabled him to signal the precise location of the word in question so that he could retrace it if necessary. Most, if not all, of Junius's sources formed part of his own library. The following list comprises a concise account of those source references to Old English material that occur regularly throughout the dictionary.[58] Additional, less frequent sources will be briefly mentioned afterwards.

---

[55]MS Jun. 2, fol. 452v: "gif his nehgebures ceap recð in on his agen geat, Si vicini sui pecus introeat per proprium suum apertum; LL. Inae R. 40. Plane videntur hisce Inæ verbis respondere Belgica, indien sijnes nae-buyrs beest ingeraeckt door sijn eygen opening. vel, raeckt sijnes nae-buyrs beest in door sijn eygen haeg-breke."

[56]See my earlier quotation on *clumian* from MS Jun. 2, fol. 52v (above, p. 316).

[57]MS Jun. 2, fol. 408r: "hwelung, Clangor, a shrill noise, as the sound of a trumpet. L. Noëllus. cum his etiam aliquam videri possunt habere affinitatem Angl. howle & Belg. huylen."

[58]It would far exceed the scope of this paper to check whether for a given source Junius used only his own transcript, or whether he also, or instead, made use of his exemplar. Further research on Junius's manuscripts may bring such details to light.

A. Printed Books[59]

"Matth.," "Marc.," "Luc.," "Joh.," + r,a:[60] the first edition of the Gospels in Old English, by John Foxe (1571).[61] Junius's copy has not been preserved.[62]

"Ps." + a,a: MS Jun. 33, Junius's annotated copy of John Spelman's edition of the continuous Old English gloss to the Psalter,[63] collated by Junius with his own Psalter manuscript, MS Jun. 27, to which he referred as "MS V."[64]

"Beda" + r,a: MS Jun. 10, Junius's copy of Abraham Wheelock's Old English and Latin edition of Bede's *Historia*

---

[59]For this section I have used Junius's own comments on his Old English sources in his *Gothicum glossarium*, sigs. ***1r–***4r, Madan et al. (1937), 962–90, the corrections and emendations to the latter in Stanley (1998), and my own observations.

[60]In my references to Junius's sources, I have used these formulae for the sake of brevity: "+" = "followed by"; "r" = a Roman numeral; "a" = an Arabic numeral. Two consecutive numerals are separated by a comma without spaces.

[61]John Foxe, ed., *The Gospels of the Fower Evangelistes* . . . (London, 1571). Foxe's edition, published at the instigation of Archbishop Parker, was based on Bodleian MS Bodley 441. Junius used it for his own edition of the Old English Gospels, which he compiled with the help of Thomas Marshall. In the process, the 1571 edition was again collated with MS Bodley 441, and also with CUL MS Ii. 2. 11, CCCC MS 140, and Bodleian MSS Hatton 38 and Auct. D. 2. 19 (the Rushworth glosses). See Skeat (1871), xv.

[62]Junius refers to the edition in the *Gothicum glossarium*, sigs. ***2v–***3r.

[63]John Spelman, ed., *Psalterium Davidis Latino-Saxonicum vetus* (London, 1640).

[64]"V" stands for Isaac Vossius, who was the owner of the Psalter when Junius made his collations. Afterwards, Vossius gave the manuscript to Junius. Spelman's edition had been based on BL MS Stowe 2, collated with manuscripts designated as "T" (the Eadwine Psalter: TCC MS R. 17. 1), "C" (CUL MS Ff. 1. 23), and "D" (BL MS Arundel 60). Junius himself added one extra collation from MS "T" to Psalm 12.

ecclesiastica gentis Anglorum,[65] which Junius annotated with underlinings and cross-references. Junius referred to Bede's preface to King Ceolwulf as "Beda in præf.," and to Pope Gregory's replies to Augustine's questions in Book I, chapter 27, as "Beda I,27. Resp."

"Chron." + year: MS Jun. 10, Wheelock's edition of Bede, which includes on pages 503–64 an edition of the Anglo-Saxon Chronicle. Junius collated the Chronicle edition with BL MS Cotton Domitian A. viii, fols. 30–70,[66] and he inserted at the beginning of MS Jun. 10 his transcription of the Old English version of the annals for 1002–56 from the Domitian manuscript.[67]

"LL." + "Inae R.," "Alvredi R.," "Foedus Alvredi & Guthruni R.," "Canuti R.," "Edouardi R.," or "Edouardi Confessoris" + a: again, MS Jun. 10, the Bede edition, in the second issue of which Wheelock included a reprinting, with additions, of William Lambarde's edition of Anglo-Saxon laws, the *Archaionomia*, first printed in 1568. "LL. Polit." + "Canuti R.," "Alvredi R.," "Edgari R.," or "Edmundi" are also references to the *Archaionomia*, for the most part to laws pertaining to the clergy.[68] Further specifications of Anglo-Saxon laws are "LL. eccles.," "Æthelstani regis LL.

---

[65]Abraham Wheelock, ed., *Historiæ ecclesiasticæ gentis Anglorum libri V. a venerabili Beda presbytero scripti* . . . (Cambridge, 1643). Although the title page of Junius's copy bears the date 1643, the copy has appended to it Wheelock's reissue (with additions) of William Lambarde's *Archaionomia*, this portion of the book having its own title page dated 1644. According to Oates (1986), 208, the version of Wheelock's Bede that included the *Archaionomia* was issued about a year after the first appearance of the Bede.

[66]Ker (1957), no. 148.

[67]Madan et al. (1937), 964 (no. 5122), incorrectly identifies MS Cotton Tiberius A. vi as the source of Junius's transcription.

[68]These are not references to Wulfstan's *Institutes of Polity*.

Exonienses,"[69] "Senatus consultum de Walliæ monticolis,"[70] "Æthelstani leges Gratanleanæ,"[71] "Foedus Æthelredi cum exercitu Anlavi,"[72] and "Canones Ælfrici."[73]

"Canones sub Edgaro R." + a: again, MS Jun. 10. Wheelock incorporated in his reissue of the *Archaionomia* an edition of the *Canons of Edgar*, which were not included in Lambarde's original publication of 1568.

"Ælfr. de Vet. test.," "Ælfr. de novo Test.": Ælfric's letter to Sigeweard, entitled *De veteri testamento et novo*, from William L'Isle's edition.[74] Neither the printed book nor a transcript is among Junius's manuscripts.[75]

B. Manuscripts

"Abus." + r: MS Jun. 48, fols. 1–6, Junius's transcript of *De duodecim abusiuis*, from Bodleian MS Hatton 115, fols. 116r–121r.[76]

---

[69]I.e., the law code V Æthelstan, drawn up at Exeter. See Liebermann (1903–16), I, 167–69.

[70]Liebermann (1903–16), I, 374–78.

[71]Liebermann (1903–16), I, 150–64.

[72]The treaty between Æthelred and Olaf, for which see Liebermann (1903–16), I, 220–25.

[73]See Junius's *Gothicum glossarium*, sig. ***2^v, where he referred to this text (now known as Ælfric's Pastoral Letter for Bishop Wulfsige of Sherborne) as one of Wheelock's additions to the *Archaionomia*. However, Junius would also have known of the text from its occurrence in MS Jun. 121, fols. 101v–110r: see Ker (1957), no. 338, art. 26.

[74]William L'Isle, *A Saxon Treatise Concerning the Old and New Testament* (London, 1623).

[75]Junius referred to the book in *Gothicum glossarium*, sig. ***2^r.

[76]Ker (1957), no. 332, art. 31. Junius also knew the text from Bodleian MS Hatton 116, pp. 329–47: Ker (1957), no. 333, art. 19.

"Ælfr. Gramm." / "gr. Ælfr." + "cap." + a: Ælfric's Old English translation of the *Excerptiones de Prisciano*, based on excerpts from Priscian's *Institutiones grammaticae* and Donatus's *Ars minor*.[77] This text does not occur among Junius's transcripts. William Somner's edition of Ælfric's *Grammar*,[78] which Junius mentioned in the *Gothicum glossarium* (sig. ***3[r]), seems rather late for Junius to have used it in his dictionary. It is more likely that Junius made use of a transcript owned by Sir Simonds D'Ewes, BL MS Harley 8, which contains Junius's annotations.[79]

"Ælfr. Gloss." + r: MS Jun. 72, fols. 1–32, a transcript of Ælfric's *Glossary*, from BL MS Cotton Julius A. ii, fols. 120v–130v,[80] collated with MS Harley 107,[81] which was at the time in the possession of Sir Simonds D'Ewes.

"Æqu. vern." + r: MS Jun. 41, pp. 1–24, Junius's transcript of Ælfric's Old English rendering of part of Bede's *De temporibus*, headed "De primo die seculi, sive de equinoctio vernali," from BL MS Cotton Tiberius A. iii, fols. 65v–73r.[82]

---

[77]See Gneuss (1990), 9–13; and Gneuss (1996b), 10–13.

[78]William Somner, *Dictionarium Saxonico-Latino-Anglicum* (Oxford, 1659), pp. 1–52 following the end of the dictionary.

[79]Collation of a passage of some length (on fol. 289r of MS Jun. 2) against the edition of Zupitza (1880), 231/11–232/2, appears to prove that Junius did indeed use D'Ewes's transcript. D'Ewes made his transcript from BL MS Harley 107, a copy of the *Grammar* that shows distinctly Kentish features. In the passage in question, only Harley 107 includes the form *lægdest*, equivalent to Zupitza 231/13, *ledest. lægdest* is the form used in Junius's quotation of the passage. On Junius's cooperation with D'Ewes, see Van Romburgh (2000).

[80]Ker (1957), no. 158.

[81]Ker (1957), no. 227, art. 1.

[82]Ker (1957), no. 186, art. 13.

"Basil. reg." + r: MS Jun. 68, pp. 1–18, Junius's transcript of the Old English version of St. Basil's *Admonitio ad filium spiritualem*, from Bodleian MS Hatton 76, fols. 55r–67v.[83]

"Basilii Magni Hexaëmeron, Cap." + r: MS Jun. 47, pp. 1–19, Junius's transcript of Ælfric's homily *Exameron Anglice*, on the six days of Creation and the fall and redemption of man, from Bodleian MS Hatton 115, fols. 1r–10r.[84]

"Boëthius": MS Jun. 12, Junius's transcript of King Alfred's translation of Boethius's *De consolatione philosophiae*, from Bodleian MS Bodley 180.[85] In the margins Junius noted the variant readings of BL MS Cotton Otho A. vi[86] (which was subsequently damaged in the Cotton fire of 1731), and on separate leaves inserted into MS Jun. 12 he transcribed the metrical passages of the Cotton manuscript.[87]

"C. Matth.," "C. Marc.," "C. Luc.," "C. Joh." + r,a: the continuous interlinear Old English gloss in the Lindisfarne Gospels, BL MS Cotton Nero D. iv,[88] which Junius identified, according to the name of the owner, as the Cotton Gospels and hence referred to as "C." Junius's entries were presumably based on his excerpts from the Lindisfarne Gospels in MS Jun. 50, fols. 1–29, and MS Jun. 76, fols. 1–51.[89]

---

[83] Ker (1957), no. 328A, art. 2.

[84] Ker (1957), no. 332, art. 1.

[85] Ker (1957), no. 305.

[86] Ker (1957), no. 167.

[87] For a facsimile of Junius's transcript of the *Meters of Boethius*, see Robinson and Stanley (1991), section 5.

[88] Ker (1957), no. 165.

[89] When a form occurred both in the Lindisfarne Gospels and in the Rushworth Gospels (on which see below under "R. Matth." etc.), Junius identified the sources as "C. & R."

"Cædmon" + a,a: MS Jun. 11, the so-called "Cædmonian" poems, published by Junius in 1655. Junius's annotated copy of the edition is MS Jun. 73.

"De Spiritu Septiformi" + a: MS Jun. 48, fols. 35–40, Junius's transcript of Wulfstan's *De septiformi spiritu*, from Bodleian MS Hatton 116, pp. 373–77.[90]

"Fulg." + r: MS Jun. 52, fols. 73–80, Junius's transcript of two Latin texts with interlinear Old English gloss from BL MS Cotton Tiberius A. iii, fols. 163v–168v.[91] The two texts are the dictum on the Rule of St. Benedict attributed to St. Fulgentius, and the partial copy of the *Memoriale qualiter in monasterio conuersari debemus*.

"Gl. Cott." + a: MS Jun. 77, Junius's transcript of a Latin–Old English glossary extending only to the letter *P*, and other glossaries, from BL MS Cotton Cleopatra A. iii.[92]

"Gl. R. pag." + a: MS Jun. 71, Junius's transcript of the glossary material in a manuscript now divided between Antwerp, Plantin-Moretus Museum, MS 16.2 (formerly MS 47) and BL MS Add. 32246.[93] Junius attributed this glossary to Archbishop Ælfric—he did not distinguish between the archbishop of Canterbury from 995 to 1005 and the grammarian and homilist of the same name—but to avoid confusion with the glossary in MS Jun. 72, he referred to it as "R," to indicate the provenance of the source manuscript from the family of his friend, the famous Antwerp painter Peter Paul Rubens.[94]

---

[90]Ker (1957), no. 333, art. 22.

[91]Ker (1957), no. 186, arts. 2 and 3.

[92]Ker (1957), no. 143.

[93]Ker (1957), no. 2. It was printed in Somner (1659), 53–80.

[94]Junius received the manuscript from Rubens's son Albert, whose father had obtained it from the library of the Plantin-Moretus family, the owners of the manuscript. See Ladd (1960).

"Greg. magnus Dialog." + r,a: MS Jun. 46, fols. i–52, Junius's transcript of the Old English version of the *Dialogues* of Pope Gregory the Great, from Bodleian MS Hatton 76, fols. 1r–54v.[95]

"Herb." + r,a: MS Jun. 58, pp. 1–141, Junius's transcript of the *Liber medicinalis*, or enlarged *Herbarium Apuleii*,[96] from Bodleian MS Hatton 76, fols. 68r–124r.[97]

"Hymn.": (1) MS Jun. 107, Junius's transcript of hymns and canticles with Old English glosses, from BL MS Cotton Vespasian D. xii, fols. 4r–120v;[98] (2) MS Jun. 108, Junius's transcript of hymns and canticles from MS Cotton Julius A. vi.[99]

"Laur. Noëllo," "Noëllus": MS Jun. 26, Junius's transcript of Laurence Nowell's *Vocabularium Saxonicum* in Bodleian MS Selden supra 63.[100]

"Lupus Serm." + r,a: MS Jun. 102, Junius's transcripts of five sermons by Wulfstan and other material, from BL MSS Cotton Nero A. i and Tiberius A. iii, CCCC MS 201, and Bodleian MS Hatton 113.[101]

"Martyrol." + date: MS Jun. 101, Junius's excerpts from Old English Martyrologies. Folios v^r–vi^r are from BL MS Cotton Julius

---

[95]Ker (1957), no. 328A, art. 1. Junius added chapter numbers in the margin of the manuscript.

[96]The transcript includes some lexicographical notes by Junius; see Stanley (1998), 168.

[97]Ker (1957), no. 328B, art. 1.

[98]Ker (1957), no. 208, art. b.

[99]Ker (1957), no. 160.

[100]For an edition of Nowell's *Vocabularium*, see Marckwardt (1952).

[101]The items transcribed by Junius are Ker (1957), no. 164, arts. 20 and 21; no. 49B, arts. 3–5; no. 331, art. 29; no. 186, art. 19 (e); and no. 49B, arts. 14–16.

A. x,[102] and fols. vi[v]–5v are from CCCC MS 196.[103]

"Med. ex quadr." + r,a: MS Jun. 58, pp. 145–64, Junius's transcript of the *Medicina de quadrupedibus*, from Bodleian MS Hatton 76, fols. 124v–130r.[104]

"Medicina, cap." + a: MS Jun. 59, fols. 1–4, Junius's transcript of *De peccatorum medicina*, from BL MS Cotton Tiberius A. iii, fols. 94v–97r.[105]

"Modus confitendi, cap." + a: MS Jun. 63, fols. i–24, Junius's transcript of confessional prayers, from MS Cotton Tiberius A. iii, fols. 44r–56v.[106]

"Monast. ind." + a: MS Jun. 52, fols. 93–102, Junius's transcript of the *Monasteriales indicia*, from MS Cotton Tiberius A. iii, fols. 97r–101v.[107]

"Mor. Praecept." + a: MS Jun. 45, fols. 4v–9r, Junius's transcript of the *Dialogues of Adrian and Ritheus*, the *Distichs of Cato*, and some notes, from BL MS Cotton Julius A. ii, fols. 137v–144v.[108]

---

[102]Ker (1957), no. 161. Junius also referred to the Julius A. x text as "Cottoniano fastor."

[103]Ker (1957), no. 47, art. 1.

[104]Ker (1957), no. 328B, art. 1.

[105]Ker (1957), no. 186, art. 21 (a)–(j).

[106]Ker (1957), no. 186, art. 9.

[107]Ker (1957), no. 186, art. 22.

[108]Ker (1957), no. 159, arts. 2, 3, and 4. See also Ker's remark (p. 202) on the significance of this transcript by Junius, in view of the damaged state of MS Julius A. ii. Another of Junius's manuscripts, MS Jun. 61, also contains excerpts from *Adrian and Ritheus* derived from MS Julius A. ii; in MS Jun. 61, these excerpts are compared with the prose *Solomon and Saturn*, from BL MS Cotton Vitellius A. xv, fols. 86v–93v (Ker [1957], no. 215, art. 3). See also Stanley (1998), 164.

"MS. resp.," "MS Alb. resp." + r: MS Jun. 104, fols. 1–21, Junius's transcript of Ælfric's *Interrogationes Sigewulfi*, from Bodleian MS Hatton 115, fols. 121r–131v, collated with MS Hatton 116, pp. 300–29.[109]

"Nathan" + a: MS Jun. 74, fols. 11v–16r, Junius's transcript of the embassy of Nathan the Jew to Tiberius (i.e., the *Vindicta Salvatoris*), from CUL MS Ii. 2. 11, fols. 193r–202r.[110]

"Nicod.": MS Jun. 74, fols. i^r–11r, Junius's transcript of the pseudo-Gospel of Nicodemus, from CUL MS Ii. 2. 11, fols. 173v–193r,[111] collated with BL MS Cotton Vitellius A. xv, fols. 60r–86v.[112]

"Observ. Lunae" + a; "Observ. de Kalendis" + name of month: MS Jun. 44, Junius's transcripts of *De observatione lunae et quae cavenda*, from BL MS Cotton Tiberius A. iii, fols. 32v–35v,[113] collated with Bodleian MS Hatton 115, fols. 148r–153v.[114]

"Octo vitia capitalia": MS Jun. 48, fols. 29–34, Junius's transcript of *De octo vitiis*, from Bodleian MS Hatton 116, pp. 329–47.[115]

"Off. episcoporum, cap." + a: presumably, MS Jun. 65, fols. 1–10, Junius's extracts from the texts describing the duties of various ranks of Christians (including bishops) in BL MS Cotton Nero A. i, fols. 70r–76v and 97r–105v.[116]

---

[109]Ker (1957), no. 332, art. 32, and no. 333, art. 18.

[110]Ker (1957), no. 20, art. 3.

[111]Ker (1957), no. 20, art. 2.

[112]Ker (1957), no. 215, art. 2.

[113]Ker (1957), no. 186, art. 7 (b).

[114]Ker (1957), no. 332, art. 35.

[115]Ker (1957), no. 333, art. 19.

[116]Stanley (1998), 169, identifies the sources of these extracts by Junius as Ker (1957), no. 164, arts. 1, 2, and 11–18.

"Off. regum, cap." + a: presumably MS Jun. 60, Junius's transcript of the coronation oath, *Sacramentum uel promissio regis in consecratione*, formerly in BL MS Cotton Vitellius A. vii, but now destroyed.[117]

"Oros." + r,a: MS Jun. 15, fols. 1–110, Junius's transcript of the Alfredian Old English translation of the *Historiae aduersum paganos* of Paulus Orosius, from BL MS Cotton Tiberius B. i, fols. 3r–111v.[118]

"Past." + r,a: MS Jun. 53, fols. 1–257, Junius's transcript of King Alfred's translation of Gregory the Great's *Regula pastoralis*, from BL MS Cotton Tiberius B. xi, which is now almost completely destroyed.[119] Junius's transcript includes variants from Bodleian MS Hatton 20 and BL MS Cotton Otho B. ii.[120]

"Prov." + r: MS Jun. 71, pp. 129–57,[121] Junius's transcript of interlinear Kentish glosses to the *Proverbs of Solomon* from BL MS Cotton Vespasian D. vi, fols. 2r–37v.[122]

---

[117]Ker (1957), no. 213, art. a. For further comments, see Stanley (1998), 168.

[118]Ker (1957), no. 191, art. 1.

[119]Ker (1957), no. 195 (excluding the portion that is now Kassel, Landesbibliothek, MS Anhang 19, which Junius did not know). See also Stanley (1998), 166.

[120]Ker (1957), nos. 324 and 175. The whole is preceded by Junius's transcript of a homily for the feast of St. Gregory from Bodleian MS Hatton 114, fols. 140r–147v (Ker [1957], no. 331, art. 59). The leaves carrying the homily transcript are now foliated v–xvii, but Junius originally numbered them separately as "1"–"13," an indication that originally they may not have been part of the manuscript.

[121]Numbered "1"–"29" by Junius as a separate part.

[122]Ker (1957), no. 207, art. a.

"Quadrag." + a: MS Jun. 85, fols. 18r–24r,[123] Ælfric's homily on the first Sunday of Lent, headed in the manuscript *Dominica I in Quadragesima*.

"R. Matth.," "R. Marc.," "R. Luc.," "R. Joh." + r,a: the continuous interlinear Old English gloss in the Rushworth Gospels, Bodleian MS Auct. D. 2. 19.[124] MS Jun. 76, fols. 52–87, contain excerpts by Junius from the Rushworth Gospels, which he had on loan from the owner in 1650.[125]

"Reg. Bened. cap." + a: MS Jun. 52, fols. 1–64, Junius's transcript of the Old English text of the *Rule* of St. Benedict, from BL MS Cotton Titus A. iv, fols. 2r–107r.[126]

"Reg. Bened. interl.": MS Jun. 92, Junius's transcript of the continuous interlinear Old English gloss to the *Rule* of St. Benedict from BL MS Cotton Tiberius A. iii, fols. 118r–163v.[127]

"Regularis Concordia, cap." + r: MS Jun. 46, fols. 53–63, Junius's transcript of the *Regularis concordia Anglicae nationis monachorum sanctimoniialiumque*, from BL MS Cotton Tiberius A. iii, fols. 3r–27v.[128] There are also references to the "Proemium Regularis Concordiae."

---

[123]Ker (1957), no. 336, art. 5.

[124]Ker (1957), no. 292.

[125]See Junius's letter of May 1650 to F. Junius Nepos, Amsterdam, Universiteitsbibliotheek, M. 92c.

[126]Ker (1957), no. 200. See also Stanley (1998), 166.

[127]Ker (1957), no. 186, art. 1. Junius interlined his transcript of the Old English text into a printed edition of the Latin version: Baudoin Moreau, ed., *Regula celeberrimi toto occidente patris s. Benedicti* . . . (Douai, 1611). See Stanley (1998), 174.

[128]Ker (1957), no. 186, art. 6. It may also be noted that MS Jun. 18, Junius's copy of John Selden's *Eadmeri monachi Cantuariensis historia nouorum siue sui sæculi libri VI* (London, 1623), includes on pp. 145–54 Selden's edition of the preface and epilogue of the *Regularis concordia*, in which Junius has entered corrections.

"Scintil.," "Scintillarius," "Liber Scint. Titulo" (+ further specification) + r: MS Jun. 40, Junius's excerpts from the bilingual Latin–Old English text of the *Liber scintillarum*, a collection of commonplaces, from BL MS Royal 7 C. iv, fols. 1r–100v.[129]

"Solil." + r: MS Jun. 70, pp. 1–48, Junius's transcript of the Old English version of St. Augustine's *Soliloquies*, from BL MS Cotton Vitellius A. xv, fols. 4r–59v.[130]

"Somn." + a: MS Jun. 43, a printed book,[131] at the front of which are inserted leaves bearing transcripts by Junius.[132] The first sixteen leaves contain Junius's transcript of *De somniorum diversitate secundum ordinem abcharii Danielis prophete* and other material relating to dreams, from BL MS Cotton Tiberius A. iii, fols. 27v–32v, 38r–39v, and 42rv.[133] The second through twelfth leaves of the transcript have been paginated "1"–"22" by Junius. The seventeenth through twenty-second leaves include Junius's transcripts of material relating to dreams from Bodleian MS Hatton 115, fols. 150v–152v, BL MS Cotton Tiberius A. iii, fols. 35v–36r and 37v–38r, and MS Hatton 115, fol. 148r.[134] The seventeenth through nineteenth leaves of the transcripts have been paginated "71"–"76" by Junius.

---

[129]Ker (1957), no. 256, art. 1. As Ker observes (p. 323), on fols. 93v, 96r, and 99v Junius made notes concerning the misbinding of one quire of the manuscript.

[130]Ker (1957), no. 215, art. 1. See Stanley (1998), 170, on the significance of the transcript.

[131]Johannes Meursius, *Roma luxurians. Sive, de luxu Romanorum liber singularis. Item, mantissa* (Copenhagen, 1631).

[132]Madan et al. (1937), 974, gives a very unclear entry on this manuscript, and it is not mentioned in Stanley (1998).

[133]Ker (1957), no. 186, art. 7 (a), (i), and (q).

[134]Ker (1957), no. 332, art. 35 (j), no. 186, art. 7 (c), and no. 332, art. 35 (a).

JUNIUS'S OLD ENGLISH DICTIONARY 335

"V. Ps." + r,r: MS Jun. 27, the Junius Psalter, a tenth-century Latin Psalter with continuous interlinear Old English gloss.[135] As noted above, "V" stands for Vossius, the former owner of the manuscript.

"Wulfstan paraen.": MS Jun. 38, fols. 1–15, Junius's transcripts of Wulfstanian texts in CCCC MS 201, pp. 19–28,[136] collated with BL MS Cotton Tiberius A. iii, fols. 88v–93v.[137]

Of the additional printed books used by Junius, the English histories printed by Twysden[138] are quoted most often, especially John of Brompton's chronicle and Latin translation of Old English laws,[139] but also the chronicles by Gervase of Canterbury, Richard of Hexham, and Thomas Stubbs, as well as William Somner's glossary of Old English terms that is appended to the book. Furthermore, there are occasional references to Henry Spelman's *Archæologus* (for example, MS Jun. 2, fol. 2r), William Dugdale's *Antiquities of Warwickshire* (fol. 331v) and *Monasticon Anglicanum* (fol. 450r), Cornelius Kilianus's *Etymologicum* (fol. 281v), Stephen Skinner's *Etymologicon* (fol. 6v),[140] Spenser's *Faerie*

---

[135]Ker (1957), no. 335. See Brenner (1908), p. X, who mentioned that Junius used this Psalter for MSS Jun. 2 and 3, which Brenner wrongly referred to as "Etymologicum."

[136]Ker (1957), no. 49B, arts. 6–13.

[137]Ker (1957), no. 186, art. 19.

[138]Roger Twysden, ed., *Historiae Anglicanae scriptores X* (London, 1652).

[139]Junius preferred this translation to that by William Lambarde, as is demonstrated by his collations in the *Archaionomia* portion of MS Jun. 10. See also Junius's *Gothicum glossarium*, sig. ***3ᵛ, where he explicitly mentions his preference for Brompton's version.

[140]Henry Spelman, *Archæologus, in modum glossarii* . . . (London, 1626); William Dugdale, *The Antiquities of Warwickshire* (London, 1656); William Dugdale, *Monasticon Anglicanum*, 3 vols. (London, 1655, 1661, and 1673); Cornelius Kilianus, *Etymologicum Teutonicae linguae* (Antwerp, 1599); Stephen

Queene (on the recto of the unnumbered Type 4 leaf preceding fol. 333), Adam of Bremen's *Historia ecclesiastica* (fol. 280v), and Ekkehard of St. Gallen's *De casibus monasterii sancti Galli* (fol. 517r).[141] Occasional references to Junius's own manuscripts and printed books include: MS Jun. 1, the *Ormulum* (for example, MS Jun. 2, fol. 276v); MSS Jun. 4 and 5, the *Etymologicum Anglicanum* (fol. 525v); MS Jun. 21, the *Theutonista* (fol. 93r);[142] MS Jun. 116c, Junius's Old High German *Glossarium D* (fol. 6v); MS Jun. 116e, Kero's Old High German glossary to the Benedictine Rule (fol. 408r); the *Observationes in Willerami . . . paraphrasin* (fol. 100r); the *Gothicum glossarium* (fol. 81v); and an "etymologicum nostrum Teutonicum" which has not been preserved.[143]

IV. EVALUATION AND FINAL HISTORY

A sample count in the *E* section of the frequency of the various sources on the Type 1 and Type 2 leaves shows that Junius began compiling his dictionary exclusively from printed books. In the *E* section the Type 1 leaves contain 179 references to the Gospels, 142 to the Psalms, and ninety-five to Bede, whereas the Type 2 leaves have only six references to the Psalms, thirteen to the Gospels, and thirty-five to Bede. Although the total number of entries on the Type 1 leaves outnumbers the total on the Type 2 leaves, the difference is nevertheless telling. A second group of sources, consisting of the Cotton glossary, Ælfric's *Glossary*, the

---

Skinner, *Etymologicon linguae Anglicanae* (London, 1671). On Junius's use of Kilianus's *Etymologicum*, see Dekker (1996).

[141] MS Jun. 20, Melchior Goldastus, *Alamannicarum rerum scriptores aliquot vetusti* (Frankfurt, 1606), contains Ekkehard's writings.

[142] Gherard van Schueren, *Vocabularium quod intitulatur Theutonista* (Cologne, 1477): an incunable Latin–Low German/Low German–Latin dictionary.

[143] For evidence of the existence of this work, see Breuker (1990), 52–53.

"Rubens" glossary, Ælfric's *Grammar*, and the Lindisfarne and Rushworth Gospels, probably necessitated the expansion of the dictionary with the Type 2 leaves, for references to these sources occur with relatively equal frequency on both types.

Bennett claimed that Junius started work on the dictionary between 1651 and 1655, but he did not explain why he believed 1651 to be the earliest possible date for Junius to have embarked on the project.[144] Considering that Junius worked with Ælfric's *Glossary* in 1648, had the Rushworth Gospels on loan in 1650, and added the Gothic entries in 1656, I am inclined to believe that the main work on the dictionary was carried out between 1643,[145] when Wheelock published his edition of Bede, and 1656, when Junius entered the Gothic words. This does not imply that work on the dictionary ceased completely after that time. Additions from Dugdale's *Monasticon Anglicanum* (of which the last volume was published in 1673) and Skinner's *Etymologicon* (published in 1671)[146] indicate that Junius continued to make additions until very late in his life.

Junius's Old English–Latin dictionary occupies a unique place in the Old English lexicographical tradition, in that, with the exception of Laurence Nowell's *Vocabularium Saxonicum*, which had no known forebears, it is the only Old English dictionary, in a period which extends into the twentieth century, that did not rely on its predecessors.[147] Junius must have known of John Joscelyn's

---

[144]See Bennett (1938), 29; also Harris (1992), 7, who calls MSS Jun. 2 and 3 "the remains of a project undertaken by Junius in the 1650s, following his return to the Continent."

[145]For corroborative evidence regarding the beginning of Junius's studies in Germanic philology, see Breuker (1990), 50.

[146]See Bennett (1938), 368–69.

[147]I have left out of consideration the lost seventeenth-century dictionary by the Dutchman Johannes de Laet; see Bekkers (1970), xviii–xxvii. On De Laet's Old English Studies, see Bremmer (1998c), pp. 154–62.

dictionary[148] through his acquaintance with Sir Simonds D'Ewes, whom he visited in 1648.[149] During this period, Junius annotated a transcript of Ælfric's *Grammar* in BL MS Harley 8, which also contains part of D'Ewes's transcript of Joscelyn's dictionary.[150] Although it is likely that Junius had started his own dictionary by that time, there are no indications that Joscelyn's work played a role in it. The same holds good for William Somner's *Dictionarium*. Somner mentioned Junius's assistance in the compilation of his *Dictionarium*,[151] but there is no evidence that Junius made any use of the *Dictionarium* in his own Old English dictionary. The reason for this is presumably the difference in design between the two dictionaries.[152] The absence of quotations and source references in many of Somner's entries caused it to be of little value for Junius's purposes, despite the fact that Somner had used material that Junius had not consulted. Moreover, since Junius concentrated on Old English, Somner's emphasis on etymological and historical information also fell outside the scope of Junius's dictionary.

Junius's extensive use of quotations to illustrate the meaning of words and phrases, together with the consistent and lucid manner of referencing and the appearance of being exhaustive, gave his dictionary a distinctly scholarly touch. It shares these characteristics with the famous humanist dictionary of Ambrogio de

---

[148]BL MSS Cotton Titus A. xv and A. xvi. On the influence of Joscelyn's dictionary, see Hetherington (1980), 25–51; Rosier (1960) and (1966); and the study by Timothy Graham in the present volume.

[149]This was first established by Timmer (1957), 143. See also Breuker (1990), 53–54.

[150]See Hetherington (1980), 107–08.

[151]See Somner (1659), sig. b2ʳ; and Hetherington (1980), 153–54 and 176.

[152]For a description of Somner's *Dictionarium*, see Hetherington (1980), 141–79.

Calepino,[153] whose work was named a *Dictionarium* on account of the many *dictiones*, or quotations from classical authors, that it contained. The influence of humanist lexicography, which aimed to display the complete lexicon, or *thesaurus*, of classical Latin,[154] is clearly present in Junius's work, in which he aimed to include the *thesaurus* of the Old English language. This very characteristic made Junius's Old English dictionary a much desired object for the next generation of scholars of Old English.

After Junius's death in 1677, Dr. John Fell (1625–86), bishop of Oxford—who as Vice-Chancellor of the university revived the university press—gave much attention to the publication of Junius's manuscripts. As Saxonists at Oxford appeared very much interested in the Old English dictionary, Fell gave it priority. Although Junius had spent his last years in Oxford preparing his manuscripts for the press,[155] the state in which he left the material was such that it still required further work to make it fit for printing. Bishop Fell assigned the task to William Nicolson, who made a transcript in which he not only used the Old English–Latin dictionary but also incorporated other material from Junius's collection.[156] Since the transcript included Old High German and some Old Frisian, it is likely that Nicolson used MS Jun. 115a, fols. 147r–337v, which is a glossary containing these two languages. This, indeed, might account for the misbinding of five leaves of this manuscript as MS Jun. 2, fols. 552–56. The results of Nicolson's efforts consist of eleven handwritten volumes, now Bodleian MSS Fell 8–18.[157] In 1681, apparently after the

---

[153] Ambrogio de Calepino, *Dictionarium* (Reggio, 1502).

[154] See Claes (1970), 25.

[155] See Wood (1721), II, 203–04 within the separately paginated "Fasti Oxonienses" at the end of the book.

[156] Bennett (1938), 218–19, mentioned Nicolson's use of MS Jun. 120, the manuscript of Gudmund Andrésson's *Lexicon Islandicum*.

[157] For which see Madan et al. (1937), 1214, nos. 8696–8706.

completion of his transcript, Nicolson left Oxford to take up an ecclesiastical post in the North, and by the time Bishop Fell died (in 1686), only a specimen of the transcript had been printed. The next person to become involved in efforts to publish the dictionary was none other than the great Saxonist George Hickes (1642–1715), who hoped that its publication would follow that of a second edition of his own *Institutiones grammaticæ*. In a letter to Arthur Charlett (1665–1722) of 16 March 1693, Hickes stated that, as he had no time for it himself, he had found a suitable publisher for the dictionary in Dr. Hugh Todd (ca. 1658–1728). Again, these efforts came to nothing. A few years later, in 1698, Hickes's correspondence with Edward Thwaites (1667–1711) reveals that Thwaites intended "to throw all the Glossaries into the Dictionary in their alphabetical order," and "mix" the result with the *Etymologicum Anglicanum*, all to be accomplished in one year.[158] In spite of Thwaites's plans, Nicolson's transcript of MSS Jun. 2 and 3 has remained unpublished.[159]

Another attempt to publish Junius's Old English–Latin dictionary was made in the eighteenth century by Edward Lye (1694–1767), who was also the editor of Junius's *Etymologicum linguae Anglicanae*. BL MSS Add. 4720–4722 contain a transcript of MSS Jun. 2 and 3, owned by Lye. The three massive double folio volumes, containing 307, 408, and 407 leaves respectively, were written in the first half of the eighteenth century and are said to have been copied at the expense of the second earl of Oxford. They were presented to the British Museum by Edward Lye on 12 November 1762.[160] Through this three-volume transcript, Junius's

---

[158]For these quotations, see Harris (1992), 8.

[159]Most of this paragraph is based on Harris (1992), 5–8, and Bennett (1938), passim.

[160]The size of the volumes and the sumptuous bindings point to a luxury transcript rather than books for easy reference. In the *British Library Catalogue of Additions to the Manuscripts 1756–1782: Additional Manuscripts 4101–5017* (London, 1977), 195, it is suggested that the books were made for Edward Harley, the

dictionary was a principal basis for Lye's own, which was still unpublished at Lye's death in 1767 but which finally appeared in two large quarto volumes in 1772, under the supervision of the Cambridge scholar Owen Manning (1721–1801).[161]

The efforts of Fell and his fellow Saxonists caused Bennett to observe, "For Junius's great lexicographical works had all been undertaken with a view to eventual publication. In his Gothic Glossary he often refers to his *Etymologicon* and his *Dictionarium Saxonicum*—evidently hoping to print them forthwith."[162] This statement is true for a number of Junius's lexicographical works, but it does not apply to the Old English dictionary. There is no evidence that Junius ever considered publication of the Old English dictionary on the basis of the material in its present state. Junius himself very clearly stated his aim when he wrote to Dugdale in 1656 that he had long been gathering an Old English dictionary *for his own private use.*[163] In the early 1660s Junius lent

---

second earl of Oxford (1689–1741). His father, Robert Harley (1661–1724), the first earl, acquired the collections of John Foxe the martyrologist, Sir Simonds D'Ewes, and the antiquary John Stow: see *DNB* s.n. "Harley, Robert," p. 1289. If the books were first made for the earl of Oxford, they must have passed from him to Edward Lye, who gave them to the British Museum. Bennett (1938), 374–75, reported that Wanley, in his annotated copy of Nicolson's *Historical Library*, described the transcripts as being at Harley's library, and that the opening folios of Add. 4720 and 4721 are in Wanley's hand.

[161]Owen Manning, ed., *Dictionarium Saxonico et Gothico-Latinum. Auctore Edvardo Lye . . .*, 2 vols. (London, 1772). See Adams (1917), 105; and Bennett (1938), 374–75.

[162]Bennett (1938), 361. I have found no evidence for Bennett's assertion that Junius often referred to his *Dictionarium Saxonicum* in the *Gothicum glossarium*. Rather, Junius often simply preceded his citations of Old English words in the *Gothicum glossarium* with the referent "Anglo-Saxonibus," and sometimes also included a citation of the source. He explained his sources in his preface (sigs. ***2r–***4r).

[163]See above, p. 318.

the work to his friend the Dutch philologist Jan van Vliet (1622–66), who used it to collate his copy of Somner's *Dictionarium*.[164] When Van Vliet issued a list of Junius's publications and manuscripts ready for the press, the Old English dictionary did not appear on the list. Instead, Van Vliet mentioned MSS Jun. 4 and 5 (the *Etymologicum Anglicanum*) and a number of works on Old High German.[165]

To Bishop Fell and his fellow Oxford Saxonists, the Old English dictionary and the *Etymologicum Anglicanum* were much more attractive options for publication in England than the Old High German glossaries, if only because Fell's activities were constantly thwarted by insufficient funds. Nicolson's transcript, which also included material from other Junius manuscripts, formed a compromise between Junius's wishes, Fell's intentions, and a shortage of funds. After the printing of a specimen by John Wallis in 1682, the transcript lost its attraction. Hickes's plans to publish Junius's work involved a new edition, while Edward Thwaites's scheme seems to have been grotesquely unrealistic. Owen Manning's publication of Lye's edition was based on an entirely different transcript, in which the Gothic, Runic, and Icelandic words were left out, and the Old English entries rearranged in alphabetical order, abridged, and supplied with Modern English translations.[166]

---

[164]Leiden, Universiteitsbibliotheek, 766 A 5.

[165]The list formed part of Van Vliet's anonymous publication, *'t Vader Ons in XX Oude Noordse en Duijtse Taelen, met d'Uijtleggingen* (Dordrecht, 1664), which was to function as an appetizer for Junius's Gothic–Anglo-Saxon Gospels and *Gothicum glossarium*, published a year later. The manuscripts that Van Vliet explicitly mentioned as being ready for the press are: MSS Jun. 4 and 5, 12, 13, 15, 42, 52 (fols. 1–70), 53, 70, 116a–c, 116e (fols. 4–48), and 116f (fols. 3–116).

[166]For additional information, including Gothic entries, Lye did not consult MSS Jun. 2 and 3, but resorted to other sources.

There has never been any real attempt at publishing Junius's Old English–Latin dictionary in the way that Junius intended the book to be used, namely as a comprehensive lexicon of the Old English language. For Junius himself, it was an incomplete project, for he must have realized that there were more Old English manuscripts to be investigated; the open spaces that he left on many of the pages of MSS Jun. 2 and 3 furnish evidence of this. Both attempts at editing the manuscripts after Junius's death failed to do credit to his method and design, which only required completion and regularization, not abridgment or expansion with other languages. For the study of Old English in the eighteenth and nineteenth centuries, MSS Jun. 2 and 3 were a lost opportunity.

WORKS CITED

Abbott (1900): T. K. Abbott, *Catalogue of the Manuscripts in the Library of Trinity College, Dublin* (Dublin: Hodges & Figgis).

Adams (1917): Eleanor N. Adams, *Old English Scholarship in England from 1566–1800*, Yale Studies in English 55 (New Haven: Yale University Press; repr. Hamden, Conn.: Archon Books, 1970).

Allison and Rogers (1989–94): A. F. Allison and D. M. Rogers, *The Contemporary Printed Literature of the English Counter-Reformation between 1558 and 1640*, 2 vols. (Aldershot: Scolar Press).

Annius (1498): Joannes Annius Viterbiensis, *Commentaria super opera diversorum auctorum de antiquitatibus loquentium* (Rome: Eucharius Silber).

Asher (1993): R. E. Asher, *National Myths in Renaissance France: Francus, Samothes and the Druids* (Edinburgh: Edinburgh University Press).

Assmann (1886): Bruno Assmann, "Abt Ælfrics angelsächsische Bearbeitung des Buches Esther," *Anglia* 9: 25–38.

——— (1889): Bruno Assmann, ed., *Angelsächsische Homilien und Heiligenleben*, Bibliothek der angelsächsischen Prosa 3 (Kassel: G. H. Wigand; repr. with supplementary introduction by Peter Clemoes, Darmstadt: Wissenschaftliche Buchgesellschaft, 1964).

Atkins (1940): Ivor Atkins, "The Origin of the Later Part of the Saxon Chronicle Known as D," *English Historical Review* 55: 8–26.

Bately (1986): Janet M. Bately, ed., *MS A: A Semi-Diplomatic Edition with Introduction and Indices*, The Anglo-Saxon Chronicle: A Collaborative Edition 3, ed. David Dumville and Simon Keynes (Cambridge: D. S. Brewer).

——— (1991): Janet Bately, *The Anglo-Saxon Chronicle: Texts and Textual Relationships*, Reading Medieval Studies, Monograph 3 (Reading: University of Reading).

Bath (1992): Michael Bath, "Anglo-Dutch Relations in the Field of the Emblem," in *Emblems in Glasgow: A Collection of Essays Drawing on the Stirling Maxwell Collection in Glasgow University Library*, ed. Alison Adams, University of Glasgow French and German Publications (Glasgow: University of Glasgow), 25–46.

Becanus (1569): Johannes Goropius Becanus, *Origenes Antwerpianae sive Cimmeriorvm Becceselana* (Antwerp: Christopher Plantin).

Bekkers (1970): Johannes Antonius Frederik Bekkers, ed., *Correspondence of John Morris with Johannes de Laet (1634–1649)* (Assen: Van Gorcum).

Belfour (1909): A. O. Belfour, ed., *Twelfth Century Homilies in MS. Bodley 343. Part I: Text and Translation*, EETS, os 137 (London: Kegan Paul, Trench, Trübner; repr. London: Oxford University Press, 1962).

Bennett (1938): J. A. W. Bennett, "The History of Old English and Old Norse Studies in England from the Time of Francis Junius till the End of the Eighteenth Century," unpublished D. Phil. thesis, University of Oxford.

——— (1948): J. A. W. Bennett, "Hickes's 'Thesaurus': A Study in Oxford Book-Production," *English Studies*, n.s., 1: 28–45.

——— (1950–51): J. A. W. Bennett, "The Beginnings of Runic Studies in England," *Saga-Book of the Viking Society for Northern Research* 13/4: 269–83.

———— (1982): J. A. W. Bennett, "The Oxford Saxonists," in *The Humane Medievalist and Other Essays in English Literature and Learning, from Chaucer to Eliot*, ed. Piero Boitani (Rome: Edizioni di Storia e Letteratura), 199–223.

Benson (1701): Thomas Benson, *Vocabularium Anglo-Saxonicum, lexico Gul. Somneri magna parte auctius* (Oxford: E Theatro Sheldoniano).

Berkhout (1985): Carl T. Berkhout, "The Pedigree of Laurence Nowell the Antiquary," *English Language Notes* 23/2: 15–26.

———— (1993–94): Carl T. Berkhout, "The Parkerian Legacy of a Scheide Manuscript: William of Malmesbury's *Gesta Regum Anglorum*," *Princeton University Library Chronicle* 55: 277–86.

———— (1998): Carl T. Berkhout, "Laurence Nowell (1530–ca. 1570)," in *Medieval Scholarship: Biographical Studies on the Formation of a Discipline*, II: *Literature and Philology*, ed. Helen Damico with Donald Fennema and Karmen Lenz (New York: Garland), 3–17.

Berkhout and Gatch (1982): Carl T. Berkhout and Milton McC. Gatch, eds., *Anglo-Saxon Scholarship: The First Three Centuries* (Boston: G. K. Hall).

Berryman (1996): Martha Berryman, "Franciscus Junius's *Etymologicum Anglicanum*: Scholarship and Historical Linguistics in the Seventeenth Century," unpublished Ph.D. dissertation, University of Minnesota.

Bethurum (1957): Dorothy Bethurum, *The Homilies of Wulfstan* (Oxford: Clarendon Press).

Bierbaumer (1985): Peter Bierbaumer, "Research into Old English Glosses: A Critical Survey," in *Problems of Old English Lexicography: Studies in Memory of Angus Cameron*, ed. Alfred Bammesberger, Eichstätter Beiträge 15 (Regensburg: F. Pustet), 65–77.

Birrell (1966): T. A. Birrell, "The Society of Antiquaries and the Taste for Old English 1705–1840," *Neophilologus* 50: 107–17.

Bischoff et al. (1988): Bernhard Bischoff, Mildred Budny, Geoffrey Harlow, M. B. Parkes, and J. D. Pheifer, eds., *The Épinal, Erfurt, Werden, and Corpus Glossaries: Épinal, Bibliothèque Municipale 72 (2); Erfurt, Wissenschaftliche Bibliothek Amplonianus 2° 42; Düsseldorf, Universitätsbibliothek Fragm. K 19: Z 9/1; Munich, Bayerische Staatsbibliothek Cgm. 187 III (e.4); Cambridge, Corpus Christi College 144*, EEMF 22 (Copenhagen: Rosenkilde & Bagger).

Black (1977): Pamela M. Black, "Laurence Nowell's 'Disappearance' in Germany and Its Bearing on the Whereabouts of His Collectanea 1568–1572," *English Historical Review* 92: 345–53.

Blom (1979): Joannes Maria Blom, *The Post-Tridentine English Primer* (Meppel: Krips Repro).

Blount (1656): Thomas Blount, *Glossographia: or a Dictionary, Interpreting All Such Hard Words, Whether Hebrew, Greek, Latin, Italian, Spanish, French, Teutonick, Belgick, British or Saxon, As Are Now Used in Our Refined English Tongue* (London: Thomas Newcomb; facsimile repr. Menston: Scolar Press, 1969).

———— (1670): Thomas Blount, *Nomo-Lexikon: A Law-Dictionary. Interpreting Such Difficult and Obscure Words and Terms, As Are Found either in Our Common or Statute, Ancient or Modern Lawes* (London: Thomas Newcomb).

Bremmer (1988): Rolf H. Bremmer, Jr., "Late Medieval and Early Modern Opinions on the Affinity between English and Frisian: The Growth of a Commonplace," *Folia Linguistica Historica* 9: 167–91.

———— (1998a): Rolf H. Bremmer, Jr., ed., *Franciscus Junius F.F. and His Circle*, Studies in Literature 21 (Amsterdam and Atlanta: Rodopi).

———— (1998b): Rolf H. Bremmer, Jr., "Retrieving Junius's Correspondence," in Bremmer (1998a), 199–235.

———— (1998c): Rolf H. Bremmer, Jr., "The Correspondence of Johannes de Laet," in *Johannes de Laet (1581–1649): A Leiden Polymath*, ed. Rolf H. Bremmer, Jr., and Paul Hoftijzer, *LIAS: Sources and Documents Relating to the Early Modern History of Ideas* 25: 139–64.

Brenner (1908): Eduard Brenner, ed., *Der altenglische Junius-Psalter: Die Interlinear-Glosse der Handschrift Junius 27 der Bodleiana zu Oxford*, Anglistische Forschungen 23 (Heidelberg: C. Winter; repr. Amsterdam: Swets & Zeitlinger, 1973).

Breuker (1990): Ph. H. Breuker, "On the Course of Franciscus Junius' Germanic Studies, with Special Reference to Frisian," in *Aspects of Old Frisian Philology*, ed. Rolf H. Bremmer, Jr., Geart van der Meer, and Oebele Vries, Amsterdamer Beiträge zur älteren Germanistik 31/32 (Amsterdam and Atlanta: Rodopi), 42–68; repr. with corrections in Bremmer (1998a), 129–57.

Briquet (1907): C. M. Briquet, *Les Filigranes: Dictionnaire historique des marques du papier dès leur apparition vers 1282 jusqu'en 1600*, 4 vols. (Paris: Picard).

British Museum (1967): *The British Museum Catalogue of Additions to the Manuscripts 1931–1935* (London: British Museum).

Britt (1928): Matthew Britt, ed., *A Dictionary of the Psalter, Containing the Vocabulary of the Psalms, Hymns, Canticles, and Miscellaneous Prayers of the Breviary Psalter* (New York: Benziger Brothers).

Bromwich (1962): John Bromwich, "The First Book Printed in Anglo-Saxon Types," *Transactions of the Cambridge Bibliographical Society* 3/4: 265–91.

Budny (1997): Mildred Budny, *Insular, Anglo-Saxon, and Early Anglo-Norman Manuscript Art at Corpus Christi College, Cambridge*, 2 vols. (Kalamazoo: Medieval Institute Publications).

Buitendijk (1942): W. J. C. Buitendijk, *Het Calvinisme in de spiegel van de Zuidnederlandse literatuur der Contra-Reformatie* (Groningen: J. B. Wolters).

Butt (1938): John Butt, "The Facilities for Antiquarian Study in the Seventeenth Century," *Essays and Studies* 24: 64–79.

Calder (1982): Daniel G. Calder, "Histories and Surveys of Old English Literature: A Chronological Review," *Anglo-Saxon England* 10: 201–44.

Camden (1586): William Camden, *Britannia siue florentissimorum regnorum, Angliæ, Scotiæ, Hiberniæ, et insularum adiacentium ex intima antiquitate chorographica descriptio* (London: R. Newbery).

———— (1603): William Camden, ed., *Anglica, Normannica, Hibernica, Cambrica, a veteribus scripta* (Frankfurt: C. Marnius).

———— (1605): William Camden, *Remaines of a Greater Worke, Concerning Britaine, the Inhabitants Thereof, Their Languages, Names, Surnames, Empreses, Wise Speeches, Poësies, and Epitaphes* (London: S. Waterson).

———— (1607): William Camden, *Britannia, siue florentissimorum regnorum Angliæ, Scotiæ, Hiberniæ, et insularum adiacentium ex intima antiquitate chorographica descriptio: nunc postremò recognita, plurimis locis magna accessione adaucta, & chartis chorographicis illustrata* (London: G. Bishop & J. Norton).

———— (1615, 1625): William Camden, *Annales rerum Anglicarum, et Hibernicarum, regnante Elizabetha*, Part I (London: S. Waterson); Parts I and II (Leiden: Elzevir).

Campbell (1938): Alistair Campbell, ed., *The Battle of Brunanburh* (London: Heinemann).

Campbell (1974): A. P. Campbell, ed., *The Tiberius Psalter, Edited from British Museum MS Cotton Tiberius C vi*, Ottawa Mediaeval Texts and Studies 2 (Ottawa: University of Ottawa Press).

Canterbury (1802): *Catalogue of the Books both Manuscript and Printed Which are Preserved in the Library of Christ Church Canterbury* (Canterbury: Canterbury Cathedral).

Carley and Tite (1997): James P. Carley and Colin G. C. Tite, eds., *Books and Collectors 1200–1700: Essays Presented to Andrew Watson* (London: British Library).

Carter (1975): Harry Carter, *A History of the Oxford University Press*, I: *To the Year 1780* (Oxford: Clarendon Press).

Casaubon (1650): Meric Casaubon, *De quatuor linguis commentationis, pars prior: quæ, de lingua Hebraica: et, de lingua Saxonica* (London: R. Mynne).

Chatelain (1721): [Henri Abraham Chatelain,] *Atlas historique, ou nouvelle introduction à l'histoire, à la chronologie et à la géographie ancienne et moderne*, 3rd edn., 7 vols. (Amsterdam: L'Honoré and Chatelain).

Claes (1970): F. Claes, *De Bronnen van drie Woordenboeken uit de Drukkerij van Plantin: het Dictionarium tetraglotton (1562), de Thesaurus Theutonicae linguae (1573) en Kiliaans eerste Dictionarium Teutonico-Latinum (1574)* (Ghent: Koninklijke Vlaamse Academie voor Taal- en Letterkunde).

Classen and Harmer (1926): E. Classen and F. E. Harmer, eds., *An Anglo-Saxon Chronicle from British Museum, Cotton MS, Tiberius B. IV* (Manchester: Manchester University Press).

Clement (1998): Richard W. Clement, "Richard Verstegan's Reinvention of Anglo-Saxon England: A Contribution from the Continent," in *Reinventing the Middle Ages and the Renaissance*, ed. William Gentrup (Turnhout: Brepols), 28–46.

Clemoes (1997): Peter Clemoes, *Ælfric's Catholic Homilies: The First Series. Text*, EETS, SS 17 (Oxford: Oxford University Press).

Collins (1982): Sarah H. Collins, "The Elstobs and the End of the Saxon Revival," in Berkhout and Gatch (1982), 107–18.

Collinson (1998): Patrick Collinson, "One of Us? William Camden and the Making of History," The Camden Society Centenary Lecture, *Transactions of the Royal Historical Society*, 6th ser., 8: 139–63.

Cook (1898–1903): Albert S. Cook, *Biblical Quotations in Old English Prose Writers*, 2 vols. (New York: Macmillan/Scribner).

Cook (1962): Joan K. Cook, "Developing Techniques in Anglo-Saxon Scholarship in the Seventeenth Century: As They Appear in the *Dictionarium Saxonico-Latino-Anglicum* of William Somner," unpublished Ph.D. dissertation, University of Toronto.

Cooke (1994): Jessica Cooke, "The Harley Manuscript 3376: A Study in Anglo-Saxon Glossography," unpublished Ph.D. thesis, University of Cambridge.

Cowell (1607): John Cowell, *The Interpreter, or, Booke Containing the Signification of Words: Wherein is Set Foorth the True Meaning of All, or the Most Part of Such Words and Termes, As Are Mentioned in the Lawe Writers, or Statutes of This Victorious and Renowned Kingdome, Requiring Any Exposition or Interpretation* (Cambridge: John Legate, 1607; facsimile repr. Amsterdam: Theatrum Orbis Terrarum/New York: Da Capo, 1970).

Cowley (1932): John D. Cowley, *A Bibliography of Abridgments, Digests, Dictionaries and Indexes of English Law to the Year 1800*, Selden Society (London: Quaritch).

Crawford (1922): S. J. Crawford, ed., *The Old English Version of the Heptateuch, Aelfric's Treatise on the Old and New Testament and His Preface to Genesis, Edited from All the Existing MSS. and Fragments with an Introduction and Three Appendices, Together with a Reprint of "A Saxon Treatise Concerning the Old and New Testament: Now First Published in Print with English of Our Times by William L'Isle of Wilburgham (1623)" and the Vulgate Text of the Heptateuch*, EETS, OS 160 (London: Oxford University Press; repr. Millwood, N.Y.: Kraus, 1990).

Cronne (1956): H. A. Cronne, "The Study and Use of Charters by English Scholars in the Seventeenth Century: Sir Henry Spelman and Sir William Dugdale," in *English Historical Scholarship in the Sixteenth and Seventeenth Centuries: A Record of the Papers Delivered at a Conference Arranged by the Dugdale Society to Commemorate the Tercentary of the Publication of Dugdale's "Antiquities of Warwickshire"*, ed. Levi Fox (London: Oxford University Press), 73–91.

Cubbin (1996): G. P. Cubbin, ed., *MS D: A Semi-Diplomatic Edition with Introduction and Notes*, The Anglo-Saxon Chronicle: A Collaborative Edition 6, ed. David Dumville and Simon Keynes (Cambridge: D. S. Brewer).

Curtis (1959): Mark H. Curtis, *Oxford and Cambridge in Transition 1558–1642: An Essay on Changing Relations between the English Universities and English Society* (Oxford: Clarendon Press).

Daly and Silcox (1990): Peter M. Daly and Mary V. Silcox, *The English Emblem: Bibliography of Secondary Literature*, Corpus Librorum Emblematum (Munich: K. G. Saur).

Dean (1941): Leonard F. Dean, "Sir Francis Bacon's Theory of Civil History-Writing," *ELH* 8: 161–83.

Dekker (1996): Kees Dekker, "'*Vide Kilian . . .*': The Role of Kiliaan's *Etymologicum* in Old English Studies between 1650 and 1665," *Anglia* 114: 514–43.

——— (1999): Kees Dekker, *The Origins of Old Germanic Studies in the Low Countries*, Brill's Studies in Intellectual History 92 (Leiden: E. J. Brill).

——— (2000): Kees Dekker, "Francis Junius (1591–1677): Copyist or Editor?" *Anglo-Saxon England* 29: 279–95.

Dickins ([1946]): [Bruce Dickins,] *Printing with Anglo-Saxon Types 1566–1715: Catalogue of a Small Exhibition at Corpus Christi College, Cambridge* (Cambridge: Corpus Christi College).

——— (1947–48): Bruce Dickins, "William L'isle the Saxonist and Three XVIIth Century Remainder-Issues," *English and Germanic Studies* 1: 53–55.

——— (1972): Bruce Dickins, "The Making of the Parker Library," *Transactions of the Cambridge Bibliographical Society* 6/1: 19–34.

DNB: Leslie Stephen and Sidney Lee, eds., *The Dictionary of National Biography*, 2nd edn., 22 vols. (London: Smith, Elder, 1908–09).

DNB Missing Persons: C. S. Nicholls, ed., *The Dictionary of National Biography: Missing Persons* (Oxford: Oxford University Press, 1993).

Dobbie (1942): Elliott Van Kirk Dobbie, ed., *The Anglo-Saxon Minor Poems*, The Anglo-Saxon Poetic Records 6 (New York: Columbia University Press).

Dodd (1737–42): Charles Dodd, *The Church History of England, from the Year 1500 to the Year 1688: Chiefly with Regard to Catholicks*, 3 vols. (Brussels [*recte* London: W. Bowyer]).

Dodwell and Clemoes (1974): C. R. Dodwell and Peter Clemoes, eds., *The Old English Illustrated Hexateuch: British Museum Cotton Claudius B. IV*, EEMF 18 (Copenhagen: Rosenkilde & Bagger).

DOE: *Dictionary of Old English* (Toronto: Pontifical Institute of Mediaeval Studies for the Dictionary of Old English Project, 1986–; issued in microfiche format).

Douglas (1951): David C. Douglas, *English Scholars 1660–1730*, 2nd edn. (London: Eyre & Spottiswoode; repr. Westport, Conn.: Greenwood Press, 1975).

Drage (1978): Elaine M. Drage, "Bishop Leofric and Exeter Cathedral Chapter (1050–1072): A Reassessment of the Manuscript Evidence," unpublished D. Phil. thesis, Oxford University.

Dumville (1983): David N. Dumville, "Some Aspects of Annalistic Writing at Canterbury in the Eleventh and Early Twelfth Centuries," *Peritia* 2: 23–57.

——— (1995): David Dumville, ed., *Facsimile of MS. F: The Domitian Bilingual*, The Anglo-Saxon Chronicle: A Collaborative Edition 1, ed. David Dumville and Simon Keynes (Cambridge: D. S. Brewer).

Edwards (1917): Caesar, *The Gallic War*, ed. and trans. H. J. Edwards, Loeb Classical Library (London: Heinemann).

Ellis (1843): Henry Ellis, ed., *Original Letters of Eminent Literary Men of the Sixteenth, Seventeenth, and Eighteenth Centuries*, Camden Society 23 (London: J. B. Nichols).

Elstob (1715): Elizabeth Elstob, *The Rudiments of Grammar for the English-Saxon Tongue, First Given in English: With an Apology for the Study of Northern Antiquities* (London: W. Bowyer; facsimile repr. Menston: Scolar Press, 1968).

Fairer (1986): David Fairer, "Anglo-Saxon Studies," in *The History of the University of Oxford*, V: *The Eighteenth Century*, ed. L. S. Sutherland and L. G. Mitchell (Oxford: Clarendon Press), 807–29.

Flower (1934): Robin Flower, "Laurence Nowell and a Recovered Anglo-Saxon Poem," *British Museum Quarterly* 8: 130–32.

——— (1935): Robin Flower, "Laurence Nowell and the Discovery of England in Tudor Times," *Proceedings of the British Academy* 21: 47–73; repr. in *British Academy Papers on Anglo-Saxon England*, ed. E. G. Stanley (Oxford: Oxford University Press, 1990), 1–27.

Flower and Smith (1941): Robin Flower and Hugh Smith, eds., *The Parker Chronicle and Laws (Corpus Christi College, Cambridge, MS. 173): A Facsimile*, EETS, os 208 (London: Oxford University Press; repr. 1973).

Flügel (1909): Ewald Flügel, "Die älteste englische Akademie," *Anglia* 32: 261–68.

Fogle (1971): French Fogle, ed., *Complete Prose Works of John Milton*, vol. V (New Haven: Yale University Press).

Förster (1910): Max Förster, "Beiträge zur mittelalterlichen Volkskunde IV," *Archiv für das Studium der neueren Sprachen und Literaturen* 125: 39–70.

Foxe (1571): John Foxe, ed., *The Gospels of the Fower Euangelistes Translated in the Olde Saxons Tyme out of Latin into the Vulgare Toung of the Saxons, Newly Collected out of Auncient Monumentes of the Sayd Saxons, and Now Published for Testimonie of the Same* (London: John Day).

Frank (1998): Roberta Frank, "When Lexicography Met the Exeter Book," in *Words and Works: Studies in Medieval English Language and Literature in Honour of Fred C. Robinson*, ed. Peter S. Baker and Nicholas Howe (Toronto: University of Toronto Press), 207–21.

Frantzen (1990): Allen J. Frantzen, *Desire for Origins: New Language, Old English, and Teaching the Tradition* (New Brunswick: Rutgers University Press).

Fussner (1962): F. Smith Fussner, *The Historical Revolution: English Historical Writing and Thought 1580–1640* (London: Routledge and Kegan Paul).

———— (1970): F. Smith Fussner, *Tudor History and the Historians* (New York: Basic Books).

Gardner (1955): William Bradford Gardner, "George Hickes and His 'Thesaurus'," *Notes and Queries* 200: 196–99.

Gelling (1973): Margaret Gelling, "Further Thoughts on Pagan Place-Names," in *Otium et Negotium: Studies in Onomatology and Library Science Presented to Olof von Feilitzen*, ed. Folke Sandgren (Stockholm: P. A. Norstedt), 109–28; repr. in *Place-Name Evidence for the Anglo-Saxon Invasion and Scandinavian Settlements*, ed. Kenneth Cameron (Nottingham: English Place-Name Society, 1977), 99–114.

Gibson (1692): Edmund Gibson, ed., *Chronicon Saxonicum* (Oxford: E Theatro Sheldoniano).

————(1698): Edmund Gibson, ed., *Reliquiæ Spelmannianæ: The Post-humous Works of Sir Henry Spelman Kt. Relating to the Laws and Antiquities of England* (Oxford: At the Theater).

Glass (1982): Sandra A. Glass, "The Saxonists' Influence on Seventeenth-Century English Literature," in Berkhout and Gatch (1982), 91–105.

Gneuss (1976): Helmut Gneuss, "Die Handschrift Cotton Otho A. XII," *Anglia* 94: 289–318. Reprinted in Gneuss (1996a).

———— (1990): Helmut Gneuss, *Die Wissenschaft von der englischen Sprache: Ihre Entwicklung bis zum Ausgang des 19. Jahrhunderts*, Sitzungsberichte der Bayerischen Akademie der Wissenschaften, phil.-hist. Klasse (Munich: Verlag der Bayerischen Akademie der Wissenschaften). (Expanded English translation in Gneuss [1996b].)

———— (1993): Helmut Gneuss, "Der älteste Katalog der angelsächsischen Handschriften und seine Nachfolger," in *Anglo-Saxonica: Beiträge zur Vor- und Frühgeschichte der englischen Sprache und zur altenglischen Literatur. Festschrift für Hans*

Schabram zum 65. Geburtstag, ed. Klaus R. Grinda and Claus-Dieter Wetzel (Munich: Wilhelm Fink), 91–106; repr. in Gneuss (1996a).

————(1996a): Helmut Gneuss, *Books and Libraries in Early England*, Collected Studies Series CS 558 (Aldershot: Variorum).

———— (1996b): Helmut Gneuss, *English Language Scholarship: A Survey and Bibliography from the Beginnings to the End of the Nineteenth Century*, Medieval & Renaissance Texts & Studies 125 (Binghamton, N.Y.: MRTS).

Godden (1979): Malcolm Godden, ed., *Ælfric's Catholic Homilies: The Second Series. Text*, EETS, SS 5 (London: Oxford University Press).

Goepp (1949): Philip H. Goepp, "Verstegan's 'Most Ancient Saxon Words'," in *Philologica: The Malone Anniversary Studies*, ed. Thomas A. Kirby and Henry Bosley Woolf (Baltimore: Johns Hopkins Press), 249–55.

Gollancz (1927): Israel Gollancz, ed., *The Cædmon Manuscript of Anglo-Saxon Biblical Poetry, Junius XI in the Bodleian Library* (Oxford: Oxford University Press).

Grafton (1990): Anthony Grafton, "Invention of Traditions and Traditions of Invention in Renaissance Europe: The Strange Case of Annius of Viterbo," in *The Transmission of Culture in Early Modern Europe*, ed. Anthony Grafton and Ann Blair (Philadelphia: University of Pennsylvania Press), 8–38.

Graham (1994): Timothy Graham, "A Parkerian Transcript of the List of Bishop Leofric's Procurements for Exeter Cathedral: Matthew Parker, the Exeter Book, and Cambridge University Library MS Ii.2.11," *Transactions of the Cambridge Bibliographical Society* 10/4: 421–55.

———— (1997a): Timothy Graham, "The Beginnings of Old English Studies: Evidence from the Manuscripts of Matthew Parker," in

Back to the Manuscripts: Papers from the Symposium "The Integrated Approach to Manuscript Studies: A New Horizon" Held at the Eighth General Meeting of the Japan Society for Medieval English Studies, Tokyo, December 1992, ed. Shuji Sato, Occasional Papers of the Centre for Medieval English Studies 1 (Tokyo: Centre for Medieval English Studies), 29–50.

—— (1997b): Timothy Graham, "Robert Talbot's 'Old Saxonice Bede': Cambridge University Library, MS Kk.3.18 and the 'Alphabetum Norwagicum' of British Library, Cotton MSS, Domitian A. IX," in Carley and Tite (1997), 295–316.

——(1997c): Timothy Graham, "Abraham Wheelock's Use of CCCC MS 41 (Old English Bede) and the Borrowing of Manuscripts from the Library of Corpus Christi College," *Cambridge Bibliographical Society Newsletter* (Summer 1997), 10–16.

—— (2000): Timothy Graham, "Early Modern Users of Claudius B. iv: Robert Talbot and William L'Isle," in *The Old English Hexateuch: Aspects and Approaches*, ed. Rebecca Barnhouse and Benjamin C. Withers (Kalamazoo: Medieval Institute Publications), 271–316.

Graham and Watson (1998): Timothy Graham and Andrew G. Watson, *The Recovery of the Past in Early Elizabethan England: Documents by John Bale and John Joscelyn from the Circle of Matthew Parker*, Cambridge Bibliographical Society Monograph 13 (Cambridge: Cambridge Bibliographical Society).

Granlund (1976): Olaus Magnus, *Historia om de Nordiska Folken*, trans. with a commentary by John Granlund, 4 vols. (Stockholm: Gidlund).

Grant (1996): Raymond J. S. Grant, *Laurence Nowell, William Lambarde, and the Laws of the Anglo-Saxons*, Costerus, n.s., 108 (Amsterdam and Atlanta: Rodopi).

Greenfield and Robinson (1980): Stanley B. Greenfield and Fred C. Robinson, *A Bibliography of Publications on Old English Literature to the End of 1972* (Toronto: University of Toronto Press).

Hahn (1983): Thomas Hahn, "The Identity of the Antiquary Laurence Nowell," *English Language Notes* 20 (3/4): 10–18.

Hamper (1827): William Hamper, ed., *The Life, Diary, and Correspondence of Sir William Dugdale, Knight, Sometime Garter Principal King of Arms* (London: Harding, Lepard).

Harley (1808): *A Catalogue of the Harleian Manuscripts, in the British Museum*, I (London: British Museum; repr. Hildesheim and New York: G. Olms, 1973).

Harris (1983): Richard L. Harris, "George Hickes, White Kennett and the Inception of the *Thesaurus Linguarum Septentrionalium*," *Bodleian Library Record* 11/3: 169–86.

——— (1992): Richard L. Harris, ed., *A Chorus of Grammars: The Correspondence of George Hickes and His Collaborators on the "Thesaurus Linguarum Septentrionalium"*, Publications of the Dictionary of Old English 4 (Toronto: Pontifical Institute of Mediaeval Studies).

Harsley (1889): Fred Harsley, ed., *Eadwine's Canterbury Psalter, Edited, with Introduction and Notes, from the Manuscript in Trinity College, Cambridge*, EETS, os 92 (London: Trübner; repr. Millwood, N.Y.: Kraus, 1987).

Hayashi (1978): Tetsuro Hayashi, *The Theory of English Lexicography 1530–1791*, Amsterdam Studies in the Theory and History of Linguistic Science Ser. III, Studies in the History of Linguistics 18 (Amsterdam: Benjamins).

Henkel and Schöne (1967): Arthur Henkel and Albrecht Schöne, eds., *Emblemata: Handbuch zur Sinnbildkunst des XVI. und XVII. Jahrhunderts*, 2 vols. (Stuttgart: J. B. Metzler).

Hetherington (1975): M. S. Hetherington, "Sir Simonds D'Ewes and Method in Old English Lexicography," *Texas Studies in Literature and Language* 17: 75–92.

———— (1980): M. S. Hetherington, *The Beginnings of Old English Lexicography* (Spicewood, Tex.: privately printed).

———— (1982): M. Sue Hetherington, "The Recovery of the Anglo-Saxon Lexicon," in Berkhout and Gatch (1982), 79–89.

Heuser (1907): W. Heuser, "Die Ancren Riwle—ein aus angelsächsischer Zeit überliefertes Denkmal," *Anglia* 30: 103–22.

Heyworth (1989): P. L. Heyworth, ed., *Letters of Humfrey Wanley, Palaeographer, Anglo-Saxonist, Librarian, 1672–1726* (Oxford: Clarendon Press).

Hickes (1689): George Hickes, *Institutiones grammaticæ Anglo-Saxonicæ, et Moeso-Gothicæ* (Oxford: E Theatro Sheldoniano; facsimile repr. Menston: Scolar Press, 1971).

———— (1703–05): George Hickes, *Linguarum vett. septentrionalium thesaurus grammatico-criticus et archæologicus* (Oxford: E Theatro Sheldoniano; facsimile repr. Menston: Scolar Press, 1970). (Vol. I of Hickes's *Antiquæ literaturæ septentrionalis libri duo*.)

Hill (1965): Christopher Hill, *Intellectual Origins of the English Revolution* (Oxford: Clarendon Press).

James (1935): M. R. James, *The Canterbury Psalter* (London: Lund, Humphries).

Jones (1943): Charles W. Jones, ed., *Bedae opera de temporibus*, Mediaeval Academy of America Publication 41 (Cambridge, Mass.: Mediaeval Academy of America).

Junius (1655a): Franciscus Junius, *Observationes in Willerami abbatis Francicam paraphrasin Cantici canticorum* (Amsterdam: Christoffel Cunradus). (See also Voorwinden [1992].)

————(1655b): Franciscus Junius, ed., *Cædmonis monachi paraphrasis poetica Genesios ac præcipuarum sacræ paginæ historiarum, abhinc annos M.LXX. Anglo-Saxonicè conscripta* (Amsterdam: Christoffel Cunradus). (See also Lucas [2000].)

Junius and Marshall (1665): Franciscus Junius and Thomas Marshall, eds., *Quatuor D. N. Jesu Christi euangeliorum versiones perantiquæ duæ, Gothica scil. et Anglo-Saxonica* (Dordrecht: H. & J. Essæi).

Kearney (1970): Hugh Kearney, *Scholars and Gentlemen: Universities and Society in Pre-Industrial Britain 1500–1700* (London: Faber and Faber).

Kennett (1693): White Kennett, "The Life of Mr. Somner," prefixed to William Somner, *A Treatise of the Roman Ports and Forts in Kent*, ed. James Brome (Oxford: At the Theater).

Kenyon (1983): John Kenyon, *The History Men: The Historical Profession in England since the Renaissance* (London: Weidenfeld and Nicolson).

Ker (1956): N. R. Ker, ed., *The Pastoral Care: King Alfred's Translation of St. Gregory's Regula Pastoralis (MS. Hatton 20 in the Bodleian Library at Oxford, MS. Cotton Tiberius B.XI in the British Museum, MS. Anhang 19 in the Landesbibliothek at Kassel)*, EEMF 6 (Copenhagen: Rosenkilde & Bagger).

————(1957): N. R. Ker, *Catalogue of Manuscripts Containing Anglo-Saxon* (Oxford: Clarendon Press; repr. with supplement, 1990).

Kerling (1984): Johan Kerling, "Scholar, Antiquary, Factotum: Franciscus Junius Revisited," in *Current Research in Dutch and Belgian Universities on Old English, Middle English and Historical Linguistics: Five Papers Read at the Sixth Philological Symposium*

Held at Utrecht on 3rd November 1984, ed. Frans Diekstra (Nijmegen: Katholieke Universiteit Nijmegen), 33–43.

Keynes (1996): Simon Keynes, "The Reconstruction of a Burnt Cottonian Manuscript: The Case of Cotton MS. Otho A. I," *The British Library Journal* 22: 113–60.

Kiernan (1990): Kevin S. Kiernan, "Reading 'Cædmon's Hymn' with Someone Else's Glosses," *Representations* 32: 157–74.

Kimmens (1979): Andrew C. Kimmens, ed., *The Stowe Psalter*, Toronto Old English Series (Toronto: University of Toronto Press).

Klaeber (1950): Frederick Klaeber, ed., *Beowulf and the Fight at Finnsburg*, 3rd edn. (Boston: D. C. Heath).

Knox (1967): R. Buick Knox, *James Ussher, Archbishop of Armagh* (Cardiff: University of Wales Press).

Kok (1785–96): Jacobus Kok, *Vaderlandsch Woordenboek*, 35 vols. (Amsterdam: J. Allart).

Krapp (1931): George Philip Krapp, ed., *The Junius Manuscript*, The Anglo-Saxon Poetic Records 1 (New York: Columbia University Press).

——— (1932): George Philip Krapp, ed., *The Paris Psalter and the Meters of Boethius*, The Anglo-Saxon Poetic Records 5 (New York: Columbia University Press).

Krusch and Levison (1920): B. Krusch and W. Levison, eds., *Passiones vitaeque sanctorum aevi Merovingici*, vol. V, Monumenta Germaniae Historica, Scriptores Rerum Merovingicarum 7 (Hanover: Hahn).

Kuhn (1965): Sherman M. Kuhn, ed., *The Vespasian Psalter* (Ann Arbor: University of Michigan Press).

Ladd (1960): C. A. Ladd, "The 'Rubens' Manuscript and *Archbishop Ælfric's Vocabulary*," *Review of English Studies*, n.s., 11: 353–64.

Lambarde (1568): William Lambarde, *Archaionomia, sive de priscis Anglorum legibus libri, sermone Anglico, vetustate antiquissimo, aliquot abhinc seculis conscripti, atque nunc demum, magno iurisperitorum, & amantium antiquitatis omnium commodo, è tenebris in lucem vocati* (London: John Day).

——— (1576): William Lambarde, *A Perambulation of Kent: Conteining the Description, Hystorie, and Customes of That Shyre* (London: Ralph Newbery).

——— (1581): William Lambarde, *Eirenarcha: or Of the Office of the Iustices of Peace* (London: R. Newbery and H. Bynneman; facsimile repr. Amsterdam: Theatrum Orbis Terrarum/New York: Da Capo, 1970).

Lee (1992): S. D. Lee, "An Edition of Ælfric's Homilies on Judith, Esther, and the Maccabees," unpublished Ph.D. thesis, University of London. Also available in electronic format at http://users.ox.ac.uk/~stuart/kings/.

——— (1993): S. D. Lee, "The Comet in the Eadwine Psalter: A Recently Discovered Seventeenth-Century Transcription," *Manuscripta* 37: 322–24.

Leinbaugh (1982): Theodore H. Leinbaugh, "Ælfric's *Sermo de Sacrificio in Die Pascae*: Anglican Polemic in the Sixteenth and Seventeenth Centuries," in Berkhout and Gatch (1982), 51–68.

Lendinara (1992): P. Lendinara, "Glosses and Glossaries," in *Anglo-Saxon Glossography: Papers Read at the International Conference Held in the Koninklijke Academie voor Wetenschappen, Letteren en Schone Kunsten van België, Brussels, 8 and 9 September 1986*, ed. R. Derolez (Brussels: Koninklijke Academie), 209–43.

Levine (1987): Joseph M. Levine, *Humanism and History: Origins of Modern English Historiography* (Ithaca: Cornell University Press).

Levy (1964): F. J. Levy, "The Making of Camden's *Britannia*," *Bibliothèque d'Humanisme et Renaissance* 26: 70–97.

Liebermann (1903–16): F. Liebermann, ed., *Die Gesetze der Angelsachsen*, 3 vols. (Halle: Niemeyer).

Lindelöf (1909): U. Lindelöf, ed., *Der Lambeth-Psalter: Eine altenglische Interlinearversion des Psalters in der Hs. 427 der erzbischöflichen Lambeth Palace Library*, I: *Text und Glossar*, Acta Societatis Scientiarum Fennicae 35/1 (Helsinki: Finnische Litteraturgesellschaft).

Lindsay (1921): W. M. Lindsay, ed., *The Corpus Glossary* (Cambridge: Cambridge University Press).

L'Isle (1623): William L'Isle, ed., *A Saxon Treatise Concerning the Old and New Testament* (London: H. Seile).

Logeman (1888): H. Logeman, ed., *The Rule of S. Benet: Latin and Anglo-Saxon Interlinear Version*, EETS, OS 90 (London: Trübner).

Loyn (1971): Henry R. Loyn, ed., *A Wulfstan Manuscript Containing Institutes, Laws and Homilies: British Museum Cotton Nero A.I*, EEMF 17 (Copenhagen: Rosenkilde & Bagger).

Lucas (1995): Peter J. Lucas, "The *Metrical Epilogue* to the Alfredian *Pastoral Care*: A Postscript from Junius," *Anglo-Saxon England* 24: 43–50.

———(1997a): Peter J. Lucas, "A Testimonye of Verye Ancient Tyme? Some Manuscript Models for the Parkerian Anglo-Saxon Type-Designs," in *Of the Making of Books: Medieval Manuscripts, Their Scribes and Readers. Essays Presented to M. B. Parkes*, ed. P. R. Robinson and Rivkah Zim (Aldershot: Scolar Press), 147–88.

———(1997b): Peter J. Lucas, "Franciscus Junius and the Versification of *Judith*. *Francisci Junii in Memoriam*: 1591–1991," in *The Preservation and Transmission of Anglo-Saxon Culture: Selected Papers from the 1991 Meeting of the International Society of Anglo-Saxonists*, ed. Paul E. Szarmach and Joel T. Rosenthal, Studies in Medieval Culture 40 (Kalamazoo: Medieval Institute Publications), 369–404.

———(1998): Peter J. Lucas, "Junius, His Printers and His Types: An Interim Report," in Bremmer (1998a), 177–97.

———(1999): Peter J. Lucas, "Parker, Lambarde and the Provision of Special Sorts for Printing Anglo-Saxon in the Sixteenth Century," *Journal of the Printing Historical Society* 28: 41–69.

——— (2000): Franciscus Junius, *Cædmonis monachi paraphrasis poetica Genesios ac præcipuarum sacræ paginæ historiarum, abhinc annos M.LXX. Anglo-Saxonicè conscripta*, ed. Peter J. Lucas, Early Studies in Germanic Philology 4 (Amsterdam and Atlanta: Rodopi).

Lutz (1981): Angelika Lutz, *Die Version G der angelsächsischen Chronik: Rekonstruktion und Edition*, Texte und Untersuchungen zur Englischen Philologie 11 (Munich: Wilhelm Fink).

——— (1982): Angelika Lutz, "Das Studium der angelsächsischen Chronik im 16. Jahrhundert: Nowell und Joscelyn," *Anglia* 100: 301–56.

———(1988): Angelika Lutz, "Zur Entstehungsgeschichte von William Somners *Dictionarium Saxonico-Latino-Anglicum*," *Anglia* 106: 1–25.

Lye (1743): Edward Lye, ed., *Francisci Junii Francisci filii Etymologicum Anglicanum* (Oxford: E Theatro Sheldoniano; facsimile repr. Los Angeles: Sherwin & Freutel, 1970).

————(1772): Edward Lye, *Dictionarium Saxonico et Gothico-Latinum* (London: E. Allen).

McKisack (1971): May McKisack, *Medieval History in the Tudor Age* (Oxford: Clarendon Press).

McKitterick (1992): David McKitterick, "The Eadwine Psalter Rediscovered," in *The Eadwine Psalter: Text, Image, and Monastic Culture in Twelfth-Century Canterbury*, ed. Margaret Gibson, T. A. Heslop, and Richard W. Pfaff, Publications of the Modern Humanities Research Association 14 (London: Modern Humanities Research Association/University Park, Pa.: Pennsylvania State University Press), 195–208.

MacLean (1884): George Edwin MacLean, "Ælfric's Version of Alcuini Interrogationes Sigeuulfi in Genesin," *Anglia* 7: 1–59.

Macray (1890): William Dunn Macray, *Annals of the Bodleian Library, Oxford, with a Notice of the Earlier Library of the University*, 2nd edn. (Oxford: Clarendon Press).

Madan et al. (1937): Falconer Madan, H. H. E. Craster, and N. Denholm-Young, *A Summary Catalogue of Western Manuscripts in the Bodleian Library at Oxford*, II/2 (Oxford: Clarendon Press).

Magnus (1555): Olaus Magnus, *Historia de gentibus septentrionalibus, earumque diuersis statibus, conditionibus, moribus, ritibus, superstitionibus, disciplinis, exercitiis, regimine, victu, bellis, structuris, instrumentis, ac mineris metallicis, & rebus mirabilibus, necnon uniuersis pene animalibus in Septentrione degentibus, eorumque natura* (Rome: Ioannes Maria de Viottis).

Malone (1963): Kemp Malone, ed., *The Nowell Codex: British Museum Cotton Vitellius A. XV, Second MS*, EEMF 12 (Copenhagen: Rosenkilde & Bagger).

Marckwardt (1952): Albert H. Marckwardt, ed., *Laurence Nowell's "Vocabularium Saxonicum"*, University of Michigan Publications,

Language and Literature 25 (Ann Arbor: University of Michigan Press; repr. New York: Kraus, 1971).

Miller (1890–98): Thomas Miller, ed., *The Old English Version of Bede's Ecclesiastical History of the English Nation*, 4 vols., EETS, OS 95–96, 110–11 (London: Kegan Paul; repr. London: Oxford University Press, 1996–97).

Milton (1670): John Milton, *The History of Britain, That Part Especially Now Call'd England: From the First Traditional Beginning, Continu'd to the Norman Conquest* (London: J. Allestry; 2nd edn. 1677, facsimile repr. with introduction by Graham Parry, Stamford: Paul Watkins, 1991).

Morison and Carter (1967): Stanley Morison, with the assistance of Harry Carter, *John Fell, the University Press and the 'Fell' Types: The Punches and Matrices Designed for Printing in the Greek, Latin, English, and Oriental Languages Bequeathed in 1686 to the University of Oxford by John Fell, D. D.* (Oxford: Clarendon Press).

Morris (1867–68): Richard Morris, ed., *Old English Homilies and Homiletic Treatises (Sawles Warde, and þe Wohunge of Ure Lauerd: Ureisuns of Ure Louerd and of Ure Lefdi, &c.) of the Twelfth and Thirteenth Centuries*, EETS, OS 29 and 34, 2 vols. (London: Trübner; repr. in one vol., Millwood, N.Y.: Kraus, 1988).

Murphy (1967): Michael Murphy, "Abraham Wheloc's Edition of Bede's *History* in Old English," *Studia Neophilologica* 39: 46–59.

———(1968): Michael Murphy, "Methods in the Study of Old English in the Sixteenth and Seventeenth Centuries," *Mediaeval Studies* 30: 345–50.

———(1982a): Michael Murphy, "Scholars at Play: A Short History of Composing in Old English," *Old English Newsletter* 15/2: 26–36.

—————— (1982b): Michael Murphy, "Antiquary to Academic: The Progress of Anglo-Saxon Scholarship," in Berkhout and Gatch (1982), 1–17.

Murphy and Barrett (1985): Michael Murphy and Edward Barrett, "Abraham Wheelock, Arabist and Saxonist," *Biography* 8: 163–85.

Myres (1958): J. N. L. Myres, "Oxford Libraries in the Seventeenth and Eighteenth Centuries," in Wormald and Wright (1958), 236–55.

Napier (1883): Arthur Napier, ed., *Wulfstan: Sammlung der ihm zu-geschriebenen Homilien nebst Untersuchungen über ihre Echtheit*, Sammlung englischer Denkmäler in kritischen Ausgaben 4 (Berlin: Weidmann; repr. Dublin: Weidmann, 1967).

—————— (1900): Arthur S. Napier, ed., *Old English Glosses Chiefly Unpublished*, Analecta Oxoniensia: Mediaeval and Modern Series 11 (Oxford: Clarendon Press).

—————— (1901): A. S. Napier, "An Old English Homily on the Observance of Sunday," in *An English Miscellany Presented to Dr. Furnivall in Honour of His Seventy-Fifth Birthday* (Oxford: Clarendon Press), 355–62.

—————— (1908–09): A. S. Napier, "The 'Ancren Riwle'," *The Modern Language Review* 4: 433–36.

Nichols (1790): John Nichols, *Bibliotheca topographica Britannica*, vol. I (London: J. Nichols; repr. New York: Kraus, 1968).

—————— (1812–15): John Nichols, *Literary Anecdotes of the Eighteenth Century; Comprizing Biographical Memoirs of William Bowyer, Printer, F. S. A. and Many of His Learned Friends; An Incidental View of the Progress and Advancement of Literature in This Kingdom during the Last Century; and Biographical Anecdotes of a Considerable Number of Eminent Writers and Ingenious Artists; with a Very Copious Index*, 9 vols. (London: Nichols and Bentley; facsimile repr. New York: AMS Press/Kraus, 1966).

Nicolson (1696–99): William Nicolson, *The English Historical Library: or, A Short View and Character of Most of the Writers Now Extant, either in Print or Manuscript; Which May Be Serviceable to the Undertakers of a General History of This Kingdom*, 3 vols. (London: A. Swall and T. Child).

Oates (1958): J. C. T. Oates, "The Libraries of Cambridge, 1570–1700," in Wormald and Wright (1958), 213–35.

———(1986): J. C. T. Oates, *Cambridge University Library: A History*, I: *From the Beginnings to the Copyright Act of Queen Anne* (Cambridge: Cambridge University Press).

Oess (1910): Guido Oess, ed., *Der altenglische Arundel-Psalter: Eine Interlinearversion in der Handschrift Arundel 60 des Britischen Museums*, Anglistische Forschungen 30 (Heidelberg: C. Winter; repr. Amsterdam: Swets & Zeitlinger, 1968).

O'Keeffe (1990): Katherine O'Brien O'Keeffe, *Visible Song: Transitional Literacy in Old English Verse*, Cambridge Studies in Anglo-Saxon England 4 (Cambridge: Cambridge University Press).

Oliphant (1966): Robert T. Oliphant, *The Harley Latin–Old English Glossary Edited from ●British Museum MS Harley 3376*, Janua Linguarum: Studia Memoriae Nicolai van Wijk Dedicata, Series Practica 20 (The Hague: Mouton).

O'Sullivan (1956): William O'Sullivan, "Ussher as a Collector of Manuscripts," *Hermathena* 88: 34–58.

Oulton (1956): J. E. L. Oulton, "Ussher's Work as a Patristic Scholar and Church Historian," *Hermathena* 88: 3–11.

Owen (1981): Gale R. Owen, *Rites and Religions of the Anglo-Saxons* (Newton Abbot: David & Charles; repr. New York: Dorset Press, 1985, and New York: Barnes & Noble, 1996).

Page (1992): R. I. Page, "The Sixteenth-Century Reception of Alfred the Great's Letter to His Bishops," *Anglia* 110: 36–64.

———— (1993): R. I. Page, *Matthew Parker and His Books*, Sandars Lectures in Bibliography 1990 (Kalamazoo: Medieval Institute Publications).

Page and Bushnell (1975): R. I. Page and G. H. S. Bushnell, *Matthew Parker's Legacy: Books and Plate* (Cambridge: Corpus Christi College).

Parker (1566): [Matthew Parker, ed.,] *A Testimonie of Antiqvitie, Shewing the Ancient Fayth in the Church of England Touching the Sacrament of the Body and Bloude of the Lord Here Publikely Preached, and Also Receaued in the Saxons Tyme, aboue 600. Yeares Agoe* (London: John Day; repr. Amsterdam: Theatrum Orbis Terrarum/New York: Da Capo, 1970).

———— (1566/67): [Matthew Parker, ed.,] *A Defence of Priestes Mariages Stablysshed by the Imperiall Lawes of the Realme of Englande, agaynst a Ciuilian, Namyng Hym Selfe Thomas Martin Doctour of the Ciuile Lawes* (London: R. Jugge).

———— (1574): Johannes Asser, *Ælfredi regis res gestæ* [ed. Matthew Parker] (London: John Day).

Parkes (1997): M. B. Parkes, "Archaizing Hands in English Manuscripts," in Carley and Tite (1997), 101–41.

Parr (1686): Richard Parr, *The Life of the Most Reverend Father in God, James Usher, Late Lord Arch-Bishop of Armagh, Primate and Metropolitan of All Ireland* (London: Nathanael Ranew).

Parry (1995): G. Parry, *The Trophies of Time: English Antiquarians of the Seventeenth Century* (Oxford: Oxford University Press).

Pat. Lat.: J.-P. Migne, ed., *Patrologia Latina*, 221 vols. (Paris, 1844–64).

Petheram (1840): John Petheram, *An Historical Sketch of the Progress and Present State of Anglo-Saxon Literature in England* (London: Edward Lumley).

Petti (1959): Anthony G. Petti, ed., *The Letters and Despatches of Richard Verstegan (c. 1550–1640)*, Publications of the Catholic Record Society 52 (London: Catholic Record Society).

——— (1963): A. G. Petti, "A Bibliography of the Writings of Richard Verstegan (c. 1550–1641)," *Recusant History* 7: 82–103.

Philip (1983): Ian Philip, *The Bodleian Library in the Seventeenth and Eighteenth Centuries*, The Lyell Lectures 1980–81 (Oxford: Clarendon Press).

Picinelli (1681): Filippo Picinelli, *Mundus symbolicus, in emblematum universitate formatus, explicatus, et tam sacris, quàm profanis eruditionibus ac sententiis illustratus* (Cologne: Hermann Demen).

Piggott (1951): Stuart Piggott, "William Camden and the *Britannia*," *Proceedings of the British Academy* 37: 199–217.

Planta (1802): J. Planta, *Catalogue of the Manuscripts in the Cottonian Library, Deposited in the British Museum* (London: British Museum).

Plummer (1892–99): Charles Plummer, ed., *Two of the Saxon Chronicles Parallel with Supplementary Extracts from the Others: A Revised Text on the Basis of an Edition by John Earle*, 2 vols. (Oxford: Clarendon Press; repr. 1952).

Pocock (1951): J. G. A. Pocock, "Robert Brady, 1627–1700: A Cambridge Historian of the Restoration," *The Cambridge Historical Journal* 10/2: 186–204.

―――― (1987): J. G. A. Pocock, *The Ancient Constitution and the Feudal Law: A Study of English Historical Thought in the Seventeenth Century. A Reissue with a Retrospect* (Cambridge: Cambridge University Press).

Pollard and Redgrave (1976–91): A. W. Pollard and G. R. Redgrave, *A Short-Title Catalogue of Books Printed in England, Scotland, & Ireland and of English Books Printed Abroad 1475–1640*, 2nd edn., rev. and enl. by W. A. Jackson, F. S. Ferguson, and Katharine F. Pantzer, 3 vols. (London: Bibliographical Society).

Pope (1967–68): John C. Pope, ed., *Homilies of Ælfric: A Supplementary Collection, Being Twenty-One Full Homilies of His Middle and Later Career for the Most Part Not Previously Edited, with Some Shorter Pieces, Mainly Passages Added to the Second and Third Series*, EETS, OS 259–60, 2 vols. (London: Oxford University Press).

Porteman (1996): Otto Vaenius, *Amorum emblemata, figuris æneis incisa studio Othonis Væni, Batavo-Lugdunensis. Emblemes of Loue, with Verses in Latin, English, and Italian*, facsimile repr. of the original Antwerp, 1608 edition with introduction by Karel Porteman, Emblem Book Facsimile Series 1 (Aldershot: Scolar Press).

Powicke (1930): F. M. Powicke, "Sir Henry Spelman and the 'Concilia'," *Proceedings of the British Academy* 16: 345–79.

―――― (1948): Maurice Powicke, "William Camden," *English Studies* 1: 67–84.

Pulsiano (1989): Phillip Pulsiano, "A *Gothic Grammar* with a Transcript of Anglo-Saxon Prayers," *Old English Newsletter* 23/1: 40–41.

―――― (1991): Phillip Pulsiano, "Old English Glossed Psalters: Editions versus Manuscripts," *Manuscripta* 35: 75–95.

von Raumer (1870): Rudolf von Raumer, *Geschichte der germanischen Philologie, vorzugsweise in Deutschland* (Munich: R. Oldenbourg).

Rawlinson (1698): Christopher Rawlinson, ed., *An. Manl. Sever. Boethii Consolationis philosophiæ libri V. Anglo-Saxonice redditi ab Alfredo, inclyto Anglo-Saxonum rege* (Oxford: E Theatro Sheldoniano).

Reddick (1990): Allen Reddick, *The Making of Johnson's Dictionary 1746–1773*, Cambridge Studies in Publishing and Printing History (Cambridge: Cambridge University Press).

Ripa (1603): Cesare Ripa, *Iconologia. Overo descrittione di diverse imagini cavate dall'antichità, e di propria inventione* (Rome: Lepido Facii; repr. with introduction by Erna Mandowsky, Hildesheim: Georg Olms, 1984).

Robinson (1993): Fred C. Robinson, *The Tomb of Beowulf and Other Essays on Old English* (Oxford: Blackwell).

Robinson and Stanley (1991): Fred C. Robinson and E. G. Stanley, eds., *Old English Verse Texts from Many Sources: A Comprehensive Collection*, EEMF 23 (Copenhagen: Rosenkilde & Bagger).

Roeder (1904): Fritz Roeder, ed., *Der altenglische Regius-Psalter: Eine Interlinearversion in Hs. Royal 2. B. 5 des Brit. Mus.*, Studien zur englischen Philologie 18 (Halle: Max Niemeyer).

Rogers (1991): David Rogers, *The Bodleian Library and Its Treasures 1320–1700* (Henley-on-Thames: Aidan Ellis).

Rombauts (1933): Edward Rombauts, *Richard Verstegen: Een polemist der Contra-Reformatie*, Koninklijke Vlaamsche Academie voor Taal-en Letterkunde, 6th Ser., 54 (Brussels: Algemeene Drukinrichting).

Rosier (1960): James L. Rosier, "The Sources of John Joscelyn's Old English–Latin Dictionary," *Anglia* 78: 28–39.

————— (1962): James L. Rosier, ed., *The Vitellius Psalter, Edited from British Museum MS Cotton Vitellius E. xviii*, Cornell Studies in English 42 (Ithaca: Cornell University Press).

————— (1966): James L. Rosier, "Lexicographical Genealogy in Old English," *Journal of English and Germanic Philology* 65: 295–302.

Rositzke (1940): Harry August Rositzke, *The C-Text of the Old English Chronicles*, Beiträge zur englischen Philologie 34 (Bochum-Langendreer: H. Pöppinghaus; repr. New York: Johnson Reprint, 1967).

Sanders (1983): Vivienne Sanders, "The Household of Archbishop Parker and the Influencing of Public Opinion," *The Journal of Ecclesiastical History* 34: 534–47.

Sanders Gale (1978): Judith Sanders Gale, "John Joscelyn's Notebook: A Study of the Contents and Sources of B. L., Cotton MS. Vitellius D. vii," unpublished M. Phil. dissertation, University of Nottingham.

Sandys (1851): Charles Sandys, *Consuetudines Kanciae: A History of Gavelkind and Other Remarkable Customs in the County of Kent* (London: J. R. Smith).

Sawyer (1968): P. H. Sawyer, *Anglo-Saxon Charters: An Annotated List and Bibliography*, Royal Historical Society Guides and Handbooks 8 (London: Royal Historical Society).

Schäfer (1982): Jürgen Schäfer, "Alt- und Mittelenglisch in der lexikographischen Tradition des 17. Jahrhunderts," in *Festschrift für Karl Schneider zum 70. Geburtstag am 18. April 1982*, ed. Ernst S. Dick and Kurt J. Jankowsky (Amsterdam and Philadelphia: J. Benjamins), 169–85.

————— (1989): Jürgen Schäfer, *Early Modern English Lexicography, I: A Survey of Monolingual Printed Glossaries and Dictionaries 1475–1640* (Oxford: Clarendon Press).

Schedius (1728): Elias Schedius, *De diis Germanis sive veteri Germanorum, Gallorum, Britannorum, Vandalorum religione syngrammata quatuor*, 2nd edn. (Halle: Officina Crugiana).

Schipper (1989): William Schipper, "The Early Dictionaries of Old English and the Worcester Tremulous Scribe," *ICU Language Research Bulletin* 4/1: 81–99.

Schmeidler (1917): Adam of Bremen, *Hamburgische Kirchengeschichte*, ed. Bernhard Schmeidler, Monumenta Germaniae Historica, Scriptores Rerum Germanicarum 2 (Hanover: Hahn).

Schoeck (1958): R. J. Schoeck, "Early Anglo-Saxon Studies and Legal Scholarship in the Renaissance," *Studies in the Renaissance* 5: 102–10.

Schröer (1885–88): Arnold Schröer, ed., *Die angelsächsischen Prosabearbeitungen der Benedictinerregel*, Bibliothek der angelsächsischen Prosa 2 (Kassel: Wigand; repr. with supplementary preface and appendix by Helmut Gneuss, Darmstadt: Wissenschaftliche Buchgesellschaft, 1964).

Scragg (1992): D. G. Scragg, ed., *The Vercelli Homilies and Related Texts*, EETS, os 300 (Oxford: Oxford University Press).

Selden (1618): John Selden, *The Historie of Tithes* ([London]; facsimile repr. Amsterdam: Theatrum Orbis Terrarum, 1969).

Serarius (1605): Nikolaus Serarius, ed., *Epistolæ s. Bonifacii martyris, primi Moguntini archiepiscopi, Germanorum apostoli: pluriumque pontificum, regum, & aliorum, nunc primùm è Cæsarę maiestatis Viennensi bibliothecâ luce, notisque donatæ* (Mainz: Balthasar Lipp).

Sharpe (1979): Kevin Sharpe, *Sir Robert Cotton, 1586–1631: History and Politics in Early Modern England*, Oxford Historical Monographs (Oxford: Oxford University Press).

———— (1982): Kevin Sharpe, "The Foundation of the Chairs of History at Oxford and Cambridge: An Episode in Jacobean Politics," *History of Universities* 2: 127–52.

———— (1997): Kevin Sharpe, "Introduction: Rewriting Sir Robert Cotton," in Wright (1997), 1–39.

Simmons and Van Ginneken-van de Kasteele (1994): J. S. G. Simmons and Bé van Ginneken-van de Kasteele, eds., *Likhachev's Watermarks: An English-Language Version*, 2 vols., Monumenta Chartæ Papyraceæ Historiam Illustrantia 15 (Amsterdam: Paper Publications Society).

Sisam (1953a): Kenneth Sisam, "Humfrey Wanley," in Kenneth Sisam, *Studies in the History of Old English Literature* (Oxford: Clarendon Press), 259–77.

———— (1953b): Kenneth Sisam, "MSS. Bodley 340 and 342: Ælfric's Catholic Homilies," in Kenneth Sisam, *Studies in the History of Old English Literature* (Oxford: Clarendon Press), 148–98.

Sisam and Sisam (1959): Celia Sisam and Kenneth Sisam, eds., *The Salisbury Psalter, Edited from Salisbury Cathedral MS. 150*, EETS, os 242 (London: Oxford University Press; repr. 1969).

Skeat (1871): Walter W. Skeat, ed., *The Gospel According to Saint Mark in Anglo-Saxon and Northumbrian Versions, Synoptically Arranged, with Collations Exhibiting All the Readings of All the MSS.* (Cambridge: Cambridge University Press).

———— (1881–1900): Walter W. Skeat, ed., *Ælfric's Lives of Saints, Being a Set of Sermons on Saints' Days Formerly Observed by the English Church, Edited from Manuscript Julius E. VII in the Cottonian Collection, with Various Readings from Other Manuscripts*, EETS, os 76, 82, 94, and 114, 4 vols. (London: Trübner; repr. in 2 vols., London: Oxford University Press, 1966).

Smith (1722): John Smith, ed., *Historiae ecclesiasticae gentis Anglorum libri quinque, auctore sancto & venerabili Baeda, presbytero Anglo-Saxone, una cum reliquis ejus operibus historicis in unum volumen collectis* (Cambridge: Typis Academicis).

Somner (1640): William Somner, *The Antiquities of Canterbury, or, A Survey of That Ancient Citie* (London: R. Thrale; 2nd edn., rev. and completed by Nicolas Battely, London: R. Knaplock, 1703, repr. with introduction by William Urry, Wakefield: EP Publishing, 1977).

——— (1659): William Somner, *Dictionarium Saxonico-Latino-Anglicum voces, phrasesque præcipuas Anglo-Saxonicas, e libris, sive manuscriptis, sive typis excusis, aliisque monumentis tum publicis tum privatis, magna diligentia collectas; cum Latina et Anglica vocum interpretatione complectens* (Oxford: W. Hall; facsimile repr. Menston: Scolar Press, 1970).

——— (1660): William Somner, *A Treatise of Gavelkind, both Name and Thing: Shewing the True Etymologie and Derivation of the One, the Nature, Antiquity, and Original of the Other* (London: R. & W. Leybourn).

——— (1726): William Somner, *A Treatise of Gavelkind, both Name and Thing: Shewing the True Etymologie and Derivation of the One, the Nature, Antiquity, and Original of the Other*, 2nd edn. (London: F. Gyles).

Speed (1611): John Speed, *The History of Great Britaine under the Conquests of the Romans, Saxons, Danes and Normans. Their Originals, Manners, Warres, Coines & Seales: with the Successions, Lives, Acts & Issues of the English Monarchs from Iulius Cæsar, to Our Most Gracious Soueraigne King Iames* (London: [W. Hall and J. Beale]).

Spelman (1626): Henry Spelman, *Archæologus, in modum glossarii ad rem antiquam posteriorem* (London: John Beale).

———(1639): Henry Spelman, *Concilia, decreta, leges, constitutiones, in re ecclesiarum orbis Britannici* (London: R. Badger).

Spelman (1640): John Spelman, ed., *Psalterium Davidis Latino-Saxonicum vetus* (London: R. Badger).

Stanley (1975): E. G. Stanley, *The Search for Anglo-Saxon Paganism* (Cambridge: D. S. Brewer).

——— (1981): E. G. Stanley, "The Scholarly Recovery of the Significance of Anglo-Saxon Records in Prose and Verse: A New Bibliography," *Anglo-Saxon England* 9: 223–62.

——— (1987): E. G. Stanley, *A Collection of Papers with Emphasis on Old English Literature* (Toronto: Pontifical Institute of Mediaeval Studies).

——— (1998): E. G. Stanley, "The Sources of Junius's Learning as Revealed in the Junius Manuscripts in the Bodleian Library," in Bremmer (1998a), 159–76.

Starnes and Noyes (1946): DeWitt T. Starnes and Gertrude E. Noyes, *The English Dictionary from Cawdrey to Johnson 1604–1755* (Chapel Hill: University of North Carolina Press).

Stone (1964): Lawrence Stone, "The Educational Revolution in England, 1560–1640," *Past and Present* 28: 41–80.

——— (1966): Lawrence Stone, "Social Mobility in England, 1500–1700," *Past and Present* 33: 16–55.

Strongman (1977): Sheila Strongman, "John Parker's Manuscripts: An Edition of the Lists in Lambeth Palace MS 737," *Transactions of the Cambridge Bibliographical Society* 7/1: 1–27.

Strype (1711): John Strype, *The Life and Acts of Matthew Parker, the First Archbishop of Canterbury in the Reign of Queen Elizabeth* (London: J. Wyat).

Styles (1956): Philip Styles, "James Ussher and His Times," *Hermathena* 88: 12–33.

Sutherland (1998): Kathryn Sutherland, "Elizabeth Elstob (1683–1756)," in *Medieval Scholarship: Biographical Studies on the Formation of a Discipline*, II: *Literature and Philology*, ed. Helen Damico with Donald Fennema and Karmen Lenz (New York: Garland), 59–73.

Swift (1712): Jonathan Swift, *A Proposal for Correcting, Improving, and Ascertaining the English Tongue; in a Letter to the Most Honourable Robert, Earl of Oxford and Mortimer, Lord High Treasurer of Great Britain* (London: Benjamin Tooke; facsimile repr. Menston: Scolar Press, 1969).

Sykes (1926): Norman Sykes, *Edmund Gibson, Bishop of London 1669–1748: A Study in Politics and Religion in the Eighteenth Century* (London: Oxford University Press).

Tanner (1930): J. R. Tanner, *Tudor Constitutional Documents A. D. 1485–1603, with an Historical Commentary*, 2nd edn. (Cambridge: Cambridge University Press; repr. 1951).

Taylor (1983): Simon Taylor, ed., *MS B: A Semi-Diplomatic Edition with Introduction and Indices*, The Anglo-Saxon Chronicle: A Collaborative Edition 4, ed. David Dumville and Simon Keynes (Cambridge: D. S. Brewer).

Thorpe (1861): Benjamin Thorpe, ed., *The Anglo-Saxon Chronicle, According to the Several Original Authorities*, I: *Original Texts*, Rolls Series 23 (London: Longman).

Thwaites (1698): Edward Thwaites, ed., *Heptateuchus, liber Job, et evangelium Nicodemi; Anglo-Saxonice. Historiæ Judith fragmentum; Dano-Saxonice* (Oxford: E Theatro Sheldoniano).

———— (1711): [Edward Thwaites, ed.,] *Grammatica Anglo-Saxonica ex Hickesiano linguarum septentrionalium thesauro excerpta* (Oxford: E Theatro Sheldoniano).

Timmer (1957): B. J. Timmer, "Junius' Stay in Friesland," *Neophilologus* 41: 141–44.

Tite (1992): Colin G. C. Tite, "'Lost or Stolen or Strayed': A Survey of Manuscripts Formerly in the Cotton Library," *The British Library Journal* 18: 107–47. Reprinted in Wright (1997), 262–306.

———— (1994): Colin G. C. Tite, *The Manuscript Library of Sir Robert Cotton*, The Panizzi Lectures 1993 (London: British Library, 1994).

Todd (1793): H. J. Todd, *Catalogue of Manuscripts in the Library of Christ Church, Canterbury* (Canterbury: Canterbury Cathedral).

Tolkien (1962): J. R. R. Tolkien, ed., *The English Text of the Ancrene Riwle: Ancrene Wisse, Edited from MS. Corpus Christi College Cambridge 402*, with an introduction by N. R. Ker, EETS, os 249 (London: Oxford University Press).

Torkar (1981): Roland Torkar, *Eine altenglische Übersetzung von Alcuins 'De Virtutibus et Vitiis,' Kap. 20 (Liebermanns Judex): Untersuchungen und Textausgabe*, Texte und Untersuchungen zur Englischen Philologie 7 (Munich: Wilhelm Fink).

Trevor-Roper (1962): H. R. Trevor-Roper, *Archbishop Laud, 1573–1645*, 2nd edn. (London: Macmillan).

———— (1971): Hugh Trevor-Roper, *Queen Elizabeth's First Historian: William Camden and the Beginnings of English 'Civil History'*, Neale Lecture in English History (London: Jonathan Cape).

Turner (1948): Alberta Turner, "Another Seventeenth-Century Anglo-Saxon Poem," *Modern Language Quarterly* 9: 389–93.

Turner (1971): D. H. Turner, ed., *The Claudius Pontificals (from Cotton MS. Claudius A. iii in the British Museum)*, Henry Bradshaw Society 97 (Chichester: Moore & Tillyer).

Tuve (1939): Rosemond Tuve, "Ancients, Moderns, and Saxons," *ELH* 6: 165–90.

Twigg (1990): John Twigg, *The University of Cambridge and the English Revolution 1625–1688*, The History of Cambridge: Texts and Studies 1 (Woodbridge: Boydell).

Twysden (1652): Roger Twysden, ed., *Historiæ Anglicanæ scriptores X* (London: James Flesher).

Urry (1977): William Urry, "Introduction: William Somner and His *Antiquities*," in repr. of Somner (1640^2).

Ussher (1639): James Ussher, *Britannicarum ecclesiarum antiquitates* (Dublin: Ex Officina Typographica Societatis Bibliopolarum).

Utley (1942): Francis Lee Utley, "Two Seventeenth-Century Anglo-Saxon Poems," *Modern Language Quarterly* 3: 243–61.

Van de Velde (1966): R. G. van de Velde, *De studie van het Gotisch in de Nederlanden: Bijdrage tot een Status quaestionis over de studie van het Gotisch en het Krimgotisch*, Koninklijke Vlaamse Academie voor Taal- en Letterkunde, 6th ser., 97 (Ghent: Koninklijke Vlaamse Academie).

Van de Waal (1952): H. van de Waal, *Drie eeuwen vaderlandsche Geschied-Uitbeelding 1500–1800: een iconologische studie*, 2 vols. (The Hague: M. Nijhoff).

Van Leeuwen (1672): Simon van Leeuwen, *Korte besgryving van het Lugdunum Batavorum nu Leyden: vervattende een verhaal van haar grond-stand, oudheid, opkomst, voort-gang, ende stads-bestier* (Leiden: Johannes van Gelder).

Van Norden (1949–50): Linda van Norden, "Sir Henry Spelman on the Chronology of the Elizabethan College of Antiquaries," *The Huntington Library Quarterly* 13: 131–60.

Van Romburgh (2000): Sophie van Romburgh, "Why Francis Junius (1591–1677) Became an Anglo-Saxonist, or, The Study of Old English for the Elevation of Dutch," *Studies in Medievalism* 11, ed. T. A. Shippey.

Van Veen (1608): Otto van Veen, *Amorum emblemata, figuris aeneis incisa studio Othonis Vaeni, Batavo-Lugdunensis. Emblemes of Love, with Verses in Latin, English, and Italian* (Antwerp: Apud auctorem).

Venezky and Healey (1980): Richard L. Venezky and Antonette diPaolo Healey, *A Microfiche Concordance to Old English* (Newark, Del.: University of Delaware; issued in microfiche format).

Venn and Venn (1922–27): John Venn and J. A. Venn, *Alumni Cantabrigienses: A Biographical List of All Known Students, Graduates and Holders of Office at the University of Cambridge, from the Earliest Times to 1900. Part I: From the Earliest Times to 1751*, 4 vols. (Cambridge: Cambridge University Press).

Verstegen (1605): Richard Verstegen, *A Restitvtion of Decayed Intelligence: in Antiquities. Concerning the Most Noble and Renovvmed English Nation* (Antwerp: Robert Bruney; facsimile reprs. Ilkley: Scolar Press, 1976, and New York: Da Capo, 1979).

———(1613): Richard Verstegen, *Nederlantsche Antiquiteyten met de bekeeringhe van eenighe der selve landen tot het kersten gheloove, deur S. Willebrordus, Apostel van Hollant, Zeelant, Sticht van Utrecht, Overijssel, ende Vrieslant, met oock eenighe deelen van Gelderlant, Cleve, Gulick, Brabandt ende Vlaenderen* (Antwerp: Gaspar Bellerus).

——— (1700): Richard Verstegen, *Antiquitates Belgicæ, of Nederlandsche oudtheden* (Amsterdam: Jacob van Royen).

Voorwinden (1992): Franciscus Junius, *Observationes in Willerami abbatis Francicam paraphrasin Cantici canticorum*, ed. Norbert Voorwinden, Early Studies in Germanic Philology 1 (Amsterdam and Atlanta: Rodopi).

Wada (1994): Yoko Wada, ed. and trans., *'Temptations' from Ancrene Wisse*, Kansai University Institute of Oriental and Occidental Studies, Sources and Materials Series 18 (Osaka: Kansai University Press).

Wanley (1705): Humfrey Wanley, *Librorum vett. septentrionalium, qui in Angliæ bibliothecis extant, nec non multorum vett. codd. septentrionalium alibi extantium catalogus historico-criticus, cum totius thesauri linguarum septentrionalium sex indicibus* (Oxford: E Theatro Sheldoniano; facsimile repr. Menston: Scolar Press, 1970). (Vol. II of George Hickes's *Antiquæ literaturæ septentrionalis libri duo.*)

Warnicke (1973): Retha M. Warnicke, *William Lambarde, Elizabethan Antiquary, 1536–1601* (London: Phillimore).

———— (1974): Retha M. Warnicke, "Note on a Court of Requests Case of 1571," *English Language Notes* 11: 250–56.

Watson (1966): Andrew G. Watson, *The Library of Sir Simonds D'Ewes* (London: British Museum).

———— (1986): Andrew G. Watson, "John Twyne of Canterbury (d. 1581) as a Collector of Medieval Manuscripts: A Preliminary Investigation," *The Library*, 6th ser., 8: 133–51.

Weber (1953): Robert Weber, ed., *Le Psautier romain et les autres anciens Psautiers latins*, Collectanea Biblica Latina 10 (Rome: Abbaye Saint-Jérôme/Vatican City: Libreria Vaticana).

Weinbrot (1993): Howard D. Weinbrot, "Politics, Taste, and National Identity: Some Uses of Tacitism in Eighteenth-Century Britain," in *Tacitus and the Tacitean Tradition*, ed. T. J. Luce and A. J. Woodman (Princeton: Princeton University Press), 169–84.

Wharton (1691): Henry Wharton, ed., *Anglia sacra, sive collectio historiarum, partim antiquitus, partim recenter scriptarum, de archiepiscopis & episcopis Angliæ, a prima fidei Christianæ susceptione ad annum MDXL*, 2 vols. (London: R. Chiswel).

Wheelock (1643): Abraham Wheelock, ed., *Historiæ ecclesiasticæ gentis Anglorum libri V. a venerabili Beda presbytero scripti . . . quibus in calce operis Saxonicam chronologiam . . . contexuimus* (Cambridge: Roger Daniel).

Whitelock (1954): Dorothy Whitelock, ed., *The Peterborough Chronicle (the Bodleian Manuscript Laud Misc. 636)*, with an appendix by Cecily Clark, EEMF 4 (Copenhagen: Rosenkilde & Bagger).

——— (1962): Dorothy Whitelock, "The Old English Bede," *Proceedings of the British Academy* 48: 57–90; repr. in *British Academy Papers on Anglo-Saxon England*, ed. E. G. Stanley (Oxford: Oxford University Press, 1990), 227–60.

——— (1979): Dorothy Whitelock, ed., *English Historical Documents* c. *500–1042*, 2nd edn. (London: Eyre Methuen).

Wildhagen (1910): Karl Wildhagen, ed., *Der Cambridger Psalter (Hs. Ff. 1. 23 University Libr. Cambridge) zum ersten Male herausgegeben mit besonderer Berücksichtigung des lateinischen Textes*, I: *Text mit Erklärungen*, Bibliothek der angelsächsischen Prosa 7 (Hamburg: H. Grand; repr. Darmstadt: Wissenschaftliche Buchgesellschaft, 1964).

Wing (1972–88): Donald Wing, *Short-Title Catalogue of Books Printed in England, Scotland, Ireland, Wales, and British America, and of English Books Printed in Other Countries, 1641–1700*, 2nd edn., 3 vols. (New York: Modern Language Association of America).

Winterbottom and Ogilvie (1975): M. Winterbottom and R. M. Ogilvie, eds., *Cornelii Taciti opera minora*, Scriptorum Classicorum Bibliotheca Oxoniensis (Oxford: Clarendon Press).

Wood (1721): Anthony Wood, *Athenæ Oxonienses: An Exact History of All the Writers and Bishops Who Have Had Their Education in the Most Antient and Famous University of Oxford, from the Fifteenth Year of King Henry the Seventh, A. D. 1500, to the Author's Death in November 1695*, 2nd edn. (London: R. Knaplock, D. Midwinter, & J. Tonson).

Woodruff (1911): C. Eveleigh Woodruff, *A Catalogue of the Manuscript Books in the Library of Christ Church, Canterbury* (Canterbury: Cross & Jackman).

Woolf (1953): Henry Bosley Woolf, "The Earliest Printing of Old English Poetry," *English Studies* 34: 113–15.

Wormald (1997): Patrick Wormald, "The Lambarde Problem: Eighty Years On," in *Alfred the Wise: Studies in Honour of Janet Bately on the Occasion of Her Sixty-Fifth Birthday*, ed. Jane Roberts and Janet L. Nelson with Malcolm Godden (Cambridge: D. S. Brewer), 237–75.

Wormald and Wright (1958): Francis Wormald and C. E. Wright, eds., *The English Library before 1700* (London: Athlone Press).

Wright (1951): C. E. Wright, "The Dispersal of the Monastic Libraries and the Beginnings of Anglo-Saxon Studies. Matthew Parker and His Circle: A Preliminary Study," *Transactions of the Cambridge Bibliographical Society* 1/3: 208–37.

——— (1958): C. E. Wright, "The Elizabethan Society of Antiquaries and the Formation of the Cottonian Library," in Wormald and Wright (1958), 176–212.

——— (1960): C. E. Wright, "Humfrey Wanley: Saxonist and Library-Keeper," *Proceedings of the British Academy* 46: 99–129.

—————— (1972): Cyril Ernest Wright, *Fontes Harleiani: A Study of the Sources of the Harleian Collection of Manuscripts Preserved in the Department of Manuscripts in the British Museum* (London: British Museum).

Wright (1997): C. J. Wright, ed., *Sir Robert Cotton as Collector: Essays on an Early Stuart Courtier and His Legacy* (London: British Library).

Wright and Wright (1966): C. E. Wright and Ruth C. Wright, eds., *The Diary of Humfrey Wanley, 1715–1726*, 2 vols. (London: Bibliographical Society).

Wülker (1885): Richard Wülker, *Grundriss zur Geschichte der angelsächsischen Litteratur: Mit einer Übersicht der angelsächsischen Sprachwissenschaft* (Leipzig: von Veit).

Zupitza (1880): Julius Zupitza, ed., *Ælfrics Grammatik und Glossar*, Sammlung englischer Denkmäler in kritischen Ausgaben 1 (Berlin: Weidmann; repr. with supplementary introduction by Helmut Gneuss, Berlin: Weidmann, 1966).

INDEX OF MANUSCRIPTS

GENERAL INDEX